Dynamics of Child Development

Dynamics of Child Development

HORACE B. ENGLISH, *The Ohio State University*

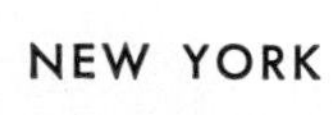

NEW YORK HOLT, RINEHART AND WINSTON, INC.

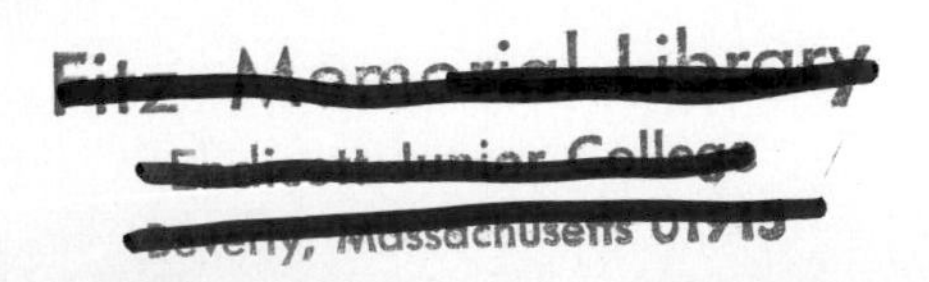

May, 1962

Library of Congress Catalog Card Number: 61-6170

22392-0311

Printed in the United States of America

TO MY FIVE CHILDREN
AND
THEIR CHILDREN

Preface

Most textbook writers, one gathers, write as if the grim visages of professional colleagues were leering over their shoulders. I have tried to exorcise this specter and to substitute the composite image of the readers for whom the book is written. No doubt the effort is only partially successful; there are passages unwittingly written to please the wrong critic, but I hope they are few.

This book is the product of a concern and a conviction. I have a deep concern for the welfare of children and a conviction that through scientific methods, more especially the methods of psychology, we have discovered and are daily discovering ways of promoting that welfare. The book is written in an effort to get those ways adopted as widely as possible, particularly by teachers and parents. The aim is thus unashamedly practical. This is not a venture in pure science but in applied science, or what we are nowadays learning to call technology.

The technology of child development is not a mere assemblage of wise hints on child care, nor is it just an organized citation of the practical deductions that can be made from a miscellaneous array of experiments. A technology is based upon and guided by scientific theories as well as by established facts.

It would be presumptuous to claim that the over-all theory or system of psychological thinking that is embodied in the text is all of one piece, free from inner inconsistencies. But there *is* a system. It is not expounded or argued for; it is incorporated and put to work.

Thus in the two chapters on authority and discipline at least nineteen important concepts of contemporary child development are embodied. The concepts are not defined or discussed as such; some are not even mentioned by name.

This is particularly apt to be the case with some of the psychoanalytical concepts, which receive considerable verbal alteration here. Yet the debt to Freud and his followers will be obvious to the informed reader. It would, however, be cheap if not dishonest to seek acceptance of ideas by appealing to the popular, rather mystical, esteem in which Freud is held. I do not want these ideas accepted because they are derived from Freud. The same argument holds against stressing the latest vocabulary from other "schools" of psychology.

The value of theoretical concepts is that they help to put the facts in significant order. It does not depend on the student's ability to state the concepts; and if the student fails to discern the "school" espoused by the author, so much the better. Emphasis can then be put on the facts and the guidance they give to action.

We cannot, however, always evade discussing theoretical issues, even some that seem to us falsely stated. It would be difficult, for example, to avoid discussing the nature-nurture problem. If the instructor does not bring it up, students will, and will reveal how much of their thinking is conditioned by misconceptions about heredity. But the test of our teaching is not whether the student can restate the proper theory about the role of nurture but whether he knows when and how to intervene to promote a child's development.

The practical aim determines also the use made of research materials. There is a wealth of fact concerning child development that is still unassimilated into a theoretical framework, or that is unrelated to the care and education of children. I do not disparage the value of such facts. But if professional psychologists have not yet been able to see the bearing of a fact upon the actions of the ultimate consumer—that is, of the teacher and parent for whom this book is written—the fact (or concept) belongs in a reference handbook, not in a textbook. Here attention is focused not on research about children but on the children themselves; research is brought in only when it helps us in our practical relations with children. For the practitioner the important consideration is not how the scientific conclusions have been reached but where he can go with them.

Very often, it is true, a description of an experiment is a useful means to understanding its meaning in application. I have often used this approach in the text; and in my classes I present other examples of the "build up" of a particular generalization. Instructors who wish to follow this plan will find the many references to the research literature helpful. Yet when we thus use experiments as a sort of elaborate illustration, we should not lose sight of the real goal: the understanding of children, actual children. Consequently the reader is constantly challenged to correlate what he reads with observation of children's behavior. There are many helpful films that show real-life situations, but they are no substitute for direct observation. (A manual on methods of studying the individual child is in preparation.)

In thus focusing attention primarily upon understanding and helping individual children, we are not proposing that future practitioners suspend critical judgment and scientific thinking. On the contrary. We are proposing to put the major emphasis upon that kind of scientific thinking that the practitioner will himself use. It is not necessary for teachers to know the details of the standardization processes for the Wechsler Intelligence Scale for Children; it is very important that they know what a WISC MA of 8½ years means, what other facts they need, how to get them, and how to weigh such facts in the light of scientific findings.

In preparing this book, I have added new material and rewritten and rearranged material drawn from my earlier *Child Psychology* in order to focus upon the theme expressed in the title: What causes children to develop as they do and what may we do about it?

For many years I have been concerned with the vocabulary of psychology and have edited a dictionary of psychological terms. But in this textbook it has been my intention to write so that almost never will the reader need to consult that tome. This book is not written to convince people that I am a scholar; it is written to be understandable.

While the several chapters have a degree of autonomy and may therefore be taught in a different order, they also give each other mutual support. The same facts or the same conclusions often appear in one chapter only to be picked up later in a quite different context. This is not careless repetition. It is a recognition that, although we discuss different topics in distinct chapters, the behavior facts belong not to a topic but to a life.

Like Dr. Spock in his celebrated book, *Infant and Child Care,* I must apologize for so often referring to the child as "him." This is grammatically correct, but may give the impression that I am less interested in girls. Not at all. Girls are not only as nice as boys, but, from a psychologist's point of view, probably more important. For the girls will grow up to be the homemakers of the next generation, and it is a truism that the home has a pre-eminent part in the development of children. But if I speak of the child as "him," then I can without confusion use "her" to refer to the mother or the teacher.[1]

The book is structured primarily as a textbook for prospective teachers or teachers-in-service. Nonetheless, the needs of parents have been kept in mind, and it is believed that they can profitably use the book either for private study or in class. Most books for parents seem to assume that their responsibility for psychological guidance ends when they have packed the youngsters off to school. I would like to think that this book will promote a little more cooperation between teachers and parents in meeting their common problems.

H. B. E.

Columbus, Ohio
January, 1961

---

[1] Believing that education in America has been overfeminized, I have opposed the use of "teacher" as a feminine noun. One must, however, recognize the facts of life: the teachers to whom this book is addressed are in overwhelming majority women, and that state of affairs is likely to continue long after the effective use of this book.

Table of Contents

Dynamics of Child Development

1

We Confront Our Problems

If you are a parent whose child has recently passed from infancy into childhood, you probably feel that you face a sort of crisis. While he was a baby you somehow mastered the knack of caring for his physical needs and made a start at meeting his relatively simple emotional and intellectual needs—probably with the help of one or more of the excellent baby books currently available. Now, rather suddenly, he passes a milestone. You can no longer treat him as a sort of animated doll. You have problems!

And if you are a teacher, you face not one or two children but a whole roomful. To the parent little Martin or little Esther may sometimes *seem* to be strangers; to you they *are* strangers. And in the year ahead you will be spending nearly a thousand hours with these strange children. You, too, have problems.

Nevertheless, the first thing to say is, Relax! Of course you want, and *need,* to learn more about children, but why be so grim about it? I'm afraid our books on child development, particularly those addressed to parents, have contributed to needless anxiety. Children can be fun; and the study of children is fascinating.

To begin with, what a fascinating variety! Think of the excitement of facing for the first time twenty or thirty or forty little individual personalities. (If you are a parent, read on. This is addressed to the teacher but it concerns you, too.)

Who is this nervous, thin, little girl in the front row, eager almost to the point of anxiety? What lies behind the dull mask of the big boy who sits slouched down in the too-small seat? Will the little boy in the second row always be so dirty? (Certainly most of the others will not always be so spruce and clean as on this opening day.) Does the girl at the back of the room really look defiant or is that your imagination? Which of these children will be the natural leaders of the class? Which child will be the bully? Do these children know how to cooperate? Which ones persevere in a task until it is finished; which flit from task to task like so many butterflies?

Are there truants or disciplinary cases here? Any "problem children"? Do some stutter or lisp or talk baby talk? Do some talk too much? Will there be a "thief" in the class? Will some of the children be surly, quarrelsome, contentious?

What is the religious background of these children? If you are a teacher in a public school you must scrupulously avoid any form of religious instruction—this is the law of our country as embodied in the Constitution. But religious attitudes, or the absence of such attitudes, form part of the total personality. You cannot—must not—teach religion, but it is foolish to ignore the effect of the children's religious beliefs on other sorts of instruction.

How about health? The children look well just now; will winter weather bring out chronic illnesses? Will some of these children be perpetually below par? There's one lad with glasses; what is he doing in the back seat? How many have visual defects that are uncorrected? How many are a little hard of hearing? Do they all get enough to eat?

And last—and perhaps least, but still very important—which are the good pupils, the quick learners? How much arithmetic do they know? What kind of grammar do they use in everyday talk? Have they learned how to study? Have any been "failed" from last year; and if so, why? These are some of the many questions a teacher must face.

These are by no means all the questions we might ask. Allport and Odbert (5) [1] took the trouble to count all the words in an unabridged dictionary that refer to human traits. They found over 18,000. As if these were not enough, slang is adding new ones every day. We should not infer that there are as many traits as there are terms; but

[1] Numbers in parentheses refer to the bibliography at the end of the book.

each term is the answer to someone's legitimate question about a person.

And if you are that unique sort of "teacher," the child's mother or father? Most of the problems are fundamentally the same. Where they are a little different, parents should give some thought to the questions as the schoolteacher must face them.

"If It Exists, It Exists in Measurable Amount"

It is not enough to ask whether a person is aggressive or unaggressive; we must ask how often or how long or how easily he is provoked to aggressiveness. That is, we must seek quantitative answers. Probably every human quality is found in at least a minimal degree in every human being. The range of variation from the least degree to the greatest—the range, e.g., from the most submissive to the most aggressive, from the most selfish to the least selfish of mortals, from the idiot to the genius—is enormous.

Most measurements in psychology are relative; that is, they don't have reference to some absolute standard. Ethel's height of fifty-six inches is defined by reference to a standard inch kept in the Bureau of Standards. Her intelligence cannot be thus defined. We have no absolute unit, no "inch" of intelligence. Instead we describe Ethel's intelligence by comparing her to other children.

Relative measurements have their limitations—you can't perform certain kinds of mathematical tricks with them, for instance. But they serve most practical purposes as well as or better than absolute measurements. Suppose you do know how tall a girl is in absolute units? Ethel's fifty-six inches, for example. What does this mean? "Well, at her age less than one girl in fifty is that tall." That statement has personal significance for Ethel, her parents, her teacher. And it is based on the same kind of relative or comparative standard that we use in measuring intelligence.

In similarly relative and meaningful terms we can seek to answer the question "How much?" for every psychological characteristic, and if we respect the limits of our techniques, these measurements have genuine significance and helpfulness.

Differences Matter

The ascertainable range of differences in human qualities is so great as to have important social consequences. A person's level of intelligence influences not only his education but the whole course and tenor of his life—the things he is interested in and the things he enjoys, quite as much as the things he can do.

Differences in personality are even more important. Take, for example, an emotional tendency such as fearfulness. Even leaving pathological instances out of account, we have at one end the child who is like Burns's mouse, a "wee, sleekit, cowrin, tim'rous beastie," and at the other extreme the child who, almost literally, does not know what it is to be afraid. Can we possibly suppose that we should treat such extremes in the same way?

Ignorance as to Individual Differences

That individuals differ, and differ tremendously, is obvious. We do not, however, adequately adjust our actions to these differences, perhaps mainly because we do not realize concretely and fully how extensive they are. How many teachers can state with any degree of confidence or accuracy the probable range of differences to be expected in the grade they teach?

One of the most tangible and easily known characteristics is height. How much difference will you find between the tallest and the shortest child? Suppose you know that the average height in the third grade is fifty-two inches. Will that knowledge enable you to adjust your activities program to the children's height? It is rather a shock to realize that you may have to be ready to deal with one child who is sixty-five inches tall—as tall as the average woman teacher—and with another who is only thirty-eight inches, hardly more than half the first.

Herewith is the picture of the largest and the smallest girl in a certain third grade (Figure 1-1). I did not hunt for an extreme case; rather, I took at random a typical class from a nearby school. It is clear enough that these two girls will not fit the same seats; clear also that they cannot compete in games on anything like equal terms.[2]

To us as adults—and those special adults known as teachers—it may seem that differences in intelligence matter still more. Perhaps. Well, what do we know about the range and variety of intelligence with which we must cope? Sixty-five experienced teachers in one of my

Figure 1-1. The Shortest and the Tallest Girl in the Class

classes were asked to state the highest and lowest mental ages likely to be found in a third grade. They were told to assume that the average *chronological age* is somewhat over 8, as it is in most school systems. Eleven of the sixty-five teachers thought that mental age 10

[2] A difference of 15 pounds is enough to move a man from, let us say, lightweight (top limit 135 pounds) clear past the welterweights to the middleweights (beginning at 147 pounds). Almost never, of course, would men from such different classifications box or wrestle with each other. Yet a difference of 15 or more pounds is not unheard of between the heaviest and the lightest child in one school class. And, of course, 15 pounds amount to more proportionately in a child's weight than in an adult's.

was as high as was likely to occur. Nine thought that 10½ was likely, twenty-four thought it might go as high as 11. Less than a third of these experienced teachers realized that a mental age of 12 is not at all uncommon in the third grade. (It will be found in one class out of three or four.)

Estimates of the lowest mental age to be expected were somewhat less varied. Four teachers out of the sixty-five thought that some mental ages might be as low as 4 or 4½ years. Nineteen put the figure at 5 or 5½. About half thought that a mental age of 6 was about right, but three thought there was little chance of a child's mental age being under 7. Here the majority were right. Although promotion policies cause much variation from one school system to another, a child with a mental age of 6, or below, is seldom found in the third grade.

It is significant that these teachers tended to overestimate the number of dull and underestimate the number of bright children they were likely to encounter. And it is clear that even with so definite a matter as intelligence, most of them were ill-informed as to the extent of their problem.[3] That they would have more precisely estimated the range and variety of other personality characteristics of pupils is unlikely, to say the least.

One purpose of this book, then, is to help teachers to a richer, more definite, and more sensitive awareness of the range and complexity of human differences. We must learn to recognize that Harriet differs from the rest of the class in her attitude to authority, that Harold is the outstanding leader on the playground, that Peter is shy with adults, that Clara is more sophisticated in her attitudes than are the other members of the class, that Mary Lou has found that the easiest way to secure fond attention is to be a little ill.

Nor can we ignore the interrelations between these qualities within the same individual. Meekness, surely, is a very different thing (or at least has a very different value) in a huge, strong boy from what it is in a small, weak one. Again, leadership combined with a sour disposition can cause an infinitely difficult problem. Affability and intelligence in the same person, on the other hand, make a doubly effective team. It is important to know that Jim is more energetic than Bill; it is equally important to know that with Jim

[3] That these teachers were not untypical may be seen from Lewis's (279) extensive investigation.

energy is subordinated to good sense, while Bill's energy overrides his judgment and gets him into trouble. And so on with all the combinations that go into the organization of personality in both childhood and the later years.

Traits in Relation to the Environmental "Field"

Even such a consideration of traits in interaction with each other fails to do justice to the rich complexity of human nature. No person is a self-contained being. His traits or characteristics are not fixed but vary according to the circumstances, the psychological "field" or "climate," in which he finds himself. The child who is bold as a lion in the arithmetic class may be retiring where football is concerned; the child who chats freely with adults may be reserved with strange children.

In principle this is again entirely obvious. The trouble is that we often fail to apply the principle in concrete instances. Thus, it is very unusual for teachers to make a careful study of the personal-social interactions of their pupils unless, or until, a "crush" or a fighting antagonism puts in its appearance. Yet such personal relations may decidedly affect not only personality development or character but even the learning of subject matter. If John detests Henry, who is good at history, he may decline to be interested in the "foul subject"; or, if he judges his chances are good, he may strive to excel in that area in order to defeat his rival.

More important, of course, is the way in which the psychological "field of forces" determines which traits of personality are to be exercised, and hence developed, and which are to be depressed or inhibited. Thus, when Sally recites in arithmetic she is supported by her schoolfellows' confident expectations; she has gained the reputation of "being good at arithmetic." Jerry's bungling efforts are depressed by derisive hoots and titters. Sally, therefore, gains not only in arithmetic but also in self-confidence—at least in classlike situations, and usually in others as well. But Jerry, unless the teacher skillfully manipulates the situation, loses out on both counts. Ability to guide personality development depends on understanding and controlling *the psychological climate in which the children live.*

The Dynamics of Child Development

Differences in traits, as we said above, are important. We do need to know what a child is like; but we need to know it in order to help him *become*. A child's traits are only part of what determines his development. They are the starting point, not the end, of the lifelong process of learning and development.

Major attention in what follows will be focused, therefore, on the dynamic *and alterable* conditions that determine behavior and growth. We shall be examining the effects on behavior of different kinds of environmental stimuli and situations. Of these environmental factors the actions and attitudes of persons are the most important. We shall examine, for example, the effects of sternness or laxity upon the child's development, or the effects of satisfaction or of deprivation of satisfactions. Against the background of such cause-and-effect relationships we can envisage the child in all his individuality and with fullness of understanding. And with enjoyment!

Rule of Thumb or Understanding?

You have, however, a right to expect practical help as well as enjoyment. But what constitutes practical help? Not rules of thumb, surely.

They won't work. Every child is different from every other child. The situations in which he finds himself—or in which you find him—differ from child to child and from hour to hour. Rules made to fit one child or one situation won't fit another. What we need is a basic understanding of how and why children act as they do, and how they can be led to change their conduct so that they will develop into mature and happy adults. It is my aim in this book to help you to deepen your understanding of children.

What Kind of Book Is This?

This, then, is not a "cookbook" to which you can refer for a recipe when Orville gives Pete a black eye. It is my hope that the study of this book will help you to think and feel differently from what you otherwise would about Orville and Pete when they are in this sort of jam. But you will still have to think and feel yourself into their situation with all its uniqueness.

Thus, in the next two chapters we shall take up the very important problem of discipline. You won't find there any directions on how many spanks to give for breaking Granny's upper dentures, or on how many hours of detention to impose for intentionally tripping a child on the school stairway.

Figure 1-2. The Wrong Use of Child Psychology

You will find, instead, a discussion of what makes a child flout authority and, more important, what makes him responsive to authority. From this discussion you will get a few hints on how to meet concrete emergencies; but the major emphasis is upon the whole pattern according to which the child is developing. In the chapters on motives you may learn a little about such things as how to get George to study his homework; but it is my hope that you will learn more about the whole process of influencing and changing the motives that control conduct.

Ours, then, is the long look. How a child behaves at age six or seven—yes, that matters. What to do to keep him from disrupting the household or the classroom—that is important, too. But what kind of man or woman he is growing up to be—that matters much more. If we understand the child's behavior, we have a better chance to help him grow up into the man or woman he is capable of becoming.

How to Use This Book

A book that seeks to take such a long look needs to be read a little differently from the way a novel is read. I have tried to write simply and with a minimum of technicalities. You won't, I hope, find it hard to see what I am trying to say. But there is a deeper level of comprehension wherein ideas are *absorbed*. This, of course, is what you are aiming for.

My colleague, Dr. Francis P. Robinson, has been finding out a great deal lately about how people study (367). He finds that even very good students often use inefficient methods. They can do so because they are bright; if they used better methods, they could do even better work. Improvement in study habits is even more important for poor students. For those of you who have been out of school for some time, the problem of proper study habits is crucial.

Let's consider, therefore, what you can easily do to improve your understanding of this book. Robinson has summarized his finding in a very modern-sounding formula: "SQ3R," or "Survey! Question! Read! Recite! Review!" Let us look at each of these in turn.

1. *Survey!* In this book each chapter opens with a brief statement of what the chapter is all about. Read that first. Then leaf through the chapter, *reading only the section headings*. Finally read the summary at the end of the chapter. The Survey should take only a minute or two but it is important.

2. *Question!* This is the heart of the SQ3R technique; it is the hardest part to make yourself do systematically. (I know, for I've worked at this myself.) But it is hard simply because you aren't used to it. You must ask yourself what the author is trying to say. *For each major section* (in this book the heading is centered like that on page

10) ask what, specifically, the questions are that the author sets out to answer *for you.* The section heading and the subheadings are very helpful at this point. Sometimes your questions will be little more than restatements of these headings, but usually you will find that you need to expand or modify them to fit them to your own personal purposes. The quality of your understanding will be in direct proportion to the pointedness and pertinence of the questions for which you seek answers. This is the chief justification of the old saying, "You get out of it just about what you put in." But a better way to put it is, "You take out just about what you actively seek to pull out."

3. *Read!* Just read; but if you have asked some good questions, you will now be reading like a good setter dog coursing over ground full of interesting traces of game. You will be "sniffing" at each sentence to see if it doesn't have the answer or part of the answer to your questions. It is marvelous to see how your reading gains in both speed and interest when you know what you are looking for.

4. *Recite!* Here Robinson has had to use an old term with rather unpleasant associations for most of us, who recall dreary hours of teacher-questioning and pupil-recitation. He means recite to yourself. *At the end of each section* tell yourself what you have found out. Writing a brief note from memory is a good way to do it.

To provide some stimulus to this process of assimilation and integration of ideas, I have interrupted the text at intervals with some of *my* questions. These should supplement (not replace!) the questions you ask yourself. And they should be answered before proceeding further with your reading. These questions are intended to challenge your thinking, not your memory. You will seldom find the answers in the text—only the raw material out of which you can fashion your own answers. Sometimes you will come to the conclusion that the question can't be answered. You may be right. But the attempt to fashion an answer is guaranteed to contribute to your understanding and insight.

A caution: it is all too easy to read a question and to say to yourself, "Yes, I know the answer—well enough, anyway." Put that to the test. *Write out* the answer. Nine times out of ten you will find not only that your answer might be wrong but that you really had no answer at all. Before you can answer you will find yourself needing to check back on the text—the best kind of review.

After some experience in answering on paper, try answering aloud.

Presently you will find that you can answer the question "in your mind"—and that now you can really *answer* and not just assure yourself that you can.

All this may sound like time-consuming business. It isn't—not if you think of how much you learn in the time spent. It has been amply proved that it pays to spend as much as 50 percent of one's study time in self-recitation (steps 4 and 5). The usual procedure of reading and then rereading is much less valuable for both retention and comprehension.

Steps 2, 3, and 4 are to be carried out for each major division of the text—in this book for each section with a centered heading.

5. *Review!* This time the whole chapter is the unit. Look over the headings, check any passages underlined, read over any notes you have taken. Read the summary again and be sure you now understand it. (If you do understand it you can write at least a paragraph about each sentence in the summary.) In step 4 you undoubtedly found weak spots in your grasp of the text; pay close attention to these in review. Watch for ideas that you missed on your first go-through.

Now to take the liberty of adding two more letters to Robinson's formula in order to bring out two important ideas. (They are probably implicit in the notion of review but they need to be spelled out.) Let's make it read SQ3RAI.

6. *Apply!* Apply what you learn. To do so makes it real, makes it meaningful, makes it stick.

If you are working with children at the present time, you have plenty of opportunity to put your new knowledge to work. Although I have explicitly disavowed the idea that the text has ready-made answers for you, there is nothing more practical than the attitudes and understandings you will explore in this book. Let these attitudes color and determine your actual behavior.

But if you are not at the moment actually dealing with children, you can still apply to hypothetical cases what you have been learning. Ask yourself what you would do in certain situations with which you are familiar. A caution: don't just take extreme or emergency cases. A child's development is affected chiefly by the day-by-day, hour-by-hour ordinary experiences he lives through.

7. *Integrate!* Closely related to the effort to apply is a final step: stand off a little and try to get an *overview* of each chapter. Try to

tie in what you have been reading with your own knowledge, whether gained by direct experience or from other reading. What does it mean? Mean to *you?* Does it help you to clarify what you already "knew" but hadn't tied together? What changes in your outlook are implied?

Finally, can you accept what the text says and make the necessary changes in your behavior? I have tried very hard to set down the best available knowledge and attitudes of contemporary psychology; there's a wealth of both scientific experiment and practical experience behind most of the ideas in this book. I hope you won't lightly discard them. But neither are they the last word. When it comes to actual dealings with a child, the last word lies with you. (Correction: Sometimes it lies with the child!)

In the end, the only things in this book that can be of value to you are the things *you* can absorb and put to work. So, as you read, stop often and ask yourself, How would this principle, if adopted, have affected my behavior in this or that remembered situation? How will it affect my behavior in future situations? What will I have to do to live up to the principle? What will happen to the child if I do? or don't?

2

Discipline and the Child's Response to Authority

Discipline—everyone talks about it, but what is it? Is it necessary? How does it work? In this chapter you won't find a set of rules on how to discipline. Instead you will find a discussion of what makes discipline work and of how different kinds of discipline affect the child's personality.

Discipline—Necessity or Delusion?

"A necessity," shrieks the daily press. Mrs. Walter Ferguson in her syndicated column well represents the advocates of "old-fashioned" discipline:

Our Overprivileged Children

Several thousand experts met recently in Washington to discuss the needs of American children. I hope it was suggested to them that what children need most is parents who can control them. . . . Many are overprivileged by being permitted to do as they please. . . .

Anyway, for years the little dears have been urged by educators to trample on the rights of their parents and teachers, while the latter are scared to protest lest the innocents would be injured. And so we've suffered from infant tyrants at home and from juveniles who are holy terrors to their neighborhoods. Children who demand too much of their parents usually demand too much of their society. . . . Our plain duty, it seems to me, is to teach them self-control.[1]

[1] Quoted by permission of the Scripps-Howard Newspaper Alliance.

That she speaks for a majority opinion may be seen from the poll taken by the National Opinion Research Center (333); when parents were asked what's wrong with the schools, three out of five condemned the lack of discipline.

Professional support for this position is not lacking. Ask school administrators the chief cause of failure among young teachers. "Poor discipline," they will tell you, and will back it up with statistics (40, 221, 322, 454).

Ask the teachers themselves. Teachers in their first years of teaching complain that they have not been helped enough in their teacher preparation to meet the problems of discipline (148). Wightman (476) found that over a third of the entries in teachers' school diaries concerned these same problems.

Finally, many research reports (40, 110, 124, 221) show that even the pupils consider teacher discipline important. And as Stott (425) found, they are very critical of their parents' discipline.

What Is This Discipline?

We have been using the word "discipline" in its ordinary sense to mean the way that the adult exerts control over children, and also to mean the orderly and obedient behavior that this control is designed to secure. The control need not always provoke resentment or resistance (though it often does) and it may be positive as well as negative or prohibitive. But in what we call "discipline" there always is an element of constraint.

Some people even find it difficult to conceive of discipline without actual punishment. Indeed, for many persons "to discipline" seems to mean simply to punish by inflicting bodily pain on a child in order to compel his obedience.

This somewhat narrow conception of discipline is certainly out of line with current educational practice. Gone, or almost gone, are the days of

> 'Readin' and writin' and 'rithmetik'
> Taught to the tune of a hick'ry stick

and despite sentimental and nostalgic yearnings for the "good old days," few people would really welcome their return.

Within living memory there has been a tremendous decline in

both the severity and the amount of corporal punishment. Thus in 1881 in St. Louis, where the law required that a record be kept, there were 141 cases of corporal punishment for each 1000 pupils—about 5 thrashings a year on the average in each classroom (115). The wisdom of a particular thrashing was occasionally questioned; but the wisdom and, indeed, the necessity of corporal punishment in general were assumed without argument. At the turn of the century, when I started to school, whippings were still fairly commonplace; I got two myself, one in the first and one in the second grade. In contrast, most of you, I am sure, have never been thrashed at school nor have ever seen a school child punished by whipping or slapping. By 1924 in St. Louis there were only 1.7 corporal punishments for each 1000 children—a reduction of 98.5 percent from the 1881 average (115). Indeed, in about one fourth of all schools, corporal punishment is not allowed at all (213).

Corporal punishment, however, is not the whole story. As Agnes Benedict (55) puts it, "Though you see no whips in the classroom, you hear voices that carry the sting of a whip." In 1956 a sizable minority (about 1 in 5) of the teachers were complaining that they did not have sufficient authorization to *enforce* discipline as it should be enforced by more or less severe punishment if needed (213).

As I write there is an almost hysterical uproar in the press and elsewhere about the need for firmer discipline in order to prevent the growth of juvenile delinquency. Fifty-five percent of the parents questioned in a Gallup Poll thought that school officials should have the right to give pupils a "licking." As so often in a crisis, the cry goes up to DO something—in effect to do almost anything, whether it will improve or worsen the situation. In this case the demand is to get tough with the delinquent (and indeed with all children regarded as potential delinquents) rather than to search out the causes of the disorder.

Or, if there is any thought at all about causes, the argument seems to run something like this: Home and school discipline have become progressively soft while juvenile delinquency has been increasing alarmingly. Soft discipline is what causes the delinquency: "After this, therefore on account of this."

Although soft discipline is by no means as common as all this implies, Radke's and Stendler's data do show that for twenty-five or thirty years there has been a fairly clear trend away from strong coerciveness and toward a more democratic control of children (359, 416, 417). Perhaps the pendulum is now swinging back toward more regimentation. At any rate we are clearly in a period of some confusion in our thinking about discipline. In such a period it is especially important to take a firm grip on basic principles. We shall presently try to see what these are.

But what we think about discipline also depends greatly upon our attitude toward offenses. About most acts of juvenile delinquency there is of course little difference of opinion. We are all against sin. But about other kinds of troublesome behavior there is a wide range of opinion.

Where Do You Stand?

Would you like to compare your attitude with those of others?

Listed below are some of the behaviors about which parents and teachers are apt to feel concerned, selected from Stogdill's much longer list of "problem behaviors." How do you feel about these behaviors? Which do you think are relatively unimportant and which are of major concern?

Before you read further record your ratings in the spaces provided below or on a separate sheet. You need not think of what to do to correct these actions; just mark them in terms of how damaging they are to a child's development. Mark the most serious 10, the next 9 and so on down to the least serious as 1.

	Rating		Rating
a. unsociableness	( )	f. disrespect to elders	( )
b. daydreaming	( )	g. excessive modesty	( )
c. rudeness	( )	h. shyness	( )
d. suspiciousness	( )	i. contradicting elders	( )
e. disobedience	( )	j. impertinence	( )

Now that you have completed your rating, look back over the list. You will note that many of the items refer to behaviors that involve some sort of conflict with adults and seem to require discipline. (See Figure 2-1, where these items are shaded.) Other items refer to behaviors indicative of various other personality traits.

A large number of specialists—child psychologists and mental hygienists—have rated these same behaviors, basing their rating on

Figure 2-1. Relative Seriousness of Children's Behavior Problems

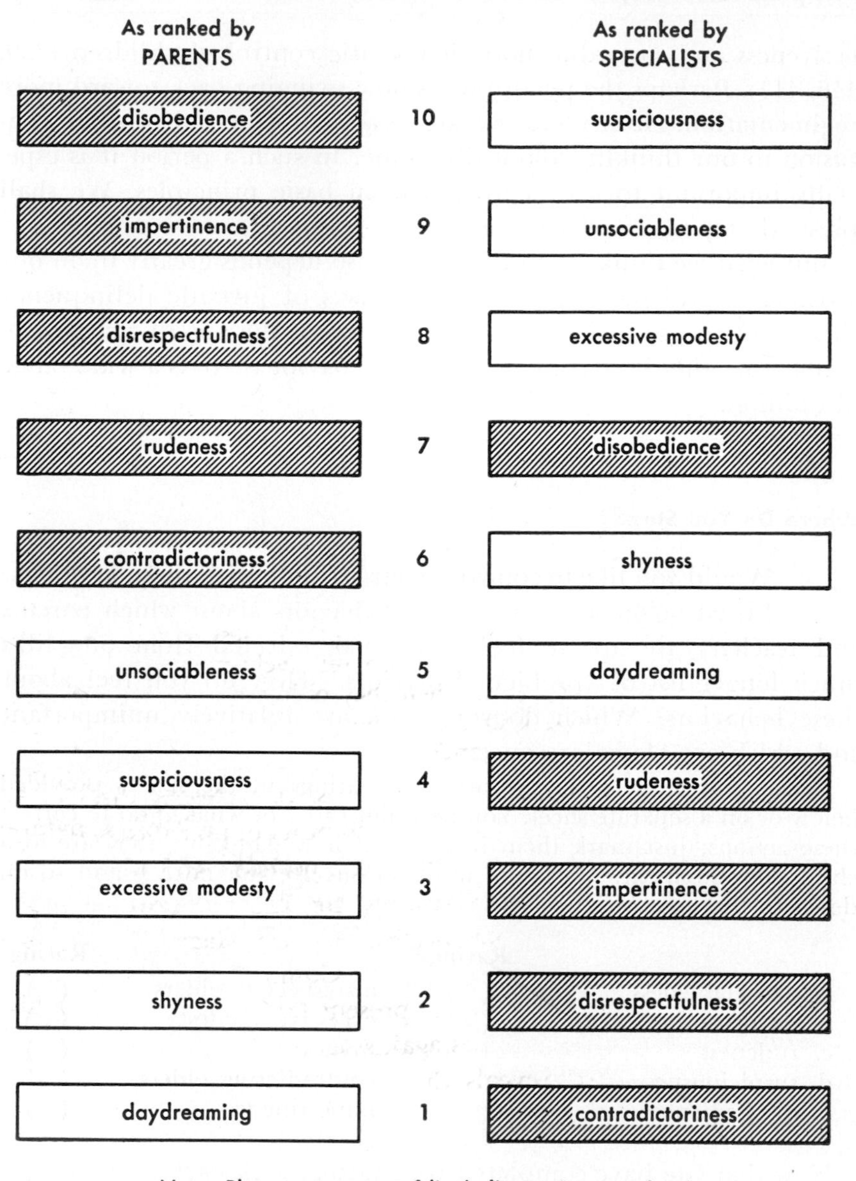

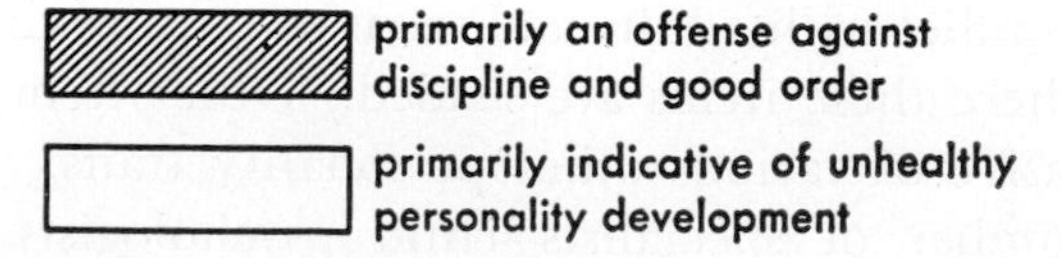

Adapted from Ralph M. Stogdill, The measurement of attitudes toward parental control and the social adjustment of children. *J. appl. Psychol.,* 1936, **20,** 259-267. The items used are selected from a longer list of problem behaviors.

their knowledge of what helps or hinders the child in what they consider to be wholesome development (421).

Note that the specialists do not consider most of the items that seem to require discipline—those shaded in Figure 2-1—very serious for the child's wholesome development; only "disobedience" gets into the top division. The average ranking of the discipline items according to the experts is only 3.4.

By averaging your own ratings for these same items, you can see how much you overestimated this sort of behavior as compared with the experts. If you were rather out of line, it may be consoling to look at the ratings made by a large group of parents. They put *all* the "discipline" items at the top; their average score for these items is 8 instead of 3.4.

QUESTIONS

(to be answered before reading further)

1. Why do the mental hygienists list suspiciousness as so serious?
2. Why do they list impertinence as a relatively minor problem?
3. Don't parents have a point when they object to impertinence? Isn't it right for children to keep a civil tongue in their heads? How would you answer such an argument?

Parents, of course, have a vested interest in reducing disciplinary behavior, so perhaps their overestimation of its importance is natural. Teachers, however, take nearly the same position and for the same reason; these behaviors make trouble for the adult in charge. A whole series of investigations beginning with Haggerty's (184) in 1925 followed by Wickman's celebrated Commonwealth Fund study (475), and coming on down to the present (352), shows that teachers take a very dim view of offenses against discipline. A recent study in southern France (487) reveals that French teachers are in this respect very like their American colleagues. In Britain also teachers hold "discipline" in high esteem (201, 454). And children, too. Whatever their actual conduct, they go along with parents and teachers in their judgment of what is "good" and "bad" (366). Fortunately, there is much evidence that, over the years, teachers have become increasingly sensitive to nondisciplinary problems, apparently largely as a result of the study of psychology (25, 214, 243, 376, 426). The same trend is found in the attitude of parents, though the change has been slower and less extensive (259, 359, 414).

So—how did you do? Were you—like many parents and teachers—most concerned about conduct that offends against discipline and good order? That would be understandable.

Understandable, but also unfortunate. For it means that you are deploring chiefly the kind of behavior which often comes merely from being "full of beans and high spirits." What we ought to be more concerned about is the child whose behavior is often praised as "good"; much so-called "goodness" is the result of lack of energy or of shyness or of morbid withdrawal from social contacts.

In contrast, the healthy, outgoing, up-and-coming child often gives us lots of trouble. At times he is almost sure to be rude and "sassy" and disobedient. I don't say these are admirable behaviors; they aren't. Yet more often than not they are merely the inevitable by-product of quite normal development. Let's not make the mistake of preferring a "good" child to one who is "good for something." Let's try to remember that a great many disciplinary situations are not really serious, troublesome though they may be at the moment.

With this much said to allay our anxieties about discipline, it remains true that there is a real problem. Let's look at it.

Is There a Substitute for Discipline?

Certainly, there is sometimes a substitute for discipline. If his Daddy's invitation to take a walk gets Bobby joyfully out into the fresh air he needs, the mother doesn't need any disciplinary measures. If a class project stimulates Janet's interest in arithmetic, her teacher doesn't need to use coercion. A good many problems of discipline can be short-circuited if we use our imaginations to find ways of making good conduct attractive. Every experienced parent or teacher knows, however, that it just isn't always possible to get the child to accept our "positive suggestions." He is too apt to have some of his own.

It is only in Utopia, moreover, that some of his goals will not be pretty undesirable. Since, for example, we cannot shield the child from movies and TV, nor from the ideas and activities of other children, we must resign ourselves to having him presently fired with ambition to be a gangster or a two-gun outlaw, and to have him play-acting accordingly. This includes doing a lot of things we wish he wouldn't.

We have barely time to breathe easier that this phase is over when some other craze catches him. If we are lucky, it may be a relatively harmless craze. If his conduct seems too far out of line, we can—and should—try counterattractions; they sometimes work. When they don't, there may be just nothing to do but put our foot down.

That's not the only time when we need discipline, either. Even if his goals are acceptable, the child may get into trouble out of sheer excessive zeal and eagerness. The three-year-old often needs to be saved from literally breaking his neck while trying some perfectly proper stunt for which he is not ready. An eighth-grader may need to be kept from imitating the college athlete to the detriment of his health. In school the intelligent, eager, and interested child often has to be tactfully held back from monopolizing discussion. In short, a child needs to be restrained even when he is doing the right thing but doing it with too much enthusiasm.

At the opposite extreme we find feeble and ineffective purposes. "Charlotte," her mother wrote me, "seems to want to do the right thing but she doesn't follow through. She wanted to play the piano but wouldn't keep up her lessons. She has tried painting, tap dancing, sewing, cooking, the oboe, and poetry. With none of these has she stuck it out long enough to gain any skill or to be of any real satisfaction to herself."

Common enough, you say? Yes, but her mother is right to be concerned. A strong personality is not likely to emerge from such capricious or aimless drift. It is not simply help in selecting goals that a child needs; he often needs a great deal of firm direction to ensure that he sticks to them. Nowhere is this more apparent than in the schoolroom.

In short, once more, discipline. We thus reach the conclusion—which to many of you doubtless has been obvious all along—that at times there is no substitute for discipline. The consequences of wrongdoing are sometimes too serious to be permitted. The child's immaturity in understanding and in his ability to control himself make it necessary for us to step in with disciplinary measures.

This does not necessarily mean punishment—we shall come to that a little later. It does not even mean that the child resists the discipline; children often welcome firm adult guidance. Nonetheless, only the perfect mother of the perfect child can always avoid a nasty little clash of wills. The clash may be a little less overt in the schoolroom but it is just as real.

QUESTIONS

1. Granted that a certain amount of rambunctious behavior is natural and a sign of high spirits, what is a teacher to do about it when it interferes with getting on with the job? Can you suggest a general principle to guide the teacher?
2. A few parents insist that they find no need for discipline with their children. Do you believe them? What do they mean?

Authority

Authority is power over the behavior of others. Psychologically it is "a relation between two or more persons such that commands, suggestions, or ideas of one of them influence the others." [2]

I introduce the topic of authority with some hesitation. A climate of opinion hostile to authority, or at least to the *word* "authority," has long been part of our culture in America. I hope my readers will postpone any tendency to reject the whole concept until the nature of authority has been set forth. Let it be said now, however, that there are many kinds of authority and many ways of exercising it. But of the *fact* of authority in human relations there can be no doubt. Authority is the basis of all discipline and of leadership as well.

The Origin of Authority [3]

To understand authority in the school, or elsewhere in life, we must consider its origin in infancy and its development primarily in the family circle. A child's response to authority has its roots deep in his earliest years. Above all other animals, the human has a prolonged and helpless infancy. During all his most plastic

[2] H. B. and A. C. English, *A Comprehensive Dictionary of Psychological and Psychoanalytical Terms* (New York: Longmans, 1958), p. 54.

[3] A semipopular statement of the role of authority in child development was published by the present writer in 1946 (135).

years, the child depends on his parents for his very survival. To them he turns for food, protection, support, and assistance of every character. And for love. Nearly every satisfaction of a baby's first few weeks is a result of adult help and guidance. Dependency is learned by association with a recurrent person whose presence and activity bring reward (418).

The child thus begins life under a sort of benevolent dictatorship. Where, even in the most totalitarian society, does any adult live under authority as complete as that which rules the conduct of infant and very young child? It is true that, after a few months, in some homes the case seems to be reversed: the child begins to reign as a veritable king.

Yet even in the most indulgent of homes, the child is apt to be not an absolute monarch but a constitutional ruler, subject to many restraints. Even for the child as king there is superior authority; moreover, his experience of ruling the roost is projected upon an earlier experience in which he was necessarily subservient to his elders. *Dependence upon superior authority and compliance with the suggestions of authority are thus among the child's earliest social responses.* This relationship is never wholly lost.

Compliance then, like dependence, is an inevitable mode of behavior, but the particular modes of compliance are not inevitable. Since compliant responses are more dynamic, more active, and therefore more important than the closely related dependency behavior, they will receive most of our attention.

In speaking of emotional and instrumental dependency Heathers (196) is making much the same distinction as we are between dependence and compliance. His experiments show that the two tendencies are distinguishable but closely related. Both Heathers and Beller (50), moreover, make the important point that children *may* grow in independence without losing their tendency to comply with authority and without losing a sort of affectional dependence.

Compliance

Compliance is the bedrock of social behavior. As infants all of us have depended upon a superior. We accepted what the superior did for us—there was nothing else we could do. A little later—only a very little later—we learned to accept the directions of the superior and to comply with them; that is, to do what we were directed to do.

Here, then, is the essential meaning of authority. We shall be embroidering the theme with all sorts of necessary embellishments but we must cling fast to this as central: *for every living human being, the first social relationship is one of recognizing and complying with the suggestions of authority.*

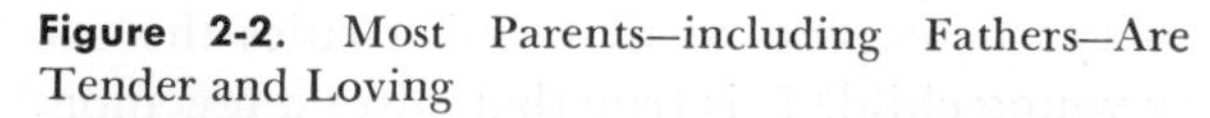

Figure 2-2. Most Parents—including Fathers—Are Tender and Loving

Some people resist recognizing this truth—we shall see why presently. Others accept this truth too eagerly—and we shall presently see why they are so eager. Like it or not, however, the early response to authority is a fundamental fact in all our lives.

In what guise does authority present itself to the infant? Fortunately, parents are usually tender and loving in the care of their children, especially when they are babies. We laugh at the Alice-in-Wonderland Duchess when she says, "Speak roughly to your little boy, and beat him when he sneezes," because this is so foreign to our treatment of the helpless young. Authority first presents itself to the infant in a mainly benign and friendly form. She who is the first authority is also the source of satisfaction and the first object of trust and of love.

By this last statement I do not mean to imply that the satisfactions the child gains from the mother are through some mysterious alchemy transformed into love. This view (which makes love a sort of derived or secondary drive) has an ancient history and is still popular in certain circles, but there is almost no direct evidence for it. I am merely saying that in early infancy the provision of satisfaction is the necessary *condition* for eliciting love.

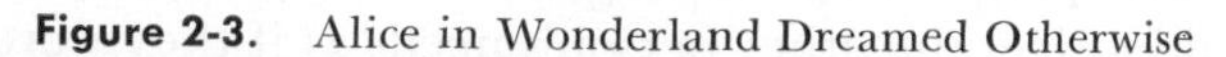

Figure 2-3. Alice in Wonderland Dreamed Otherwise

In his article "The Nature of Love" Harry Harlow (191) has recently shown that the primary satisfaction that leads to love need not be what we usually think of as biological. In monkeys the mother who provides milk but does not cuddle is less loved than the mother who cuddles but does not feed the infant. In human beings the effective satisfactions may be even further removed from the biologically useful. The mother who plays with the babe and who talks to him also provides intense satisfactions.

Identification

Now one of the things we do when we love someone is to identify ourselves with that person. That is, we tend to perceive the other person as in some sense an extension of ourselves; with that other person we enjoy a peculiar unity of purpose and feeling. We tend to feel the other person's needs as if they were our own. As Harry Overstreet (342, p. 103) puts it, "the love of a person implies not the possession of that person, but the affirmation of that person." Compliance with his wishes, yielding to his direction, does not seem to us self-abasement or loss of independence; we ourselves *want* to do these things. His goals become our goals.

Figure 2-4. "Show Daddy how big you are!"

In the very young, the beloved person's suggestions are simply carried out with satisfaction. The mother says, "Show Daddy how big you are!" and the child complies with a happy smile. Later the identification becomes more conscious. We feel that to yield to the beloved authority is the way to attain some of our own most enduring purposes and values. This has been recognized in religion, where identification with Supreme Authority is set forth as nobler than mere obedience. Thus we find such expressions as these: "I have no will, but to do the will of my Father in Heaven"; and "In His service is perfect freedom." Discipline in this case is a form of discipleship.

On a more mundane level, the identification with a beloved parent (or with society as a parent-substitute) is the motivation for a large part of our socially useful activities. Indeed, one may question whether without it society would not fall apart.

It is common to suppose that love of others is developed late and as a sort of counterpoise of an early or innate love of self. Clearly, however, love of self cannot arise until one has a self to love. Now the child is not born with a self; he gains his sense of selfhood through contact with the beloved mother, the "psychological organizer," as Bowlby (68) puts it, of the babe's unformed psyche. (See also Baldwin [30], Murphy [325], Spitz [409, 411] and Ausubel [22].) Long before he has a sharply defined self of his own to love, he is aware of the tender ministrations of another self who is "good." He builds his picture of his own self largely in the image of the loving parent.

Thus in infancy love of others is not opposed to love of self; and in a deeper sense I do not think it is so at any age. The fundamental fact is not that in loving one gives up or loses part of one's self ("altruism"); it is, rather, that love and identification with another are the essential bases for having a self at all. Outgoing love is earlier and more basic than self-love.

How early does it appear? Bridges (74) finds evidence for the appearance of a distinct emotion of affection at about eight months. But this emotion is a refinement of an earlier-appearing, vague, emotional pattern which she calls delight. When we have delight in the attending adult, as we do as early as the third or fourth month, we have the basis for the loving identification of later months and years.

The topic of identification has been dealt with extensively, especially in connection with family relationships. See, for example, Symonds (433), Levy and Munroe (272), Taft (434), Benne (57), Courtney (111), Hutt and Miller (215), and Stoke (423). How important it is for wholesome development, even for physical health, has been shown by a number of studies (68, 409, 410).[4]

It is clear that the fact of identification with the person in authority must have a profound effect upon the way the child reacts to authority. If, as seems to be true, the foundation stones of authority

[4] It may be noted that "identification" has two common meanings. We are using the term to mean that a child feels himself to be in some way identical with his mother or other beloved person. The other meaning does not deal with self but with two others who are reacted to as if they were the same—the child often reacts to the teacher as if she were the mother. Both meanings are useful and unlikely to be confused.

are hewn out of the hard rock of a necessary dependence, the cement by which they are bound together is love. *Attraction, not compulsion,* says Morton (323) *is the primary condition of the growth, if not the origin, of authority.*

Compliance and affection grow together out of the same soil, are displayed toward the same loving and powerful adult. In early infancy they are probably not distinct reactions; and throughout life they are closely connected. For most of us the basic social response is compliance with an authority who is loved.

Oppositional Behavior

Now that's a beautiful picture as we have sketched it, but if it is to correspond to reality we shall have to put in a few dark shadings. We have spoken of the mother's tender care of the child and of the satisfactions which she brings him. But from the child's point of view, the attending mother is also, and inevitably, responsible for deprivations and dissatisfactions as well as for satisfactions. Hence she becomes the object also of resistance, displeasure, and anger.

Oppositional behavior or resistance to the parent's authority thus begins early—in the nursery, if not in the bassinet. According to a series of careful psychological studies, certain manifestations of resistance reach their peak at about age two or three (84, 271, 364, 371). It is at this time that the child is most likely to resist even the simplest suggestion or request—and for no apparent reason. At least this is so in our culture; it might not prove to be so in another culture.[5]

In any case, resistance to authority does not just cease when the child passes his fourth birthday. Every mother's son and daughter displays a little resistance; some more, some less. A Swiss study of 12,000 pupils between six and fifteen found 17 percent of them ha-

[5] The concept of "culture" is an important one in psychology. Culture is the totality of the ways of life of a particular social group: the complex tissue of habits and skills and ways of earning a living, and the tools and machines used in this pursuit; institutions such as church, school, and government; and, of special interest for psychology, the beliefs, ideas, and customs of a society. Within the pattern of a larger culture, such as that of a nation, subcultures may be distinguished: the culture of a locality, of a religious group, even of so small a unit as a family. The individual lives in constant interaction with his culture, is molded by it. No other animal has a real culture; man is inconceivable without one.

bitually in rebellion against the authority figures in their lives, boys more than girls in the ratio of three to one.

Besides being a great nuisance, this negativism of our beloved children hurts our feelings. It may help us if we realize that a good deal of the resistance of the two- and three-year-old springs from the simple fact that he just doesn't understand what we want him to do.[6]

Much of it, moreover, can be avoided. Some of the child's resistance is to the inevitable limitations of life. But a large part of it develops when someone interferes with what he is doing or deprives him of something he wants. More often than not, oppositional behavior is really counteropposition; from the child's point of view it is the adult who first opposes him.

Parents—who believe, of course, that their actions are practically always "reasonable"—are usually quite unaware of the degree to which they frustrate the young child. The older child sometimes gets the point of the regulations; at least he has had a lot of practice in taking interference in his stride. (Psychologists like to speak of his developing "frustration tolerance.") But the young child doesn't appreciate adult motives and hasn't learned to accept interference. He has been accustomed, as an infant, to being treated like a doll; now we seek to "socialize" him, to get him to "behave himself."

Thus, we insist that the child shall not eat between meals although he may be hungry, shall not destroy "property" (whatever that is), shall not fight but instead "cooperate" or even give in to brothers and sisters and to other playmates, shall keep quiet when father is reading or mother is resting. (Above all in most homes, he must not touch his genitals.) No wonder the child sometimes strikes back, literally or in angry words, against so many and such rigid prohibitions.

Most of these things children must indeed learn, but we should be careful lest we make the pace of learning too fast. Thus, a limited amount of cooperation can be taught to three-year-olds, but it does no good to cram it down their throats. Real cooperativeness must wait. There will be fewer negativistic personalities around when parents ease up a little on the speed of socialization.

---

[6] A parent of a mentally deficient child comments that the retarded child remains much longer in this period of not understanding our simple requests and thus has a longer time in which to acquire the habits of negativism.

In all of this we need a sense of proportion. In most cases, resistance merely means that a child has grown up enough to make a choice, and that his choice, unhappily, happens to differ from ours. I say "unhappily" because it does tend to make us unhappy. Yet it should not. As David Levy (271) says, this oppositional behavior is part of the "general movement towards autonomy of the whole per-

Figure 2-5. "Oh Mommy, see all the nice No, No's!"

son, the first flowering of self-determination, and should be regarded as one of the protective and self-propelling functions that enables the child to overcome [excessive] infantile dependency." We may as well get used to the fact that our children don't ever completely identify themselves with us; they early show signs of wanting to be independent. We wouldn't want it to be otherwise. Resistance is thus by no means always a bad sign.

Hostility

Yet let's face it. We can't always avoid interfering with the child, and we can't interfere and not have him feel anger and resentment. As a result, an attitude of hostility slowly develops toward us.

That's an unpleasant idea and most of us tend to reject it at first. We admit that a child may display sharp anger, but the anger is temporary. Hostility, however, we don't like to ascribe to an innocent child. Yet I heard no objection when I suggested that the child develops an attitude of love out of his experience of parental helpfulness and goodness. Isn't it just as reasonable to think that he learns hostility from thwarting and frustrating? Of course I am saying that he feels *both* love and hostility.

Perhaps this is the place to make clear how I am using the terms "love" and "hostility." They refer to the more or less permanent or lasting attitudes or sentiments which result from repeatedly feeling affection or anger. Despite all the differences between the manifold varieties of love—love of mother or father, love of mate, love of comrades, love of pets, love of country, love of God—it is usually held that a common element runs through them all. All genuine love responses belong together in one class. All the varieties of feeling which lie at the opposite pole from love, ranging from mild dislike down to violent hatred, seem equally to have a common quality. And it is only common-sense realism to face the fact that all children feel hostility for those who repeatedly frustrate and thwart them, just as they love those who bring them satisfactions or facilitate their struggle to satisfy their needs.

We have tried in the preceding discussion to direct attention to the dynamic interactions between the adult authority-figure and the child, and the way these influence the child's development. Perhaps it will help if we present here in outline form a structural analysis of the authority-situation—that is, a listing of its elements.

I do not suggest that you memorize this outline. It should help your understanding if you first find illustrations of each kind of behavior. Then you should consider, for each of these elements, when it occurs and what effects it has. As our discussion has implied, these elements are not of equal importance, but all of them occur and are influential in constituting the total complex of the authority-relation. Moreover, they form a system—that is to say, each of these behaviors affects the tendency to make the others.

THE AUTHORITY COMPLEX

I. The Objective Relationship: an adult, superior in knowledge and power, and a dependent child

II. The Adult's Behavior
- A. Nurture—the direct provision of satisfaction to the child (feeding, rocking, patting, and later smiling, etc.)
  1. Volunteered or proferred
  2. Yielded to appeal or demand
  3. Given as reward
- B. Directive or controlling behavior
  1. Physical constraints (*not* including inflicting pain)
  2. Orders, imperatives
  3. Requests
  4. Appeals
  5. Suggestions
  6. Aggressions
     - a. Physical attack (inflicting pain)
     - b. Deprivation of satisfaction
- C. Clarification and information-giving

III. The Child's Overt Responses to Adult Behavior
- A. Passive acceptance
- B. Compliance
- C. Submission
- D. Resistance
- E. Avoidance
- F. Appeal

IV. The Child's Feeling Responses
- A. Ranging from love to hostility and hatred
- B. Ranging from delighted approval to violent disapproval of parent behavior
- C. Moods

The form of this outline has been influenced by the analysis of Roger G. Barker and Herbert F. Wright, *Midwest and its Children*. Evanston, Ill.: Row, 1954.

Ambivalence

Early in life then, the mother, as the primal source of authority whose wishes are so lovingly complied with, becomes also the authority whose wishes or demands may be resisted as hateful. Compliance and love, opposition and hostility, spring from the same source in the infant's dependence upon the parent for satisfaction and dissatisfaction. These are the basic components of authority.

Figure 2-6. Our Reactions to Authority Fall Somewhere on the Sphere between the Poles of Love and Hostility

Because of their common origin these apparently divergent responses are closely connected throughout our lives. We cannot resist authority wholeheartedly: to resist is to be already half prepared to comply. Have you not yourself seen how easily children pass from love to hate and perhaps back again, all within a few minutes? We cannot accept anyone as authority without some degree of love but also not without some degree of hate, nor can we hate without love. This concept of ambivalence, as you probably know, is a major one of psychoanalysis. Indeed, it is an old concept, long recognized by poets. Congreve long ago wrote, "Heaven has no rage like love to hatred turned," and a perceptive modern poet-essayist, Rebecca West (473), speaks of "our fluctuating partisanship to love and hate," adding, "However much we hate we also love." In "A Long Day's Journey into Night" Eugene O'Neill tells us that hate does not invalidate love; love does not exorcise hate. They coexist without resolution.

Yet it is not a simple ambivalence. Sometimes a child complies readily, yet with hatred in his heart; his dull, sullen submission is quite unlike the joyful obedience of the child who loves and identifies himself with his parents. Sometimes even the most loving child resists. And even the bitter rebel feels the pull of authority. And of course the reaction of a child to the father's authority more often than not is quite different from his reaction to his mother's.

Compliance and resistance, love and hate, submission and revolt—all these are woven into a complex and individual pattern.

QUESTIONS

1. Even if it be granted that a child's earliest social reaction is one of compliance with authority, to what extent need this be reflected in his adult life?
2. It was admitted that in another culture the peak of resistance might come at another time than age three. What cultural factors might cause a shift?
3. Do you accept the view that a common thread runs through all kinds of love? What kind of evidence would bear on the question?
4. Isn't it an exaggeration to suppose that all children hate parents? Have you ever in fact known any child younger than ten who really *hated* his parents? How can one tell?

Different Homes, Different Authority

Children respond alike to authority because they have been treated so much alike. All of us are born as babies and have attending mothers; and all of us are dependent for many years upon adult care. The similarity of experience thus involved imposes a great similarity in our responses to those in authority. We all learn the same lessons because the same things happen to us.

Yet even infants do not have exactly the same experiences, and as they grow older their experiences grow even more diverse. Despite all the pressure for conformity, parents still cling to their right to have their own ideas about how to bring up children; and even when their ideologies are similar, their personalities are different. Hence arise parallel differences in their children's reactions to their authority (77).

Mrs. Jenkins is conspicuously fair-minded, just, and self-sacrificing. Moreover, she is a very attractive and lovable person—altogether the most glorious person her son Weldon, now seventeen, has ever known. Her authority has been steady and at times pretty firm, but reasonable. As a result, Weldon has always been comfortable about authority. Although, for example, he is capable of criticizing the errors of his schoolteachers, he usually falls into step with their suggestions or requests, and finds a real satisfaction in doing so.

Mrs. Brubaker is another extremely attractive mother, and her son Gordon is no less devoted to her than is Weldon to his mother. Mrs. Brubaker, however, is obviously too lenient and indulgent with Gordon. There are few conflicts between the two: Gordon is usually pleased to accept his mother's authority—why should he not be when she usually wants him to do just the things which please him anyway? But Gordon finds it difficult to adjust to anyone else's authority, particularly if the authority is a bit stern or exacting. In kindergarten, after an initial period of adjustment, he got along pretty well with his teacher, who was a very gentle and permissive person—like his mother, you see. But later teachers found him touchy and resentful.

It is easy to see how the personalities of these two mothers have given a sort of halo to the kind of authority they represent. Their kind is expected and preferred.

There are innumerable varieties in the home pattern of authority. In most homes we have not one but two patterns, one for each parent. Inconsistency in parental control may even present a whole covey of authority-patterns until, in extreme cases, the poor child can frame no dependable image of authority at all.

If you are a teacher or anyone who works directly with children, you will inevitably meet the products of these patterns. Let us look at a few. If we take as our examples homes in which certain behavior is carried to extremes it may be easier to judge the effect of that sort of behavior in milder cases.

The Overregulated Home

One of the commonest varieties is the home in which the parents try to regulate every detail of the child's daily living. Sometimes this excessive regulation is due to the parents' love of power but more often it comes from too great solicitude—i.e, actually from love that is somewhat misdirected—or from a distorted sense of values. One mother put the case for most of her type: "If I don't tell Jim exactly what to do and how to do it, he just doesn't get things done right."

Anyone who has had a hand in bringing up children knows how right she is. Nonetheless, so much regimentation misses its mark. What is it that this mother is trying to get done? Is it the picking up of playthings, the wearing of snow boots when it is slushy, the use of good manners or good grammar? All worthy objectives no doubt. And more easily attained if we issue detailed orders and then see that they are carried out.

Yet of course these are not the real things. What we really want is to have our child grow in resourcefulness, self-dependence, and initiative. Well yes, neatness, too, and politeness and all the rest; but we want him to do these things for himself and by himself. And of course we know, when we stop to think, that we don't get this by regimentation.

Stopping to think is a luxury, however, when guests are expected for dinner and Jim's toys are strewn over the dining room floor and the last touches have to be put on the dessert. It is terribly hard to get out of the habit of doing things for a child as if he were a baby, perhaps even harder to get out of the habit of ordering him around till *he* does things—all in the name of efficiency. One of the chief values of nursery school and kindergarten is that it gives the child a chance to do things without so many and such restrictive orders. But in most schools, when the child leaves the kindergarten for the first grade, he finds himself again in a highly regimented environment—as restrictive as the home, perhaps even more so, and with regulations less acceptable because they do not emanate from love.

QUESTIONS

1. How much regulation is too much? How can you tell?
2. Don't children invariably think themselves overregulated? Looking back on your own home, did you feel that way? How do you feel now?
3. Children used to "Stand! Turn! March!" from school with military precision. Nowadays it is all much more informal. But is there really less regulation?

Loveless Authority

In many homes the orders are not only too many and too restrictive; they are imposed in a harsh and unaffectionate manner. A few parents actually do not love their children, though of course they protest that they do. Others probably do love them but it is hard to believe it when we see them "disciplining" their children. Try keeping a record for a week—I am suggesting that you make an actual written record—of all the methods you see in public places—busses, parks, stores—whereby a parent is controlling a child's behavior. Count the gentle means of control, the quiet gesture, the pleasant word, the meaningful smile. Count also the unkind yanks, the strident commands, the threats, the blows. What is the relative frequency? All is not yet sweetness and light in the rearing of children.

Authority begins, we remember, in a union of compliance with love. In our dealings with the very young infant we recognize that it is impossible to show him too much tenderness, and there is almost nothing we won't do for his happiness or comfort. But by the time he is two years old, his capacity to move around and his growing capacity "to have ideas of his own" about what to do bring him into conflict with authority—that is, with us. This, as we saw earlier, is inevitable and natural—a sort of psychological growing pains. We need to meet the little one's puny attempts at independence or resistance with a sense of humor. And with love. As Rabindranath Tagore says, "For he only may chastise who loves."

A great many mothers, however, though they manifest their love in countless ways, do not let it show when they are most sharply enacting their role as authority. Love at other times is all right, they seem to say, but when we discipline we have to be severe. Thus in-

Figure 2-7. Contrasted Parental Behaviors

stead of authority evoking loving compliance, it brings forth only subservient obedience. A sort of "divorce" breaks the union of love with authority.

Some parents—I am afraid a great many—even believe that the best way to punish a child is to withdraw all signs of love when he does not conform to orders. Perhaps worst of all are those who seem to make the continuance of love contingent on achievement or on good behavior and thus fill the child with a wordless anxiety lest he fail to live up to unstated or vaguely defined standards. Instead of learning how to cope with the actual task, the child must strive to learn what will bring him parental love or save him from parental disapproval. The whole learning process is distorted (80). And in nearly all cases of problem behavior and of delinquency we find a feeling of parental rejection playing a great part.

If there is enough counterbalancing evidence that his parents do love him—the evidence must be visible to the child himself—this form of punishment may have little ill effect. The child just doesn't believe it when he is threatened with loss of love. (In that case, how effective do you think the threat will be?) But those who use this threat run a considerable risk.

Starting to school sometimes creates a special problem. In an astonishing number of cases studied in our psychological clinics, the child is found to believe that his parents are sending him to school to get rid of him. One three-year-old defined nursery school as "Where your mama sends you so you won't be in the way." This he interpreted, reasonably enough, as desertion and the withdrawal of her love. No wonder that he sat silent, withdrawn, hating teacher and school and all that went with it.

Of course, he was probably mistaken. Mostly so, that is; for beyond question there was a small element of truth in what he believed. We often *do* want to get children out from under our feet. No matter how much we love them, they can be quite a nuisance. Naturally, however, we can't expect the children to understand the subtle shadings involved in all this; they are apt to feel that we just don't want them around. Now if the children, however wrongly and even only part of the time, *feel* rejected, love and authority move too far apart.

The school situation itself may not help things. The teacher of course becomes a sort of substitute mother, but with what a difference! Behind her she does not have the years of loving helpfulness which support the mother's authority. Her initial kindness is apt to be followed promptly by some fairly peremptory orders—after all, she has from twenty to forty children to manage, and quiet gentleness sometimes takes time. Even in the best of cases, the teacher's authority is apt to bear down a little more heavily than that of the home. For the child who has already begun at home to experience the divorce of love from authority, strictness at school has an intensified effect.

When authority presents itself in a loveless guise, the child is blocked from identifying himself with the person in authority. To comply with his mother's or teacher's authority, therefore, is not to find satisfaction by accepting her goal as his own; to comply means giving up his own goals merely because he must. So, if he can, he rebels. Even when he recognizes that his parents' authority is wise and just, it seems to him an unlovely thing that limits his freedom. As I pointed out earlier, a *little* opposition to authority is natural and helpful in the process of growing up. But the child is to be pitied who feels that he must always resist, that if he ever complies with anyone's suggestions he is surrendering his own independence.

A vicious circle results. When he sallies forth from his home, the rebel, whether the active, aggressive type, or the sullen passive resister, creates an atmosphere in which it is very difficult for persons in authority to give him love. The teacher at school finds it very hard to "accept" a child who defies her, flouts her authority, weakens her position with the other children. So the poor youngster who defies his teacher because he feels rejected at home now finds the teacher, too, rejecting him. No wonder that eventually he cannot think of authority as anything but hostile.

At least, this often seems to be the case. Yet even for such tragic children, lurking in the background is a craving to find, once more as in the blessed days of infancy, authority that is the source of good, authority that can be loved. The success with which young rebels and young delinquents are often cured in such places as the George Junior Republics and Boys' Towns, where they find themselves accepted, attests to this fact.

QUESTIONS

1. What was the ratio of kind to unkind treatment that you observed?
2. How do you show a child that you love or accept him at the moment he is defying you and you feel that you must exact obedience?

3. The text speaks of clinic cases who feel rejected. Of course these are unusual. How about those who never get to the clinics?

Overaffectionate Authority

In many homes, especially in really good homes, the error lies in the opposite direction. Authority is too personal, too wrapped up and bound by the ties of affection; it centers too much in the beloved mother (or occasionally the father). Overdependency is rewarded at the expense of independence (418). The child's self is so closely linked with the parent that further growth tends to be inhibited.

This is natural enough; yet it represents a stage in development which must be overcome. A young friend of mine has lost position after position because he cannot work for a man whom he does not look upon as a sort of father. He gets stubborn and mulish, resistant to even the mildest and most reasonable of suggestions.

The famous psychiatrist, Edward S. Strecker, has written a whole book, *Their Mothers' Sons* (428), devoted to showing the evils of what he calls "momism," the excessive dependence upon the authority of a beloved mother. The good doctor has been accused of exaggeration; probably "momism" is not quite so common as he implies. But he has a point. Where love is almost the sole basis of relation to one's parents we get slavish conformity. Overdependency is rewarded and the development of independence is retarded (418). It is a terrible handicap in adult life to be able to recognize authority only in persons one can love.

David Ausubel's (22) description of a child as becoming "satellized" is perhaps less journalistic. Such a child unhesitatingly accepts parent values, becomes excessively dependent upon the parent for direction and approval. Later the child may assume a satellite relation to some other authority-figure, even to a peer. The lieutenant of a juvenile gang is a good example of such a satellite.

In the culture of our own country the mother usually continues, to the greater or less exclusion of the father, to be both the authority-figure and the love-figure for a longer time than is the case in Europe. She is the dispenser of rewards, the giver of protection and comfort; but she is also the rule giver and the dispenser of punishments. Ours is a matriarchal society. (Many European observers see America as a culture in active revolt against the father. See, for example, Louis Dermigny's recent book, *U.S.A.—Essai de mythologie americaine.)*

Little by little, of course, the father begins to assume the authority-role. But this new authority-figure is not so easily invested, at the stage of late childhood, with the affection that the primary authority-figure carries. In Europe the father begins to play an important role as authority much earlier at a time when fathers are more likely to be direct sources of affectionate satisfaction. The shift from maternal to paternal authority is more gradual.

Sooner or later a child must learn that authority need not be lodged solely in the beloved father or mother. Other persons, less beloved, sometimes take their place. There can be all sorts of substitute parent-figures, from baby sitters or grandmothers to schoolteachers and scoutmasters. It is good also for older brothers and sisters to exercise a limited amount of authority.

And then, of course, a child needs to recognize the authority of the social group. Hard as it may be for the adult to have a "mere child" challenge his authority in the name of what "the gang says," it is a sign of the child's growth. Moreover, not to accept the coauthority of the gang is to risk losing one's authority altogether.

Impersonal Authority

Eventually, also, the child must learn the value of impersonal authority. He must learn to respect the authority of facts and things, of reason, and of critical, reflective thinking. He must be willing to accept the authority of impersonal law, of impersonal truth, and of ideals (143).

True, the impersonal is easier to accept as authority when it comes to us cloaked in the garb of the personal. That, no doubt, is the reason we so often personify such ideals as "Justice" or "Mercy." Since authority originates in a personal relation it can seldom become completely impersonal. And direct personal authority remains for every one of us a major influence throughout our lives.

But it can be too influential. In our own time we have seen whole nations hypnotized by a dynamic personality into the acceptance of dangerous and irrational ideas and ideals. If America ever slips down the road to dictatorship it will be in large part because we have not learned to go beyond the kind of authority that is exercised by a beloved human personality. The founders of our democracy had good reason to surround political leadership with so many checks and balances.

It is thus pure gain when the child finds authority outside the immediate family. When he finds authority outside the circle of strong personal affection, he is taking an important step toward depersonalizing his response to authority. Naturally the step cannot be too long nor be taken too fast. The teacher, for example, as a substitute for parental authority, should not be a cold-blooded, impersonal machine. Only if a great deal of affection pervades the new relation will an adequate transfer of authority from parent to teacher take place.

But the loss, if not the danger, of basing authority chiefly upon an appeal to affection must be squarely faced. There is a kind of child who is, we are told, "very easily managed—no disciplinary problem at all. All he needs is kindness." Of course that is *not* all he needs. Such an affection-demanding and affectionate child requires very careful handling if he is to develop a more mature differentiation between affection and submission. Though the self originates in identification with another, *excessive* identification means a failure to develop one's own self.

QUESTIONS

1. What can a mother who really loves her child do to avoid "momism" without running into the dangers of rejection?
2. How can teachers help the child who is too dependent on love for authority?

The Bossy Home

In many homes there is strong emphasis upon obedience as the very heart and center of the relation of the child to his parents—obedience enforced when need be by coercion and punishment. This attitude is called authoritarianism and has been made the object of extensive study in recent years. Bossiness may be used to describe the overt *means* used to enforce obedience. It is theoretically possible for parents to be somewhat bossy and to use many repressive restraints without being basically authoritarian in attitude. But bossy techniques have a reflex effect upon the attitude, and the two are seldom separate. Usually, the home that insists upon implicit obedience is also overregulated as well; the rules are not only strict but numerous.

Bossiness is far from being a sign of a strong, secure relation of authority between parent and child. On the contrary, it is when our authority is weak that we try to bolster it up with bossy demands for obedience—"or else!" Genuine authority is a psychological relation, a two-way bridge of communication between the leader and the led. There is no single kind of act which is the act of exercising true authority. Any act of the person in authority which the child finds helpful strengthens the authority-relation. It is not too much to say that *real authority does not need to be asserted: it is accepted and it works.* It does not require—indeed, it is damaged by—bossy behavior.

Bossy behavior, however, can often get quick results. Through coercion we can compel obedience which seems to fit the immediate situation, even though this may be at the expense of the child's long-term needs, especially of his need to develop initiative and spontaneity and *self*-discipline.

Some bossy parents are uneasy about it. They recognize that some day the child must learn to manage himself, and they are only too aware that he is not making much progress under a regime of parental domination. Meanwhile, however, the immediate problem, they feel, must be met. As one mother put it in an open-forum discussion of discipline: "I've tried leading my son but it just doesn't work. All he seems to understand is force." At which many heads were nodded in agreement.

A little later in the discussion she was to sharpen up the problem: "If my child does not recognize my authority and follow my leadership, how can I control him without using force? You can't just let a child run wild."

With the last, of course, we all agree. And there are few parents who don't sympathize with the questioner. Yet when we spread the problem out so that we can think about it calmly, it is easy to see at least the main outline of the answer. How can we expect a child to recognize a real authority relationship who has known only authoritative dominance? True, this mother *briefly* tried "leading the child," but at the first failure she regressed to her familiar pattern of coercion. She gave him very little chance to learn to recognize her authority and leadership.

I suppose we always have to compromise a little between doing the things which get results in the immediate situation and doing the things which help the child's long-term development. But this mother's "compromise" almost wholly neglects the latter. A child has to *learn* to recognize authority. It is a natural enough thing for him to learn, but, as we have been emphasizing, there's nothing automatic or instantaneous about it. Like all learning, it takes time and experience. Moreover, we cannot expect the learning to be perfect, especially if we haven't provided the favorable conditions for it. Bossiness doesn't help much in building a sound authority relation between parent and child.

If a parent has been relying too much on authoritativeness, as a great many do, both parent and teacher have a nice problem. The child has become accustomed to heeding only when someone "lays down the law." He has come to recognize authority only when it is dressed up in the trappings of an authoritative, domineering manner. Thus when one lays aside this manner, there's a danger that the child will ignore the authority.

We shouldn't just give up at the first failure. The real basis of authority is the child's awareness of superiority and the fact that the superiority is used to give him satisfaction. That can be built up. Not, of course, by argument or even by reminding him in so many words that he will be better off if he does what the adult suggests. There's no magical technique to fit every situation. The important thing is to get the child to *feel* the steady effect of authority's loving support of *his* purposes.

The problem is more difficult when the adult's domineering techniques spring from an inner desire to be boss. None of us is above a little hankering to display our superiority, to exercise dominance over others. If one doesn't watch out, the hankering gets out of hand. Instead of using superiority to promote the child's development, a person winds up cherishing authority and the ability to compel obedience as ends in themselves. He ends up by being *authoritarian.*

What are the earmarks of the authoritarian? Listen to the mother who snarls: "It's none of your business why. You do as I tell you and don't ask questions." Does she give this order primarily to get the child to do something that would be satisfying or good for him, or to inflate her own sense of power? Insistence upon implicit and undeviating obedience, upon obedience for obedience's sake, upon "respect" for one's authority—in all these the desire to wield power over others is more important than concern for the child's development.

Some parents, and practically all teachers, who have the authoritarian attitude justify it on the ground of concern for the child. They say, and they even seem to believe, that it serves the child's moral development to stand in fear and awe of authority. We don't need to question the sincerity of the belief that undeviating authority is good for the child, but we may question whether the belief does not originate in love of power rather than in concern for what happens to the child who is thus drastically regimented.

For we are beginning to get concrete evidence of the bad effects of authoritarianism. People often defend it, as we noted a little earlier, on the grounds that at least it gets results. Even this is pretty doubtful as is shown in the famous experiment of Lewin, Lippitt, and White (278).

A Real-Life Experiment. In this experiment the boys belonging to a club-workshop were systematically exposed to three different kinds of leadership. In one the adult leader planned all the details of a club project, gave each boy his task, supervised the work rather carefully. He was friendly and pleasant and the work itself was fun; but there was no doubt at all who was boss. This was autocratic or authoritative leadership.

In the second type of leadership, if we can call it that, the adult exercised no real control at all. If one of the boys asked for help, he was more or less tactfully brushed off. Most of the time the "leader" sat idly by, allowing the project to take its own course. This the experimenters called the *"laissez-faire"* or "let-alone" policy.

In the third type of leadership, the adult participated with the boys in planning and carrying on the project. This was called democratic leadership.

While all this was going on, a concealed motion-picture camera and an observer recorded the details of what took place. The results should not have surprised anyone but apparently they have.

What is your guess, how did authoritative direction work? Would you say, "The boys didn't like it but they got a lot done, because there was no horseplay and they knew what to do"? That was the guess of one parent; it is half right. Right that the boys didn't like the autocratic leadership, wrong that they tended to business and got a *lot* done. Quotas were met, but only when the leader kept the pressure high. The boys vented their objection to so much regimentation not only against the leader but against the project and the other boys. They quarreled a lot, were rude to each other, were careless and spoiled material, showed increasing loss of interest and general disorder, and were frequently absent. It just isn't true that regimentation is efficient.

How, then, about the "let-alone" policy? Logically we would expect it to be more like democratic than autocratic leadership. Unfortunately, it didn't come out that way. "Laissez faire" seems to have about the same kinds of results as autocracy. Too little control evoked much the same kind of misconduct as too much. Disorder and quarreling we might have expected. But there was also the same sort of slackness and lack of interest.

The alternative to authoritativeness, even for the short run, is not the surrender of authority but the exercise of democratic or cooperative authority. By every sort of test which could be devised, the boys in the experiment reacted best under a democratic leader. They did more work, they quarreled less, they obviously enjoyed their activity more (as shown by more faithful attendance).

A Field Study of Real Homes. In a study carried out over a four-year period by the Council for Research in the Social Studies of Columbia University, children from strict, authoritarian homes were compared with those from highly "permissive" homes (463, 464). Only "good" homes were considered, homes in which both parents lived with their children and in which there were no cases of delinquency or "problem behavior" in the usual sense. Unless the home visitors were convinced that the children were wanted and were given plenty of love, the homes were excluded. Careful distinction was made between "strictness" and harshness or cruelty and between "permissiveness" and carelessness and neglect. To repeat—here were two kinds of *good* homes, but homes of sharply contrasted, even rather extreme, kinds of discipline.

For example, the permissive homes were those in which the parents believed—and acted on their beliefs—that "children can well make most of their decisions for themselves; parents should respect the child's developing inner self-direction. Children need freedom; their own experience will tell them what works well and what does not; they will naturally model themselves after their parents if they love these parents; scolding and spanking do more harm than good." In such homes the children eat about as they like, sleep when sleepy, are not required to keep their toys orderly, usually work out their quarrels with their brothers and sisters in their own way, may tell off their parents—or anyone else—if they feel like it. In short, these homes correspond to the stereotyped picture of "everything goes," the so-called progressive or overprivileged home of which Mrs. Ferguson was speaking at the beginning of this chapter.

We can more briefly characterize the "strict" home. It is the typical "old-fashioned" home of many strictly enforced rules. Quarrels are repressed, boisterous play is strictly regulated, no impudence is permitted, politeness is taught and insisted on. In such homes parents often explain the necessity of rules but do not formulate them cooperatively with the children; obedience rather than reasoning is the primary concern.

Surprisingly enough in view of all the clamor in the public press about excessive freedom, it proved difficult to find homes that met the criteria of permissiveness. Homes of occasional indulgence, yes, very many of these. Inconsistently permissive homes, not a few. But homes where the parents really carried through on this line were hard to find. On the other hand, strict homes, consistently strict homes, were much more common—about 3 to 1 in suburban Westchester County, New York. Most homes, of course, fall in between; but to evaluate the effect of a given treatment it is often desirable to look at extremes. The children compared were matched for age, sex, education, and intelligence as well as for the above-mentioned lack of pronounced problem behavior.

How, then, did the children from these sharply contrasting kinds of homes differ? First, children from permissive homes were far more likely to be spontaneous, creative, and original; children from strict homes, to be conventional and stereotyped in their ideas and in executing them. Related to this was the tendency of the "permissives" to be more independent; the "stricts," to be dependent. For example, given a chance to play as they liked in a room full of attractive toys, the children from strict homes kept turning to the adult to see if they were "doing all right." By a ratio of 4 to 1, the "stricts" were more frequently found extremely dependent upon adults.

It is perhaps not surprising that freedom should help a child to be more independent and spontaneous. But it is a little surprising to find that children from strict and well-regulated homes are less likely to be considerate, cooperative, friendly, and popular with their fellows. (The "permissives" win by a ratio of 3 to 1.)

As we know also from previous studies (e.g., 399), children from strictly regulated homes, where they are not free to express resentments directly, become touchy and too easily upset—especially when away from home.

Finally, the "permissives" more often showed good sense in solving difficult problems. The "stricts" seemed to be divided into two groups: those who gave up too easily, and those who stuck bullishly at it (often using the same method over and over) long after it was apparent that the method would fail. The "permissives" used more varied methods, but when it was clear that the problem was beyond them they gave up with good grace.

There have been more than a score of other investigations, studying in all several thousand persons. Despite many differences in the way the researches were designed, a pretty consistent picture begins to emerge. In the first place, children brought up in authoritarian homes tend strongly to become authoritarian themselves. As the authors say in summary of one very extensive investigation:

> An authoritarian, exploitive parent-child relationship is apt to carry over into a power-oriented, exploitively dependent attitude towards one's sex partner and one's God, and may well culminate in a political philosophy and social outlook which has no room for anything but a desperate clinging to what appears to be strong and a disdainful rejection of whatever is relegated to the bottom. Conventionality, rigidity, repressive denial and the ensuing break-through of one's weakness, fear, and dependency are but other aspects of the same fundamental personality pattern. [4]

From other investigations come reports showing that adults and adolescents who have grown up in regimented authoritarian homes (and schools) are more likely to be quarrelsome, nervous, less able to face reality, less happy, excessively dependent, giving up too easily in the face of difficulties, and, in general, maladjusted (17, 24, 31, 150, 280, 305, 321, 462, 477). Even the intellectual development of children is hampered in such homes (97, 247). It is from highly authoritarian homes, moreover, that the largest percentage of delinquents comes. Although the authoritarian atmosphere, with its corollary of severe punishment, is not the only cause of delinquency, it is an important contributing influence. The current almost hysterical cry for a "get-tough" policy as a preventive of delinquency is not only not supported by facts, it is directly contrary to the facts.

It must be emphasized that authoritarianism is very prevalent, even in democratic America. In a summary of an intensive study of a small midwestern city—a study in which, among other things, a record was kept for an entire day of everything done by and to selected children—Barker and Wright tell us, "There is in this description of how grownups behave with these Midwest children, and of how the children behaved, the picture of a beneficent, yet dominative, but not characteristically subjugating, bridling, conflictive, hostile, indulgent, or rejective situation. There is the picture of an authoritarian social regimen which was at the same time a benevolent one" (39).

We should be careful not to overinterpret all these studies. The authoritarian home does, indeed, *tend* to breed authoritarianism in the children, thus creating a vicious cycle. But the empirical data do not justify a fatalistic attitude. Even allowing for the effect of imperfect measures, correlations between parent and child authoritarianism are seldom higher than $r = .60$. (See, e.g., Lyle and Levitt [289], whose results are fairly typical.) Such correlations make clear that many influences other than just the home play their part in educating the authoritarian. (Indeed, the correlations show that only about a third of the differences in authoritarianism in people can be predicted by knowing how authoritarian their parents were. But that is quite a lot.) We make ourselves authoritarian, or we unmake much of the authoritarianism implanted by parents, by the way we live and let ourselves think and feel. The whole of one's life pattern is involved in becoming or not becoming authoritarian.

QUESTIONS

1. Is there any difference between wanting to be recognized as authority and in being an authoritarian?
2. Is it possible for parents or teachers to be bossy without being authoritarian? If *you* make the distinction, do you think the child recognizes it?

3. Would not a person who seemed pretty liberal in the culture of Nazi Germany seem quite authoritarian in our culture? What does your answer imply for the psychological nature of authoritarianism?
4. In the Lewin, Lippitt, and White experiment several of the boys acted much better under autocracy. How would you explain this? What significance does this have (beyond the rather sterile comment that people differ)?
5. What are the effects of the school as we find it today upon children from authoritarian and from nonauthoritarian homes?

Other Varieties of Authority

There are innumerable other varieties in the home pattern of authority.[7] There is the home where undeviating submission is so drastically exacted that the child is either cowed or only inwardly resistant. There is the home where excessive resistance is tolerated, even encouraged, where impertinence and insolence are mistaken for strength. There is the home where authority is infirm and weak, to be wheedled, cajoled, or circumvented. A few modern mothers try to reason with their child almost before he can talk; others seem to think that the louder they shout the more prompt and the more certain the child's obedience. Some parents try to enforce obedience by the threat of withdrawing love, others depend upon anger and punishment. Some parents are so casual and indifferent that they seem to have—indeed, do have—but little authority. In most homes, perhaps, authority seems to the child somewhat arbitrary and capricious.

In all of this it is to be noted that the important thing is the way adult authority is perceived by the child rather than the way it is perceived by the adult—and fathers, mothers, and children are very likely to perceive a particular authority-situation in very different ways (489). Most of us would be shocked if we were to learn how our authority looks to our children.

[7] The patterns of parental authority have had much study. See, e.g., Champney (97, 98), Radke (359), and Baldwin, *et al.* (29).

Authority and the Feeling of Guilt

All homes tend in some measure to breed in the child a feeling of guilt. In some homes this is the major element of the child's feeling in relation to his parents' authority. Hedged in by innumerable restrictions—as, perhaps, he must be, and at any rate certainly is—the child inevitably finds himself violating parental injunctions. Equally inevitably, he is made to feel how shameful it is to have thus fallen short of "proper" or "good" behavior, how sorry he should be to have thus grieved his beloved parents. The shocked horror with which some parents greet a lie or a bit of obscenity has given many a small child a deep feeling of unworthiness.

A little later he finds himself violating the code of the school and of the larger social group, and of the precepts of religion; and again he may be severely reprimanded or made to feel how despicable his behavior is. Onto a child's growing sense of selfhood is thus grafted a feeling of inadequacy, of anxiety, and of guilt.[8]

An ineffective effort to get rid of an excessive feeling of guilt is, we are now beginning to see, a major root of neurosis and of many distortions of personality. Guilt and anxiety are painful feelings, too painful to be long endured. Yet the child is not wise enough to know what to do about it.

Various societies have found different ways of ridding themselves of the discomfort of these feelings of guilt. In the classic Greek tragedies, the hero always suffered for his violation of moral law, but he was represented as feeling no remorse because he was driven to his misdeeds by inexorable fate. So the spectators, viewing the tragic hero suffering but guiltless, went away relieved of a sense of guilt for their own lesser offenses and encouraged to endure their own lesser sufferings. (This is what Aristotle meant by the drama as "catharsis.")

The ancient Hebrews had a magical ceremony in which they put all the sins of the people upon a "scapegoat" which was then driven forth into the wilderness to suffer and die; thus the people were freed from past sin. And in other cultures there are similar expiatory rites and ceremonies to take away not only guilt but the sense of guilt.

The Western world, however, has a very mixed attitude toward the sense of guilt. This is shown in religion. Both the Christian and the Jewish faiths declare the need for repentance, which is usually taken to mean

[8] Following a somewhat parallel line of reasoning, the psychoanalytic doctrine of the superego arrives at the same conclusion.

a deep awareness of one's own failures and unworthiness. In some circles, indeed, a groveling admission of depravity is required as prelude to admission into the "fellowship of the saints." On the other hand, the doctrine of the atonement is clearly intended to *relieve* the believer of his sense of guilt and remorse. We can't seem quite to make up our minds whether guilt feelings are good or bad.

The same ambiguity infects our treatment of criminals and delinquents. They must feel guilty, must repent, and be deeply remorseful, yet they must also become self-respecting. And in this respect, as in many others, I am afraid that we regard children as merely one species of young delinquent.

There are many reasons for our divided mind about guilt feelings. For one thing, feeling our own guilt, we find a satisfaction in having others reveal theirs. Then, too, when a child has thwarted us or hurt our feelings, it is very satisfying to receive his expressions of regret. Moreover, the suppliant child is an appealing figure who brings out our tenderness and allows us to luxuriate in the experience of comforting him.

Equally important, probably, is our belief that a sense of guilt helps to prevent future wrongdoing. This is undoubtedly part of the reason why we so often insist upon an "apology." There is clinical evidence, however, that when children have too strong a sense of guilt they are less likely to reform than to feel compelled to repeat their offenses again and again. (See, for example, 254.) The great theologian, Sören Kierkegaard (249), makes the same point when he writes: "Despairing over sin means one accepts one's sinful state and therefore will have nothing to do with good. . . . Despair over sin . . . secures against any aspiration after good."

When, on the other hand, the offender finds himself "accepted" by the person in authority despite full knowledge of the misconduct, the compulsion to continue to offend is wiped out. There have been startling cures of long-standing delinquencies based upon this principle of "acceptance" by the person in authority *before* repentance takes place. In the story of the woman taken in adultery, Jesus does not ask for repentance: "Doth no man accuse you? Neither do I accuse you. Go and sin no more." The traditional formula—feel guilty, repent, reform, and *then* be forgiven—seems to invert the proper order. Note, however, that the child offender himself must recognize that although you accept him you do not accept his misconduct.

Psychologically what the child needs is forgiveness first, *so that he may learn to do better.*

In more general terms, what the child needs is a release from anxiety so that he may learn to face his problems and solve them realistically. There are, of course, many causes of guilt feeling, but they are all connected with the child's anxiety in relation to authority. However loving it may be, an authority which is at the same time too exacting, which constantly holds before the child the mirror of an impossible perfection, does not permit him to be free of anxiety. And the anxious child does not learn or learns only slowly.

When we find that the child has a strongly anxious or "guilty" sense of his responsibility to authority, our task is a delicate one. Retaliatory punishment, which is always bad, is particularly so in these cases. In most cases it merely increases his anxious sense of guilt; but in some cases it relieves guilt (the child feels he has paid the price) in such a way that the child feels free to resume his misconduct. Any suggestion that we are hurt and disappointed in his behavior tends to make things worse. Even his own self-criticism, otherwise so valuable, will often lead this kind of child to self-recrimination and anxiety. As much as any other—perhaps more—such a child needs for a time the security that comes from a strong guiding hand, one which as far as possible *prevents* wrongdoing. But more than that, when he does get involved in what he feels to be offenses against authority, they must somehow be "accepted" without being condoned—or rather, the *child* must continue to be accepted and to feel accepted, while the offenses are not. On the constructive side, we should help the child to replace his preoccupation about *wrong*-doing with a realization of how many right-doings there are which can be fascinating and satisfying.

QUESTIONS

1. Is the sense of guilt wholly bad?
2. Granting that anxiety can be excessive, will a person try to overcome his misbehavior unless he has some anxiety or fear?

Wholesome Authority

So many evil or defective patterns of home authority! How about describing the home where authority is good? A fair request but difficult. Of course, I have implied what makes authority good by describing what makes it bad. Consider what was said about loveless compared with overaffectionate authority on page 37 ff and 41 ff. Doesn't that help you see how love and authority ought to be combined?

But I hesitate to set up a static picture of the home where authority, like the third bear's bed in the story of Goldilocks, is "just right." What is good for one child may be much less good for another. What is good at one stage in the child's development is downright bad at another. What one parent does supremely well, another would do badly no matter how hard he tried. There just isn't any single type of good authority.

Yet of course there must be, and are, criteria by means of which you can decide what makes your authority good. I would like to postpone a statement of those criteria until the end of the next chapter. Let's finish our present discussion of the varieties of parental authority by saying merely that there are as many *kinds* of good homes as of bad homes—and I truly believe, more of them.

Early Experiences Count

Everyone knows that "as the twig is bent the tree's inclined." But haven't we played up early experience too strongly? It is possible, certainly, to be much too fatalistic about bad beginnings. But early experience does count. The kind of habits of responding to authority which a child forms in his first few years tends, *unless modified,* to determine how he will react to later circumstances. Early experience tends to create later experience in its own image; later events are reacted to in terms of what one has already learned to do.

Notice, then, what happens when a child leaves his home for the larger world of the school and the neighborhood. He carries with him his pattern of reacting to authority. Thus he will react to some new authority-figure, say the teacher, in more or less the way he has been reacting to his parents. His comrade, meanwhile, will be reacting in the light of *his* experiences with *his* parents—in quite a different way.

Let's take the effect of a traditional "strict disciplinarian" teacher upon three different children. To a fairly sharp reprimand Ann responds with cringing submission, combined with a hurt appeal to the teacher for signs of affection. Susan ignores the reprimand until it becomes even more severe. Obviously she believes in sailing as close as possible to the submerged reefs of punishment; once she "gets the teacher's number," she is astute in judging just how far to go. Billy is openly defiant. It is clear, is it not, that the psychological value of the "same" reprimand is entirely different for these three children, and that identical treatment, far from making them more alike, will make them more and more different? Each has reacted to the reprimand in the light of his own earlier experience with authority. Even within the same family, no two children have the same experiences, thus the same relation, with authority.

Changing the Pattern

It is difficult, then, to change the early or primal patterns of behavior, and it is important to notice why. It is difficult because we have to select the influences which, in the light of each child's background, will be effective in his particular case in producing desirable changes. The pattern of his reaction to authority tends to remain much the same because we seldom take the trouble to understand it.

Here is an excellent place for the teacher to promote a little parent-teacher cooperation. Many a mother is objective enough to see that her child's picture of authority could be improved. All by herself, however, it is not easy to make the changes—she has some habits of her own, and so has the child's other parent. Why not talk it over with the mother and plan a program for both home and school?

Even when such teamwork is not possible, the school can accomplish a great deal, as seen directly in Levitt's study (266) and indirectly in Harold Anderson's (9). (See also 41, 42, 284.) But to correct a child's false conceptions of authority calls for highly individual treatment. And note that I say *treatment* rather than sermonizing. The child's picture of authority rests squarely upon personal experience and can be changed very little except by further experience. Charles needs to feel warm affection coupled with firm control over his conduct. Henry needs to learn that he cannot wheedle you into changing your mind. Janet needs to have reasons carefully set forth.

Even the needs that are common to nearly all children must be met by means adjusted to the individual. Every child needs to find security in authority, yet he also needs to become independent. To meet this need calls for a blend of adult guidance, on the one hand, and opportunities for personal initiative, on the other. But the blend has to be judicious and adjusted to the individual. Every child needs to find a worthy source of authority, someone who can actually help him; but the kind of help each child requires varies. Every child needs to see the person in authority—the mother, the father, the teacher—acting consistently; yet while being consistent the adult must also act with due regard to the personality of the child.

What about Democracy?

Authority and discipline are not just for children. They begin in the home, true enough, but they run through all our social life. What are dictatorship and totalitarianism but the carrying over into the political sphere of the habits of domination and obedience which rule in so many homes? Authoritarianism in the home is the seedbed of authoritarianism in the state. (See Schaffner's study of Germany [375] and Benedict's study of Japan [56].) Nor is this primitive spirit confined to politics or to countries abroad; it crops up continually in our own land in the advocacy of all manner of repressive controls over our fellow citizens.

Yet part of the time I have been actually urging the parent and teacher to increase their authority. You have a perfect right to ask whether so much authority can be reconciled with democracy. Isn't this whole notion of "disciplined obedience" too much like totalitarianism to square with our professed social ideals?

If I seem to straddle on this issue a bit, it only shows I'm a good American. As a nation we are peculiarly ambivalent about authority. We pay more than mere lip service to the idea of "rugged individualism" and "sturdy independence"; we really believe in them. On the other hand, we want in our children—and elsewhere—discipline, obedience, and even the uncritical acceptance of our authority; and we cling to an industrial system where large masses of men are dependent upon the will of a few. It really looks as if we mean that discipline is for others and rugged individualism is for ourselves (79).

There are perfectly good historical reasons why we think like that. The religion of colonial days was strongly authoritarian; it stressed especially the Father-child relation. Yet our national history began with the rejection of the authority of the British Crown. The most vocal of the Founding Fathers believed that all political authority was at best a necessary evil to be kept at a minimum. Hence the famous system of "checks and balances" in our Constitution: no one was to have too much authority. Yet, during the same period, family life was sternly authoritative and was defended as such.

Then came the move to the West. The pioneer was truly a rugged individualist, but family life and religion remained authoritative. Still later came wave after wave of immigrants—most of them fleeing from the authority of the kings and potentates of the Old World. But they also brought with them, and still do, the peasant idea of the all-powerful father.

Their children, however, in their desire to become "good Americans," felt compelled to resist the authority of the old folks with their old-country speech and ideas. Thus the second-generation American reinforces one strand in the complex ideology of American culture. The rejection of authority is part of the American tradition. (Compare Gorer's analysis in *The American people* [174].)

But it is only a part! For not only do we act authoritatively; we defend authoritarianism with a good bit of fervor (162, 456). "Discipline" is still a magic word in home, school, and factory. Apparently we think to solve the problem of authority by shouting contradictory slogans.

This head-in-the-sand attitude is unfortunate. We need to take a hard look at the problem of authority. For it is clear that the persistence of the authority reactions, bred in the home, creates a special difficulty for a democratic society. Under autocracy all anyone has to do is to find out who is in authority and obey; *in a democracy each of us must learn how to fuse his own authority with that of others in cooperative enterprise.*

We seem to be caught in a vicious circle. As we have seen, each and every human being starts life under the benevolent authority of his parents. For years the infant's lack of maturity imposes upon him a more or less willing, but anyway necessary, submission to authority. How is he to grow out of this?

It is not easy for parents to help. Habits of *submission* they can and do impose, often long after these habits cease to be helpful. Parents can even reinforce them by the exercise of compulsion (275). But how can they *compel* a child to *cooperate?* To cooperate one has to be free, and freedom cannot be imposed; though it can be permitted, in a very real sense it must be inwardly won.

Even to permit freedom to children is difficult enough. We ourselves grew up under the sheltering wings of authority, grew up accepting it, and learning early to exercise it over our own "inferiors." If the family of our own childhood was autocratic—as it probably was—we are all the more likely to feel a desperate, though perhaps unconscious, need to dominate others as we were dominated. Even when we are intellectually convinced of the need to grant children greater freedom, our need to dominate keeps breaking through. As the child grows older, moreover, it is sometimes difficult to divest ourselves of those habits of affectionate control of his behavior which were appropriate at an earlier period.

The teacher, however, has a chance to start afresh without such specific habits clustering about each child. She has not formed the habit of pandering affectionately to Billy-Boy's helplessness, of severely regimenting Mabel's obstreperousness. And the child also, despite his tendency to transfer from parent to teacher his response to authority, soon learns that he has a new personality to deal with, a new embodiment of authority. The stage is thus set in the school for a revision of old habit patterns, for moving away from subservience toward intelligent, cooperative self-regulation.

But what happens? School readers bombard the children with stories which emphasize the values of conformity and obedience. (See the excellent study by Child, *et al.* [103].) Teachers, compelled to ride herd on thirty to fifty squirming youngsters, are tempted to maintain the necessary order by force and coercion. It is far easier to take over the autocratic pattern of the home to which the children are so thoroughly accustomed than to lead them in the path of independence. Thus the rigidly ordered, teacher-directed regime of the traditional school offers little scope for the children's development of democratic followership, let alone of democratic leadership. By the time they reach adolescence, far too many children have settled down to a comfortable acceptance of benevolently authoritative leadership.

In a study of adolescent leaders Ronald Lippitt (285) found that from 70 to 80 percent of their actions fell into the classification of "ordering," "pressuring," and so on. Yet this evoked comparatively little resistance; most of the followers were satisfied or dependently apathetic. Such patterns of human relationship, Lippitt wrote a little sadly, can hardly be expected to serve as the backbone for the democracy many of us have talked about so hopefully.

And when they become adults? Society reinforces in innumerable ways the tendency to dependence and compliance long after childhood and adolescence have passed. Industry in our civilization, says a distinguished industrial consultant (304), is organized along authoritative lines. In a fundamental and pervasive sense, the subordinate is dependent upon his superior for his job; for the continuity of his employment; for promotion with its accompanying satisfactions in the form of increased pay, responsibility, and prestige; and for a host of other personal and social satisfactions to be obtained in the work situation.

Labor organizations, it is true, represent an attempt to reduce this dependence of the worker upon management. In this attempt, however, the unions are working against certain deeply rooted attitudes of the workers themselves. "Fair treatment" rather than independence seems to be the goal of a large proportion of industrial workers.

Now "fair treatment" psychologically means a relationship in which compliance with orders from those in authority brings rewards and approval. It is, in short, a yearning for a continuance of that linkage between compliance and affection which characterizes infancy. Labor-union policies designed to secure *independence* thus meet resistance from many of the very persons the policies are intended to benefit. Intuitively recognizing this situation, union leadership sometimes seeks to substitute dependence upon the union for dependence upon management—psychologically not much of a change! The development of independence and cooperation is evidently a peculiarly difficult problem within the structure of industrial society.

Without using the term, we have been implying that our problem is the persistence of "infantile" reactions—in this case of infantile authority-dependence-affection-hostility reactions. Perhaps, then, we ought to add explicitly that infantile responses are not necessarily bad. Breathing, for example, is clearly an infantile reaction, but we haven't developed any better way of behaving in order to oxygenate our blood. Infantile reactions to authority are to be deprecated only when we know that it is possible for people to modify them for the better—in which event we call these other responses more mature.

Fortunately more and more teachers as well as some parents are coming to see themselves as leaders and guides rather than as task-mistresses or order-givers. The Scouts, the Y's, and other youth organizations are giving thoughtful attention to their leadership functions. A few great industries also are training their foremen as democratic authorities. Most important of all, an increasing number of parents have come to see their authority in a new light. A psychology of democratic leadership is clearly in the making.

What Is Democratic Leadership?

In our description, a few pages back, of the experiment with different types of leadership, we spoke of the adult's participating with the boys in planning. That is perhaps a rather superficial description. I have seen "planning sessions" in which the leader knew all along where he wanted the group to come out, and, under the *forms* of democracy, he manipulated the group until his purpose was accepted. Children are apt to see through that sort of "democracy" more often than those who perpetrate it realize.

When we act in the true democratic spirit we try to find the genuine purposes of those we lead. True, the child does not always know his own purposes; our task in that case is to help him recognize them.

We need, however, to have genuine faith in his potentialities for growth. *Autocratic authority takes advantage of the child's weakness to secure compliance, even subservience. Democratic authority seeks to release the child's strength and energy in constructive directions and to develop initiative and intelligent self-direction.*

It will be evident that I am not advocating that we surrender our authority. In the first place, we cannot. Children crave and naturally seek authority. There is point to the kindergartner's plaintive query:

"Do we have to do what we want to do again today?" As John Dewey (121) says: "Docility, desire for direction, love for protective control are stronger . . . . traits of human nature than is insubordination." [9] So long as we adults are actually superior, so long *must* we be authority to children. Authority exists as a fact in our relation to them. And the existence of authority provides a needed element to the stability and security of the child's world. When children are reared under an extreme laissez-faire regime, they grow up feeling rootless and indecisive, lacking in self-confidence and self-acceptance (192).

Authority enables you to exercise direct control over children without too much constraint and conflict. It enables you to help them work together cooperatively rather than competitively. It is not when your authority is strong but when it is weak that you must frequently resort to the use of force and punishment and threats.

Authority and the Mores

Authority is important, moreover, not only in the immediate control of conduct but in the transmission of ideas and ideals, the whole complex of traditional ways which make up our customs and mores. Authority gives enormous prestige to the suggestions of parents and of teachers—including the "suggestions" that are carried by their own behavior as well as those they make in so many words. Far more than we commonly realize, our notions of what is good and bad, right and wrong, proper and improper, are unwittingly absorbed early in life from those in authority. However much we value direct experience we must recognize that there simply isn't time enough for a child to have all the necessary direct experiences, to examine them critically, and to generalize from them. Whether we like it or not—and there are obvious dangers—the child inevitably takes over from authority the greater bulk of his ideology. It is not too much to say that the whole tissue of culture, which more than anything else distinguishes human societies from those of the animals, could hardly be transmitted from generation to generation were it not for the facilitating effect of authority.

Valuable, indeed inevitable, as authority is thus seen to be, the

[9] This is the same John Dewey who is accused by some newspaper critics of modern education of proposing the abandonment of all discipline.

dangers of its abuse remain. Authority gives security to a child, but if we are not careful it can be a spurious security, the security of dependence rather than the security which dares to strike out on one's own. There is consequently a tremendous challenge to parents and teachers to be wise in their use of authority, to choose wisely the things they say and the things they do—for always they are investing both words and deeds with some of the prestige of their authority.

But even more important is their responsibility, of which we spoke earlier, to help the child develop more mature attitudes toward authority. Specifically, they may use their authority to encourage a thoughtful and critical challenge to authority—even including their own—and the critical examination of authoritative and traditional ideas in the light of facts.

Summary

Nearly everyone agrees that "good discipline" is important, but the concrete problems that arise in this area are better understood if we think of the parent or the teacher not as a disciplinarian but as a leader. Ability to lead depends most of all upon the children's reaction to authority.

Authority has its origin in the universal experiences of the human infant which lead him to react to adult superiority with a complex of interwoven attitudes: (1) *dependence-compliance,* (2) *resistance,* (3) *love,* (4) *hatred.* These are combined in many different patterns according to the child's differing experiences with adults. The authority-pattern is first formed in the home and is transferred almost intact to the school, where it determines the way in which the child accepts the teacher's leadership.

The parent's or the teacher's authority must be carefully distinguished from authoritativeness: authority is a *relation* which exists; authoritativeness or bossiness is a way of acting which tries to bolster up the authority which is felt to be inadequate.

One of the commonest mistakes is to attempt to strengthen one's authority by authoritative or bossy behavior; it seldom works out that way. More serious, however, is the attitude of cherishing one's authority for the pleasure it gives us to be boss. Such authoritarianism cramps the wholesome development of the child.

3

Authority in Conflict Situations

What should you do when a child resists your authority? Resort to punishment? Most of us do. When to punish and how are thus important questions. In this chapter they are subjected to careful psychological analysis.

But punishment is never the whole answer. We do not want children to be merely "disciplined"; we want them to grow up to be "self-disciplined." The relationship between discipline and self-discipline is made clear.

Sources of Conflict

Most children are ready, many of them too ready, to comply with adult directions—most of the time. I know it seldom looks like that. Disobedience is dreadfully noticeable and uncomfortable whereas cheerful compliance goes unremarked.

But put it to the test. Make what psychologists call a time sample. Watch a small group of children (you will find three or four quite enough!) under competent adult leadership. Simply count every time the children respond positively to the adult's suggestions and every time one of them responds negatively or shows any sign of resistance. Unless the situation is decidedly abnormal, you will find, as others have, that compliance outruns resistance in frequency. A sort of half-automatic response to authority is natural and pretty satisfying to a child.

Good Behavior Wears Thin

But however compliant a child is, he does not want forever to be told what to do. Even if you are at pains not to frustrate any of his other desires, sooner or later you frustrate his desire to have a little independence. The very routines of school life—most of them necessary routines—are bound eventually to generate antagonism and conflict. As Fritz Redl (362) says, "Hyperorganization and compulsive order hamper all normal pleasure for everyday interplay and undermine the morale of an otherwise quite willing group."

Figure 3-1.

Now this is hardly a new idea. I'm sure it is to be found in the Bible and other ancient writings. Over fifty years ago Theodate Smith (402) made it the object of scientific investigation.

Apparently the picture has not greatly changed since then. Wright (484), in his study of hour-to-hour behavior in a midwestern town, took a sample of fifty consecutive episodes in which an adult and a child were interacting. In 34 percent of these episodes the adult dominated the child's behavior. In twelve episodes the adult positively resisted what the child did; in six the adult was aggressive. In five other episodes (10 percent) the adult deigned to accompany his or her request with a "please." Thus thirty-one interactions (62 percent) put some sort of pressure on the child. In only 28 percent of the episodes was the adult directly seeking to satisfy a child's immediate desires or needs.

More than twice as many attempts to get the child to conform to adult dictates as attempts to help the child directly get something *he* wants! The critics who are always harping on the theme of pampering children or of "letting them do just what they want" must have been looking at different parents! In 89 percent of all the episodes in this study, the power and decision lay in the adults' hands.

As we have repeatedly emphasized, such preponderance of adult control of the children's behavior is not necessarily unreasonable or ill-advised. Children need control. Sometimes their actions threaten to produce immediate effects of such consequence that they have to be controlled even if this does some damage to the child's pursuit of long-term developmental goals (393). What we need to see is the psychic cost to the child of such control—however beneficent or necessary it may be.

Many disciplinary conflicts, moreover, are caused by poor adult leadership. Jerry, who really wants to learn to play the piano, asks to be excused from practicing today in order to join the gang in shooting baskets. He is told that basketball can wait. No, it *can't* wait; the fellows will go away. Let practice wait until that tomorrow which never comes. His mother insists. So Jerry slams open the piano and smashes out a few discords to show what he thinks of her.

The alternative in such situations is not to surrender authority but rather to use it in the right way. It would be a better use of authority to help Jerry plan a schedule so that he can have both basketball and piano practice. True authority, it bears repeating, brings the child richer satisfaction, helps him *to attain more of his own goals* than he could without the help of authority. His response to authority is his faith that this is so.

The school is often guilty of using authority to impose on children an unnatural mode of activity—or, too often, of inactivity. Fixed seats, a carefully regulated timetable, long periods of "keeping quiet" undoubtedly play their part in building up toward revolt. Nor can we ignore the fact that many pupils come to school with very bad habits of followership and with attitudes of hostility toward adult authority.

I do not mean to imply that teacher or parent must relax all rules.

Do you remember the effect of laissez-faire leadership in the Lewin, Lippitt, and White experiment? We should also bear in mind, however, how strong the pressure is that we put upon children. A great deal of what we call naughtiness, misconduct, or "problem behavior" is directly the result of too much adult control. A little timely relaxation often goes a long way in preventing an explosion. And, as shown by the Lewin, Lippitt, and White experiment (278), it is enormously worth while to develop a cooperative democratic spirit in all concerned (including oneself). If it has no other virtues, the method will avoid a lot of trouble.

The Emergency Treatment of Conflict

Yet only a perfect teacher in a far more perfect world than ours is going to avoid all disciplinary conflicts. (Even more is this true of a parent in a home where there are several children.) What, then, are you going to do *at the time?*

Let's take a concrete case. Hal is happily engaged in annoying Mabel in the seat ahead of him. Nothing serious—just a nudge now and then, or a snide remark—but Mabel doesn't like it. Trouble impends. You speak quietly to Hal and ask him to desist. He doesn't stop. Now what are you going to do? And why?

"Do I dare to let him get away with it?" Your request was certainly reasonable. You wanted to teach Hal considerateness. You wanted to save Mabel from annoyance, and to head off retaliation on her part. You had an eye on the peace and quiet of the schoolroom. Worthy motives, every one.

But is the situation serious enough to make an issue of it? What would happen if you were to say, "Well, Mabel, it looks as if Hal is out to annoy you and me this morning. Can you take it or do you want to move your seat?"

The immediate response of many teachers is to ask, "But wouldn't I lose my authority if I let him get away with it?" Would you? Does your authority really rest upon so fragile a basis as the insistence upon unvarying obedience?

Look at it positively. If you refuse to take every minor disobedience or small annoyance seriously, will even small children lose their real respect for you? Will it cause them to forget your real helpfulness, your real superiority? Surely you can't think so. Yet it is these last which are the solid bases of your authority. Nor will these children mistake tolerance for approval. If all your authority amounts to is that the child knows he will be punished if he defies it too far, you had better go ahead and lose it. Hal would know perfectly well that you thoroughly disapproved; and your amused or serene tolerance is more likely to give him second thoughts than any punishment.

True, if you let Hal get away with it this time, he will probably try it again. He probably will anyhow, even if you punish him. Somewhere, to be sure, you must draw the line. But draw the line, not in terms of how great a disobedience *you* can tolerate, but in terms of what sorts of conduct under the circumstances are intolerable. Whether to put the heat on Hal might well depend upon the way he is feeling, or upon the kind of day he has had. (Usually, of course, it actually depends upon the way *you* feel, the kind of day *you* have had.) Draw the line not to save your own ego, or to save face with the other children, but to ensure the kind of situation that promotes pupil development. There are better ways of teaching Hal considerateness than by coercing him into leaving Mabel alone. Considerateness comes from a warm heart and not from a paddle-warmed bottom.

QUESTIONS

1. Give examples of overcontrol leading to misbehavior. In each case, consider whether there was any really practical alternative.
2. What should be a teacher's attitude if she decides to ignore a disciplinary situation?
3. Do you agree that disciplinary conflicts in school are inevitable? If you do, describe a few cases and make clear why they couldn't be avoided.
4. Analyze an example of punishment that you are inclined to believe was justified. Show why. What did the punishment cause the child to do?

Coercion and Punishment

All very well, but there are times when you *do* have to put your foot down—i.e., to use *coercion.* Coercion is compelling obedience by punishment or the threat of punishment. And by *punishment* we mean deliberately inflicting dissatisfaction upon a person as a penalty for some act or failure to act. These are just the ordinary dictionary meanings.

The Varieties of Punishment

Note first how very broad the notion of punishment is. Corporal punishment, deprivation of "pleasures," scolding and reproof, failure to gain a sought-for goal, lack of success, pain as a "natural consequence" of failure, withdrawal of affection, shame, social isolation, solitary confinement, extra tasks, and Heaven alone knows what else—all these are supposed to work as "punishments." There may be a common psychological factor running through all these varied things called punishment; it is doubtful, to say the least.

This may be the place to remind the reader that psychology is the study of *what a person does.* Now punishment is not something the child does; it is done to him. The psychology of punishment, therefore, begins when we ask what the child does in response to punishment. Does anyone really believe that there is any one kind of response that is made to all the varied kinds of things called punishment?

Is Punishment Ethically Justifiable?

Punishment, as thus defined, has an ugly sound. For the more powerful or more powerfully placed person deliberately to hurt one less powerful is repugnant to our better instincts. Whenever we find ourselves *enjoying* passing out punishment, it is time to take ourselves in hand. Punishment not only sounds ugly; it is ugly. It can be ethically defended only when it can be shown that punishment really serves the child's interests.

Who decides that? Generally the parent—a party to the dispute. Quite obviously, the ethics of the situation are against the indiscriminate use of punishment. It is a sort of court of last resort. Yet few of us are willing to dispense with punishment even in theory, let alone in practice. We say that it is necessary.

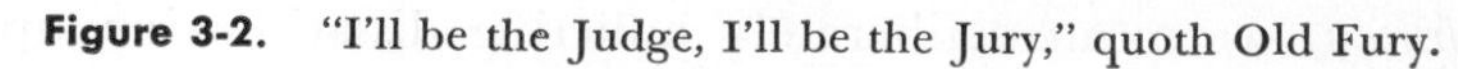

Figure 3-2. "I'll be the Judge, I'll be the Jury," quoth Old Fury.

Is Punishment Necessary?

What does punishment accomplish? We say that it is sometimes necessary to teach a child what is right and what is wrong and to teach him to act accordingly. We say that it is necessary to keep order. And we say that it is necessary to develop in the child a due and proper restraint of his own conduct, that is, to develop self-discipline. These three, I think, pretty well cover all the reasons commonly given for punishment. All the respectable ones: there are still "adults" who will openly punish a child to "show him who is running things around here."

Does Punishment Help Us Learn?

An immense amount of experimental work with animals has been devoted to this question. In the typical experiment, the punishment consists of an electric shock whenever the animal makes an "incorrect" response in a puzzle box or a maze. The "punishment" thus consists in a vigorous "signal" to the animal that he is on the wrong track. Rather strict parallels to such learning also occur in everyday human learning; in infants and young children they doubtless form a very large proportion of everything learned. It is popular nowadays to speak of such learning as "conditioning." (Even laymen are being taught to speak of "reinforcement conditioning.")

In a crowded tenement district one hot summer evening a father sat on the curb smoking, while around him played a yelling mob of children. Ever and anon a truck rumbled by, or a taxi hurtled through the mean and rather narrow street. To the other children the man paid little heed, but whenever the youngest, a toddler of perhaps nineteen months, came within a foot of the curb, the father reached out a grimy paw, turned the child over, and administered a resounding but not brutal smack upon the traditional place for smacks, then calmly resumed his smoking. Not a word was spoken, no emotion was displayed. He simply and methodically "punished" the child whenever he got too near the dangerous street.

Presently one could see the child start toward the street, hesitate, and turn away. Once he even put his hands on his "spanker" before he turned back. Obviously the child was being "conditioned" as objectively as any rat in a puzzle box to regard the edge of the curb as a bad place to be. (It is doubtful that either rat or infant in such cases is learning to regard his own behavior as "wrong." It was the curb that was wrong. Both these organisms seem to be pretty object-minded or place-minded.)

Both mice and men, then, learn under the influence of the good or ill effects of their own behavior. But the relation is not simple. One experimenter (447) had a group of orphanage children trying to learn some material by heart. Every time a child got an item right, he received a penny; when he got it wrong, a penny was taken away. Since even a few pennies meant a lot to these children, it was expected that they would learn the right answers quickly, and unlearn the wrong ones. Instead, in many cases, despite the repeated punishment, they seemed to become fixated on their errors.

Another experimenter (Estes, 142) found much the same thing

when he tried to teach white rats to solve some rather difficult "rat problems." They got stalled on an ineffective solution and, though rather severely punished every time, kept trying that "solution" over and over. Apparently punishment, instead of warning them away from error, prevented them from facing reality with an adaptive problem-solving attitude. It isn't easy to intimidate even a docile white rat into correct behavior.

Everyday life is full of parallel examples with human beings. A businessman facing failure may resort to alcohol, although he recognizes that he thereby incapacitates himself for solving his problem. A child finding himself rejected or unloved by his parents may resort to bed-wetting or exhibitionism, although even he can see how these behaviors only lead to more rejection. Surely it is one of the saddest facts of human experience that men, like rats, often persist in errors, even though the errors clearly lead to ill effects.

Associate Punishment with the Offense

If you want punishment to teach the child to avoid doing something, you have to be sure that the act and its painful consequences are closely connected in his mind. If you have ever tried to train a dog, you know what I mean. Dog hairs on the sofa may constitute proof enough that Spunky was there; but dogs have good ears and after one or two punishments Spunky gets off the couch before you get there. And how can you punish him effectively unless you can catch him in the act?

Even then it isn't easy to get Spunky to make the right association between what he was doing and your punishment. Suppose that you catch him chewing your bedroom slippers and whip him. If Spunky could talk he might well ask you what you are punishing him for. Was it because he was in the bedroom, because he was chewing, because he had a slipper, or just because? Spunky doesn't ask those questions, of course, but neither does he usually act as if he had the correct answer. As a result of your whipping he may avoid the bedroom but happily chew slippers anywhere else. More likely, however, he will just tend to be a little shy of you.

Of course it is easier with a child. You can *tell* him what you are whipping him for. Only don't be too sure he will get the point.

It is sometimes said that the best punishment is to let the child feel the "natural consequences" of his own misdeeds, without the intervention of the adult. Generally, however, the natural consequences are so far in the future that we cannot wait. Consider the delayed result of not learning 6 + 2 in computing income tax. Since, moreover, such "natural consequences" too seldom occur "naturally," the next step is to cause the child to *believe* that he is hurting himself although you are actually responsible. That is a neat trick, if you can work it—which you seldom can. In any case, is it honest? Besides, the very considerable ingenuity required might be much better spent in planning situations that will help the child to learn *approved* ways of acting rather than in devising traps that will catch him when he goes astray.

Punishment is not effective in deterring a child from future wrongdoing unless the penalty is directly related—for the child—*to the misconduct;* and this it seldom is. Only in the rare case where the effort to avoid punishment *automatically* causes the child to "cease and desist" does punishment lead straight to "reform." A somewhat more positive way to put it is this: *Punishment helps the child to learn only when the effort to avoid punishment leads him directly to do the right thing with real satisfaction.* That doesn't often occur.

Punishment as a Social Signal

But punishment, we are told, is a *cue* or guide to what is right, or more specifically, to what is wrong. Murder, we imply, must be a very dreadful crime or it would not be punished so severely. Walking on the grass, by contrast, is a minor offense to be lightly punished.[1] Punishment is thus roughly parallel to the signal "Wrong" or to the electric shock of the laboratory experiment. It serves as a vivid link between the disapproved act and society's verdict on it. We know all too well, however, that almost as often as not the fact that an act is forbidden only makes it more attractive. In any case,

[1] Just why it is supposed to be so useful to inform a child that a certain act is only mildly wrong is a fascinating question in both ethics and psychology. If it is wrong at all, don't we want the child to avoid the act? One is forcibly reminded of Captain Marryat's excuse for the illegitimate baby—it was such a little one! Are we trying to teach the child to estimate just how much wrongdoing he can get away with without being too badly hurt—that is, punished?

isn't there some way less primitive than punishment to help a child understand our abhorrence of wrongdoing?

Children themselves, however, quickly get to the stage where they use the possibility of punishment as a measure of wrongfulness. They will often test you out to see how far they can go. In some cases, moreover, they even seem to feel the *need* for punishment as a means of testing the limits. If you let them break the law without punishing them, they become anxious. Punishment may serve to clarify the limits and thus allay tension and anxiety.

Again, however, we must ask ourselves whether punishment is the only way to define the limits. If we take the trouble to understand what is perplexing the child, we can help him to find the limits and thus relieve his anxiety without punishment.

It is true that if the child accepts authority whether of parents, of teachers, or of society, punishment may really help to deter him from wrongdoing. This use of punishment, however, although of some value as a sort of flaming social signal, fails to touch the really difficult cases of those who deny or challenge the authority of parents or of society. The really naughty child and the school offender, the juvenile delinquent, and the criminal may know full well that their conduct is condemned by parents, by teachers, by society, by authority in general. Their reply is, "So what?" Punishment, in such cases, if it has any effect, seems designed to make the child reject authority all the more.

Emotional Effects

We must not forget that disciplinary punishment is an *inter*personal phenomenon. The child of five who is slapped for being impudent certainly knows as little as does the rat in a maze experiment about *what* he is being punished for; indeed, he knows less, for the rat can at least identify the locality that leads to punishment, whereas the "locality" of impudence is a mystery to the five-year-old. Even so, the child is definitely aware that the adult authority in his world is deliberately cracking down on him.

The interpersonal character of such "discipline" thus introduces a complication. As Fritz Redl says, the natural reaction to being hurt is to focus aggression on the source of the hurt. When punishment is imposed by authority, it becomes one of the attributes of authority. It is not quite true, as one is often tempted to say, that a child learns *nothing* from punishment. He learns that persons in authority sometimes hurt him—deliberately hurt him. Even if he grants the "justice" of the penalty (and that is asking much of the understanding and the feelings of the child), he is still learning that authority, in addition to being loving and kind—if indeed it *is* that—is also severe and harsh. *The one thing almost invariably learned during punishment is some degree of emotional antagonism toward the person inflicting it.*

Nor is this emotional antagonism of trifling significance. True, for most children it is, so to speak, canceled out by other experiences. The parent who punishes is the same person who is often generous and loving and kind. The teacher who punishes, on the other hand, has much less than the parent of this counterbalancing background of affection. In either case the hurt frequently remains, and our psychological clinics have many clients whose maladjustments seem to hark back to severe discipline, especially in the home.

A concrete example may help to clarify the issue:

> When I was in the second grade I thought I saw a water wheel in the grain of the wood of the teacher's desk just in front of me. With my slate pencil I set to work "improving" the picture. For thus "deliberately scratching" the teacher's desk, I was whipped. At home, brooding over the injustice, I burst out, "I don't care, Miss Swan is an old fool." For such "impudence" I promptly got a second thrashing.
>
> Now what was accomplished here? Certainly neither of the whippings seriously impaired my physical well-being. But Miss Swan needed no ruler across my shoulders to interrupt my attempts at "creative art." A word would have helped me to realize the fault, and would have guided future behavior as well or better—and it needn't have been a cross word, either.
>
> My mother's punishment was even less justified. She missed a royal chance to help me understand adults, to help me gain tolerance of others. For this I needed an opportunity to air my grievance in a sympathetic atmosphere. But instead of lessening my grievance, she increased it.

Reporting on their intensive study of child-rearing practices in 379 families, Sears, Maccoby, and Levin (381) have this to say about punishment:

> The unhappy effects of punishment have run like a dismal thread through our findings. Mothers who punished toilet accidents severely

ended up with bed-wetting children. Mothers who punished dependency to get rid of it had more dependent children than mothers who did not punish. Mothers who punished aggressive behavior severely had more aggressive children than mothers who punished lightly. They also had more dependent children. Harsh physical punishment was associated with high childhood aggressiveness and with the development of feeding problems.

We must conclude, then, that punishment as *an aid to learning* is a pretty poor one. It works as a deterrent only in a limited range of cases, and then not invariably. And that's the nice way of putting it. A better way might be to say that very few children are permanently intimidated into goodness by punishment. It may indeed serve to tell the docile and obedient what is expected of them by authority, but it seems an unnecessarily harsh and unimaginative technique for this purpose. And it does not help to reform those who are in rebellion against authority; more often it merely makes them more rebellious. Finally, it damages the emotional relationship between the punisher and the punished.[2]

A strong indictment, surely, and one that seems to leave little room for punishment. Yet the whole human race relies on punishment, and always has. Mankind often persists in error for a long time, but it is scarcely likely that we should be so persistently and so unanimously wrong. There must be *some* value in punishment. And so there is.

Punishment as an Emergency Control

As I pointed out earlier, there is no escape from occasionally having to interfere with children's activities. We may have to prevent them from directly harming themselves, from learning bad habits, from interfering with others. When we cannot control disapproved behavior by other means, we may find it necessary to put an end to it by punishment or the fear of punishment. Coercion is, in other words, a sometimes necessary and a sometimes effective way of *keeping order,* or of preventing the child from harming himself or others, physically or otherwise. Punishment is thus to be looked on as an emergency method of stopping a person's behavior *then and there.*

[2] Lewin (273) comes to much the same conclusion from his theory of personality.

But what if the child is not overtly misbehaving but is *thinking* and *feeling* the wrong way? Do you really want to punish him for that? Even totalitarian countries do not find "thought police" overly effective, and it is one of the glories of our Anglo-American tradition that punishment and the law are concerned only with overt acts, not with thoughts or feelings. The child's thinking and feeling are indeed important, but punishment is not the way to alter them. There is something both ludicrous and morally offensive in punishing a person for his thoughts, even more for his feelings.

This suggests another consideration. Little children often tend to *act out* their thoughts and feelings. For this they may be punished by some parents. Later, they often restrict themselves to verbal expressions of their emotions. When they get still older, however, they learn "to keep their mouths shut"—at least part of the time. Now, if it is illegitimate to punish a child for his inner thoughts, is it legitimate to punish his outwardly expressed thoughts and feelings? The answer must be that it is legitimate only if the child's outward expression creates a situation that really cannot be allowed to continue and that can be checked *only* by punishment.

Parents often ask me whether they should punish the child who gets angry at them, strikes them, or says, "I hate you!" Well, what is the purpose of punishment? To stop an intolerable act. Now is it so intolerable if Fred strikes his father or mother? Surely one can, usually, keep from being physically hurt. What hurts, of course, is that the child should feel like that. But will punishment make him *feel* less hateful?

It is a little different when Fred attacks his sister or brother. That may provoke retaliation and an ugly situation may develop. It is sometimes necessary to step in to keep the peace. Not always, however; there seems to be no general rule. Sometimes you will do well just to ignore these flashes of anger.

We shall deal more fully with this question in the chapters on emotion. But you must remember that punishment *never* decreases the feelings of resentment or anger; hence clearly it does not solve this problem but makes it worse. The most punishment can do is to keep angry feelings from spilling over into dangerous *acts.*

This brings us back to the justification of any punishment: punishment and coercion have as their true purpose *the inhibition of misconduct at the time it is happening.*

QUESTIONS

1. What is the main difference psychologically between punishment in the form of an electric shock given to a white rat who goes down the wrong alley in a maze, and a smart slap on the wrist of a two-year-old who is trying to pull the table cover (and dishes!) off the table?
2. Did you ever receive a punishment that did you good? Explain fully.
3. If a rat is given a shock when he takes the wrong fork in a maze, the punishment leads him—almost forces him—into taking the right fork. Describe circumstances where punishment of a child *directly* leads to doing what is right.
4. What are the advantages and the disadvantages of having ready a list of the punishments that might be used in a given grade? Give examples.

The Right Kind of Punishment

Promptness

If we look at punishment in this way it should not be too hard to find the right kind. In the first place, since it is an emergency measure, we have to make use of a punishment which is at hand. Well, certainly that seems an easy recommendation to follow, for we generally do use the first punishment to pop into our heads. If our first impulse is not always judicious, at least it has the virtue of being—as recommended—prompt.

Exactly the opposite advice, however, is sometimes given: Never punish until we—the punisher *and* the punished—have had a chance to cool off. Obviously, this advice is based on a faulty notion of what punishment is for. Delayed punishment is almost a contradiction in terms; it is really a form of revenge, a way of getting even. Delayed punishment does not stop the culprit's misconduct; it has already stopped! And if punishment is to have reformative effects it must, as we noted earlier, be very immediate.

Moreover, delayed punishment is more likely to damage the adult-child relation. A child can readily understand—and perhaps excuse—a parent, or even a teacher, who hurts him in a moment of irritation or anger; it is hard to excuse one who is, as it seems to him, *deliberately* cruel. I must confess that I agree with him. Of course,

I accept the claim that punishment is well-intended cruelty; the child seldom does.

By a prompt punishment, however, I do not mean one which is just momentary; it may last for some time. Most punishments clearly do. If you have a headache and Granville persists in playing his harmonica, you may have a perfect right to "punish" him by impounding the harmonica. That punishment is prompt and may last for quite a long time, especially as the child reckons time. But it is not delayed punishment. You don't wait until the misconduct has ceased and then begin to punish. Punishment is legitimate only if *begun* at the time the misconduct is taking place. (This, of course, rules out the practice of having father impose the punishment when he gets home after a hard day's work.)

Severity

Second, you need a punishment that will actually stop the misconduct. This means that you should not try to make the punishment correspond in severity with the "enormity" of the offense. Instead, you should make the severity just great enough to break down the child's resistance to authority *at the time.* Now resistance varies from child to child and from occasion to occasion. A child engrossed in a television program will resist the call to go to bed more strenuously than one who just happens not to feel like sleeping, though both may, in fact, refuse to go. The child watching the TV will doubtless have to be more severely coerced or punished in order to pry him loose. The treatment is rougher not because he is "naughtier"—he isn't—but simply because it takes more punishment to secure compliance.

In school two cases of "disorderly conduct" that from the outside look almost exactly alike may have to be very differently treated because the two children are different: a scolding for Catherine is a crushing punishment; for Sally Lou a deprivation of some privilege is more effective.

But if the punishment has to be really severe, surely we must ask whether obedience is worth it; and also why it is so difficult to obtain. (You probably won't have time, however, to reflect on these questions until after the emergency has been met—that is, after punishment has been inflicted and obedience obtained.)

Side Effects

Third, we must select a punishment which does not have too many "side effects" in addition to the one intended. Obviously this requirement severely limits the other two. If you are thinking of the child's development instead of the present emergency only, this is apt to be a decisive point. Many a punishment is immediately effective but has, in connection with other instances, bad long-time effects. Thus frequent and severe punishment may go far to crush a child's spirit. Or, for another child, it may create bitter rebellion.

Take the perennial issue of corporal punishment. It can be prompt (our first principle); and it can be effective (our second principle). What, however, are its side effects? That depends.

As far as very young children are concerned, the side effects of physical punishment do not differ from those following any other kind. Older children, however, are apt to be humiliated by a whipping. Their self-respect is injured. We should find some other way of restraining them.

Punishment and Rejection

With any kind of punishment, the great danger is that you may make the child feel that you are rejecting him. Never let him draw that conclusion if you can help it. Never threaten him—or seem to threaten him—with the loss of your love if he is "bad."

Now that's precisely what isolation as a punishment sometimes does. When a parent sends Tim to his room because he persists in annoying his sister, Tim is likely to feel that the parent does not consider him fit to associate with the rest of the family. When a teacher banishes a child from the class, she frequently says in so many words that he is making an intolerable nuisance of himself and that he must stay away until he is fit to associate with others again.

Note that it is social, not mere physical, isolation which hurts.

Scorn, ridicule, and sarcasm are apt to drive a wedge between the child and his associates as well as between you and the child. They are thus socially isolating and may seriously endanger his feeling of security. No punishment for bad conduct should be allowed to cause the child to feel that *he is exiled or banished from association with others.*

Some theorists believe that the threat of loss of love is the basis of conscience and a major means to socialization. Most of this thinking is based on a study of badly disturbed children and neurotics. I am willing to concede that neurotic conscience often has a strong component of anxiety. But I cannot agree that jittery, pervasive anxiety, a half-conscious fear of losing what most makes life worth while is the basis of a healthy acceptance of necessary social rules.

Punishment and Aggression

Another common side effect of punishment is aggression.

When you punish a child, it looks to him like hostility on your part; he therefore reacts with counterhostility. Sometimes, of course, knowing that he does not dare show this counterhostility against you, he "displaces" it onto his playmates or his pets. But nearly always punishment generates aggression—at some times more than at others, depending on the circumstances (223).

Punishment because the child has been aggressive is particularly apt to start a vicious circle. Bobby has been fighting; when you punish him for that, you make him still more likely to break out with further aggression, which then has to be punished, and so "round and round." Punishment, far from restoring order, causes it to be hopelessly lost. Any punishment which creates a situation calling for further punishment is bad.

The side effects of punishment depend on the whole pattern of the child's life, on his age, on his psychological make-up, on the family pattern, even somewhat on the attitudes which prevail in the community. (More than "somewhat" in the case of older children.) Punishment is a highly individual matter.

We thus turn our backs squarely on the celebrated advice in *The Mikado* to "let the punishment fit the crime." Indeed, nothing could be more stupid than to have a standing list of punishments "appro-

Figure 3-3. What does this accomplish?

priate" for each kind of offense. Even the more modern notion of "making the punishment fit the criminal" needs to be taken with much reservation.

The trouble in all these cases is that we are trying to make punishment do something it is ill-fitted to do—to reform the child's behavior. *Punishment by itself is an inhibitive, not a reformative, agency.*

Constructive Measures

Indeed, you have to be on your toes to make sure that your punishments do not get in the way of reform—they do so more often than you might think. And you should not expect punishment to effect the reform directly. This means, I think, that you must relegate punishment to a very secondary place. Your primary concern is not with *punishing offenses* but with *treating offenders*. It can hardly be too strongly urged, then, that your task is not even half begun when you punish a child and let it go at that. Nothing constructive at all is likely to come out of punishment. The real job comes *after* punishment.

Not, however, immediately after! On the theory that you should "strike while the iron is hot," many people try to explain the reason for the punishment immediately before or after it is inflicted. Nothing could be more ineffective. Just when a child is full of resentment and hurt self-esteem, smarting both literally and figuratively, how can you expect him to attend to and accept the teachings of "wisdom and morality"? You are trying to get him to see the connection between his misconduct and the dissatisfaction it is sure to bring him. You seldom succeed. Stimulation applied to the bottom of the spinal column seldom produces rational thought at the top. If the child makes any connection at all under these circumstances it is to associate the moral code you are arguing for with his own anger and resentment. Contrary to all the folklore, a good switching just does not "larn 'em to behave." The evidence is pretty conclusive that pain and fear and anger do not facilitate learning; they disrupt it. Indeed, it would be hard to devise a more unfavorable situation for learning than that which immediately follows upon conflict and punishment.

You do have to inhibit or break up antisocial behavior once in a while, and you may need to take strenuous measures to do so. That done, give the child a chance to get over it. Don't try then and there "to point a moral or adorn a tale." Wait!

Is that all? Well, in other cases where a child's activity is blocked off by external circumstances we encourage him in "constructive persistence." But when we put the roadblock there ourselves, we call such persistence "willfulness" or "disobedience." Buster, age two, is abusing a toy truck and refuses to heed your warning. So you take it from him and put it on a high shelf. Are we to encourage his "persistence" if it takes the form of pulling up a chair and reclaiming the forbidden truck?

No, hardly, though I hope most of you will take at least a grim

Figure 3-4. "What do you want him to do? Brood over his troubles?"

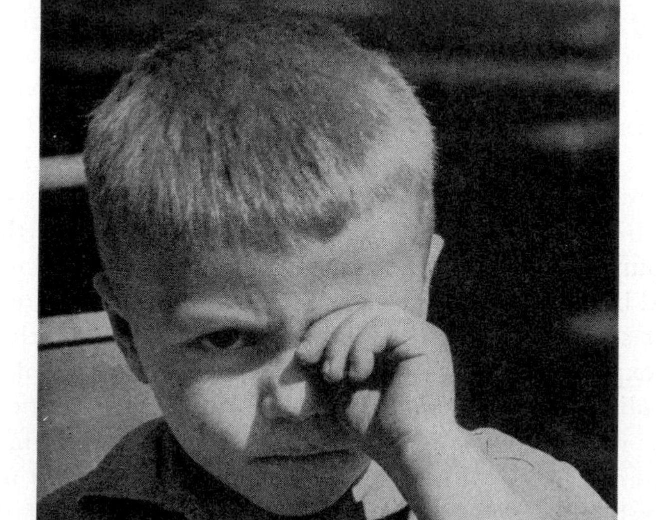

satisfaction in the fact that Buster doesn't give in easily. Still you can't let him get away with it. What, then, to do?

Suppose we follow through the parallel of punishment with some other form of frustration. If his son has just lost out in a contest at school and is feeling pretty low, a father will often take the lad to a show or go hunting with him. If he is feeling low after punishment, why not treat him the same way? After a punishment has served its legitimate purpose of preventing some bad conduct or other, what do we want the child to do? Sit and brood over his troubles, nurse his sense of frustration? Or seek something wholesome to do?

Our disinclination to give a child, who has just been punished, a chance to do something satisfactory to him seems to have several roots, all of them rather discreditable. We don't want him "to think he's getting away with it"; we want him to recognize our own superior power. (Well, he *will* do that.) We want to be sure the child really feels our disapprobation of his conduct. (But he is likely, rather, to feel that we have rejected him.) We are afraid that if we give him something nice to do, he won't have paid a big enough price for his misdeeds. (The old "an-eye-for-an-eye" doctrine.) In all this we are misconstruing the true value of punishment, which is that of a mere inhibitor. Once it has served that purpose, there is no reason why the child should not be helped to find happy and satisfactory activities. Indeed, there is every reason why he should be. When we get the motives of revenge and sadism out of our systems, there will be fewer punishments, and those we do inflict will better serve their limited but legitimate purpose.

I am by no means suggesting that you pamper the child by offering him something on a silver platter. He should be encouraged, rather, himself to search for "something fun to do." But it does little good just to encourage him with words. If you want to make the encouragement stick, you've got to see to it that it does some good to try. Choking off bad conduct by punishment without providing any acceptable alternatives is just inviting trouble. The best thing we can do for a child is to see that his environment provides him with *rich opportunities for legitimate need-satisfaction if he goes after them.*

In school the principle is the same, though it may take more imagination to apply it. Here is a group of boys who have had to be punished for "horsing around." They resent the punishment. So now, according to what I have been saying, you have to find them "something fun to do."

But in all probability they were "horsing around" in the first place because nothing within the range of school activities seemed "fun to do." Before you resorted to punishment, in utter desperation, you had already tried to find interesting but constructive activities—and had failed. Something that will divert these boys from their boredom won't be easier to find just because they have been punished.

Of course, one answer is the old one—punish only as a last resort. But occasionally the last resort *is* necessary. Then what? I refuse to believe that there is *nothing* within the range of school activities that can hold these boys. (If there is nothing, the boys should not be in this particular school.) Immediately after the punishment you can make changes in schedule or in work assignments that *will* give the boys a chance to find some satisfaction.

Note I spoke of "work assignments." The idea is not to "sweeten them up" after punishment by offering a treat, but to restructure the situation so that satisfactory and constructive effort can take place. It won't always work, but it is worth trying for.

Later, you can try to get the child to see why certain kinds of behavior must be avoided. Use an instance of his own behavior by all means; moral education must be very concrete. But don't refer at all to the fact that you had to punish him for it. What you are after is that he make a firm connection between a certain situation (the baby is trying to snatch away the toy the child is playing with, for example) and the right thing to do in that situation (not to strike the baby, for one thing). Punishment has no relationship to such correct behavior.

Admittedly this policy leaves us with one of the supposed purposes of punishment still unfulfilled—that of teaching the child why his behavior was wrong. But as we pointed out earlier, nothing we can do immediately after punishment is likely to have much effect along these lines.

That is, none that is useful. I was severely cracked on the knuckles in the first grade for spelling the word "horse" as h-o-r-c-e. As a result it was years before I really knew how to spell that word. (It is significant, moreover, that the only other incident I recall from that grade is when Artie Gardner, to my great glee, successfully defied this teacher.)

Nowadays, of course, punishment for a failure to learn, especially a corporal punishment such as striking the knuckles with a ruler, is nearly inconceivable. When we punish in today's schools, we say it is only for misconduct. Perhaps so. Yet why we make a distinction between punishment for "academic failure" and punishment for "misconduct" is not easy to see. Surely we ought rather to recognize that misconduct is just as truly "failure to learn" as is academic failure. And it will help us to a due humility if we recognize further that "failure to learn" is generally a corollary of "failure to teach effectively." Do we want to chastise the child for *our* failures?

I must insist once more that it is not a matter of corporal punishment versus other forms. To substitute sarcastic reproof for a ruler is far from an improvement. It is not my knuckles I resent after over fifty years but the teacher's stupidity. What I needed was to get the idea that a certain word was spelled h-o-r-s-e. What I got from my punishment was an agitated uncertainty as between *c* and *s*. Right behavior, whether in spelling or arithmetic or morals, should be the direct and unhesitating sequel of the appropriate social stimulus. Worry about punishment in this connection is nothing but a disturbance.

Our long discussion of punishment may be briefly summed up in the words of a Sunday school pupil's definition of a lie: "A lie," he said, "is an abomination unto the Lord—and an ever-present help in time of trouble." We cannot quite get along without coercive measures, but we can and should resort to them as little as possible. For coercion and punishment seldom if ever directly contribute to constructive outcomes, and often directly hinder them. We shall have a healthier and happier tomorrow in proportion as we cease to imbue children at home and at school with the notion of revenge, of retribution, and of penalties for misconduct.

Discipline Versus Self-Discipline

All along my treatment of "discipline" has been highly critical—some of you may think unduly so. The trouble is that discipline is such a negative concept. It is more important to want to do the right thing—and to know how!—than to be afraid of doing the wrong thing. The growth of personality and of character is more a matter of *enrichment than of disciplinary restraint.*

Obedience or Self-Direction?

Even so, I do not suggest that you encourage "undisciplined conduct." The question is, How is this to be avoided? There seem two alternatives. On the one hand is the old doctrine of unhesitating obedience, in action and even in thought, enforced by coercion and punishment. On the other hand, there is self-control, self-discipline.

The child's behavior may be defined in terms of its nearness to one of the three corners of the "Triangle of Discipline." (See Figure 3-5.) Wholly undisciplined behavior is farther from either of the other two corners because it is truly an opposite of both sorts of discipline. But it must not be overlooked that "Disciplined" and "Self-Disciplined" are also at opposite angles, though less distantly related.

Nearly everyone admits that self-control is more to be desired than obedience. And a great many people have begun to realize that intelligent self-direction is an even better way to describe what we want our children to attain.

Figure 3-5. The Triangle of Discipline

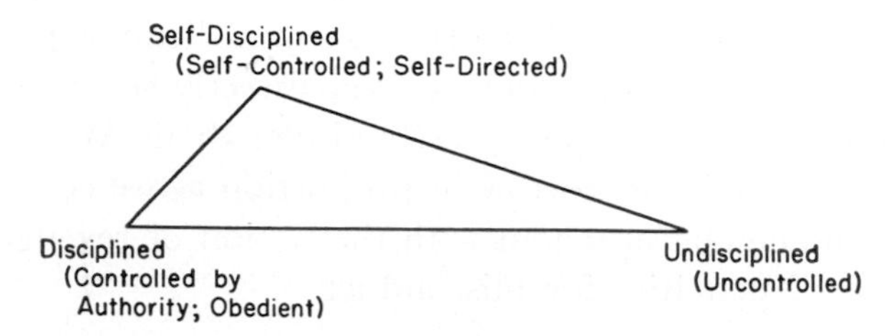

But ought not children be taught to obey? Yes and no. I am not one of those who believe that there should be *no* rules which children must obey. (Frankly, I have never met anyone else who really so believed, or who acted on such a belief.) External discipline and obedience are a valuable, even necessary, means whereby we control children's behavior. We should, therefore, train children in obedience.

But how? Many people seem to think that children learn to obey only under coercion and the threat of punishment. The result is to give the child the feeling that rules are inherently hateful. Some children learn that it is no use to resist; they become spineless and submissive. Others, perhaps because of tougher fiber or as a result of less persistent parental pressure, learn that rules are to be obeyed when the authority-figure has his eye on them and when the heat is on. Obedience with such children is obviously highly unreliable.

There is, however, another kind of obedience—obedience that springs from the whole relation of the child to authority. I do not speak of the joyful compliance of the child who is—at the moment—closely identified with the authority-figure. That is more than obedience (and, of course, much better). I am speaking of obedience where the child would rather do something else, but does obey out of trust and faith in the authority-figure. Now how is such obedience instilled?

I think we have already seen the answer. The whole experience of the child must teach him that when rules and commands are followed, the results are likely to be more satisfactory—to him. The child must learn that obedience pays off—not every time, naturally, but in the long run.

Of course that's what we tell him. But telling is not enough. There must be abundant direct experience of the fact. And it must *be* the fact; too often it is not. The exercise of authority is selfish, concerned with the comfort and needs of the adult. Authority deserves obedience only when it is exercised in order to help the child more fully attain his own goals, fulfill his own needs. Trust in the goodness and usefulness of authority should begin very early, and should be continually reinforced.

The two ways of teaching obedience are thus in stark contrast. Fortunately, however, they are not wholly antagonistic. A certain amount of coercion may be employed and the child discovers to his reluctant surprise that "Mother was right—this *is* OK." A little coercion now and then won't break a child's spirit or convert him into a persistent rebel. And a little coercion may certainly be needed when the child's recognition of authority is somewhat inadequate. The trouble arises not if we merely use coercion occasionally to get an immediate result, but if we habitually rely on it as a means of instilling the habit of obedience.

Over and above this, we need to remember that obedience is merely a means to an end, to be exacted only when the end makes it necessary. Obedience is not a *primary* virtue or end in itself.

Self-discipline is. To help children become self-disciplined persons is one of the chief goals of education. How do we do it?

First let's be sure that we are clear about the difference between self-discipline and external discipline. Self-discipline means that the child himself restrains a present impulse in order to attain a more distant goal. Discipline by another person means that the present impulse is inhibited by what someone else does or threatens to do to him. Self-discipline is something the child does; external discipline is done to him. Psychologically, they are thus very different.

Self-discipline, like anything else, is learned only by the child's own action—what the adult does helps the development of self-discipline only as it evokes *in the child* genuinely self-controlling behavior. Does punishment or coercion do that? Is there not indeed a genuine contradiction between his controlling of himself and being controlled or coerced by others? Surely it is obvious that, just to the extent that coercion is actually successful in its goal of controlling the child, it rules out the possibility of his learning there and then the lesson of *self*-control.[3] Any favorable effect of external discipline on self-discipline must therefore be indirect.

A fair case, however, for such indirect benefits of external discipline can be made. In the first place, unless we do something to keep things under control, children may get in the *habit* of unruly and chaotic behavior. All of us have seen children who are not essentially bad but who habitually give in to every passing impulse. Nothing could be more unfavorable to the growth of real self-direction. Discipline from outside may help to check the development of these bad habits and thus *keep the way open* for self-discipline. This is a negative benefit but it is not negligible.

I once visited the class of a young teacher who was an enthusiastic but uncritical believer in the virtues of freedom and self-expression. The program for the day apparently was the reading of original verse by members of the class. Half the class paid no attention but were engaged in small groups of four or five in only slightly subdued conversation—indulging in random and mostly personal remarks. Others who listened to the verse often interrupted or made insulting noises and "Bronx Cheers." Not more than five out of perhaps thirty children were pursuing the supposed program. More important, not more than five were displaying a genuine axis of self-directed behavior. The others were reacting to the whim of the moment.

Now such anarchic, capricious behavior is just as foreign to self-discipline as is regimented behavior—perhaps more so. The teacher's defense was that so long as the children had no chance to choose for themselves, they could not gain that *ability* to choose which is the heart of self-discipline. That is quite true. But the way the situation was actually structured, they were *not* choosing, however free they were to do so. Instead, they were acquiring a variety of bad habits—socially and even ethically bad—including as the chief bad habit that of aimless drift and thoughtless (or, literally, thought-free) impulsiveness, which lies at the very opposite pole from self-discipline.

---

[3] And let's not forget that the bad feeling and resentment caused by punishment are radically unfavorable to learning anything.

Self-discipline does not grow, then, when the child yields to every passing inclination, nor when he yields, with or without constraint, to authority. It grows when he successfully masters and integrates his own unruly and conflicting impulses. It is our task to create a social situation in which the children *utilize* freedom for genuine choice. Freedom which does not lead to successful self-control leads away from the development of character. *Every undisciplined act is a loss.*

The Earmarks of Good Discipline

In Chapter 2, I promised to summarize the characteristics of good discipline. The preceding paragraph comes very close to providing that summary. I think that every parent or teacher can well afford to ponder it and to take it to heart. Good discipline helps to create situations in which the child can learn to direct his own behavior.

But scattered through these two chapters are a number of concrete characterizations of what makes authority wholesome. At the risk of being bromidic, perhaps I should assemble these ideas here in one place. If, however, these statements are taken as dogmas or rules to be mechanically applied, they will fail of their purpose. Take them instead as stimuli for thoughtful consideration of your relationship to the children under your guidance.

I. First of all, good authority gives security and stability to the growing child. He is aware of his weaknesses and his inabilities; he needs the security of a loving helper.

II. Good authority helps the child to attain *his own purposes* better than he could if he "followed too much the devices and desires of his own heart." Good authority is not truly restrictive; when it restrains the child's conduct at one point, it is only to release his energies in other and more fruitful directions. Good authority seldom says, "Don't do that!" It inquires, "Wouldn't it be better to do this instead?"

Good authority helps the child because it guides him away from the errors and mistakes which would otherwise keep him from attaining his goals. It helps him to attain his purposes because it helps him to avoid conflict with others. Good authority saves the child from the hampering effects of a sense of guilt.

III. Good authority enables the child to play his part in society as a *follower,* without resentment or without feeling loss of selfhood. Where the child has learned to identify himself with authority, he can feel that accepting the leadership of that authority is a means to his own best purposes. Followership—which is so essential to the very existence of society—is not a despised necessity but a welcomed activity.

It cannot be too much emphasized that this aspect of authority, unless carefully guarded, leads us easily down the primrose path to authoritarianism and dictatorship. Unless identification with authority is properly balanced with independence, it is very dangerous. Yet without that identification, social life, in which each of us inevitably yields to the direction of others at many points, would be a succession of frustrations and irritations.

IV. Good authority is a great "teacher." The prestige of authority enables us to teach the child much that he would never have time to learn from direct experience. Through our authority we teach manners and morals, attitudes and ideas. Good authority presents a sound model which the child may copy, for good authority teaches as much by example as by precept.

V. Finally, good authority is self-limiting, even self-liquidating. We accept the necessity of adult control, but we see the role of such control in a new light, no longer primarily negative, and certainly not as an end in itself. The adults' control of children's behavior is a means whereby they can create a social situation in which the children *utilize freedom for genuine self-direction.* The area of freedom expands as fast as the children move into that area with self-disciplined choice. Abundant evidence exists that when we thus give them a chance for growth under freedom they steadily develop in self-discipline. *The true measure of the value of "discipline" is the rapidity with which it renders itself unnecessary.*

Summary

Resistance to authority is often a reflection of adults' failure to exercise positive motivation. In large part this failure is due to too much regimentation of the child's behavior; but too *little* leadership also leads to various sorts of unfortunate behavior. To avert conflict, adults need to display an authority which seeks to harmonize the children's purposes, not to dominate them or impose their own. Such authority does not restrict; rather, it releases the children's energies in constructive directions.

Disciplinary conflicts, however, can't always be avoided. Here coercion and punishment enter the picture. What good does punishment do? It is a very slim aid to reform. Punishment seems to be justifiable almost exclusively as a *means of preventing, then and there, forms of misconduct which cannot otherwise be controlled.* To accomplish this purpose, punishment must be not merely prompt but practically simultaneous with the misconduct. It should be adjusted not to the "crime," nor even to the "criminal," but to the difficulty of checking the offensive acts. And it must interfere as little as possible with the rest of the child's behavior.

Punishment thus conceived is purely negative. Constructive guidance of the child's behavior is best divorced from punishment. And the less we need to fall back on coercion and punishment the better.

Discipline imposed upon a child is to be viewed as at best a necessary nuisance. Self-discipline, however, is a positive virtue of the highest importance. Discipline by others does very little to promote self-discipline, but positive leadership by adults may create social situations in which children utilize freedom to gain practice in self-direction and thus learn self-discipline. Good discipline is self-liquidating.

4

Emotion in Children

Emoting as a way of acting, as a way of getting along in the world, may be either good or bad. How do children learn or unlearn their emotional behavior?

To their first day of school some children bring anxious dread, even stark terror; to the fear of the untried is often added the prospect (so it seems to the child) of being abandoned by the mother. Other children come full of triumphant pride in being big enough at last to go to school. Some bring into the schoolroom hostility to the teacher, some a shy affection; some bring an eager zest, some a whiny craving for attention.

Sharp differences in emotional behavior thus mark the first day of school, and continue to mark every day until the children pass before the rostrum to receive their high school diplomas—some elated, some cynical, some pretending boredom, some with naked joy at release from school, some sad and fearful for the days ahead.

What Is Emotion? [1]

What are these emotions that we see our children display? Despite the fact that the word "emotion" is on every tongue, it is surprisingly

[1] The theory of emotion that follows is essentially my own (137), though it has obvious affinities with the views of R. S. Woodworth and N. Cameron (86). It does not pretend to be a complete statement; only as much is presented here as is needed for an orientation to the problems of emotional development in children.

difficult to say what it really is. The difficulty is not that we lack concrete facts but that it is hard to arrange them in a meaningful pattern.

Whatever else it is, however, emotion is a very active way of behaving. *Emotion is "emoting"*; emoting is fearing, loving, hating, delighting, joying, trusting, and so on through a long list. All these emotions are ways of *acting*.

A very complex way of acting, of course. As you probably learned in your elementary psychology course, the distinguishing feature of this complex is the *internal behavior* of "visceral" or autonomic response—a sort of internal adaptation of ourselves to the emotive situation. Indeed, this internal behavior is more than the distinguishing feature; all the other activities of emotion are organized in reference to it.

These other activities, however, are equally part of emotion. They include the *overt responses* by means of which we cope with the physical features of the emotive situation, and the whole gamut of *emotional communication* by means of which we cope with the social features of the situation: facial expressions, gestures and postures, as well as emotional expression in words.

All of these are what are called organismic or personal activities—that is, they are things done by an organism and apparently have a quality not found except in the activity of a person or other living being. Some of them (e.g., the secretion of adrenin), usually studied in physiology, are called physiological activities; others (e.g., a threatening gesture) are studied in psychology and may be called psychological responses or behavior or acts. Emotion clearly includes both kinds; or rather, as Kantor (241) puts it, both kinds of processes are "participants" in the total psychological response.

In my view, however, it will not do to say that emoting is *nothing but* a series of such responses as have been listed above. A whole is more than the sum of its parts. Just as a triangle is more than a combination of lines, just as a melody is more than a succession of tones, so an emotion is more than a combination of organismic activities. Emoting is precisely the *whole* that is constituted by the parts; it is the "wholeness aspect" of those complex actions that are organized about the responses of internal adaptation.

Take a specific kind of emoting such as fearing, loving, or being anxious, disgusted, or trusting. What we have been saying is that trusting is the *integration,* the *wholeness* of the responses we demonstrably make when we trust. "Joying" is likewise simply the particular unity of activities found when we "joy." A specific emoting is not some mysterious essence distinct from the ways of acting that can be discerned in operation; the ways of acting in their totality *are* the emoting. Fear, anger, disgust, courage, and compassion are simply you in action in as many different ways.

To think of anger or fear or joy as being particular ways of living gives us a richer concept than to think of them as some sort of "mental content"—as feelings—locked up in each individual's mind and inaccessible to anyone else save indirectly. Joy remains joy no matter how it is analyzed.

But the analysis of emoting into its component parts has practical as well as theoretical value. It is often possible to alter one or another of the components and thus to gain a measure of control over the whole emotional process. Knowing what the parts are is a great help in changing the whole which is emotion.

The concept of emotion as an integration of a variety of organismic activties is, however, incomplete. If emotion is to be fully understood, it must be seen in its context. As John Anderson (12) puts it, "When we say a person is angry, we describe a total property of a system."

Let us take a concrete example. It is clear that a mother's love for her child differs from the child's love for her. Yet mankind persists in calling both experiences by the same name, evidently perceiving in them a basic identity.[2] I suggest that the similarity between the two kinds of love lies in the *pattern* of personal or organismic activities that we have been describing. Conceivably, in a given case, precisely the same pattern of activities might characterize a mother-child love and a child-mother love.

But the two experiences in total cannot possibly be the same. They differ because the experience of loving is never an event by itself. It is always an experience of loving *someone.* The mother's love is the love of her child; the child is an intrinsic part of her loving. Similarly the child's love is not some sort of abstract loving, but a loving

[2] Modern and Western mankind, that is. I do not know whether other peoples have different names for these experiences. The argument, in any case, would not be affected by the fact that other peoples perceive difference where we see similarity. Both similarity and difference are real and must be accounted for.

of his mother. The event of loving is defined in its very inmost nature by the object loved.

Furthermore, a mother's love is inextricably entangled with the whole of her life experience, whereas the child's loving is part of a still undeveloped life space; it is almost—not quite—a thing by itself. Thus the two loves differ sharply, however similar the organismic pattern of activities may be.

According to this view (which expresses the position of what is known as field theory), an emotion taken by itself as an integrate of organismic activities is an abstraction from the richness of concrete reality. But abstractions are frequently useful. It may be true that for a full understanding of emoting, we must take into account the wider context of the emotional event. It is also true that we can often gain in our understanding by thinking about a part of the whole event and treating it *as if* the part were somewhat distinct from the larger field.

Specifically, it is often worth while to turn our attention away from the unique quality of a Mrs. Thackeray's love for her son Jamie and the equally unique quality of her love for Carl. She does love them differently, of course; but her love for her two sons shows great similarities also, similarities in the kinds of integrated patterns of personal activity we have just been describing.

The similarities are there even when we observe two mothers and even across the gap between two cultures. When, shortly after the war, I accompanied Corporal Yoshio Inoye to his home in a remote village in the interior of Kyushu, his mother fell upon his neck with tears and sobs of joy no different from those with which Mrs. Thackeray greeted the return to Tulsa of Sergeant Carl Thackeray. The similarities in the pattern of behavior may be important, even decisive. Emoting as the totality of certain patterns of activity is not the whole truth; but it is a useful part of the truth.

This already extremely abbreviated statement of the nature of emotion may be summarized as follows: Emotion is a very complex way of acting. It integrates a variety of organismic activities, both physiological and psychological, around the activities of internal adaptation—those often misleadingly called "visceral." But this integration of organismic activities can only be fully described when it is seen as part of the whole personality and life experience of the individual, and as having reference to an object.

QUESTIONS

1. Does the discussion of "emotion" and "emotional" seriously conflict with the way you are accustomed to use these terms in everyday speech?
2. How does it differ from the treatment of emotion in the textbook of elementary psychology you studied?
3. Our next topic is about emotional problems. Try to see how one might conceive of an emotional problem as a disturbance in the pattern of behavior.

Some Emotional Problems

Occasions for emotion are, of course, ever present. Whenever anything goes wrong, whenever he feels imposed on, the child is apt to become emotional. The emotional outburst, moreover, is all too likely to outlive the immediate occasion. It becomes an emotional problem with a considerable life span.

No such permanent effect was to be seen when Judy spilled her milk on four-year-old Maybelle's dress. Maybelle yelled loudly and slapped Judy's hands. Half an hour later, however, they were happily cooperating in sandpile play. In contrast is the situation in a fourth grade where Arthur, though by no means a star reader himself, had the bright idea one morning of ridiculing Grandison's bumbling oral reading. Already sensitive to his inadequacy, Grandison became very angry. Naturally this was Arthur's cue to continue ribbing at every opportunity. Before the teacher knew what was happening, a full-blown feud began to develop, with most of the children taking sides.

Like other troubles, moreover, emotional problems seldom come singly. Instead they are likely to interweave with other problems in so complex a way that it is sometimes difficult to tell which is cause and which is effect. The difficulties associated with physical growth and the even greater difficulties associated with ill-health are complicated by the emotional problems they generate. Emotional habits may be set up which in turn interfere with health and normal growth. (On this, more in Chapter 5.)

Billy Boy developed rheumatic fever when he was seven and spent the biggest part of a year in bed. With careful tutoring by his mother he easily kept pace with his schoolmates, even got ahead a little. But he became very dependent upon his mother's devoted attendance. If he wanted a drink, a picture book, one of his many toys, he had only to ask for it and his mother would bring it to him. These services were, of course, made more or less necessary by his illness; but they were accompanied by indulgent and affectionate attention which convinced Billy Boy that he was the center of the universe. Neither Billy nor his mother could easily change their attitudes when his restored health made them no longer necessary.

Of course the attitudes were never really necessary. An invalid can be cared for in ways that make him feel loved without making him so dependent. He can be encouraged to do for himself whatever lies within the limits of his physical condition and can be praised for doing it. It is not without significance that this invalid was called "Billy Boy." His mother was indulgent and overprotective. Billy's illness merely accentuated a trend present from the beginning.

Differences in intelligence may also cause emotional distress. To be the smartest among your companions can give rise to just as much emotional distress as to be the dull one—as many of you can testify. And this emotional distress can keep you from using your intelligence, may even interfere with its further development.

"Bozo" is the bully of Grade VI. His profanity and rough speech match his swaggering walk. Clearly he glories in being a tough guy. In class he barely skirts around the edges of impudence. He refuses to recite or makes some smart-aleck reply. Yet his written work is usually fairly adequate and his intelligence test shows him to be of very superior ability.

Bozo's school history is an interesting one. In the kindergarten he was aggressive, or at least self-assertive, but not at all unpleasant. In both the first and second grades he was unfortunate enough to have teachers so eager to help him develop his very real intellectual ability that they were insensitive to his social relations. Bozo, or rather John Henry, as he was then called, became teacher's pet. One day toward the end of the second grade, three of his classmates taunted him: "Yah, yah, teacher's pet, teacher's pet!" John Henry waded in with flailing fists and thoroughly beat up all three, partly by virtue of the fact that he was, like most children of advanced intelligence, big for his age, but partly by virtue of his indignation.

This was the beginning of John Henry's metamorphosis into "Bozo." The word that he had "licked three kids in his grade at once" spread. The social approval of his fellows was far more satisfying than the pallid approval of his teacher. The syllogism, though hardly put into words, was clearly apparent to Bozo: "Doing good work in school may get teacher's approval, but makes the kids hate me. But I can be a hero by being a tough guy."

The result is apparent. Bozo's schoolwork has steadily grown worse.

Though one cannot be sure, there are indications that his superiority in intelligence has lessened. Meanwhile Bozo is not really happy in his role. At eleven he is no longer satisfied to have kids somewhat fearful and subservient. He is intelligent enough to realize that this kind of leadership is inadequate.

It is interesting to speculate what would have happened had John Henry been put in a group of children of more nearly equal intellectual potential. His natural aggressiveness, one suspects, might well have made him respond to the challenge of intellectual achievement. As it is, his anti-intellectualism and his social domineering attitudes are pretty well established and will not easily be modified.

It is probably unnecessary to illustrate at any length the many other ways in which emotional problems interact with other kinds. Failure in schoolwork may lead to depressed or angry frustration; or in reverse, frustration at home, grief at the loss of a puppy, or worry about an absent parent may be the cause of school failure. In the classroom Julius neglects study of his spelling list for the fun of teasing Genevieve; and Genevieve thereupon becomes so enraged she cannot work and may precipitate a scene that upsets the whole room —including, of course, the teacher.

Research supports our everyday impression. Thus, among children referred to a child guidance clinic for fearfulness, it was found that this was seldom the only symptom; 65 percent of the fearful ones showed sleep disturbances; 34 percent, temper tantrums; 33 percent nail biting; 29 percent, enuresis; 18 percent, whining and crying (to a definitely abnormal degree); and 6 percent, stuttering (240). Stutterers were found in one study to show from one to seventeen symptoms of emotional disturbance (318). It may be said that these are "problem children." But the normal children of the California Guidance Study—normal, but all the same, they had many emotional problems—present the same sort of picture (292).

There is no question, then, that the problems of emotion are important. Indeed, the harassed teacher or parent is to be forgiven if she thinks that no other kind of problem is real.

Popular use of the term "emotional problem" includes two really different kinds of case. First, we have the case where a child emotes because he is upset by a recurring difficulty or trouble. Thus a child who has never learned to accept authority without resistance will, when the pressure is put upon him at school, display many emotional responses. (And, needless to add, he excites emotion in the teacher and others!) In a sense, he may be said to present an emotional problem. But the emotion in this case is a symptom of an underlying problem which is not essentially emotional—the problem of his relation to authority. Problems of this sort are more properly called personality problems.

The second case is the child whose adjustment is hindered by improper or injudicious habits of emoting. A child whose typical reaction is irritableness, anxiety, fear, or belligerency may be profitably discussed as a problem directly of emotion. The problem is one of how the child emotes. (Compare the similar distinction made by H. D. Meyer [311].)

The distinction is not a hard and fast one. In the end, all serious problems of adjustment become emotional, and certainly no problem is merely a problem of how one emotes. But, although the distinction is only one of degree, it calls attention to a difference in one's procedure. Where we have problems of emotion in the second sense, our attention centers on helping the child learn better ways of emoting. And that is the theme of this chapter.

QUESTIONS

1. What is the common element present in all cases of emotion so far discussed?
2. The foregoing discussion is guilty of a serious distortion of emphasis: look back to see if you can tell what it is.

Emotion—Constructive or Destructive?

It is too bad, however, to think of emotions as always creating ugly problems. Emotional behavior can have a positive value as well. To teach Charles, who is nine, how to master his fears (not merely how to avoid them) is a good first step. But more is needed. Even the "negative" emotions must be put to work. Fears need to be transmuted into intelligent caution, anger must be channeled into constructive attempts to remove obstacles, disgust needs to be used to keep our environment clean and wholesome, sorrow and pain should play their part in enlarging our sympathy and our compassion for others.

And beyond this, emotion is a necessary element in the good life. It is hardly likely that any reader of this book will question that children need not only to receive but to give love. But this is not all. Courage, gaiety, humor, joyfulness, and the zest of living—surely these, too, are to be encouraged and developed in our children. As John Macmurray says, in the emotional life there is a great capacity for growth and development (293, ch. 2). Education both *of* and *for* emotion is a great part of our task. We shall return to this topic in the next chapter.

The Development of Emotion

The Primitive Emotions of the Baby

Can you remember the first time you ever held a very young baby in your arms? How jerky, how spasmodic and uncoordinated his movements were. And how "all-over"! His whole body seemed one diffuse squirming.

You may choose for yourself whether to say that all of the newborn's behavior is emotional, or that none of it is. Certainly anyone would be hard pressed to pick out certain activities and say, "These are emotional"; and of others, "These are not." The newborn's behavior is what we speak of as "undifferentiated." Nothing that is *specifically* emotional has had time yet to develop out of what William James (222) called the "great blooming, buzzing confusion" of the newborn's awareness.

Presently, however, the infant becomes more discriminating. You can see that he is attending now to this, now to that, stimulus. A sort of vague excitement breaks what Arthur Jersild calls the "somnolence of the new-born." This excitement is the beginning, the ancestor as it were, of all later forms of emoting. And it is all the emotion the young baby has.

The Psychoanalytic Viewpoint

The last statement may seem to reject rather summarily the position of many psychoanalysts (as also of many mothers), attributing distinct emotions to the newborn, and even to the fetus. Sigmund Freud (153), for example, supposes that the fetus can at least experience pleasure and unpleasure. Some of his followers go much further. Loretta Bender (54) does not hesitate to say that the child comes into the world "lonely and afraid;" Otto Rank (360) and many others endow the newborn with anxiety; and Susan Isaacs

(218) says that "fears and angers, love and hate, are there from the beginning."

The psychoanalysts do not claim to have observed these emotions in newly delivered infants. Rather, they have reconstructed what the emotions of the newborn infant *must be like* from what their adult patients on the analytic couch tell them. They hold, in other words, that their explorations of the psychic life—conscious and unconscious—of disturbed older children and adults reveal facts that can be understood only if we ascribe emotional experience to the newborn. This is a legitimate way of arguing, but hazardous. As the psychiatrist Hendrick says, such ascriptions are "far more a projection of analytic theory and adult passions than scientific observation" (199, p. 33). Moreover, many psychoanalysts, especially the neo-Freudians, differently interpret the same clinical observations.

What we know, moreover, about the development at birth of the higher nervous centers counts strongly, though not conclusively, against this position. Freud himself in other contexts spoke of the infant as incomplete and unfinished. We have seen that emoting is the *integration* of many activities around the internal responses. The neural mechanisms for such integration are quite undeveloped at birth. (See the evidence cited by Furfey *et al.* [160], Irwin [217], Taylor [436].)

Direct Factual Evidence

We should like to appeal to direct observation for a decision as to how much, if any, emotion an infant displays at birth or soon thereafter. Unfortunately such observation is extremely difficult. An emotion, as we have seen, is a highly structured, complex, total behavior. Many of the activities that constitute it are invisible and must be indirectly observed.

What we usually do when we study emoting is to observe certain patterns of overt behavior that are so regularly a part of a particular emoting that they can be taken as signs. But what would you look for as evidence of fear or rage in a babe of four hours—or four days? There is very little pattern in the behavior of infants, and the sorts of cues we usually rely on in judging emotion are missing.

The same difficulty is met in reporting the occurrence of emotion in animals; yet, as Hebb (197) has pointed out, considerable reliability in identifying their emotions is possible. Indeed, the curator of one of the world's largest zoos says that if a keeper cannot judge the emotions of the large animals, he won't live long. Careful and objective observers can make similarly reliable reports of the emotional behavior of infants, and many have done so.

We have a number of experimental studies dealing especially with fear in infancy (217, 355, 356, 390, 391, 436). Unanimously they report that there is in infancy no specific kind of response associated with what would ordinarily be fear-provoking stimuli.

It is possible to argue that these investigations were conceived in too narrow a spirit. Perhaps they did not succeed in setting up experimental situations that were likely to arouse anxiety in infants. This argument is not likely to be made after reading what they did. For example, Sherman gave the infant a sudden push or dropped it two or three feet. Others used loud noises and the like. Is there anything more likely to scare a six-day-old baby?

Another approach is to observe babies under a wide variety of *natural* circumstances, seeking for the first, or at least a very early, manifestation of emotion. A survey has been made of more than two-score monographs and handbooks for facts of this sort. They are presented in Table 1.

In drawing up the table, I made no effort to track down anecdotal reports; these are known to be quite unreliable. Reliance was on reports of scientific observers who were giving particular attention to the very earliest days of the infant. I quote anything that looks at all like emotion, including much that the observer on the spot doubted was even rudimentary emoting (355, 436).

While these reports are based on careful and responsible observation, they represent very different levels of analysis. One author will use such detailed description as "arches the back" whereas another will summarize in such terms as "anticipatory excitement." But for our present purposes the differences in manner of report are not important.

Table 1 is *not* a table of norms showing the ages at which infants on the average first display this or that behavior. It is merely a summary showing that *one or more* infants behaved thus and so under certain not too exactly defined circumstances. How many other infants do the same the data do not show. The whole focus is upon the general line of development, not upon the normal development of an individual child.

Interpretations in the table in square brackets are mine, otherwise they are those of the investigators cited in the next column.

The table shows that emotional behavior is beginning in these early months, but only beginning. When this is all that experienced scientific observers can find, it is evident that the emotional repertory of the infant is at first pretty meager. K. C. Pratt (355) summarizes the practically unanimous verdict: "It seems certain that such well coordinated reactions as those implied by the terms love, rage, and fear, do not exist [in the newborn infant]." As Nancy Bayley (44) points out, the development of emotion must wait upon experience and a concurrent development in the intellectual sphere. One reacts emotionally to situations only as one is able to discriminate something in the situation as "disturbing." Like Al Capp's hero, Li'l Abner, the infant can't be emotional about the situation, he's too ignorant to perceive anything to emote about. Orlansky (340) and Bousfield and Orbison (67) have an incisive analysis of the material bearing on this issue.

The factual evidence, then, seems pretty conclusive against the psychoanalytic view that well-marked emotions function at birth. It is possible, however, that the problem is chiefly semantic. When Susan Isaacs (218) says that "fears and angers . . . are there from the beginning" does she mean quite the same thing as does Bridges (74), who finds no anger until about the sixth month? May it not be that the psychoanalysts are merely emphasizing the genetic continuity of life experiences? Are they saying that when certain kinds of emotion-related experiences happen to an infant, even to a newborn infant, they affect his later emotional growth, even though, then and there, they do not generate emotional behavior?

Something very like this interpretation has long enabled many of us to accept the closely related doctrine of infantile sexuality, which at first was such a shock to common sense. To say that a certain infantile experience is "sexual" is not necessarily to say that the infant is behaving as an adult does in sexual experiences, but that the infant's behavior is such as to *influence* his later sexuality. The way an infant loves his mother certainly differs from the way a man loves his mate; but the Freudians have impressive clinical evidence that the infantile or childish experience of loving the mother may explicitly affect the adult experience of mate-love.

Table 1.

Emotion-Related Behavior in the First Six Months

FIRST MONTH

Situation	Response	Interpretation	Observer
Tactual stimulation	Crying		Bridges (76)
Tactual stimulation	Checked breathing	Excitement?	Blatz, Bott, & Millichamp (60)
Painful deep pressure	Faster breathing, limb movements	Excitement	Blatz, Bott, & Millichamp (60)
Difficult evacuation	Crying	[Pain]	Bridges (76)
Loud noise	Checked breathing		Blatz, Bott, & Millichamp (60)
Loud noise	Crying		Bridges (76)
Loud noise	Blinking		Stern (419)
Holding nose	Turning head, arching back		Stern (419)
Holding nose	Slashing with arm		Landis and Hunt (258)
Restraint of arm	Stiffening body		Stern (419)
Being dropped	Upward extension of arms, clutching (crying infrequent)		Stern (419)
[Not stated]	Excited crying	Excitement	Blatz, Bott, & Millichamp (60)
Discomfort	A specific cry	"Discomfort?"	Gesell, Castner, & Thompson (167)
Pain	A specific cry	Pain	Gesell, Castner, & Thompson (167)
Hunger	A specific cry	Hunger	Gesell, Castner, & Thompson (167)
Distress	Irregular crying and kicking	Distress?	Blatz, Bott, & Millichamp (60)
Any obtrusive stimulus	Jerky movements, Moro reflex	"Startle?"	Goodenough (172)

SECOND MONTH

Situation	Response	Interpretation	Observer
Loud sound	Jerky movements	Startle	Blatz, Bott, & Millichamp (60) Goodenough (172)
Loud sound	Sigh	Fright	Bridges (76)
Adult face	Visual regard	[Interest?]	Carmichael (89)
Another child crying	Vigorous crying	[Sympathy?]	Bridges (76)

THIRD MONTH

Situation	Response	Interpretation	Observer
Unusual bodily position	Crying	Distress	Blatz, Bott, & Millichamp (60)
Toy dropped	Crying	[Frustration?]	Blatz, Bott, & Millichamp (60)
Sounds	Body tension		Landis and Hunt (258)
Sounds	Head turning	[Interest?]	Blatz, Bott, & Millichamp (60) Gesell, Castner, & Thompson (167)
Presence of strangers	Crying	Fear	Pratt, Nelson, & Sun (356)
Smiling face	Smiling, cooing	Delight, pleasure	Bridges (76), Buehler (81) and Shirley (394)
Perceiving bottle, etc.	"Anticipatory excitement"		Dockeray (123)
Unexpected tactile	Crying		Pratt, Nelson, & Sun (356)
Unexpected tactile	Laughter		Carmichael (89)

FOURTH MONTH

Situation	Response	Interpretation	Observer
Return to crib	Cries louder than for hunger		Carmichael (89)

Situation	Response	Interpretation	Observer
[Not stated]	Sucks thumb	Active displeasure	Bridges (76)
Frustration without unpleasant bodily contact	Crying		Bridges (76)
[Not stated]	Defensive movements		Bridges (76)
Bodily discomfort	Crying *less*		Blatz, Bott, & Millichamp (60)
FIFTH MONTH			
Strangers		Fear	Buehler (81)
[Not stated]	Clapping hands, crowing, laughing, smacking	Joy	Buehler (81)
Song sung	Crying	?	Carmichael (89)
Song sung	Vigorous bodily movements	Eagerness	Gesell, Castner, & Thompson (167)
[Not stated]	Vocalization	Eagerness	Gesell, Castner, & Thompson (167)
Appearance of bottle not immediately given, or adult who does not come to babe	Crying	Anticipation?	Bridges (76)
[Not stated]	Signs of pleasure more numerous than earlier		Bayley (44)
Toy replaced	[Not stated]	Joy, pleasure	Bridges (76)
Toy disappears	Crying	[Distress]	Bridges (76)
Toy disappears	[Not stated]	Distress	Blatz, Bott, & Millichamp (60)
[Not stated]	Pushes things away		Bridges (76)

SIXTH MONTH

Situation	Response	Interpretation	Observer
[Not stated]	Playful patting, banging		Bridges (76), Dockeray (123)
[Not stated]	Vocalization	Satisfaction	Bayley (44)
Angry versus friendly tones	"Distinguished by babe"		Bridges (76)
[Various]	Laughing		Bridges (76)
Familiar face	Smiling		Shirley (394)
Strange face	Crying		Shirley (394)
Strange face	Grave look, then smile		Pratt, Nelson, & Sun (356)
Strange face	Visual regard		Blatz, Bott, & Millichamp (60)
Certain foods	Rejection	[Disgust]	Blatz, Bott, & Millichamp (60)

The crucial experiences affecting emotion may sometimes, in this view, occur even before birth. Studies at the Fels Institute and elsewhere seem to show that certain kinds of maternal activity result in a sort of overstimulation of the fetus, and that this overstimulation, if frequent, makes for an excitable infant after birth (156, 175, 178, 187, 407, 479). The fetal experience may thus be of direct effect upon later emotional behavior. The events of very early *post partum* existence may be similarly influential.

This line of thinking seems to narrow the gap between the psychoanalytic theory and the empirical facts of child development. Even though it may not be wholly acceptable to some psychoanalysts, it preserves the essential features of their argument. On the other hand, it seems vital to the understanding of emotional growth to see how slow and gradual is the process of differentiation as it is described in the empirical research findings.

With the psychoanalysts, then, we concede that very early experience affects emotional growth; but, with those who directly observe infant behavior, we insist that distinctively emotional behavior is not present at first and develops with experience, out of undifferentiated beginnings.

Varied Emotions Develop

Gradually two new patterns do begin to appear, namely, distress and delight. At first both emotions are elicited only by direct physical stimuli: for distress, by such things as colic or hunger, wet diapers, cold or painful objects on the skin, sudden loud noises or sudden shifts in position, forcible hampering of movements; for delight, by such things as general comfort, sucking, being snugly held, warmth, being rocked. Gradually social stimuli begin to play a part. Patting (aside from relieving stomach gas) is probably pleasant because it satisfies the infant's social needs. By the third or fourth month it is quite clear that the infant is responding to persons as persons—e.g., the babe smiles in return to a smiling face (413).

Katherine Bridges, on the basis of an extensive study (74, 75), has given us perhaps the best description of the way these two behaviors are outwardly manifested: distress by tightening of muscles, checking of breath, change in facial color, trembling, and crying; delight by relaxing of muscles, gurgling of saliva, by free and easy movements, and by soft vocalization. (See also Bakwin [26].)

As the infant develops, other emotions grow out of distress and delight. If there is a sudden shock, the emoting is not merely distress but that special form of distress we call fear. If someone interferes with the infant, we get that form of distress called anger. Out of delight, at about one year, grows a specialized form of emoting called elation, and another that is recognized as affection.

Toward the end of the first year the differentiation of emotions has proceeded to the point that fairly reliable recognition is possible, as is seen in Goodenough's experiment (173). She used pictures of a German child of ten months photographed in natural situations in rather old-fashioned clothes. Twelve situations were described very briefly by the photographer and the presumed emotion is given. (For example, "Slight obstinacy. His mother wanted him to give her his hand, but he would not because she had just taken a toy away from him.") The task of the subjects, sixty-eight American students in a class in child development, was to match each photograph with one of the descriptions. A judgment was deemed correct if the picture and the description were of the same group—e.g., any of the three descriptions of astonishment (a′, a″, a‴) were allowed for Picture A. The results are set forth in Table 2.

The table may be read and interpreted as follows: There were three descriptions of a situation in which the child was astonished. Picture A was one of these situations and sixty-four of the sixty-eight judges correctly matched it with one or other of the three astonishment descriptions. Picture B was of obstinacy. Nine people matched this with a description of anger—for which there was no picture. Sixty-one judges correctly matched C′ with a roguishness description, but only twenty-nine so identified C″.

With twelve descriptions all told, of which three were for astonishment, for Picture A there was a 3 in 12 chance of its being correctly matched by pure guessing. This is to be compared with the 64 in 68 or 94 percent correct matches attained.

There were two verbal characterizations of obstinacy, thus two chances in twelve of chance success compared with better than fifty-fifty actual success. That is, the observers were three times as correct as would be expected from sheer guessing.

The failure of the observers to assess correctly the picture of fear

Table 2.

Number of Times Still Photographs Are Matched with Verbal Characterizations of the Situation—68 Judges

	Verbal Characterization of Situation	Picture Corresponding to Verbal Characterization									
		A	B	C′	C″	D′	D″	E	F	Judgments	Percent correct
a′ a″ a‴	Astonishment—three descriptions	(64)	10	2	16	3	13	6	1	115	56
b′ b″	Obstinacy—two descriptions	2	(38)	2			1	41	5	89	43
c′ c″	Roguishness—two descriptions	1		(61)	(29)	16	1	6	2	116	75
d′ d″	Pleasure—two descriptions			1	14	(49)	(53)		3	120	85
e	Fear or dislike	1	11	1				(14)		27	52
f	Crying for something to be done			1				1	(48)	50	96
g	Anger (no picture shown)		9							9	0
	No. of matches	68	68	68	59[a]	68	68	68	59[a]	(526)	67+
	Percent correct	94	56	90	49	72	78	21	81		
				Av. 69		Av. 75					

Correct matches are in parentheses.

[a] Data from 9 judges missing.

Rearranged from F. L. Goodenough, The expression of the emotions in infancy. *Child Develpm.,* 1931, 2, 96-101.

is interesting. Since we can be sure from other evidence that recognizable fear does manifest itself by this age, the particular fear in this case was probably somewhat mixed with other elements. All the other pictures were clearly identified well beyond the guessing level.

If the table is read the other way—across the horizontal lines—we see again that the matchings are correct far beyond chance. Not only are the pictures given the right description but, on the whole, the right descriptions are given to the right picture. (Even fear. When the judges thought a picture showed fear, they were right in over half the cases. Chance would give 1 in 8.) Although a description of anger was included, in only 9 cases out of a total of 526 did any one suppose it to match one of the pictures, and all of these made the minor error of confusing the picture of obstinacy with anger. In all, slightly over two thirds of the judgments were correct—a figure far in excess of what it would be if the judges were simply guessing.

Bridges (74, 76) gives us in Figure 4-1 a schematic picture of the order and approximate ages at which emotions develop. Each emotion is conceived as differentiating out of the emotion above it. You will note that "excitement," which is the granddaddy of all emotions—every emotion is a kind of excitement, isn't it?—continues to be exhibited as a special emotion in its own right. (In the diagram, "excitement" is found at every stage.) Nor does simple distress cease to be found just because the specialized forms, anger, fear, and disgust, have evolved out of it.

Of course all these emotions change in *quality* as a child grows older. The excitement of a ten-day-old is not entirely the same as that of even a ten-month-old baby. In infants, the pattern of anger is crying or a primitive tantrum; in older children, anger shows itself in a variety of ways (49, 171, 231). But there is a real relationship—the way the older child emotes is influenced by the way he emoted when he was younger. Variety in emotional behavior is described in many places—the following are merely samples: for sympathy, Murphy (329); for joy and delight, Leuba (264), Brackett (70), Washburn (461), Kenderdine (246), Jersild, Markey, and Jersild (232), Brambaugh (72); for jealousy, Ding and Jersild (122), Levy (267), Sewell (386). Emotions, especially those of very young children, are less distinct than might be guessed from the fact that we give them distinct names. Even in ourselves, let alone in infants, it is often difficult to say just what sort of emoting is going on. *One emotion grades into another by imperceptible degrees, as colors do in the rainbow.* You can, to be sure, tell a *typical* anger from a typical distress, but in between are many gradations that are hard to distinguish. It is the same with anger and fear, with delight and joy, or with joy and elation—at the extremes they are different enough but in between are very many

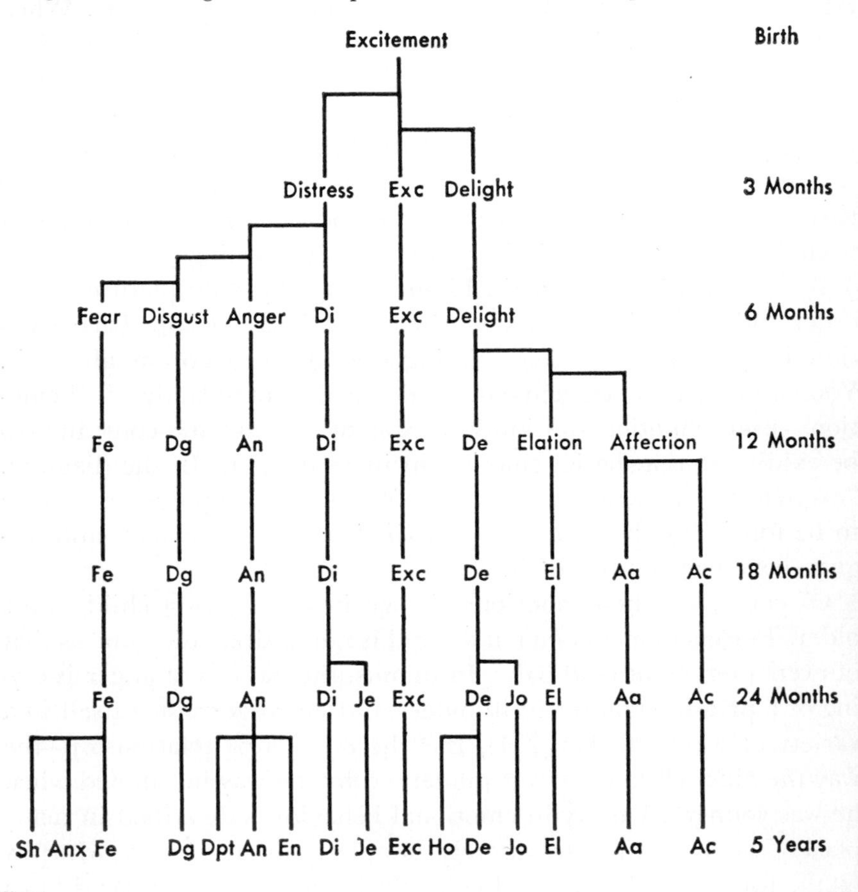

Figure 4-1. Diagrammatic Representation of the Development of Emotion

Key:

Aa = Affection for adults	De = Delight	El = Elation	Ho = Hope
Ac = Affection for children	Dg = Disgust	En = Envy	Je = Jealousy
An = Anger	Di = Distress	Exc = Excitement	Jo = Joy
Anx = Anxiety	Dpt = Disappointment	Fe = Fear	Sh = Shame

Combined from two diagrams by K. M. B. Bridges, *J. genet. Psychol.*, 1930, **37**, 524, and *Child Develpm.*, 1932, **3**, 340.

intermediate ways of acting.[3] Nonetheless, little by little the child begins to show recognizably different emotions.

The first step, then, toward greater emotional maturity is the development of a greater number and variety of emotions. Little as we may like the behavior in question, it is a step forward when a child begins to express disgust for the spinach instead of showing the less differentiated distress out of which disgust has developed. (According to the chart in Figure 4-1, you may expect disgust to appear at about six months, and according to my experience with babies spinach is one thing likely to bring it out.) As the child matures he develops a *joy* out of the simpler *delight* of the young infant. The changes are a little subtle but are to be welcomed and encouraged when we recognize them.

Individual Variability

But children do not develop these varieties of emotion in a uniform fashion. Within the general pattern there are many individual peculiarities. As you know, no two people emote just alike. They have learned to emote the way they do as a result of life experience, chiefly in childhood. Such experience, of course, differs from child to child. Even within one family, children have greatly different emotion-forming experiences. Thus joy and satisfaction, fear and disgust, and all the rest come to be manifested in most varied forms.

Certainly the pattern of *visible* or *overt behavior* is highly individual. Thus Florence Goodenough (171), in her study of anger in young children, lists kicking, stamping, jumping up and down, throwing oneself on the floor, holding one's breath, pulling, struggling, turning the head, pouting, frowning, throwing objects, grabbing, biting, striking, crying, screaming—and a number of other behaviors. Of course, few children are so talented as to display *all* these forms of angry behavior. Probably no child is. When we try to think of all these acts as one emotion, it is somewhat bewildering.

[3] Faced with a similar problem, some scientists in the field of color have abandoned color names such as "vermillion" or "pea green" and have substituted arbitrary numbers. They speak of "color 17." One suspects, however, that it will be a long time before even the driest of technical treatises substitutes "Emotional pattern No. 42" for "Joy," or "No. 18" for "Jealousy."

Yet I think you will grant that these *are* all parts of an anger pattern.

The pattern of fear is almost as varied (391, 394, 395). While there are fewer investigations of other emotions, they all tell the same story: great variety, and growing greater with age, in the overt behavior of the several emotions.

That part of the emotional response which is less visible because it is "in our insides," as the Scots say, is not quite so variable. A Bantu child in Central Africa, a Russian child on the banks of the Volga, and an American child from Cedar Rapids probably have the same sinking feeling in the pit of the stomach when they are afraid. Yet even here there is some variability. Some children lose their appetite (or their dinners) when they get excited, others do not. And a child who at age two loses appetite when promised a food treat—some children actually do this—may at age six become very much excited and manifest anything but a loss of appetite (75). Evidently the behavior of our "insides" can be altered by experience even though it can't be voluntarily controlled very fully.

The situations that stir children to emote are as various as the kinds of behavior. We psychologists are accustomed to saying that the cause of fear is "an abrupt stimulus for which the child has no ready-prepared response" (132, 453). But this formula doesn't mean that the causes of fear are all alike. Fear can be excited by almost anything; it depends on the child's previous experience whether he will have a "ready response" for it.

Sudden loud noises, for example, will usually evoke fear in a young child. If, however, he has been subjected to many such noises, they cease to be, for him, sudden and unexpected. My fourth child at fifteen months had nerves of iron when it came to "fearful" noises; her older brothers had seen to it that there just weren't any noises she was not used to (132).

On the other hand, depending again on the child's experience, things that once passed without special notice become "unusual" and "fearful." Very young children are delighted with snakes, older ones are likely to have learned to fear them. As Harold and Mary Jones (236) say, fear is simply the response a person makes in a total situation that requires a sudden new adjustment he is unprepared to make. Whether a child is prepared to adjust depends as much on his general level of development and on his individual experiences as it does on the specific stimulus. As he develops, his intelligence matures, and his perceptions become enriched through experience. New things startle him because he is mature enough to realize that they *are* new and potentially dangerous, but is not mature enough to know how to cope with them. The intelligent, imaginative child is therefore likely to show more fears than does the average child of his age; he sees more possibilities.

So, too, with anger and rage; there is great variety in what causes them. Nearly any child gets angry when there is conflict with other children over toys or activities. Orders from adults often cause anger; some children even go into a temper tantrum over Mother's enforcement of routine physical habits. Many children fly into a rage at their own failure: trying to start the bath water when the faucet is turned too tight, or making a drawing come out the way it was supposed to. Anger is aroused when the child (or the adult) is restrained from doing what he wants to do. But what the child wants to do varies from child to child, depending on previous experience. So, conspicuously, does his idea as to what constitutes restraint or interference (171). This last is often a nasty problem for teachers: some children fly off the handle at the slightest restraint; others are less touchy.

We have dealt chiefly with fear and anger because there is a greater wealth of careful observation of these emotions. But there is also an impressive array of investigations dealing with others. All tell the same story. Increasingly as the child grows older, both the occasions for emotion and the modes of manifestation (inner and outer) become greatly varied.

Besides this wide variation in the *kind* of situation that brings on emotion there is also a wide range of susceptibility (168, 394). You have probably yourself observed that some babies frighten easily almost from birth, while others are nearly fearless; some are excitable, others stolid or placid. There is some reason to think that these differences are due to differences in the functioning of the endocrine glands. The early differences tend to persist, though they are subject to modification as a result of experience (407, 443).

Universal Characteristics

Practically important though these differences are, we ought not to exaggerate them. Some things nearly all of us do the same way. There is a characteristically human way of living, and this acts upon our specifically human nature to produce characteristically human ways of emoting. Even vastly different people all over the world treat their children more alike than some popular anthropology would lead one to think.

So we find in every land and clime that three-months-old babies smile in response to the close proximity of a human face (413, 461). In Samoa and in Nebraska, children find themselves faced by baffling and sudden changes—and cry out in fear (though if they are old enough, the cry will be in Polynesian or American respectively). White children and Dakota Indians fear many of the same things (458). In Tibet and in Connecticut, children are thwarted and interfered with—and angrily resist. It is hard to imagine a society in which this would not be so.

And yet the note of caution. By the sixth month some of the universal character of smiling is lost; depending on the child's individual experience, the faces of some adults bring out a smile, those of others bring crying (413, 461).

The culture also makes a difference. In some societies, parents sternly repress angry behavior even in infants; in other societies, infantile rage is encouraged. In prewar Germany the culture encouraged a kind of blustering anger on the part of adult males toward servants, children, wives, and other "inferiors"; and this behavior was found, therefore, in men who would otherwise be judged gentlemen. In America such behavior usually is limited to people of poor breeding.

In Western culture, children are taught to feel disgust at filth and certain smells, so that these reactions are for them "normal"; in most of the world today such disgust is mere finicalness and is relatively uncommon—as it was in the lives of our ancestors only a few generations ago. Very considerable differences in the emotional characteristics of different societies are thus engendered by tradition and culture.

Ruth McKenny in "Paris! City of Children" paints an amusing but significant picture of the way culture molds the life of children.

> Georges was, take him all in all, the most civilized human being, aged two-plus years, I have ever known. He had occasional lapses, of course. . . . But these were exceptions. Georges was nearly always polite, gay and charming. He shook hands with other little boys he met in the park, he came when *Maman* called, he brushed the mud off his white shoes and took extreme care not to drip ice cream down the front of his ruffled yellow or pink silk shirt. He sat patiently while Grandma curled his hair and tied it with a blue-satin bow.
>
> "*Doucement,*" "*doucement.*" ["gently, gently"] They've been telling him that since the day he was born. Besides, they expect him to behave with a certain *noblesse oblige*. Georges has so much love, he must be responsible to it.
>
> Of course *doucement, doucement* works both ways. Georges was a two-year-old lamb, not a lion. He fell down one afternoon on the graveled path in the park; both Georges and Madame Dumontier sobbed piteously, Georges wore a large bandage over the skinned knee for days, and the whole episode left everybody shattered.[4]

Despite such cultural differences, the picture which emerges is that of a kernel of universal emotional behavior patterns based on innate factors and growing out of the universal experiences of the race. We may, if we like, speak of the inevitable maturing of such behavior tendencies; it is equally proper, however, to speak of them as inevitably learned. *All* behavior has its innate basis and all behavior has been modified by experience—that is, has been learned. *In their quality, there are no differences between the primary and universal behavior patterns and those which are learned in response to more individual or special circumstances of life.* What we may call the primary emotional behavior patterns have been fairly well established by the age of three; most of the changes thereafter are due to specific environmental circumstances of the sort usually referred to as learning. John Anderson summarizes a long series of field studies: "[Our data show that] emotions and feelings change greatly in the early years and have stabilized by entrance to school or shortly thereafter" (16).

---

[4] Reprinted by permission of the author. Copyright © 1953 by the Curtis Publishing Co.

QUESTIONS

1. If a particular named emotion changes in quality as the child grows older, what justification is there for saying it is the same?
2. What does the text mean by "culture"?
3. The text says there is no difference in *quality* between primary and acquired emotions. Are there any other differences? What value is there in making a distinction?
4. Are any emotional behaviors "instinctive"? What does this mean?
5. Are any emotional behaviors universal at age eight? at age eighty?

Learning to Emote

As the previous discussion has implied, a child is busily engaged in learning to emote from his very beginning. Three kinds of change take place.

First, there may be a change in the sort of situation that calls forth the emotion. On the positive side, a child learns to fear or hate or delight in objects that earlier did not thus excite him. Or negatively, he may learn not to fear, hate, or delight in objects or situations that formerly caused him to emote. You can readily think of innumerable examples.

Second, as a result of his experiences, a child adds or subtracts reactions to the pattern which makes up this or that emotion. You doubtless have long ago learned not to respond to something fearful with a protruded lower lip followed by a thin, explosive wail; nonetheless that was your response when you were an infant. Nowadays you probably react with a barely noticeable trembling of hands or knees. The apparently aimless thrashing about of the arms and legs in infantile anger gives way in early childhood to blows, then—in part—to angry words, and later to more subtle verbal aggressions. (The classic studies of anger in children are by Goodenough [171] and Jersild and Markey [231], but they are confirmed by many other studies dealing with particular problems.)

A third type of change consists in combining various emotions. Anger and fear are very often combined, frequently with disgust added. Indeed, any of our emotions can be mixed with almost any other.

It is amazing how little we know about how to produce changes in emotion. Of course, there are a few ideas. Thus popular psychology speaks of learning "by association": "the burnt child dreads the fire" —that is, the sight of fire evokes fear because of its previous association with a fear-provoking pain.

Emotional Conditioning

Some years ago this kind of learning was given the fancy new name "conditioning," and was elevated into the position of being the all-sufficient principle of learning. Pavlov, a great Russian physiologist, showed that a dog could be made to drool saliva when a bell was rung, simply by first ringing the bell just before the dog was fed. You may find it a little hard to see why this was an exciting discovery; after all, if you are used to a dinner bell calling you to meals, you can easily detect the "conditioned salivary response" in yourself.

Pavlov's significance, however, lay in his use of this discovery as a means of probing for some of the conditions under which behavior is changed. His work set loose a lot of theorizing and some very interesting experimenting. Watson and Rayner (466) performed a famous experiment showing that emotional as well as other kinds of behavior can be conditioned in children. They caused Albert, a well-adjusted infant who was happily playing with a white rat, to be badly scared by a crashing noise; thereafter he cried and retreated in obvious fear whenever the rat was brought near him. Moreover, the fear transferred to somewhat similar objects, such as a rabbit. The experiment has since been repeated in various forms, not always successfully, but often enough to show that learning of this type actually occurs.

The principle of conditioning is implicitly recognized by a people who, we may be sure, have never heard of Pavlov's or Watson's famous experiments. When the primitive Arapesh of New Guinea seek to wean a child (at two or three years of age), the mother holds a piece of taro in her hands while the child is suckling and chants: "Good taro, good taro, would you eat, would you eat?" And when the child releases the breast for a moment, a bit of taro is slipped into its mouth (308). Many similar applications of the principle from everyday experiences will occur to most readers. On the other hand, we are often very blind to the possibilities of *unfortunate* conditioning. Punishing a child for not drinking his milk (or for not spelling a word) is apt to condition him *against* the milk (or the spelling).

The principle of conditioning may also be applied in reverse. Finding that five-year-old Peter was afraid of furry animals and fur coats and feathers, Mary C. Jones (238) set out to decondition him. He was exposed simultaneously to two stimuli, a fear-exciting rabbit and pleasure-exciting food. Care was taken, however, to ensure that the latter was the stronger by keeping the rabbit at first at a considerable distance. Little by little on successive days the rabbit was brought nearer and nearer while Peter was happily eating, until finally the day came when Peter greeted him—"Hi! Rabbit"—patted him, and feared him no more.

And not only the rabbit! "By 'unconditioning' to the rabbit," writes Mrs. Jones, "Peter has been helped to overcome many superfluous fears, some completely, others to a less degree. His tolerance for strange animals and unfamiliar situations has apparently increased." A different white rabbit, worms, feathers, and various furry objects were now accepted with relative equanimity.

This outcome is generally and properly spoken of as the extinction of fear; but it is just as properly spoken of as the acquisition of a friendly feeling toward the rabbit. Important to note is the fact that this technique is double-edged and requires careful handling. Had the rabbit been too rapidly introduced, Peter, instead of transferring his *liking* from food to pet, might well have transferred his *aversion* from rabbit to food. Aversions to food are frequently set up in exactly this way. Many a child has been turned against orange juice, for example, by being given castor oil with it.

Later studies of conditioning, however, have shown that it is far from being the delightfully simple principle it appeared to be in John B. Watson's popular book of 1928, *The Psychological Care of Infant and Child* (465). What is properly called conditioning (as with Pavlov's dogs or even with Watson's Albert) takes place in a highly artificial situation *where nearly all competing stimuli are excluded.* The animal is compelled to react to just one isolated bit of the environment with a rigid and stereotyped response. No wonder the process often seems a bit stupid. One is tempted to say that conditioning is the way we learn when all better ways are ruled out.

Nonetheless, something not unlike it does take place in ordinary life; but it is far from representative of all sorts of learning, whether of children or even of the white rat, so beloved of psychological experimenters. Everyday learning is not a simple linking of isolated stimulus with isolated response. This is particularly true of most emotional learning.

But since conditioning does exist, we should try to see how it works. E. L. Thorndike (445) has suggested that association or conditioning takes place only when the stimuli or objects *belong together;* the suggestion seems peculiarly apt for emotional conditioning. Objects (or events) that *seem to the child to belong in an emotion-exciting situation* take on the prevailing emotional value of the total situation; and this shift or transfer may take place without any special "intent to learn," or even without the child's realization that he is learning.

It is clear how important this sort of learning can be. Emotional conditioning alters the child's behavior under circumstances that rule out much opportunity to understand what is going on or his own reaction to it. It is "blind" learning. Irrational and unreasoning likes and dislikes, fears, antipathies, attractions may thus be set up in even very young children, *and unless dislodged they may become permanent.* A very great deal of any child's emotional learning is definitely accidental.

QUESTIONS

1. Can you make deliberate use of conditioning in training emotions?
2. What are some of the limitations?
3. Why is conditioning "blind"? Does it have to be?

Emotional Climate

Does the accidental nature of emotional learning mean that we can do nothing about it? Not at all. For one thing you can make every effort to ensure that the total environmental "atmosphere" shall be such that the right kind of "accidents" have a chance to happen. The effect of "atmosphere" in determining emotional response has been verified by a number of investigations. Take the case of Peter and the cure of his fear of rabbits. Peter's deconditioning took place in an atmosphere of confidence and security. This made it possible for him to overcome his fear. Goodenough, in the study of anger already referred to, found that "a major factor in determining the frequency with which anger is displayed by children is to be found in . . . the so-called home atmosphere." (See also 126, 141, 340, 347.)

Indeed, the effect of the emotional context lies open to even casual observation. An infant secure in its mother's lap will gurgle with delight at antics designed to amuse him. Deprived of that secure position, he may be frightened by the same behavior.

One of my daughters, then fifteen months old, was terrified when she came suddenly upon patent leather dancing shoes, glistening strangely in a pool of bright sunlight. She fled at once to the "sanctuary" of her familiar high chair. Once there, she allowed the shoes to be slipped over her own and played with them happily. However, when child and slippers were removed from the safety of the high chair to the floor, the fear returned, though with lessened force (132).

The same principle holds as the child grows older. As Alfred Baldwin (28) points out, young children who are "high" with pleasure are very easily upset. In the feverish excitement of a basketball game, the emotional responses of the crowd are heightened: a trivial episode brings quick anger, perhaps a brawl. Nor are adults immune. In the surcharged atmosphere of a religious revival, the evangelist has been able to play on the emotions of the congregation as an organist on his keyboard, evoking in turn groans and sobs of despair, anger, pity, and finally jubilation over the repentance of sinners. When we read about the revival, away from the crowd and the emotional climate it created, we cannot imagine how the evangelist's exhortations could have had such effect.

Clinical studies of problem children abound in evidence that much of their difficulty comes from tension and discord in the home (396). On the other hand, studies of normal homes and of schools indicate the value of a prevailing atmosphere of relaxation and calm. (For a study of schools, see 69.) Thus even the tension naturally associated with going to a hospital is much less if the child comes from a home characterized by trust and security (220). It is apparent, then, that emotional learning depends less upon a single emotional crisis than upon the emotional climate.

Single Emotional Upsets

I am not implying, however, that you should needlessly expose a child to intense emotional upheavals—not even to one. These *can* do real harm. The classical example is that of a man who suffered from claustrophobia, or fear of being in a small, enclosed space. In the course of his treatment he was led to remember that as a child he had been bitten while locked up in a small room with a strange dog. The incident had long since been "forgotten," but ever since he had feared closed spaces without knowing why.

Cases like this led the great psychiatrist, Sigmund Freud, to set forth his theory that "nervous breakdowns" and the maladjustments called "neuroses" are due to some intensely upsetting incident in infancy (153). The theory gained an enormous vogue. People talked freely of their "phobias" and speculated even more freely about the emotional "traumas" that must have caused them.

As sophisticated after-dinner conversation this was probably harmless enough. Not so harmless was its effect on young parents, who worried a great deal lest they expose their child to some emotional trauma which would make him a neurotic, or "scar" him emotionally for life. Any punishment, of course, was *out*—sometimes even sharp reprimand was deemed to be potentially "traumatic." In their formative years the little darlings had to be most tenderly sheltered. The anxiety thus generated in the parents was often transmitted to the children and did more damage than the emotional shock the parents were trying to guard against.

Freud meanwhile was finding that his original theory needed supplement (154, 155). A traumatic episode by itself, he discovered, does not lead to "nervous difficulties" or neurosis. It has to be *sustained* by an anxious brooding or fantasy about the original incident. Indeed, in many cases, the "original incident" underlying the neurosis turns out itself to be completely imaginary; but, from much dwelling on it, the incident comes to be believed in as if it had really happened. The shocking experience, therefore, is not so important as the way the child or adult looks back upon it.[5]

In neurosis, memory of the traumatic event is repressed. This adds

[5] For discussion of the changes in psychoanalytic thinking about trauma, see Fenichel (145), Horney (209), and Misbach (316).

a complication. Ordinarily, when a child has a frightening experience with an object or a place, he soon has a nonfrightening experience with the same or a similar object and the fearfulness is canceled out. But when memory of an event is repressed, the fearful cannot be compared with the nonfearful experience, thus shutting off the former from the test of reality. The original anxiety remains associated with the original cause, and because of repression cannot be "learned away."

It is hard enough, even without repression, to soften the effects of really violent experiences. The deconditioning technique described on page 122 is dangerous in such cases. Suppose that a child has been so terrified by a dog that the mere sight of one causes convulsive shrieks and vomiting. To try to cure him by introducing the dog at a safe distance while the child is eating, as Mrs. Jones did with Peter and the rabbit, is to risk a digestive upset, if nothing worse. Many traumatic experiences are not unlearned, as Ruth Munroe (324) points out, because we do not dare expose the child to the kind of situation that would eventually bring about unlearning; the intermediate reactions are too drastic.

We do not deny, then, the obvious fact that traumatic experiences can have serious and lasting effects. Such cases should have professional attention.

It should also be obvious, however, that not every intense and disturbing experience is destined to make for lasting trouble. Otherwise, what a terrific burden of conditioned emotional abnormalities we should all be carrying around with us! We should, indeed, all be neurotics. But thousands upon thousands of children have been terribly frightened by a dog and develop no "phobia," or anything like it, even in milder form. Renaud and Estess (363) found that normal adults have had almost as many traumatic experiences in childhood as have neurotics.

Conditioned emotions in childhood, although they certainly occur, do not make lasting trouble *unless they are sustained and nourished* by the atmosphere of home, school, and playground. For permanent learning, emotional climate is ordinarily more important than even a very intense specific incident.

Intense experiences and emotional shocks do, of course, have an influence. They are part, but only part, of the total emotional climate which forms the child's personality. By all means, then, avoid subjecting a child to great shocks and tensions; but don't worry too much if he has to meet some childish crisis. If he has a secure emotional background, it will carry him through the shock without serious or enduring damage.

A very practical implication of this matter of the emotional climate takes us back to the problem of punishment that we discussed in the last chapter. What happens when, as a fairly consistent policy, you try to reform the child's behavior by punishment? What kind of emotional climate are you setting up? Obviously one dominated by pain, fear, and frustration. This emotional coloring is apt to be splashed over everything in the punishing situation.

We like to think that the emotional coloring rubs off onto the child's misbehavior—that the *misbehavior* takes on the dark color of an act that brings pain. Usually this is not the case, especially with a young child. The misdeed is over before the punishment descends upon him. It's not the naughtiness that is dyed a painful hue. It's you! You are the central figure in the punishment situation. The emotion you induce inevitably spreads to you.[6]

And if you try to preach high ideals at this time, you usually succeed merely in making these ideals hateful, too. Is it any wonder? They are preached in an atmosphere of pain and resentment and humiliation.

Emotional climate can, however, be used constructively. The first introduction of anything that seems likely to be disturbing—a new food, a medicine, even a new sort of clothes, a new subject in school, a new playmate—should be made in a situation where the child is secure, at ease, and happy. More generally, let us set it down that *no effort to keep either home or school a genuinely happy and pleasant place can be considered excessive.*

Imitation in Emotional Learning

In addition to providing a child with a general emotional atmosphere, we also give him specific models of emoting to copy. This he proceeds to do. Who has not seen a child imitating his

6 If you are a teacher, you can get the principal to inflict the actual physical punishment. If you are a mother, you can postpone the punishment "till your father gets home." Does such a dodge really help?

father's puzzled frown or the faint suggestion of a swagger in his walk? Or who has not noticed him imitating his mother's irritable scolding or her weary discouragement? Fortunately, he will also imitate our joy and delight, our humor, and our determination and courage if we set such models.

Nowadays a new set of models for imitation has entered the home by way of the TV screen. Years ago the extensive studies sponsored by the Payne Fund showed that very many children were deliberately copying the emotions depicted on the motion-picture screen (101). For most children the impact of TV is far greater than that of the movies, simply because it is more constant. The comic books provide another set of models. If we don't like the models set before children, let's remember the old adage that Nature abhors a vacuum and see to it that they have other models to imitate.

Ourselves, for one thing. Even when a child enters the gang age and when, to hear him talk, everything parents do is "crummy," he generally harbors a tremendous admiration for them. Teachers often come not far behind. (Sometimes even ahead!) We may not exactly be the child's heroes but to a surprising degree we furnish him with some of his most important standards.

Other adults may also be imitated, and so may other children. Fears, antipathies, and prejudices sometimes grow to prodigious strength without any direct experience with the offending object, merely by imitating the emotings of close associates. Thus Hagman (186) found that nursery school children resembled their mothers in fears more than in intelligence—the correlation for parent-child fears was .66. Pratt (354) found the number of fears in a group increased with its size, indicating that the fears were being acquired by imitation. The glee of other children in anticipation of some treat imparts itself to the child who doesn't know what it is all about. Dislike of the teacher is quickly transmitted to the new pupil. Waves of contagious emotion often sweep across a classroom. We may notice how this disrupts schoolwork; we should also remember that it is a way of learning to emote.

It is not just emotional *outbursts* that are imitated. The quiet absorption of the habitual emotional tone of those about him is even more important for a child's development. Emotion is less often *taught* than *caught*. A fearful child may learn calmness from being

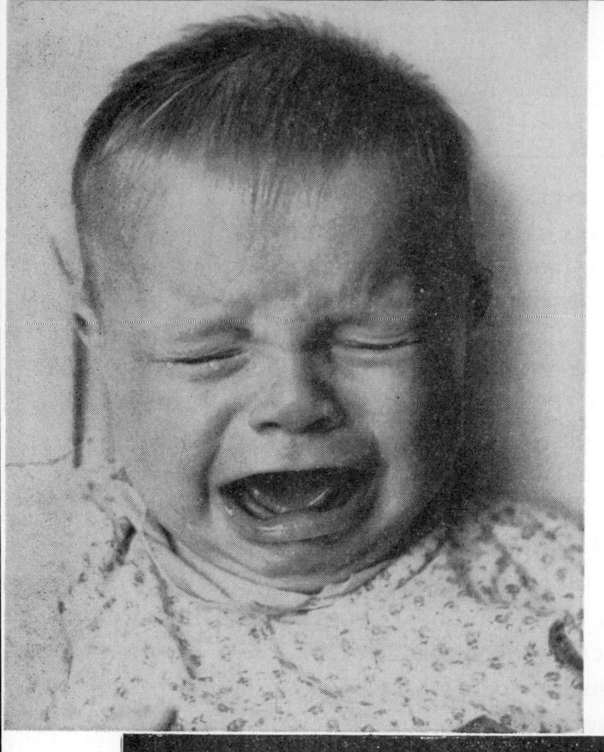

Figure 4-2. One Way of Learning to Emote

You can hardly help sharing these little fellows' feelings. An infant, seeing another person's feeling, still less can avoid imitating it.

near a calm child. However, the reverse is even more likely, since fearfulness is usually more dynamic than calmness.

It is thus fortunate that parents and teachers have the sort of prestige with their children of which we were speaking. As Breckenridge and Vincent (73) point out, on the basis of extensive observation at the Merrill Palmer Nursery school, it means that teachers and parents can provide models for the child's emotional learning more easily than some childish companion. Gaiety or severity, nervous tension or calm, fearfulness—most of it depends on adults. The flurried teacher or mother "teaches" the child to be jumpy; the quiet, calm one helps the child to meet life without excessive emotionality.

But how the notion of emotional suppression and control continues to haunt us even when we know better! It was not until the foregoing paragraphs were written that I realized how negative were their implications. A passing mention of gaiety, the rest of the discussion implying that the adult, in setting the emotional tone, should tone *down* the child's emotion.

Clearly this is only half the story. It *is* important for a child to have as his models persons who are calm and relaxed; it is just as important that he have about him persons who also emote spontaneously, persons who enrich their own lives by appropriate feeling, persons whose emotions are positive and effective ways of getting things done. Joy, pleasure, enthusiasm, and gaiety should well forth spontaneously when they are appropriate; and so should anger, disgust, sympathy, and, yes, even fear. Let us give the child a chance to learn by imitation how to emote effectively as well as how not to emote. We shall have more to say about this in the next chapter when we discuss suppression.

QUESTIONS

1. How does emotional climate differ from conditioning?
2. Is learning to emote as a result of trauma more like conditioning or more like emotional climate?
3. In order to keep the home "genuinely happy," must one allow the child to do what he likes? What are the conditions required for a happy emotional climate?
4. For what kind of behavior does the parent form the model of imitation? For what kind of behavior do playmates more often form the model?

Words Affect Emotions

If you have tried to allay the fears of a child by reassuring words, you have probably had reason to doubt the effectiveness of language in dealing with emotion. All the same, language plays a most important part in emotional development. Words can be used to stir up emotions about things, people, and events that the child has never even experienced.

In fact, between the ages of five and ten, children are more apt to be afraid of things they haven't experienced than of those they have. They fear "animals," though they have never been attacked by any animals, let alone the "bears," "wolves," and "lions" of their anxiety; they fear "criminals," "burglars," "bad men," "ghosts," and "witches," though they have never seen any of these portentous creatures; they fear "death" even though no deathlike separation from loved ones has fallen to their lot. In short, their fears are aroused by words.

For fear, at least, the evocation of emotion by symbols, chiefly verbal symbols, is very fully documented. In the Jersild and Holmes study (230), parents representing 119 families and 136 children reported the fears actually observed during the period of twenty-one days. Table 3 lists the situations in which a child showed fear one or more times. Undoubtedly parents failed to notice some fears—and no tally could be made of the fears experienced when the child was alone! But trends are fairly clear. Fears of tangible objects, fears due to the sheer sensory qualities of the situations decline with age, and fears of imaginary objects and of objects or situations perceived as "threatening" (in which perception there is a large verbal-symbolic factor) greatly increase.[7] Parallel results were found by a number of other investigators (129, 131, 186, 216, 261, 354, 358, 478).

Usually a child learns this sort of fear from the remarks of some stupid adult or miseducated playmate. "Are you afraid of the dark, Jackie?" asks the visitor to make conversation. That's a new idea to Jackie, aged two and a half, and he turns it over in his little head wonderingly. Presently he listens to stories that emphasize the terror

[7] Actually the case is not so different for adults. Epictetus long ago remarked: "What disturbs and alarms man are not things but his fancies and opinions about things."

Table 3.

Relative Frequency of Situations in Which Children Were Afraid, as Reported by Parents

Situation in which fear was shown						
Age in months	0–11	12–23	24–35	36–47	48–59	60–97
Number of children	8	23	45	46	21	9
1. Animals (not including imaginary animals)	25	35	40	46	41	0
2. Specific objects (not described as being strange)	12	9	9	4	0	0
3. Sudden rapid motion, lights, flashes, shadows, reflections	25	17	38	13	9	0
4. Noises	75	61	56	37	23	0
5. Pain and tactual shock	25	52	20	15	14	56
6. Strangeness	25	39	29	6	18	0
7. Danger of bodily injury, falling	38	35	33	35	32	33
8. Sympathy with another child	0	0	4	2	9	0
9. Loss of property	0	0	0	2	0	0
10. The imaginary: dreams, robbers, ridicule, death, being alone, imaginary creatures	0	30	35	20	45	56

Adapted from A. T. Jersild and F. B. Holmes, Children's fears, *Child Developm. Monogr.*, 1935, no. 20.

others feel in the dark. James Whitcomb Riley's "Orphant Annie" tells how *in the dark* "the Gobble-uns'll git *you* if you don't watch out." By purely verbal stimulation and without any actual frightening event, a full-blown fear of the dark may thus be set up. In one school, over half the children worried about nonpromotion although only 1 percent had ever been failed (229). Whether it came from parents, fellow pupils, or the teacher, the stimulus to worry was clearly verbal. The same is often true of other emotions.

Equally familiar, when we come to think about it, is the way in which words modify our emotional responses to actual objects or situations. Inform someone who is idly examining a harmless-looking metal object that it is a hand grenade which will explode if he sets off the trigger, and you will easily enough create a healthy "concern," if not acute terror.

The Arapesh of New Guinea develop a truly remarkable tribal unity by a kind of verbal conditioning. To a child happily eating, the mother says: "See that woman; she's your aunt. She's good. She gives you food. She's good, good." Everyone in the village is thus made "good" (308).

But why look to such faraway places for illustration? What mother has not smacked her lips and said "Good, good!" in an effort to put across a new food? It works, too. Words sometimes have almost magic power to *change the way we look at things* and hence to change our ways of reacting to them emotionally.

Of course, it is possible to mismanage the effort to alter emotional behavior by verbal means. You can cause an object to take on a new emotional value easier than you can strip an object of an old one. For example, if a child is already afraid of doctors, telling him, "Now don't be afraid, the nice doctor won't hurt you" may merely make the child more fearful than ever. When a parent's reassurance does work, it is usually because the child absorbs some of the parent's obvious lack of fear (19). Sometimes, too, verbal reassurance reminds the child of the parent's protective strength. There is truth also in the poet's notion that we may "come to have our fears loved away" (374). But usually reassurance has little effect on fear.

"Rational explanation" also fails. Take the child who begs for ice cream at an amusement park. You won't get far by telling him, "The ice cream here is dirty, and besides you aren't really hungry." You merely remind him that even dirty ice cream tastes good and that he *is* hungry. Your words may excite the very emotion you seek to diminish.

A more subtle, indirect approach is necessary if we are to break down an emotional habit by means of words. We can, for instance, tell the child stories about doctors and how nice they are, doing this well in advance of the time the doctor is needed. If the situation is skillfully handled it will build up a favorable picture of doctors in the child's mind. Playing doctor or nurse with toy stethoscopes and other instruments is still better. The trick is to help the child beforehand to get a different perspective on the situation.

Such reappraisal works for adults, too. The foot stuck out to trip you won't be an occasion for "righteous anger," if you hold back your annoyance long enough to see it as an accident or at worst a childish prank. When you reappraise or revalue the situation, the whole emotional picture changes. And language plays the central role in thus enabling you to "see" things in a new light.

For none of us reacts emotionally to the objectively real facts or situation. We react to the situation *as we apprehend or take it to be.* As Ernst Cassirer (92) says, man not only does not, he cannot, confront reality face to face. Between him and reality there is always the verbal symbol. It is all very well to say, "Sticks and stones may break my bones, But names will never hurt me." It isn't really so. Indeed, most of our adult emotions—good or bad—are so much influenced by the way we describe the situation to ourselves that we can really be said to react to words more than to things or events.

It is different with the very young child. He is an emotional "realist" and far more likely to react to things as they are. For the infant, a "pin prick is a pin prick." Wordsworth might well have been thinking of a child when he wrote,

> A primrose by a river's brim,
> A yellow primrose was to him,
> And it was nothing more.

As the child grows older, however, his emotional reactions are more and more affected by verbalization; more and more he responds to things as described or as thought about in words.

At first the words that arouse emotion are quite concrete. The eight-year-old may never have seen the tiger that gives him nightmares; but "tiger" is a concrete noun. The child who is delighted with the prospect of a "holiday" is reacting to the prospect of concrete activities like "swimming."

Only gradually do highly abstract words come to stir up feeling. It has been shown, for example, that such words as "duty" or "gratitude" are simply too abstract for a child under ten or eleven. They do not stir him to emotion, at least not to appropriate emotion. The child does indeed appreciate—at the moment—what you do for him, but he is incapable of generalizing from a lot of similar situations to such a complex emotion as gratitude. To demand that a seven-year-old feel "grateful" is to waste one's breath.

The child may learn to parrot the word, of course; and by imitation or conditioning this word can acquire some sort of emotional feeling tone. Yet it remains empty intellectually. It is like the experience of the deaf old lady who told the parson: "I could not hear much of your sermon, but I did catch that blessed word, Mesopotamia, and was greatly comforted." A great deal of religious and character education misses its mark by associating emotion and fine feeling and noble aspiration with mere words that are about as empty of real significance to the child as was "Mesopotamia" to the old lady. To insist on reverence, for example, when the child is too young to know what it is all about is to run the risk that later, when he *is* able to understand intellectually what reverence is, he will *feel* only the flat and intellectually empty emotion which he earlier learned to associate with the mere word.

We must wait, then, upon the growth of understanding before we try too hard to evoke emotion in connection with lofty abstractions. Yet when a child can really respond to the abstract, when he can respond *meaningfully* to such abstract symbols as "patriotism," "gratitude," "cooperativeness," or "fair play," his emotional as well as his intellectual life is expanded and enriched. When the *rightness* of fair play is immediately *felt,* a big step forward in emotional maturity has been attained.

QUESTIONS

1. Three types of change in emotion were listed on page 120. For which kind of change are words effective?
2. Why is it that it is easier to use words to induce emoting than to inhibit it?

3. "He didn't mean to hurt you" is an effort to secure reappraisal of the anger-provoking situation by means of words. What other technique could one use?

Mastering the Emotional Situation

Is there anything we can do while we wait for the child to mature to the point where his emotions are influenced by abstract ideas and notions? Certainly there is. A child can learn to face the emotion-arousing situation and deal effectively with it. Take the case of fear, where we have a considerable number of experimental studies. In these experiments no effort was made to get the child to achieve direct control over his *fears;* instead, he was taught how to master the *situation* giving rise to fear. One group of children showed more than normal fear of high places. The youngsters were taught to walk a plank resting on the floor. It was then raised a few inches at a time. Presently these three-year-olds were gaily walking the length of the plank six feet above the floor. *They found that they knew what to do* when faced with the formerly fearful situation, so they were no longer afraid (128).

One child, however, said, "I'll do it for *you* but I won't do it for Mom." Inquiry disclosed that, although his fears were genuine enough, the little rascal was consciously using them to control his mother. Quite aside from such conscious use of fear, Glenn Heathers (195) found that children most dependent on their mothers were most inclined to be fearful. Depending on mom is, of course, just the converse of learning to master the situation for oneself and thus remove fear.

Children in another group were afraid of the dark. The experimenter played ball with them, one at a time, and managed to throw the ball into a dark room. The dark-fearful child refused to go after it. He was first shown a light hanging very near the door and shown how to turn it on. All of the children learned to do this and thus to retrieve the ball.

Next the light was moved further away from the door, so that a few steps had to be taken in the dark. However, most of the children balked at going into the dark room to turn on the light. At this point many parents would make the mistake of trying to encourage the child. That seldom helps. Ridicule helps even less. Forcing the child to enter the dark room definitely makes him worse in most cases. Dr. Frances Holmes (207), whose experiment I am quoting, followed another tack. She put the emphasis upon the child's ability to do the needful: not "Go ahead, the dark won't hurt" but "Go ahead, you know how to turn on the light. Here, I'll help you find it this time and next time you can find it yourself." This worked. Then the light was moved a little further from the door. Eventually each child went clear across the dark room alone to turn on the light, and thus little by little lost his fear of the dark in general.

A child (or an adult) is not apt to be afraid in a situation he knows how to deal with. Fear of the water disappears as one gains enough mastery to take only a few swimming strokes. The reason that seasoned soldiers are less fearful in battle than raw recruits is not that the veteran doesn't sense the danger or is less reluctant to be killed, but mainly that he knows better what to do.

Anger also is quickly brought under control as soon as the child gains the skills he needs to meet the anger-provoking situation. But it is harder to learn this in the case of anger because another person is nearly always involved and his reactions aren't so easily controlled. By the same token it is harder to give a good concrete illustration. I could give an example of a good way to deal with fear of the dark because we can control darkness.

What, however, is a teacher or a playground director to do when a big bully of seven plus tyrannizes over six-year-old Rex? It's of little use to tell Rex that the thing to do is not to get angry but to "master the situation." Rex will scarcely thank you for the advice. *You,* of course, can control the bully—while you are around; but Rex will still have his problem.

There is really no pat answer, although the general principle holds that anger is controlled by controlling the anger-arousing circumstances rather than suppressing the response. Even at age six Rex can begin practicing that principle. Indeed, it would be better if he began at an earlier age. From earliest childhood our youngsters are learning what to do when another child interferes with them. They learn to substitute verbal combat for blows. They learn "fair play" and sportsmanship. They learn, too, many techniques for getting their own way, of diverting the other child (or even the adult!) who seeks to take away the toy they are playing with. Anger is thus kept low or is channeled into constructive ways of handling the situation.

Several hours spent in observation at a nursery school are very instructive. You can almost tell how long a child has been in the group by the number of times he shows that he can prevent others from thwarting him. Every nursery school has one or two geniuses at this sort of diplomacy.

In India we find an instructive contrast. As Lois Murphy (330) points out, in a sensitive study made under UNESCO auspices, Indian children are constantly in the company of adults or older children. "You bring up your children, we live with ours," an official of the Department of Education told Mrs. Murphy. Weaning is late, toilet training is almost nonexistent, and the child seldom meets a new and therefore potentially frustrating experience without the support of a trusted adult.

> Since an enormous proportion of the population has no property, little children are not exposed to the anxious, tense no-no's that are heard dozens of times a day by toddlers in our middle-class families when they are being taught not to touch breakable ash trays and other bric-a-brac, not to pull table cloths off the dining table, not to tear up magazines and books, not to get into mother's bureau drawers or knitting bag or sewing basket.
>
> This means that Indian children are not exposed to so much frustration, pressure from adults, conflict with authority; anger and aggression are not stimulated, there is little or no evidence of the "resistance," temper tantrums, and hitting back at the world common among our two- to four-year-olds. [326]

As a result of so much shielding from anger-stirring circumstances, Indian children grow up to be notably more gentle than ours. But also as a result, they grow up not having learned how to deal with provocations to anger. Thus in their late adolescence and in adult life, as I found in my own year of teaching in the Indian subcontinent, when anger does break through, it often has an explosive and uncontrollable character. There is evident value in the long, slow process of learning how to handle anger-arousing situations which American children have to live through.

Most of that learning takes place in face-to-face play with other children. Adults can help—we could help more if we spent less time in "correcting" children who get into a hair-pulling scrape and more in encouraging them to find ways of harmonious behavior. We usually try to "persuade" Billy not to interfere with Robert; it is more important in the long run that Robert learn how to get around Billy's annoying tactics, or even how to enlist Billy's cooperation. If the adult in the situation merely suppresses Billy, Robert does not learn, or learns merely to yell for help.

Controlling the situation is equally effective for disgust, envy, jealousy, and distress. Does it work also with the emotions that develop out of delight? Yes, it does. The almost prostrating joy over the new bicycle gradually takes on a different tone as the child learns to ride it; mastery of the situation, we see, brings with it a constructive change in even joyful emoting. Familiarity may not breed contempt but, by teaching the child how to master the situation, it does lessen not only fear or anger or disgust, but joy as well. Nor is this regrettable. As he masters the situation, as he makes his adjustment to whatever it is that has stirred him up, he is ready to move on to new experiences, new achievements. Continued mere enjoyment of that which he has already mastered is just as stultifying to improvement as a stereotyped or enduring anger or fear.

QUESTIONS

1. Which aspect of emotional behavior is modified when one "masters the situation"?
2. When you know what to do about it, a high place isn't "scary," is it? Isn't this prevention rather than control?
3. Is it fair to say that a child who has learned not to fear the dark has modified his emotion? Should we not say he has learned not to emote? Why?

Play as an Indirect Mastering of Emotive Situations

One of the primary values of play is that it helps children to gain a sense of mastery over what would otherwise be emotional situations. How this can be deliberately utilized by parents or teachers is interestingly set forth in a popular article, "Dramatic Lessons for Youngsters" by Margaret Gayle (165). For example, a child who was to take a journey alone play-acted under her mother's guidance the various experiences she was about to meet and thereby gained the poise of a seasoned traveler.

In another case, a frightening encounter in a park with what the

Figure 4-3. Play Acting for Mastery of Emotion

newspapers call a "molester" was re-enacted, and the children, with some suggestions, planned and acted out the way to meet this situation. Drama and dramatic play as a means of altering the children's emotional pattern is a resource parents and teachers would do well to exploit more fully.

Play Therapy. Psychologists in recent years have been making extensive use of play for both diagnosis and correction of deep-seated emotional difficulties. A child is encouraged by various special techniques to enact in play the emotional attitudes he usually represses—particularly hostility to parents.

The conventional explanation is that this acts as a "catharsis"—i.e., it allows the child "to get it out of his system." This explanation is open to grave objection. According to this view, the best cure for hostility should be the direct display of actual hostility. But you know that when a child merely gives way to his anger he is learning to give way to anger. *Emoting is just as habit-forming as any other behavior.* Play therapy works in part because it is *play,* not the real thing. The hostility expressed in play is not the same thing as the hostility it stands for.

Why play works this way is by no means wholly clear. Part of the explanation, however, is related to the child's ambivalence, of which we spoke in Chapter 2. Normally a child has mixed but balanced feelings toward his parents so that sometimes anger and affection chase each other across his countenance like shadow and sunlight on a field in April. In many problem children, on the other hand, hatred and hostility have gained too great superiority over love; the normal bipolarity is disturbed. Play therapy, therefore, seeks to restore a normal balance between the child's natural love and his equally natural hostility.

How does it do this? When hostile feeling is expressed in the words or other symbols of play, the child is likely to be reminded that he also has the contradictory attitude of affection. Thus when the doll-child is made to cry out to the doll-mother, "I want to kill you," the childish director of this little drama is being reminded that, although he does hate, he also loves, his real mother. In the real-life situation, however, the rush of anger and hostility is often too headlong to permit such saving afterthoughts or afterfeelings.

Ordinary play, even when it involves acting out hostility, does not seem to reduce the feeling as well as does the carefully arranged situation of play therapy. There is something about the fact that an adult (who is obviously an authority-figure, like a parent) *permits* the child to act out his feelings. The permissive atmosphere favors the emergence of the feelings of *affection* along with the permitted feelings of *animosity*. It is as if, when the child is permitted to feel whatever he wants to feel, he discovers that he wants to feel affection as well as anger. And it is the integration of the hostility feeling with the feeling of affection which gives play therapy its real value.

Should you attempt play therapy with children in your own classes? I wish I might say so; but it will seldom work. Whatever the reason, it usually takes a *substitute* authority-figure to relax the ordinary controls. You cannot (at least usually) effectively play the double role of teacher and therapist. Just at the surface level, consider that you must, as teacher, continue to be something of a "controller" of the children's life. (As the experiment on democratic atmosphere showed [see page 46], children have a deep-seated *need* for firm guidance.) But as therapist one must be willing to permit almost anything; controls are deliberately relaxed.

It can be most confusing to the child to react first to the teacher as guide and authority, then to the teacher as permissive therapist, then back to authority once more. Still deeper emotional confusions, moreover, are almost certainly involved where authority and permissive therapy are jumbled together.

It is doubtful, moreover, that it would usually succeed in so large a group as a class, though a few experts have managed it. Each child has his individual problems which he needs to work out. Often play therapy implies that he needs to be permitted—temporarily—to act in a decidedly obstreperous way to the person in authority. Can you permit this with upward of thirty other children (most of them with quite different needs and problems) looking on with keen interest? The fact that few parents would know how to accept such a classroom is also a valid consideration.

Psychodrama. The so-called psychodrama is an allied technique used for older children and adults. Persons with emotion-laden problems first re-enact scenes from real life, often with the other persons involved participating again in their original roles. Thus a child re-enacts with his mother a situation in which they were in conflict. Then, when all have seen the futility of the behavior they had indulged in, they work out and practice on the stage more constructive ways of conducting themselves.

For best results there has to be an audience of at least one person who is reacting to what happens on the stage as he would to any other stage production. This means that he can identify himself with the performers yet also maintain a certain detachment. Thus he can perceive the inner consistency of the stage character's behavior even when he disapproves of it. In short, in the psychodrama there is acceptance of what is portrayed.

Acceptance. Acceptance has come to be a very important idea in the psychological treatment of problem behavior. We seem to need someone to "accept" our misconduct before we can readily learn to change it. "Acceptance" is not merely a sort of middle ground between condoning and condemning; it has a positive quality of its own. It is, of course, almost the exact opposite of disciplinary coercion. The latter says, "Stop doing that!" The former says, "I see how you feel about it. What do you want to do?" Much current psychotherapy emphasizes, and probably all psychotherapy has actually employed, the principle of "acceptance." We don't fully understand the dynamics of acceptance but there is little doubt that it works.

The teacher may participate in the psychodrama in order to learn how to improve her own behavior at the same time the child learns to improve his, but she cannot usually be the director of the therapy. Play therapy and psychodrama, when needed, should be directed by an outsider, and a professionally trained one at that.

Ordinary play, however, and ordinary dramatizing (which should be play) have many values in the education of emotion and you should be most alert to take advantage of them. This you may often do by playing with the children. Play *therapy,* as the name implies, is used to *cure* bad conduct. You can use ordinary play, in contrast, to show children how to act in socially acceptable ways and how to *avoid* what is socially inacceptable, as with the girl being prepared for her trip. Throw yourself into this play with spontaneity and freedom and remember that in childhood emotional subtleties may not be understood. Don't be afraid to be too dramatic. In the lingo of the theater, "It goes down better with a little ham."

QUESTIONS

1. Have I drawn too strict a line between play and play therapy? Suppose you find a child enacting a mother-child relation. Is this or isn't it play therapy? Can play be therapeutic without being play therapy?
2. Does play lose its value as a means of educating emotion when the adult controls it? What are the values and the limitations of adult guidance of play?

Summary

Despite great individual variability, there is a fairly regular pattern of development in emoting. Although innate factors play a part, most of the achievement of emotional maturity is due to experience and learning. The highly advertised conditioning of emotion undoubtedly plays a part, especially in bringing about many of our seemingly irrational and mysterious emotional reactions. But imitation and the absorption of emotional behavior from the psychological climate play a more important role.

Language is a more important means of modifying and manipulating a child's emotions than is usually recognized. It is chiefly by means of language that the child is led to reappraise the nature of emotion-arousing objects or circumstances.

Learning to cope directly with the circumstances helps the child to master his fears or other emotings. Play and drama often help the child to more mature control of the emotive situation; and they also teach quite straightforwardly what some of the more mature emotional responses are.

5

Emotion as a Social Process

Emotion plays a large part in social interaction: when we emote not only do we act upon others, we react to them. How do children learn to communicate their emotions to others and to understand the emoting of others?

What constitutes emotional maturity? What are the changes in emotional behavior as a child grows up? Is moderation the answer? How much emotional control is desirable and how can it be achieved?

Suppose that you observe several children all exposed to what looks like the same painful stimulus—say a definite prick with a sterile needle or pin, strong enough to hurt but not to injure the child. First, a wee baby, a few days old. Second, an older infant, say eight months. Third, a three-year-old. Fourth, a nine-year-old.

What happens in each case? In the very young infant, you get an all-over response: undirected thrashing of arms and legs, crying. In the older infant the pinprick brings out a more useful response—the baby tries to get away from the painful stimulus or to brush it off. In both cases the response is highly predictable just from knowing the immediate physical stimulus. The whole thing is impersonal.

When we come to somewhat older children, however, the outcome is not so certain. What a three-year-old will do depends upon circumstances, chiefly personal or social circumstances. He may plead with you not to hurt him; or he may angrily attack you, verbally or with blows. A still older child may "show his manhood" by trying not to flinch. If baby brother is wielding the pin, big sister "considers the source" and tempers her annoyance with scorn or amusement.

In short, the pinprick is no longer merely a pinprick but part of a highly complex social situation. Its stimulus value has undergone a great change. The "who" of emotive stimulation becomes at least as important as the "what." As the child grows older, *things and impersonal circumstances matter less, persons matter more.*

In the growth of emotional behavior a child thus faces two problems. The first is that of sizing up how the people around him are emoting. Whether the other person is friendly or hostile, delighted or disgusted, confident or fearful, is of great importance to the child—as it is to you and me and everyone else. So it is that the child must learn to understand tones, facial expressions, gestures, postures, and the emotional as well as the intellectual meaning of words. He shows maturity to the extent that he correctly appraises these emotional expressions.

The child's second problem is that of communicating to others how *he* is emoting. Emotional behavior is largely directed at other people. It is true, of course, that we do not always *want* to show our emotions; indeed, we would often give a great deal to conceal them. Yet most of the time emoting is a way of dealing with a situation in which people play a part; and all unwittingly, perhaps, our emoting is a way of getting them to help us. As Asch says, most of our interaction with other persons is through emotion, or through that kind of thinking which takes account of others' emotions (20, p. 142).

At first, the child's emoting is more likely to take the form of direct action. Later it is more likely to take the form of so-called expressive behavior (61, 171, 231). The nursery school tike strikes out blindly with fists or feet at anyone who interferes with him; the school child uses *words* to tell the other child off, or to plead with the adult to let him alone. Many a child—even a quite young child—has learned that his merry laugh or infectious grin is a wonderful way of getting things from adults. Emotional behavior becomes, with increasing maturity, more and more an instrument of social intercourse, a way of getting things done in a social situation, of influencing and being influenced by people.

QUESTIONS

1. Language, it has been said, is often designed to conceal rather than reveal thought. Certainly as adults we often express an emotion we do not feel. How about children?
2. Granted that emoting often does get a child something, isn't it stretching the point to suppose that's *why* he is emoting?
3. If emoting is a complex dominated by the internal responses by means of which a person adapts *himself* to the situation, isn't it inconsistent to say that emoting is a way of getting others to change the situation?

Emotion as Language

We all know that words—even emotional words like "Whee!" or "Boo!"—have to be learned; it is almost equally true of other kinds of emotional expression. There is, to be sure, a sort of core of natural emotional expressiveness which seems to need no learning. Children blind from birth, who have no chance to see the facial expressions of others, nonetheless frown and smile recognizably like ordinary children; but just the same the blind children's emotional expressions are less extensive and less subtle than those of children who can learn by seeing others emote. In other words, some emotional expressions are natural but children improve upon nature by learning (127, 158, 173, 442).

Communicating Emotions

The finer shadings of emotional communication, then, have to be learned just as other forms of language have to be learned. The emotions of little children are indeed, as we often say, an open book; but it is a book written in a childish scrawl and communicating only the simplest sort of "emotional story." Because young children have not learned to show counterfeit emotions, what they communicate is true as far as it goes. It does not go very far, however, for they haven't learned by voice and word and gesture to convey their own emotional states with any degree of finesse or delicacy.

Indeed, very young babies tell hardly any kind of emotional story at all. Even "experts"—nurses, doctors, psychologists—are unable to tell which emotion the infants are displaying unless they know what has upset the child (391).

By ten months, however, the infant's little repertoire of emotional expressions has sufficiently advanced so that at least his own mother can fairly well tell whether he is feeling such simple things as hunger, pain, fright, delight, or affection. The advance in expressiveness continues as the child grows older. Investigators have found that there is a steady gain throughout childhood in what might be called emotional vocabulary—that is, as they grow older, children are better at communicating to others how they feel, not only by words but by gesture and the whole range of emotional expression (171, 172, 256, 257). They learn little tricks of conventional expression—but of course they don't learn them all at once nor do they learn them very accurately. Children need help, then, in acquiring flexible and expressive emotional "language." You can help them by direct instruction, and even more by setting good examples. For many parents and teachers this means an effort to loosen up and become more expressive themselves.

Make-believe as Emotional Expression

But there are many kinds of emotive situations to which we don't want to expose a child—they are too drastic. Nor do we feel comfortable in manifesting certain real emotional responses in the child's presence—the model is not one we wish to set up for imitation. Yet the child should not remain ignorant of these emotions.

Here play-acting and make-believe come to our aid. Even the higher animals learn in this way—the playful growling and the carefully controlled biting of a puppy or a kitten come at once to mind. Play is clearly a means of learning how to act emotionally.

In addition to its direct educational value, a child's make-believe emotion affords the watchful adult an opportunity to learn something of his inner life. In art, in storytelling and dramatics, and in free play, children often act out emotions that, for one reason or another, have been denied *direct* expression. Such acting out is a sort of unintentional communication of feeling. Long recognized by novelists and other sensitive observers of child nature, this tendency to "project one's inner life" outward upon external circumstances forms the basis of what are called "projective tests." A young child may be given household toys and dolls representing a family and asked to make a game with these ("projective doll play"). An older child is encouraged to tell a story about a picture ("thematic apperception test"). Their off-guard or unconstrained behavior in such a situation can be very revealing. But it is no mere child's play to interpret what is revealed by a child's play; it is a very difficult and professional task.

Thus, I once observed three-year-old Wanda acting out the part of a mother spanking her doll-daughter. Now how was I to interpret this? Should I have said, "Ah, ha! So that's how her mother treats *her?*" Well, I'd have been wrong. Her mother has never used corporal punishment.

Should I, then, have surmised that this behavior reflects some "repressed sadism" or "unconscious cruelty"? Not without other evidence. Actually, this interpretation would have been far from the mark in Wanda's case.

There was a more commonplace explanation—and from observing this little girl in many situations I am sure it was the correct one. Moreover, like many commonplace explanations in psychology, it is full of significance for us if we use it. This little girl's play showed, first of all, that she understood certain traditional or "literary" notions about the "cruel mother." For a child of three this points to a very considerable social maturity. In the second place, the play revealed this three-year-old's quite real talent as a "playwright" and "actress." She was, in short, putting on a good show according to the rules.

"There is a natural temptation," say Breckenridge and Vincent (73), "for amateurs or novices, people who have just discovered, for example, that a stormy picture may, on occasion, mean a stormy inner life, to 'interpret' everything children do. This is a great mistake since accurate interpretation of the meaning of 'projected' emotions requires expert training. Far more harm than good results from false interpretations." Moreover, preoccupation with ultrasophisticated interpretations may cause teachers to overlook more mundane motivations and more reliable explanations.

I do not, therefore, advise teachers or parents to try to read too much "deep stuff" into a child's play. Projective interpretations are tricky.

> Things are seldom what they seem,
> Skim milk masquerades as cream.

How a child plays with dolls *may* reveal how he feels toward father and mother; but his play may have quite a different motive, or, indeed, several motives.

Few of us can resist the tendency to find our own emotions in the child's behavior. Because they are so deeply involved with their children, this is particularly true of parents—but it is also true of good teachers. When it comes to using projective materials, the chances are good that it will be the parents or the teachers who do the projecting rather than the child. Instead of reading out of the child's behavior what the *child* has projected into it, they are likely to project into what the child is doing their own obsessions, repressions, and expectations.

Do I urge, then, that you ignore the significance of what we may call indirect emotional behavior? By no means. But I believe you will get further if you cultivate a sensitive awareness of children's needs at an *informed common-sense level* and leave "deep-level" interpretation, when it is needed, to the specialist.[1]

QUESTIONS

1. If it is proved (as the text maintains) that children do not express emotion very well, how are we to explain the common conviction that they are so "expressive"?
2. What does it mean to cultivate a common-sense sensitivity to children's feeling? How does one cultivate such sensitivity?
3. If the teacher or parent is advised against using projective tests, why discuss them here? Can you see any use of the idea of "projection" for the layman?
4. How much is a child's emotional expression natural? Do we need to teach emotional expression?

---

[1] My caution in respect to projective techniques is not to be mistaken for hostility. As a matter of fact, I look forward to the time when they can be sufficiently simplified for less highly professionalized use. But the extraordinary range and delicacy of the indirect behaviors that must be evaluated make simplification dangerous, and progress toward it accordingly slow. For a more optimistic appraisal, consult the account by Murphy and Horowitz (331).

Understanding Emotional Language

If it is important for a child to learn to communicate his emotions, it is even more important that he be able to interpret the emotional expressions of others. This also takes learning. I realize that there is a bit of folklore which holds that a child doesn't need to learn this, that he is a better judge of emotions than an adult or an older child. Scientific investigations do not confirm this notion (257, 460).

It is true that children (and domestic pets, too) sometimes have an uncomfortable habit of seeing through sham endearments and insincere reassurances. Such perceptiveness proves that we adults are bad actors rather than that the child is a good judge. When we insincerely say, "What a pretty child!" although we are actually shrinking with disgust at his filthy condition, the child is likely to react to the shrinking instead of to the honeyed words.

Or rather, the child, being somewhat unanalytical, reacts to the adult's *whole* behavior, not just to that part which he is intended to see. The child does not exactly see through the insincerity; he does not, as a rule, realize that someone is trying to fool him. He simply reacts to the *whole* of the would-be deceiver's conduct. As a result, he is not fooled by the trickery. Quite literally, the child is too undiscriminating to be deceived.

That same lack of discrimination also prevents the child from recognizing perfectly sincere but subtle shadings in a person's emotional behavior. Throughout childhood, however, there is a steady growth in ability to understand the other fellow's emotion—some psychologists call this "empathy"—and hence growth in social sensitivity (81, 164, 147, 244, 435).

The growth is not steady for all children, however; for some it is very irregular. The problem is particularly acute in the first school years. Children go to school with a limited experience with people outside their own family. They have learned, little by little, to interpret father's weary and discouraged slouch, mother's gaiety or crossness. But they do not know how to react to unfamiliar people. Every family has its own emotional peculiarities, its own "dialect" of emotional communication. There are also national and regional dialects in emotional communication which are quite as striking and as important as the dialects of verbal language. The "vivacious Italian" and the "repressed and taciturn Yankee" differ almost as much in their emotional as in their verbal language. Nor should we neglect social class as a cause of differences in emotional expression.

Thus when the child encounters the teacher with her quite different emotional idiom, there are grave problems of communication. She may come from another part of the country; she is quite likely to belong to a different social layer; at the very least she comes from a different home. Where mother is gay the teacher may be sober—or perhaps vice versa. Where mother scolds loudly—when she really means it—the teacher may talk so quietly and softly that she surely doesn't expect one to pay much attention. Or where mother's face is quick to light up with a smile or darken with a frown, teacher's mask never seems to change. The child thus finds great difficulty in understanding the teacher's emotional expressions. (But perhaps most troublesome of all to the child is the teacher who, by every gesture and expression, tells only too clearly the story of worry, of unhappiness, of desperate earnestness, of her own emotional tension.)

It is not only the teacher whose emotional dialect is mysterious. Other children can be frighteningly difficult to understand. School confronts the child with an enormous increase in the number and variety of contacts with other children; indeed, for many a child it is the first extensive experience with children outside his own family. No wonder, then, that he is frequently bewildered by the differences in emotional expression that greet him at school. It remains a persistent problem throughout the school years.

Training in Emotional Expression

How much do you do—on purpose—to meet this set of problems? Children need help in learning both to express their own emotions and to understand those of others (183). Consider first the expression of emotion in words. Undoubtedly we teach children a great deal by example—and I wager that we don't like part of what we thus teach. We hear echoed in the children our own cross tones, our impatience, our discouragement—hear and know it for our own, and are a bit ashamed. Again by our example we may teach the child the language of emotional clichés and tired platitudes instead of encouraging the astonishing emotional vigor that children sometimes manifest.

One difficulty is that when we set out intentionally to teach speech to a child, we are mostly interested in practical or intellectual ends. We want him to know the names of *things* and the verbs that tell him what he must do. We are often more interested in having him know that this flower is a "pansy" than in having him appreciate the delicate humor with which it mimics human faces. The function of speech in communicating or in stirring emotion is left to chance learning. How often do we help children to understand the *emotional* shadings of the language of everyday life? Oh yes, we feel free to correct gross errors, and we do our feeble best to keep the child from even hearing profanity and "bad" expressions. When the child does hear and use such language, we show our horror or even punish him. All quite negative. Seldom do we try to help the child attain a rich vocabulary for expressing emotion.

How can we go about that? Begin, for one thing, with the child's everyday experiences. Next, *encourage* emotional expression instead of slapping it down, as most of us do a good share of the time. We should not be so much concerned at first as to whether Gordon has written something that strikes a responsive chord in adults. Rather, we should ask whether he has truly expressed himself. Needless to say, it is fatal at this point to raise the question whether it is "nice" for him to feel that way or "nice" to say so if he does.

Later we can help him to see the social role of his expressions, to see how certain forms of speech add to his effectiveness. He can even be helped to see that if he behaves emotionally in certain ways, he can partly control the ways parents and playmates react emotionally to him. A large order? Of course it is, if you expect to do it all at once. But even at two years, children know very well that crying brings comforting from mother—they will save the cry after a bump until they have run to her.

If this is true of crying (and of overt emotional reactions, too) it is even more true of verbal language. Some people even believe that language was invented in order to enable us to control the emotions of others.

Archaic language, however, and poetic figures of speech based on alien ways and cultures won't help Jimmy to express his feelings to the little boy next door. For that you must be prepared for crudities of expression and for crudities of feeling. Indeed in general, *only as we accept, can we hope to improve, the child's emotional behavior.* Otherwise we shall find ourselves teaching artificial emotions. Only quite a little later can we make the propriety of a child's feeling the way he does the subject of open consideration. Help him first to express his feelings in effective and socially acceptable ways.

Speech is not the only expression of emotion in which children need education. Nor are art and music the only outlets for creative emotion. Facial expression, postures, gestures, and overt muscular behavior are all media for emotional behavior. Emotion involves a person's whole being. Yet except when we reprove a child who is far out of line, how little attention we give to all these things.

A generation ago the school did make an effort in "declamations" or oratorical contests to teach the language of posture and gesture as well as the "proper" intonation. Unfortunately the expressions were stereotyped and exaggerated, and this form of public torture was finally abandoned. But we have done too little to replace it with something better. We should capitalize much more than we do on the child's dramatic play and his natural love of "pretending" as means whereby he can gain greater command over the language of emotions, both to express himself and to understand others.

We can also directly demonstrate effective ways of showing emotion. How? Have you ever smacked your lips to show the baby that the food was good? Actually you were probably more successful in showing him how to express delight in food than in persuading him to like the stuff. You were teaching him emotional expression by example.

You are right, too, in somewhat exaggerating the emotional expressions you set before the very young child. He is, as yet, incapable of subtlety. Some caution, however, should be exercised lest in fun you teach the child forms of emoting he can do without. He may know you are only joking when you threaten and scold ferociously; but he is also learning that this is a way people sometimes act when in earnest.

In the main, however, the emphasis needs to shift to the positive. Don't be too much afraid of teaching the "wrong" emotional expression. Rather, be sure that the child is acquiring a grasp of "standard" or conventional emotional idioms, so that he can really use them. Then, on top of that, give him plenty of chances to learn how to get along with people—including you—whose "emotional dialects" differ from his own.

I hate to say it, but another part of our job of emotional education is teaching the child when and how to conceal or dissemble his emotions. Undeviating truthfulness is hard to take from anyone, whether it be truthfulness in ideas or in feeling. So the child has to learn to suppress all outward signs of emotion in some circumstances, and he has to learn to show counterfeit emotions in others. He must learn not to laugh when a visitor slips on a rug; he must learn to conceal his impatience and his irritation at gushing remarks about "the dear little fellow," and even to smile at people he dislikes.

Most of us, however, are strangely reluctant to give children direct instruction in how or when to dissemble their feelings. Indeed, we tend to lecture them upon the virtues of complete frankness and truthfulness, though we know quite well that it is a starkly impossible social ideal. The fact is that we tell children to behave emotionally in ways we don't ourselves believe in and don't even try to live up to. This, of course, confuses them, and makes them wonder about this "truth" we talk about. And meanwhile, they fail to learn when it is proper to dissemble and how to do it effectively.

It would be difficult to overstate the importance of emotional expression in a child's development. A versatile, flexible, and appropriately sensitive ability to express (or to dissemble) emotion, and to understand emotion in others (be the emotional language verbal, gestural, or postural) is far more important to the happiness and success of most people than the ability to convey or understand ideas.

QUESTIONS

1. Have the other kinds of emotional expressions changed since Shakespeare's day as much as, or more than, the verbal language?
2. Is not sincerity of emotion of primary importance? How, then, can we justify teaching the child faked emotion?
3. Before you read the next section, ask yourself what you mean when you call someone emotionally immature. How does an emotionally mature nine-year-old differ from an emotionally immature one?

Emotional Maturity

It is an interesting fact that while we all speak glibly enough about the lack of emotional maturity, we find it difficult to say what the opposite quality, maturity, is. What must a child do if he is to be called emotionally mature?

If we are talking about physical maturity the answer is fairly easy. As the anthropometrist Wilton Krogman says (255), maturity is just the stage reached by most people at the termination of the maturation-growth process. But will this work for emotional maturity?

Isn't the very phrase a contradiction in terms? As someone has said, emotions don't mature, they explode. Emotion seems in its very nature to be immature.

That is certainly a tempting point of view. Just think of certain

Figure 5-1. Age and Sex Differences in Proportion of Outbursts Involving Display of Undirected Energy

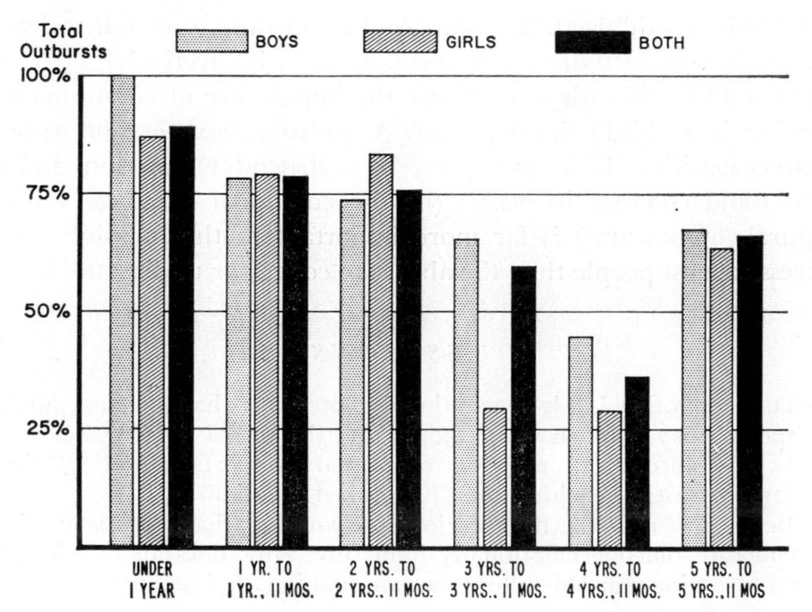

The graph includes cases in which the child's behavior may have been designed to affect others but in which there was neither direct resistance nor attack.

Adapted from Florence L. Goodenough, Anger in young children. *Univ. of Minn. Inst. Child Welf. Monogr.,* 1931, no. 9.

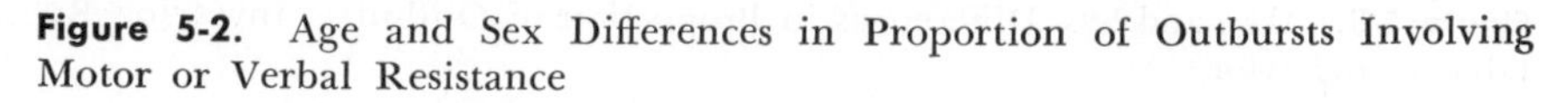

Figure 5-2. Age and Sex Differences in Proportion of Outbursts Involving Motor or Verbal Resistance

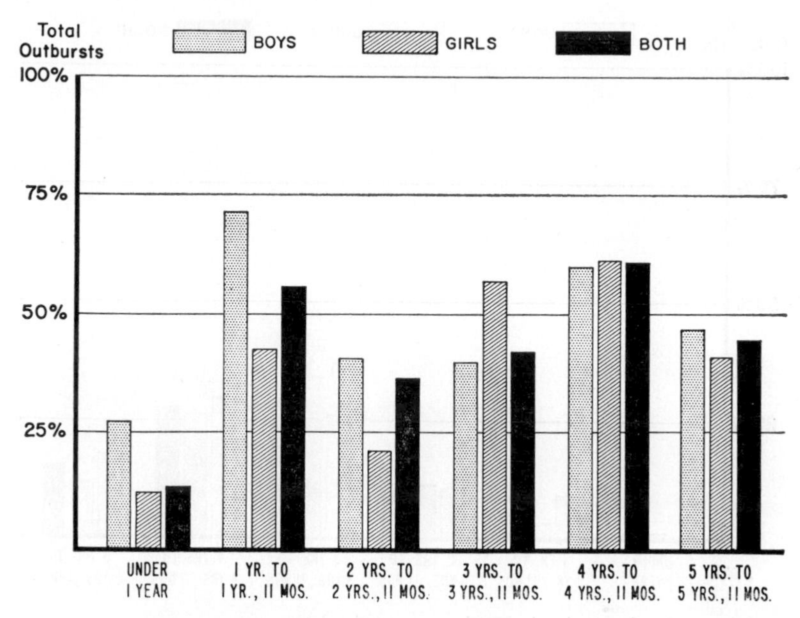

The graph does not include unverbalized vocalizations unless they were accompanied by evidences of resistant character. but it does include all cases of verbal refusal with or without motor accompaniment.

Adapted from Goodenough, Anger in young children.

emotional behaviors you have recently seen some of your friends indulge in. Undoubtedly immature, weren't they?

But think again! Haven't you seen an example of righteous indignation, of what Davis and Havighurst call adaptive anxiety (114), of a noble passion, of a pure and uplifting joy? And however ill we think of adults, I think we will have to admit that these emotions are essentially adult, mature. Perhaps, after all, the differences in emotion as we grow from infancy into adulthood are the criterion we need. With that in mind, let's take a look at a detailed study of age changes in one emotion; it may yield the clues we need as to the direction of emotional growth and maturity.

Florence Goodenough (171) secured the cooperation of forty-five mothers in carefully recording the angry behavior of their children for a month. Nearly 1900 outbursts of anger were reported. Interesting age trends are apparent in the graphs in Figures 5-1, 5-2, and

Figure 5-3. Age and Sex Differences in Proportion of Outbursts Involving Retaliative Behavior

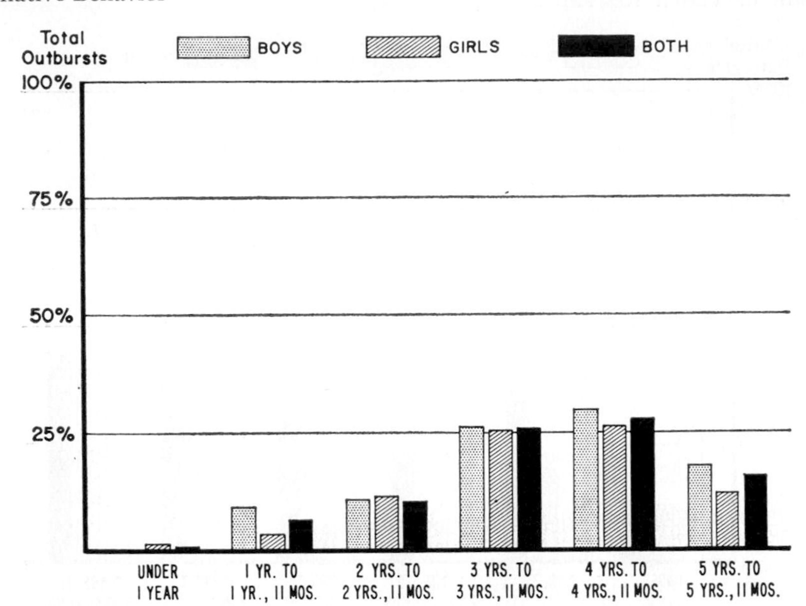

Adapted from Goodenough, Anger in young children.

5-3, which show the proportion of certain kinds of anger outbursts to the total number.[2]

As might be expected, undirected energy outbursts decline with age. What Goodenough classifies as angry resistant behavior, however, shows no relation to age after the first year. The nature of the difficulty rather than the child's age (or sex) determines whether the behavior will be resistant. Retaliatory behavior, on the other hand, increases fairly rapidly with age.

An amusing fact is that angry *crying,* the most frequently reported form of vocal behavior, is found more frequently in boys than in girls at every age up to four years. It would be interesting to find just when the sex ratio is reversed for this behavior—if indeed it is! Boys are taught that crying won't get them anywhere; but, as someone has said, it would be a dirty trick to tell girls that.

Verbal attacks and rejoinders, of course, become increasingly prevalent in both sexes. Verbal refusal rises from 3.31 percent in two-

[2] "It will be noted that these general types of behavior are not mutually exclusive since more than one form frequently appears during a single episode" (171, p. 57).

year-olds to 35.1 percent in four-year-olds. Threatening rises from 1.6 percent to 9.7 percent. Calling names rises from 1.4 to 18 percent. The findings of Ammons and Ammons (6) are concordant.

Of course, we need to broaden our inquiry from the one emotion and we need to compare persons over a wider age range—infants with young children, young children with older, children with adults. When we do this we discover certain characteristic differences; and these tell us what emotional maturity is.

Maturity and the Occasions of Emotion

The immature person is limited in the *kinds* of situations that cause emotion. In contrast a mature person is sensitive to a wide range of emotional possibilities. The infant, obviously im-

Figure 5-4. It Depends on How You See It

mature, reacts to a relatively simple stimulation of his senses—simple lights, sounds, pressures, and so on. The older child reacts to more complex objects, and to the whole situation. The Halloween mask is a terrifying object for a two-year-old; later he sees the same mask as something worn by brother Jack and hence only exciting, not fearful.

The wider context becomes even more important for the adult. Hamlet's melancholic response was not just to the skull he held in his hands but to "poor Yorick, I knew him." The young woman's delight in the engagement ring is not primarily because of its intrinsic beauty as a here-and-now perceived object (as would be the joy of a three-year-old), but because of its symbolic value of the happy days to come—or of the envy and admiration of her friends.

It is clear, then, that part of what we mean by emotional maturity is sensitivity to a wider range of emotional possibilities. We don't exactly cease to feel emotion in the simpler situation. We still are apt to feel a bit angry over a barked shin or a bruised knuckle, but we are also likely to be a little ashamed of such "childishness." And Heaven forbid that we cease to feel delight in simple sensuous pleasures: the warmth of a spring sun, a cooling drink, the smell of new-mown hay.

In the main, however, the simpler situation gets taken up into a larger whole. If you hurt your shin while hurrying to a child's assistance, you think nothing of it. Situations, persons, objects that once aroused fear or anger no longer do so because we know more about them; but, vice versa, some situations that once aroused no fear now do so because we know enough to realize their fearful nature. Feeling and emotion, as Arthur Jersild puts it, depend upon what seems to us at stake.

In short, as we grow older, social, symbolic, and imaginative stimuli play an increasing role. Our emotional behavior, like all our action, more and more reaches back into the past and forward into the future. The adult human is a "time binder," reacting here and now to what has been or to what is yet to come.

On the whole, then, our emotional life becomes more flexible and adaptable when it is guided by imagination and thought as well as by perception. True, thought *can* be erroneous, imagination *can* be mere wish-fulfilling. But they can also enable us to bring to bear upon the present situation a whole range of relevant considerations. We help children to become emotionally mature when we help them to guide emotion by thought. We shall meet this theme again in the chapters on personality development.

Maturity as Emotional Control

If you listen to parents talk about emotion, you are apt to get the impression that the only problem is how to control emotion, if not to suppress it outright. In schools, too. As Lois Murphy (328) points out, we are all so concerned with a well-ordered routine that we almost make freedom from emotion the standard of "goodness" to which children must conform. Those psychologists who define emotion as disorganized behavior would seem to agree. Indeed, nearly everyone is apt to speak disparagingly of anyone who is "emotional."

Yet we do not characterize as immature the mother's fear when her child's life is in danger, even though the fear be very intense, almost prostrating. Again, there's nothing necessarily immature in a good hearty belly laugh—the Mrs. Grundys to the contrary notwithstanding. Nor is it immature to feel with the poet, "On with the dance! let joy be unconfined."

Nonetheless, the advocates of emotional control have a point. Fear, anger, disgust, jealousy, scorn, distrust, insecurity, anxiety—what a catalog! Such behaviors don't improve a person's social standing. They interfere with his thinking and with constructive efforts to meet the situation. They wear him out—and those around him.

Certainly, moreover, wild and woolly emotionality is immature. It may be tolerated in an infant, but it gets a child into trouble when he is "old enough to know better." In an infant or a very young child, boiling rage at being thwarted is normal and may seem "cute." If an older child acts like this we speak, with troubled brow, of a temper tantrum or a behavior problem. Should an adult act like that, we suggest a sanitarium. If emotional control is not the whole story, it is a large part of emotional maturity (140). Perhaps, then, we ought to teach youngsters to suppress their emotions. Well, let's see.

How Suppression Works [3]

An old bit of verse expresses much of the folk wisdom about suppression:

I was angry with my friend:
I told my wrath, my wrath did end.
I was angry with my foe:
I told it not, my wrath did grow.

To which perhaps I may add:

I was angry with my foe:
I told my wrath, his wrath did grow.

Have you ever noticed what you yourself do when you try to suppress an emotion? Prominent in any emotion, as we saw in the previous chapter, is a stirred-up internal state. You can do precious little to suppress the activities of this "department of the interior." It is quite useless to say: "Be still, little heart, be still."

The outward expressions of emotion are almost, though not quite, as uncontrollable. What would you not give, sometimes, to be able to inhibit a telltale blush, or a tremor in voice or knees! How often have you not instantly regretted some vigorous exclamation of scorn, disgust, or incredulity? It slipped out, you say, before you could stop it.

But there is another part of emotion which you *can* control. At least you can learn to control it. You can suppress the outward activities that are a part of emotion. And this is what we teach our children. We teach them that they must be able to control their impulse to run from danger. We try to teach them to count ten before starting a fight. In short, we tend to teach the child to suppress the activities by means of which it is possible to *alter the emotion-arousing circumstances.*

So what happens? Well, sometimes things work out all right. The occasion for emotion changes of itself. The big bully gets tired of teasing. Mother ceases to give all her attention to that nauseating

[3] Note that the term is "suppression," which means "putting an end to an activity." This is not at all the same thing as "repression," which the psychoanalysts have taught us to understand as meaning "restricting an activity to the unconscious." In their view a repressed activity is *not* suppressed—i.e, put an end to—but is merely transferred to a different sphere.

new baby and notices that her big little boy is there, too. The dreadful sounds in the stilly night just fade away.

Moreover, if the child—or anyone else—can learn to "give himself time to think," the situation often doesn't look the same. The gravestone looks less like a ghost, the insult seems more trifling, the whimpering child does not seem to be actually hurt—and the whole course of emotion changes. The habit of delaying overt reaction long enough to find out "what the score is" is helpful. We may set it down as one of the signs of growing up emotionally.

It's a good thing—but it doesn't always work. Delay or no delay, the emotive situation does not always change by itself—at least not so that you can notice it. And so the emotional tension gets stronger and stronger, until finally the bursting point is reached.

The reason is clear. You are restraining yourself from doing anything constructive. So the external circumstances just keep on arousing the internal responses. The so-called visceral and glandular responses are as strong as ever. They *prepare* you to take vigorous action, but you suppress that action. Sometimes it is someone else who does the suppressing. I have seen a father restrain a child bodily from running away from a dog that was barking at him. Most of us know that the best way to treat such a dog is precisely not to run away. This child's fear responses were evoked in full force; they demanded action, but his father was preventing action. Instead of his fear diminishing, as the father had hoped, it grew steadily stronger. We don't want to encourage our children in the habit of stewing emotionally in their glandular juices while not attempting to do anything constructive about the cause of it all.

Is Suppression Desirable?

We have been talking hitherto only of the distress-avoidance group of emotions. It is these which cry out, at times, for control if not suppression. Not all emotions, however, are of this description; joy, excitement, affection, elation, mirth, delight—these are emotings as truly as anger and fear. Would we wish human life to be free from cheerfulness, exultation, courage, amusement and laughter, merriment, rejoicing, or the transports of love? Do we want to give up the emotional stimulation and release of an exciting sport or a beautiful scene, of music, drama, poetry, and art? Is the ideal of conduct the stolid lack of feeling of the cigar-store wooden Indian?

For most of us the immediate answer is an emphatic "No!" Yet on reflection we find ourselves championing moderation and self-control (though certainly not complete suppression) even of these emotions that seem to give worth and value to life. Mature emotion is characterized as *modulated, graded, versatile, and adaptive, suitable to the circumstances.*

The issue raised is a very old one. It is basic to the controversy in philosophy betwen Stoicism and Epicureanism; in the arts, between Classicism and Romanticism; in politics, it is reflected in the struggle between Order and Freedom, Dictatorship and Democracy. In one form or another, that battle has been waged in every generation for at least two thousand years: does happiness consist in restraint or expression?

Signs are not lacking that the current is running today toward restraint. Political dictatorship is more pervasive, if somewhat less savage, than the world has known in a thousand years. And even in the democracies there is that call for greater rigor and "discipline" in home and school, of which we spoke in Chapter 2.

But I cannot believe that this is the main stream of human evolution. Consider the enormously extended interest in art, music, literature in our day. These have only limited utilitarian value; they exist to give men pleasure.

The same is true of play and recreation—and modern man is playing as never before in history. True, the play is often commercialized and for many is mere spectatorship. Yet it is hard to find Puritan repression in a crowd of 70,000 people standing on their seats to applaud a brilliant open-field run. Even watching TV or a movie is scarcely a mode of self-restraint. On the whole, the modern temper has chosen full and exciting expression and abundant living as its goal.

The Positive Development of Emotion

If that be so, how poorly we perform our tasks! The eager joy and zest for life of the young child is cut down. Little by little—at home, at school, in countless other ways—the child learns to curb his feelings, to live more meagerly in feeling and emoting. As Lawrence Frank (149) points out, the child develops—he learns, he is *taught*—a lack of sensitivity to emotional stimulation. As a result he may seem to be emotionally stable and well behaved, but he is also emotionally rigid. (Or would "frigid" be more descriptive?)

We take very seriously the teaching of emotional *restraints* but not the teaching of emotional *expression,* and the guidance of emotional development for richness of living. We worry about emotional shock or trauma but not about emotional shallowness. We talk about "socially approved" and not about "socially effective" emotion. How many times lately have you encouraged emotional behavior compared with the times you have discouraged it? How much thought have you given to what you can do to bring about *positive* emotional growth?

One thing seems fairly clear: a child cannot learn how to emote appropriately and effectively without a lot of spontaneous practice. That is sometimes pretty rough on the parent or the teacher. We cannot expect spontaneous emotional responses to occur at the times, in the degree, or even of the kind, that suits our own convenience. We must be prepared to encounter emoting that is sometimes ugly, self-centered, and misguided, and, despite that, to be ready to encourage further experiments in spontaneous emotion.

> Emotional education should be a considered effort to teach children to feel for themselves, in the same sense that their intellectual training should be an effort to teach them to think for themselves. . . . We have to realize how feeble and ineffective our own emotional life is . . . . Then we shall perhaps begin to discover what we can do to develop in children the rich capacity for a spontaneous emotional life which has been so stunted in ourselves. One of the first results of such a fundamental change of attitude would be, I doubt not, that we should recognize that it is as ridiculous to put the emotional training of children in the hands of teachers whose emotional life is of a low grade or poorly developed, as it is to commit their intellectual education to teachers who are intellectually unintelligent and stupid.
>
> The suppression of offensive expressions of emotion (which is in the main what we still aim at) makes no difference to the *quality* of human life. If a man's nature is crude, it must of necessity be restrained, if only for the convenience of others. But the business of education is to make such restraints unnecessary by the refinement of the [individual's] nature.
>
> [The] expressions of emotion in activity—whether in speech or song or movement—are at first crude and indiscriminate. The business of education is not to alter their spontaneous character but to refine and subtilize them, maintaining their spontaneous character so that the development

of grace and fineness in activity is still without other motive than the joy of expression.[4]

Of course, the other side of the coin is that the child must see how his emotions work socially. For this, understanding of his own emotions is a prime necessity. Emoting is socially a circular process: the child's emotion stimulates emotions in those around him, and not always the emotions the child wants. Little Ronald may feel like singing a joyful song but he has to learn that Big Sister, who is absorbed in a TV program, is disturbed. Even spontaneous happiness

Figure 5-5. Let's Not All Sing Like the Birdies Sing

has its socially unacceptable forms or occasions. A child has to learn that there are times when others don't feel like sharing his gaiety.

We should, however, not leave him to the mercy of negative learning, of finding out that certain emotions are *not* acceptable. Instead, we should arrange situations that will call forth emotion which is at once spontaneous and socially acceptable. All this he can learn best if he has warm and friendly relationships with responsive personalities—those of his own age as well as adults. In such company we need not shelter him from emotional experiences; instead, we can expose him to situations that call them forth.

[4] From John Macmurray, *Reason and Emotion.* London: Faber and Faber, Ltd., 1935, pp. 69-70, 72, 73. By permission of the author and the publishers.

In such an atmosphere there is little danger of merely passive enjoyment. And this is well, for it is just as unwholesome to *enjoy* one's emotions without doing anything as it is helplessly to *suffer* them—and far more tempting. The emotions that develop out of "delight" are pleasant. So, for that matter, are those that develop out of distress, when they are not too intense—hence the popularity of roller coasters and big-game hunting. It is fatally easy to make such pleasant experiences the end or goal of our conduct, to seek emotional thrills for their own sake. That is not maturity. Except as it plays a part in recreation, that is pure infantilism or at best sentimentality.

The picture of emotional maturity that emerges is not, then, that of tight-lipped suppression of all natural feeling and expression, of Stoic calm and indifference, of obedience and "discipline." Neither is it that of unrestrained expressionism, or of a mawkish sentimentality in which one seeks merely to enjoy one's own feelings. *Emotion, like any other kind of behavior, is a way of getting things done.* Like any other kind of behavior, therefore, it can be excessive or deficient, judiciously directed or wide of the mark. Simple suppression, however, is clearly not the mark of emotional maturity nor a goal of emotional education. In a mature person, emoting is a positive mode of adjustment, the servant of the individual's purposes and goals. Parents and teachers need to be alert for opportunities to further and to guide the child's growth in emotional maturity.

Summary

The traditional and subjective view of emotion has obscured its essentially social character. The "who" of emotional stimulation is as important as the "what." Much of our emotional behavior is essentially a kind of language designed to have effect on others. With increasing maturity, emoting becomes a way of getting things done with people.

For the most part emotional language has to be learned. Children gradually learn the standardized words, facial expressions, and gestures that convey to others how they are emoting. In play and make-believe, also, they often convey emotions not otherwise communicated.

The child's understanding of the way others emote grows with experience and training. Many problems arise when the child is faced with a teacher or with other children who speak an "emotional language" he cannot understand. The school has an important task in teaching children to understand emoting in others and to express emotion in ways acceptable to those outside the family circle.

Gradually the child develops emotional behavior that is more nearly suited to the circumstances. It is instigated by a wider range of emotive circumstances; symbolic stimuli enable him to respond emotionally not only to the here and now but to the past and future. Mature behavior is modulated, versatile, and adaptive.

That there is a due and proper amount of emotionality is admitted by all. But how is emotionality to be controlled? Outright suppression is usually ineffective, and in any case not desirable. Emotional control is essentially a matter of learning socially acceptable ways of acting. Opportunities for emoting in acceptable and effective fashion should be provided.

6

Motivation in Childhood

Why children act as they do is obviously both an interesting and an important topic. Are they born with ineradicable motives? Or does society make them what they are?

What happens when the child's motives are frustrated? What is the effect on his personality when motives are satisfied? How shall we deal with the frustrations involved in punishment?

Let two or three friends get together for a talk and sooner or later they will begin dissecting the motives of an absent acquaintance. There is no more popular indoor sport than the discussion of people's motives. Of other people's motives, of course! As William James says, our *own* actions and impulses "shine with their own sufficient light." They don't need any explanation.

Not so the actions of others—including those of children. True, we sometimes speak of the child's guileless innocence, implying that his motives are simple and apparent; but in the next breath we may confess our inability to understand what moves him to such "odd" behavior.

There are many reasons why a child's behavior is hard to understand, especially that of our neighbors' children. Of course they have been brought up so outlandishly that we can't expect them to act like our own well-behaved children. But even our own children may move toward goals that possess for them a self-evident fascination utterly hidden from us.

What adult, for example, can understand the attractiveness of the objects that fill the pockets of a boy of nine? What adult can comprehend a child's goals from observing the indirect routes he takes in traveling toward them? If we ask the child, he is likely to think us rather stupid. Obviously, he seems to imply, these are desirable goals and obviously this is the way to get there. His attitude to our questioning is apt to be like that which William James attributed to the broody hen to whom "the notion would probably seem monstrous that there should be a person in the world to whom a nestful of eggs was not the utterly fascinating and precious and never-to-be-too-much-sat-upon object which it is to her."

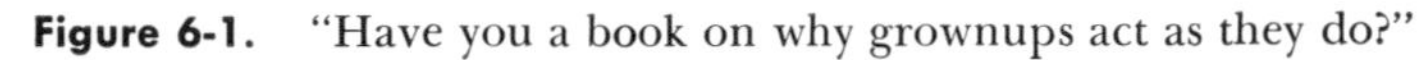

Figure 6-1. "Have you a book on why grownups act as they do?"

Perhaps we ought to recognize that our behavior is no less mysterious to the child than is his to us. Moreover, there are no literal "child psychologists" to write textbooks for other children on the strange behavior of adults.[1] Much of the mystery proceeds from the

[1] Liberman's "A Child's Guide to a Parent's Mind" (281) is a brave try to show us how we might look to children; but that is for our enlightenment, not our children's.

simple fact that we are adults and that he is a child. Age makes a difference in motivation, as in so many other things.

Yet there are general principles of motivation that apply to all sorts and conditions of mankind—including children. Perhaps, then, it will be profitable to examine some of these to see what light they throw on the motives of these young creatures, so like us at times, yet at others so mysteriously different.

What Is Motivation?

Motivation is so supremely important that mankind has invented a bewildering variety of terms to refer to it. I hesitate to give a list lest it be supposed that I expect you to memorize definitions for each. That is far from my intent. For the benefit of the curious, however, I give a partial catalog: aim, ambition, appetite, attitude, complex, craving, desire, drive, emotion, goal, habit, impulse, incentive, instinct, interest, libido, motive, need, passion, purpose, sentiment, set, tendency, urge, valence, value, want. Valence and complex are the only terms in this list that were more or less invented by psychologists for technical use; all the rest, even libido, come from literature and everyday life.

Each of these terms has a particular context in which it is somewhat more appropriate than the others. Take these four terms: goal, valence, need, impulse. *Goal* stresses the kind of condition toward which the person is drawn, whereas *valence* is used to indicate roughly the extent to which a given condition "pulls" or "repels" him. *Need* emphasizes that motivation depends upon a shortage or deficit in the organism, whereas *impulse* emphasizes the tendency to active correction of the shortage. The four terms are thus by no means synonymous, but the basic fact to which they all refer is the same. All motivation probably involves a shortage of something *(need);* and motivation tends to correct the shortage *(impulse),* doing so by moving the individual toward a state of affairs (the *goal)* that has a given amount of attraction *(valence).*

It is motivation in an inclusive sense with which we shall be concerned in this chapter; and in referring to it we shall freely use such of the above terms as may in context help to make our meaning clear.

Early Foundations

In his first few months the baby's behavior is mostly directed by a few organic needs: hunger, thirst, excretion, sleep, and general muscular activity. These are vital needs; throughout life they remain very powerful, particularly when blocked or frustrated. Yet almost from the first other needs move the babe. Sometimes the little scamp would rather play than eat. He's curious and exploratory—everything he touches is handled, looked at, and put in his mouth. He shows rudimentary esthetic needs, too—the sheer sensory pleasure in color or lights or sounds or smells, and later in rhythmic sounds and color patterns. These gather strength more slowly and are seldom strong enough to compete with organic needs, but every child shows in one way or another that he needs and enjoys the esthetically pleasing.

He has social needs, too, even as an infant. Much of his play is social. Even in the first weeks there are the beginnings of the need to be independent. And there is the contrasted need for someone to cuddle up to (191).

Temperamental factors—which certainly influence, when they do not determine, the acquisition of motives—also manifest themselves in the first few months. There are great individual differences in placidity and irritability, activity level, and tolerance or nontolerance of discomfort and stress. (Ausubel [22, p. 113] cites a considerable number of research studies.)

Berne (58) found that all the behavior of seven children, aged two to four, observed over a period of five hundred hours, could be attributed to one or more of the following motives: the needs for food, drink, sleep, excretion, movement, touching, vocalization, observation, quiescence, self-determination, self-superiority, cooperation, "self-conformance," "others-conformance," and "aloof observation of others." The classification is not perfect, and many of these are far from truly primitive needs; yet when we find all these needs fairly well differentiated as early as ages two to four, we have a clue to the richness of infantile motivation. All in all, the infant has a rather impressive repertory of simple motives on which to base later development.

Heredity and Motives

The question of the role of heredity is a hardy perennial that comes up in nearly every discussion of psychology. We might as well face it here.

Which motives, if any, are hereditary or innate and which are acquired? Let me pose a counterquestion: Why do you want to know? Can you understand a child's motives better by probing into hereditary origins? Let's try it on a concrete case. Why does Charles, age eight, prefer his Erector set to his water colors?

Figure 6-2.

Can we really explain the preference by going back to the motivations of his infancy? He did have motives even then; that is, there were things he wanted to do. As we have just said, even an infant has an impressive repertory of motives—for an infant. But Charles's behavior as an infant was *relatively* unchoosing, *relatively* unselective; that is, *relatively* unmotivated as compared with his present behavior. A stick was about as pleasing as a piece of the Erector set. The system of motives at birth and in infancy is less rich, the needs are far less sharply defined, and the modes of satisfaction are less clearly outlined than they become in the course of development.

Alleged Signs of Innate Preference

The Chinese, we are told, used to place before the year-old child certain objects symbolic of various vocations; his choice was supposed to indicate the vocation for which he was destined. One suspects that there was quite a lot of finagling to make sure that the infant chose what his father wanted him to choose. At any rate, it does not appear that this was a very successful method of vocational guidance. Neither inclination nor capacity is well developed at such an early age.

To return to Charles—we do not deny that he may have been from birth more inclined to mechanics than to art, though it would be difficult to find any real evidence. If Charles really did have a natural bent, at eight months it was pretty unspecific, so that it could easily have been channeled in this direction or that. By itself the hereditary bent would not explain the present behavior very fully. In short, the further we push back toward *"original motives," the less help we get in explaining just why a person does this rather than that.* At best the explanation in terms of hereditary inclination is partial, impoverished, incomplete.

The Interaction of Nature and Nurture

All of which is not to say that heredity plays no part. The biological inheritance with which we start out in life is comprised in "a minute package of chemicals," the zygote or fertilized egg. How complex this package of chemicals is, however, may be seen if we compare the zygote with an electronic computer or "mechanical brain." If you feed a certain code into the latter, it will issue "orders" to be carried out by another machine in a prescribed time and manner. The code book prescribing the development of a human being would require many thousand volumes, and to issue all the orders at the right time, the most compact computer yet designed would fill every building in metropolitan Chicago.

Yet the fertilized egg that contains all these "directions" for growth is barely visible to good eyes.

Our heredity, then, provides us with myriads of potentialities for development. Some of these hereditary potentialities are purely individual; they are what start a person off in life as a unique being. Other hereditary potentialities are common to the species. A dry mouth is "thirstful," an empty stomach is "hungerful," blows and wounds are painful; these are innate tendencies and no conditioning or learning by experience or acquisition of traits is required to explain their presence in all human beings.

True, in certain complex situations the relation between a certain stimulus and a need may not find direct expression. In the excitement of a basketball game a smack on the nose may well go unheeded. Yet the blow on the nose always hurts and has its part in motivating the player's behavior. There are indeed *natural* arousers of needs or motives.

And there are natural need-satisfiers, too. A cold compress helps to relieve the "need" in the injured nose, however much it fails to relieve the indignation provoked by the blow. Food, and food alone, satisfies hunger. No amount of conditioning or social pressure will make us accept good music or good company as a substitute for food, although, as we all know, they can temporarily divert us from food or can greatly *enhance* the satisfaction of food. A hard core of something laid down in our very natures *helps* to account for what satisfies our needs.

For every kind of need? Yes. The natural *basis* exists even in cases where the satisfactions do not seem very "natural." I grant that a natural tendency for Pete to find satisfaction in hanging up his hat or in saying "Thank you" may be difficult to see with the naked eye. A long and sometimes painful training is required to produce these virtuous behaviors.

But even such an obviously artificial virtue as politeness cannot be, as Gardner Murphy (325, p. 127) phrases it, merely pumped into a child as air is pumped into an empty football. You don't just put politeness into Pete, can't just "ram it down his throat." You spend a great deal of time helping Pete to *grow* and change so that he will want to be polite. You don't by your training *create* new motives; you alter or modify those already at work.

The motives already at work are not, however, simple innate

motives. They too have developed from still earlier ones, and so on back to birth if you have the patience to try to unravel the process of change so far back. But note that today's motives are not merely modified copies of the originals; they are the *progeny* of the earlier ones. The eight-year-old Charles's motive to play with mechanical toys has indeed grown out of an earlier interest, but it has *grown* and is by so much a richer, stronger, more complex motive.

The Natural Growth of Motives

The distinction, then, between innate and acquired motives does not hold up very well. Another distinction is more useful. The Topsy of *Uncle Tom's Cabin* could declare that she wasn't "brung up" at all; she "jist growed." Some of our well-developed motives are like that; they come about in all of us by a process of natural growth in ordinary life circumstances. Like weeds, they need no cultivation. Others—most of the virtues, for example—require a good deal of fostering care.

But the "natural" motives are not necessarily more powerful and they are not unchanging. Take even such a motive as hunger. Some years ago I became acquainted with a young Englishman studying in Rome. He was living on one scanty meal a day and suffering agonies of hunger, yet holding on until he could finish his studies. (He had money at home but could not get at it because of exchange restrictions.) Hunger was powerful but not so powerful as his "acquired" zeal for knowledge of Etruscan archeology. (Pride, I may add, was also strong in this young man of upper-class family, but his pride yielded to hunger when I offered him a dinner.) The "naturalness" of a motive is no measure of its strength.

And, of course, the "natural" motives are modified all the time just as the "cultivated" motives are. Four-year-old Sue's hunger is by no means the same as her hunger when she was a small baby. It comes in a different rhythm ("Thank heaven, no more 2 A.M. feedings!"), is both stimulated and satisfied by different foods, leads to markedly different activities. By the time she is sixteen her hunger will be still more different, and food, to be acceptable, may have to be served with all the refinements of civilization.

Nor will she get less satisfaction because her hunger motive is thus refined. "Primitive" satisfactions are not the strongest or the most gratifying. Most of us like for a change to "get back to Nature"; but for day-to-day satisfaction we prefer warm clothes to a savage's loin cloth, a soft bed to a shakedown of branches, filet mignon or even hamburger to pemmican or a handful of dried peas. The artificial satisfactions prove quite as powerful as the primitive.

Man's satisfactions in sex are not less but greater because, in all known social groups, he has surrounded sex with elaborate rituals and cultural controls—i.e., has enormously modified the natural motive. Neither man nor child finds his greatest satisfactions in a state of nature.

We may reasonably conclude, then, that both what we want or need and what we find satisfying to our wants are determined, not so much by heredity as *by the kind of life we lead.* There is no special class of inborn motives, powerful and ineradicable, constituting "human nature." Most of what seems "human nature" seems so merely because it is firmly embedded in our *culture,* and in accustomed ways of acting.

Most of us feel, for example, that the desire for goods and the fear of want are inevitable and "natural" motives. And so they are—for us; the culture of our Western world is impregnated with these motives. Yet there are whole societies in which these motives are almost absent or play but a subordinate role. Thus the Sioux Indians placed almost no value on goods or possessions. A man might steal a horse to prove his courage; but he then was expected to give it away (315). Competitive trading did not exist. In such societies, it is the strong desire for material goods which seems "*un*natural."

It is intriguing to ask ourselves what will happen to the "naturalness" of these motives in our own society as economic security becomes more and more nearly universal. The fear of want, at least, will surely gradually become weaker and, perhaps to a lesser degree, so will the desire for goods. Which motives will take their place as the dominant "natural" motives is an interesting speculation. Whatever they may be, we can be sure that they will be correlated with the then-existing culture—that is, with the conditions of life then prevailing.

Large-scale cultural influences, however, are not the only cause of "natural" motives. Smaller groups, even of individuals, play their part. The teacher or parent who continually stresses competition must expect to find the children "naturally" trying to outdo each other, often by hook or by crook. The parent who makes affection the keynote of the home will have children who are strongly motivated by loyalty and love. *For the individual child that motive is strongest which has been most often effectively appealed to in his experience.*

Thus it is human experience rather than some mystic innate human nature that gives color and direction to the needs themselves. For the dictum "You can't change human nature" we must substitute "You can change human nature by changing the conditions that produce it." The school has a responsibility to help bring about such change.

The above discussion has a somewhat intricate pattern; yet the elements from which it is woven are quite simple. The problem is, Why does this child act so much like other children, yet also in a manner that seems to be qualitatively unique? The answer is almost too obvious to deserve to be put in writing: The similarities come from similarities in *both* heredity *and* experience, the differences from both or either.

The tiny structures in the zygote that determine an organism's heredity are called genes. Now our genes are human genes, and in innumerable ways they resemble those of all other human beings. That makes for similarity in human behavior. Our genes also resemble the genes of the others in our family. That makes for family resemblances. But the genes of each individual are also peculiar to himself. That makes for individual differences.

The same is true of environment. There are universal human experiences—such as the dependence of the infant upon adults, stressed in an earlier chapter. There are also, quite obviously, enormous differences in environment; in the final analysis we recognize that no two persons—not even Siamese twins—ever have exactly the same experiences.

When we observe a Melanesian child from New Guinea acting "strangely"—that is, differently from one of our own children—we may ask whether the difference is mainly due to the heredity of the race, or to the physical or cultural environment of the race; or to family heredity, or to family habits; or to personal heredity; or to some "accident" of personal experience. If we observe that the Melanesian child behaves in some ways like an American child, we can only conclude that in relevant respects our children have heredity similar to that of the Melanesian (both are human) and also similar environment (both must be nourished and protected, and in many other ways are treated the same). The case is not different if we take two children living in the same block in a midwestern city. Because both are human and because they hear the same slightly nasal speech, they grow up speaking like Midwesterners. But one of them may have been born with a cleft palate which makes his speech different, and the other may have been encouraged to continue his baby talk. It is clear that the conditions that make for similarity are harder to meet than those that make for difference. It is for this reason that the list of truly universal behaviors—what we used to call instincts—is so very short.

QUESTIONS

1. In the light of the definition of motive, how would one justify classifying sentiments under that heading?
2. Which of these two statements accords with the discussion in the text?
   a. "Heredity merely defines what we can learn under certain conditions of Nurture."
   b. "Nurture merely develops what is provided first by Nature."
3. On page 172 is a list of motives found in two-year-olds. Can you add any found in all normal American school children between ages six and ten? in *all* children anywhere?
4. Suppose that you had grown up in a society just like the one in which you did grow up, except that neither you nor anyone else had ever felt pinched for lack of material things. What do you think would be the most important motive in your life? Can you relate this to your childhood experiences? How would it differ from the motive which is now dominant?

Deprivation and Frustration

From his first wailing breath—itself a response to the deprivation of the oxygen hitherto drawn from the mother's blood stream—the man-child is destined to suffer privation and deprivation.[2] Hunger

[2] It is sometimes more convenient to speak of privation when the means to satisfaction of a need are *absent;* deprivation when the means to need-satisfaction are *taken away;* and frustration when need-satisfaction is *blocked*. There is probably no basic difference, except that a social element is usually involved in frustration. The obstruction when a motive of one's own blocks another is better spoken of as *conflict*. This will be dealt with in Chapter 13.

sets in, but food may be delayed in obedience to a sacred "feeding schedule," or for other reasons. Being dressed interferes with the urge to physical activities or with the urge to sleep. Objects are rudely removed from exploration in the baby's mouth, delightful toys slip from the unskilled hands and are lost to sight. Toilet training, attempted before the child can possibly conform, is all too often one long series of frustrations and punishments. When the child begins to crawl or walk about, "No, no's!" increase in number and frequency. And by most parents the child's natural tendency to find gratification in the stimulation of genital organs is almost savagely repressed.

No wonder that in some forms of mental breakdown the patient seems to yearn for a return to the comfort of the mother's womb, that first home in which all needs are effortlessly supplied and there are no frustrations. But that is abnormality. If we are to be whole human beings we must learn to confront and master privation and frustration by our own efforts.

An Experiment in Frustration

A brief description of a famous experiment will illustrate the sort of fact-finding that underlies modern psychology, and at the same time will show us something of what happens when children are obstructed in their goal-seeking activities (35).

A special room was furnished with a number of interesting toys: a child's chair, a Teddy bear, a doll, a cup and saucer, a small truck and trailer, a teapot, an ironing board and iron, a telephone receiver, a box of crayons, writing paper, a motorboat, a sailboat, a frog, and a fishing pole. The thirty children of the experiment, aged three to four, were brought to this room one at a time for thirty minutes of free play. All seemed to enjoy themselves. An observer kept a record of what they did and scored their play according to a careful standard to show the degree of maturity displayed. The first day each child had thirty minutes of such play.

When each child was brought back the next day he found that the playroom had been enlarged by the removal of a partition and the toys used the day before had been moved into what looked like a child's dream of paradise (see Figure 6-4).

Figure 6-3. Free-Play Situation

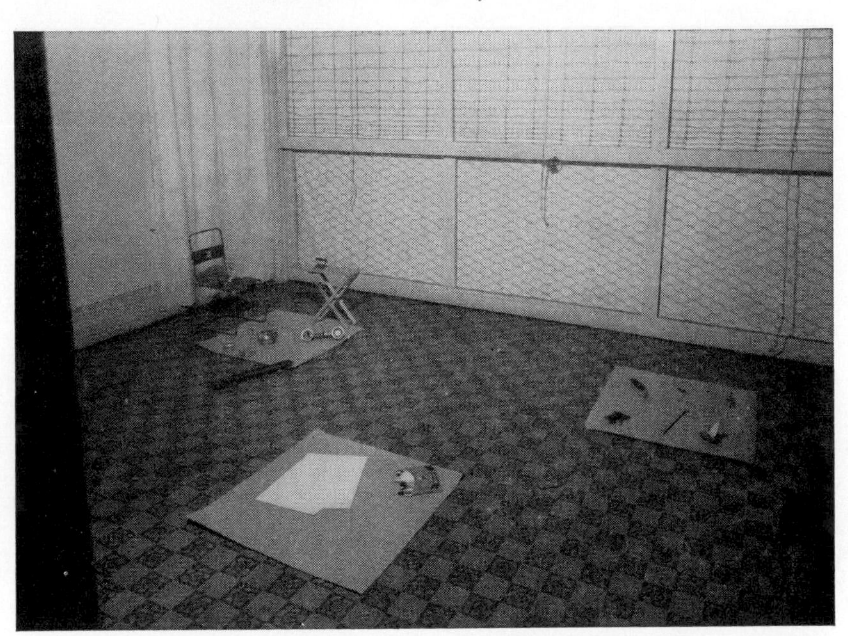

From *Univ. of Ia. Stud. Child Welf.*, 1941, **18**, no. 1, p. 51.

In the added part of the room was a dollhouse, brightly painted and decorated, and big enough for the child to enter through a doorway. Inside were a bed on which the doll was lying and a chair in which the Teddy bear sat. The ironing board with the iron on it stood against one wall, and the telephone, this time on its base with a dial and bell, was in the corner. There were a stove with cooking utensils, and a cupboard. The house had electric lights, curtains, and a carpet.

Outside the house was a laundry line on which the doll's clothes hung. A rubber bunny sat near the house. A large delivery truck (twenty-three inches long) stood near the house, and behind it was the small truck and trailer used the previous day. Nearby was a child's table prepared for a luncheon party. On the table were cups, saucers, dishes, spoons, forks, knives, a small empty teapot, and a large teapot with water in it.

In the other corner of the new part of the room was a toy lake (three feet across) filled with real water. It contained an island with

Figure 6-4. Prefrustration Situation

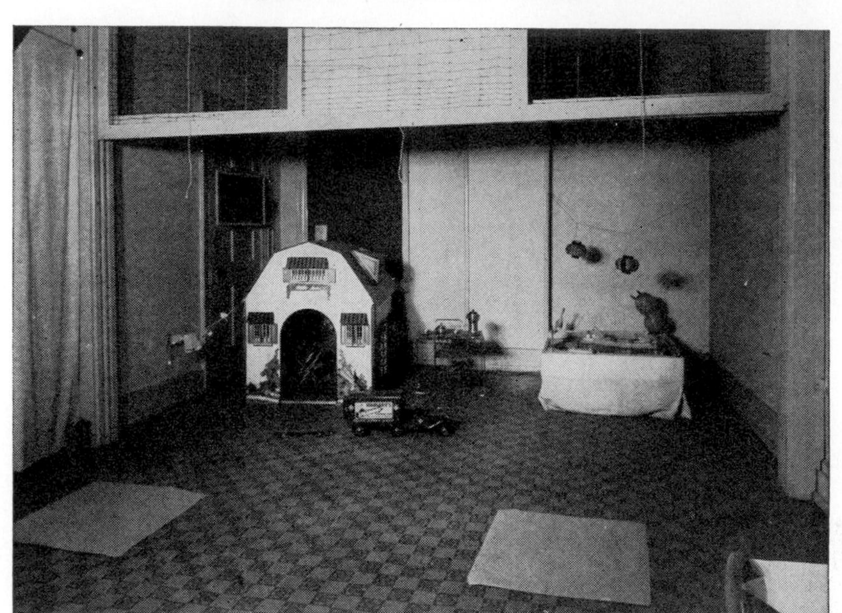

From *Univ. of Ia. Stud. Child Welf.*, 1941, **18**, no. 1, p. 55.

a lighthouse, a wharf, a ferry boat, small boats, fishes, ducks, and frogs. The lake had sand beaches.

Each child found the setup thrilling—what normal child would not?—and was encouraged to play as he liked. This was the prefrustration situation.

After a time, the experimenter gathered all the toys that had been used in the initial period and distributed them to their original positions at the other end of the playroom. Then calling or leading the child, he suggested, "Now let's play in the other end," and proceeded to lower a stout wire screen which cut off all access to the new delights, though leaving them fully visible. To make clear to the child that the other end of the playroom was now out of bounds, the screen was locked with a heavy padlock.

There followed thirty minutes called the "Frustration Period," during which the child was allowed free play with the original toys, their meagerness now in contrast with the visible delights beyond the screen. Again the child's activities were carefully recorded and scored to show how mature they were.

Figure 6-5. Frustration Situation

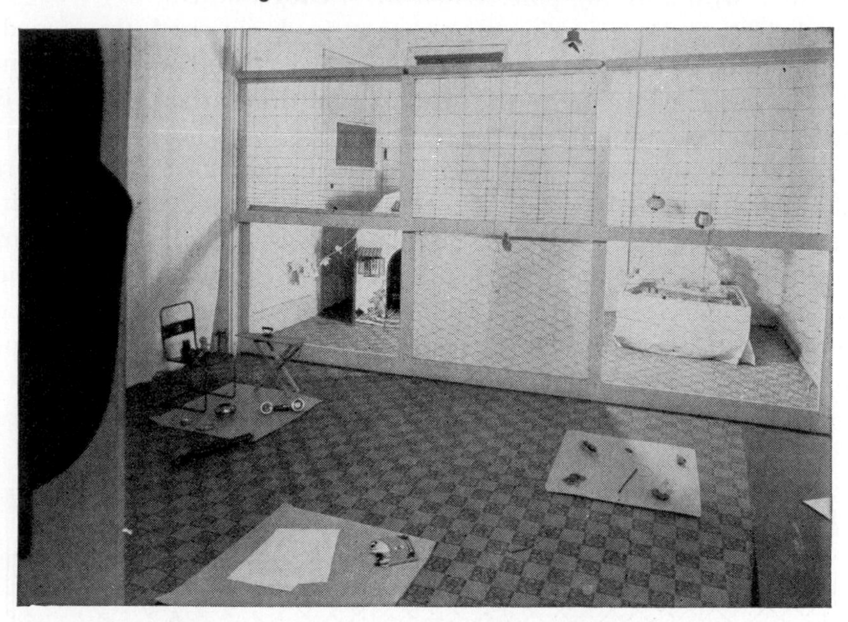

From *Univ. of Ia. Stud. Child Welf.*, 1941, **18,** no. 1, p. 57.

At the end of this period the experimenter asked whether the child wished to leave—and every one assented. Each was thoroughly bored. At this point, however, the partition was raised and the child joyfully hurried back to the fine toys at the other end of the room. (This was done to counteract any undesirable aftereffects of the frustration experience.)

Such was the experiment: first the child played normally with ordinary playthings, then was given a taste of unusual delights, only to have these suddenly and capriciously denied him.[3] It was frustrating all right. What happened?

What Children Do When Frustrated.

a) In this experiment nearly all the children made some sort of effort to get around the frustrating barrier. They tried to lift the screen, to climb over it, to open the lock, or to pull the toys

[3] The experiment has since been repeated by Block and Martin (62) with parallel results.

to them with a fishing pole. When these efforts failed, they tried to get help from the experimenter; they coaxed, reasoned, threatened, even assaulted him, to get him to help overcome the obstruction. I think we may generalize this: the natural thing when frustrated is to try to "get around" the frustration cause.

b) When the attack on the barrier failed, most of the youngsters showed disrupted behavior. Some "went all to pieces." They stuttered. They were restless and unable to direct their behavior purposefully. They complained loudly, stuck out their tongues at the unattainable Utopia, or "displaced their aggression" by destroying objects. Others whimpered or cried, sucked their thumbs. One went to sleep.

Figure 6-6. Behavior under Frustration

c) Finally, some of the children looked around for a substitute activity. In the experiment there were few satisfactory opportunities of this sort. The children could look out the window, walk around the room, or try to talk to the experimenter, who was laconic and uninterested. Or they could go back, as all eventually did, to play with the relatively meager toys which they had had in the first free-play period.

Originally these toys had been at least mildly enjoyed; now they could only remind the child of the new delights from which he had been so arbitrarily removed. Under such conditions of frustration, the play was very different.

It will be remembered that their activities in the free-play period had been carefully and objectively recorded and rated on a scale of "maturity." With the aid of this scale it was possible to compare a child's behavior in the free-play and the frustration periods.

Sylvia, for example, spent seventy seconds in the free-play period happily making a clay elephant. She used a little peg for an eye, made the elephant sit up. This behavior was rated 6 (out of a possible 8). In the frustration period she again played with the clay—if we can call the ten seconds she spent idly manipulating it "play." The constructiveness of this activity was rated 2.

Twenty-two of the thirty children in the experiment showed a similar loss of constructiveness or maturity. For the group as a whole, the average loss during the frustration period was such that the four-year-olds played more like two-year-olds. Such a going back to the kind of behavior characteristic of an earlier age is called regression.

Shall we then conclude that frustration always causes regression toward less mature behavior? That is too free a generalization. In the first place, these were quite young children. Would the result have been similar with older children?

In the second place, the dice were loaded against these children. Paradise was still in view but was totally unattainable. There was nothing warmly satisfying left to do. If, as Murphy (325) asks, the "field" in which they were free to operate had been richer, might not their behavior have seemed less regressive or immature? If, after being driven from their temporary Garden of Eden, the children in this experiment had been let out on the playground, would they not have run faster, slid down the slide more courageously, or thrown the ball more vigorously? In short, in some circumstances does not disappointment lead to behavior that is more, not less, mature?

That apparently was the case with a modification of this experiment, in which the frustration was administered to the children in pairs instead of singly (486). Most of the behavior in the frustration period showed the same sort of deterioration, but in one respect there was improvement: there was better cooperation between the two children than they had shown in the prefrustration period. Misery loves company. When the frustration was shared, it had lesser consequence.

Finally, as always, we should take note of individual differences. Of the thirty children in the experiment, three showed no net loss, and five actually improved in constructiveness during the frustration period.

The Frustration-Aggression Theory

An even more famous theory about frustration was put forward by Dollard and his associates to the effect that frustration breeds not regression but aggression (125). How does this theory accord with the experiment described above? Not too well. Certainly much of the behavior found in the Frustration Period was aggressive; but certainly much of the behavior seemed strikingly unaggressive.

Dollard *et al.* had an answer to that. Where no direct aggression is evident, we must look for some sort of "displaced" or indirect aggression. Displaced aggression is familiar enough—the man "chewed out" by his boss goes home to take it out on his wife. Or as one perspicacious youngster put it, "When little children can't get what they want, they cry; when grownups can't get what they want, they hit little children and make *them* cry." Indirect aggression is a little more complex but familiar enough, too. The child who is punished by his father may suddenly begin to lavish affection on his mother as a not-too-subtle way of saying to the former, "I hate you."

Now many of the behaviors exhibited in the frustration experiment were of just this sort, or at least could be so interpreted. But it is a little difficult to speak of aggression, even indirect aggression, when a child just lies down and goes to sleep with his thumb—this happened, you remember, in the experiment. Nor does aggression seem to account for the loss of constructiveness in play that was found.

Scott's little book *Aggression* (378), summarizing his own and others' studies of animals, is illuminating on this point, since indirect aggression, if there is any, is more easily observed in animals than in man. Scott finds that for each species there are certain rather simple, natural causes of fighting, or aggression. But on top of this there is grafted a sort of habitual aggressiveness in specific situations directed toward specific persons. The billy goat that was once my prize possession had learned that girls would fly in terror before his charge; to males he was polite and unaggressive. Similarly a watchdog is very aggressive toward intruders on his home domain but elsewhere may be very mild.

Where does frustration enter this picture? Scott finds that frustration lowers the animal's threshold for aggression; he reacts with more violence or to lesser stimuli. (The chained watchdog reacts more violently than he would if at large.) But the frustration still vents itself aggressively chiefly on the objects or situations for which aggression is a learned response. Frustration is not so much a direct cause as an intensifier of an aggression already present.

Human aggressiveness is quite parallel. Our aggressions also are found chiefly in those situations where we have learned to be aggressive. In the family circle children learn most readily to be aggressive with siblings. Once this is learned, frustration—almost any frustration—may trigger an aggressive reaction. ("I wasn't doing a thing, mama, and he up and poked me real hard.") But it is too easy an excuse to say, "Oh well, I guess it is just some frustration working itself out." We should ask instead, "Now why did frustration take this particular direction?"

A thorough critical examination (see, e.g., 276, 291, 346, 373, 491) makes it clear that the frustration-aggression hypothesis is too sweeping. Aggression is indeed usually but not always linked with frustration.

What makes the difference? Probably a number of things. Frustration tolerance, for one thing—some people have learned to tolerate frustration without "blowing their stack" either outwardly or inwardly. The extent to which the child understands and accepts the inevitability of the particular frustration, for another. The extent to which one's life in general is full of satisfaction—even a quite intense frustration can be endured if one has a generally satisfying life.

Otis and McCandless (341) found that certain experimentally induced frustrations caused more aggression if the children were known to be rather domineering and power-seeking. On the other hand, children high in a need for affection were less influenced by the frustration.

Neither regression nor aggression, then, seems to be the inevitable and direct effect of frustration. Rather, the direct effect of frustration seems to be to induce a sort of tension—and the stronger the frustration the greater the tension, as seen in Kiyoko Hoashi's experiment

(204). In this state a person tends to respond to stimuli that might not otherwise arouse him. If the situation permits, the tension may lead to a constructive attack on the problem. (You may call this sublimated aggression, if you like, but it does not seem to me to make the case any clearer.) If the situation does not permit such a solution, the tension may lead to regression *or* to aggression, or it may dissipate itself in any of a variety of activities.[4]

Most of these indirect effects of frustration are at best only partially satisfactory. Yet if something really satisfactory to do turns up, the tension may even have beneficial results.

Much depends on the individual. The history of mankind is full of examples of those who have been inspired by frustration to more vigorous and more creative attacks on their problems; it is full also of those who, like the children in the experiment described above, have regressed to defeatism. Some of this difference may be due to obscure differences in bodily constitution. But much more depends upon how, as children, they learned to react to obstruction. A large part of what we mean by maturity is the ability to react constructively to disappointment.

How to Deal with Frustration

As we have seen, the most natural thing to do when frustrated is to make a frontal attack on the cause. Thus most of the children in the experiment made a valiant effort to get around the barrier. Some of them kept this up for some time and with varying techniques.

That, of course, is what we like to see.[5] "Keep on trying," we tell the child. "If one way doesn't work, try another." But a child won't try and try again, won't expect success to follow effort unless we see to it that a vigorous and intelligent attack on obstacles usually "pays off."

This is precisely what was done by Ruth Updegraff and Marjorie Keister at the University of Iowa Child Welfare Station (452). They

[4] See the experimental studies of Dembo (118), Fajans (144), Rodnik and Klebanoff (368), Sears (382, 383), Sherman and Jost (392), and Yarrow (488).

[5] At least this is the American pattern. A Japanese child psychologist, Professor Sadao Nagashima, tells me that our encouragement of sturdy self-dependence in the very young is one of the most striking differences between his country and ours.

took children who were immature and lacking in persistence in the face of an obstacle or a difficult task. In a number of training sessions these children were set to work upon tasks in which they would experience increasing success—success visible to the children themselves. As a result, they ceased to sulk or cry, were less dependent, less "emotional" when faced with a baffling problem. They had learned confidence in their own efforts.

I need hardly point out that this experiment is rich with suggestion of a practical course to be pursued. It is usually possible—but I don't say easy—to plan things so that a child has many and varied success experiences. It is very much worth doing.

That being granted, it must be admitted that we can't *always* fix things so that a child succeeds. Some barriers cannot be overcome no matter how optimistically and energetically they are attacked. In school there are children who cannot do well *any* sort of classroom task; no matter how much the teacher tries to soften the blow, they know themselves to be failures. In such situations the child somehow learns to find his satisfactions in doing something else.

Unfortunately the substitute activities induced by frustration usually don't work very well. If you have just been locked out of a delightful playroom, "looking out the window" isn't much fun, even though it is all you can find to do. Sylvia, looking wistfully through the fence at the lake and sandy beach, turned to the "hunk of old clay" with no great enthusiasm. As a result she displayed none of the creative imagination that marked her earlier work with the clay; she merely dabbed at it as a much younger child would and declared, "Clay's no fun."

Sometimes a substitute satisfaction is worse than merely immature and partial. It gets a child into trouble. Bobby's mother took the truck away from him because he was abusing it. Frustrated, he attacked his mother with his fists. That was a partial satisfaction, all right, but with most mothers it would lead to retaliation and thus to further frustration.

Or again, a school child who fails in his academic work often seeks the acclaim of his fellows by becoming the class tough. That the satisfaction obtained is only partial and gets him into trouble needs little elaboration. (I may add that lots of the substitute satisfactions of adult life also are self-defeating—for example, a drunken spree as a substitute satisfaction when one has failed in a business deal or lost an argument with one's wife.)

Figure 6-7. How Long Will Bobby's Satisfaction Last?

We cannot ensure that the child will always be free from frustration—perhaps we would not want to, if we could. But we can help him learn to manage his frustrations. To manage frustrations does not mean to endure silently and without complaint. It means to know how to find substitute activities that really do yield satisfaction. It means learning to get right out of the frustrating situation whenever possible and into a situation where one can do really satisfying things. In short, whenever we find it necessary to thwart a child's purposeful activity, we should be at great pains to provide him with *alternative activities of high motivating value.*

QUESTIONS

1. Give an example when frustration has led to a beneficial result. (See page 188, line 2.)
2. The routine of school cannot be interrupted every time a child gets bored. What can a teacher do to keep the children from regressing to less mature behavior?
3. If there is a child who is truly unable to do well anything that is required in a particular class, what do you think should be done about his grade placement?

Long-Time Effects of Deprivation

All too often parents and teachers are moved by a sort of ascetic spirit, by a belief that it is good—for the other fellow—"to learn to do without." But whatever the virtues of *self*-denial when practiced as a means of religious grace or in order to help others, there is little value in privation and deprivation as such. On the contrary, there is a sizable body of evidence that deprivation has injurious effects on personality development.

Most of the intentional experiments have been made on animals, of course; few of us carry our ascetic beliefs far enough to want to expose children experimentally to intense deprivation.[6] But wars provide all-too-vivid illustrations of what happens when children are subjected to prolonged privation. At the International Children's Center (Bavaria) "unattached" children rescued from concentration camps after World War II could eat all they wanted, yet they persisted in taking pieces of bread and hiding them under their pillows.

> The children were aware that they would continue to be well fed. They understood, too, that the hidden pieces of bread would bring bugs and dirt. They even agreed to monitor themselves. "We understand why it should not be done," volunteered a fifteen-year-old boy to the Center's director. "But, whatever we do, we can't stop it entirely. You see, when bread has meant so much to you, you just can't do without it. It isn't a question of being hungry. It's just that you've got to have it, *yours,* amid *your* belongings, to nibble when you want a bit, something just to touch." And then he explained how each night, in the concentration camp, he had hugged his one chunk of bread, trying desperately to save some of

[6] Beach and Jaynes (48) have a comprehensive survey of the effects of early deprivation on animal behavior.

it against the next day's hunger pangs, but inevitably, on waking the next morning, finding that he had eaten it all.

Starvation had raised bread to an even greater importance than its necessity for physical survival. All a child's emotional longings—for parental love, for identity, for physical pleasure, for gaiety, for a feeling of participation in the world around him—had been forced to seek satisfaction in the simplest of symbols, a chunk of bread. [169]

Deprivation and Problem Behavior

Relevant here, also, are the findings from our clinics for problem children that unfulfillment of the child's need for love and security leads to attention-getting behavior, hostility, truancy, lying, stealing, and sex misbehavior. The studies of the Character Education Inquiry show that children who are poor are—forgivably enough, of course—more likely to be dishonest and selfish and less likely to be generous (100).

Some of these effects of privation are undoubtedly indirect. Thus the greater dishonesty of the children who have been deprived is in part a matter of direct learning. Tempted to theft by unsatisfied wants, the child is thereby learning how to steal and, simultaneously, acquiring various antisocial concepts. But there is also a *generalized* emotional attitude which tends to develop out of continued deprivation, that of getting and grabbing to satisfy one's wants, and this attitude is easily channeled in the direction of theft or other forms of selfishness. Nearly all the other character traits that are sequels to persistent frustration and privation are also unfavorable.

The School of Hard Knocks

An ancient tradition bids us beware of spoiling a child by indulging him too much. We don't want him to grow up "soft," and we fear that unless he attends the "School of Hard Knocks" he will not learn to react manfully to the inevitable disappointments of life. Perhaps the Spartans were the first to build up this attitude into a full-blown philosophy of life. The body, they argued, can be trained by graduated exposure to cold, fatigue, or pain. Why not the mind?

This may be an appropriate philosophy for a soldier-state. At any rate the Spartans tried it. They gave up almost every other kind of achievement and tried to toughen their sons—and their daughters, too, for that matter—for war, by means of deprivation. How did it work? Well, we still speak of Spartan fare, but that gift to our vocabulary is about their chief contribution to history. Even as warriors the Spartans did not last very long. The Spartan training at best made men who could endure, not men who could achieve.

During World War II Coventry was the first British city to be almost paralyzed by bombing. Rich and poor alike were reduced to a common level. Now who, do you suppose, most steadily endured the deprivations of destroyed homes, of loss of the conveniences of modern life—heat, light, running water? *Mass Observation,* a sort of public opinion poll which asks no questions but seeks to record what people say in public places, was on the spot to find out. It was the desperately poor people who were driven to panic by loss of their tragically meager belongings; the well-to-do, though they had lost so much more, had far greater fortitude in the emergency.

It is not merely in such major calamities that a difference is found. In a typical American city, Coons (109) found that children of low sociometric status (i.e., of low popularity, really) were less able to withstand frustration. It is the person who has proof in his own experience that life on the whole is good who has the strength to meet great disappointment and still hang on.

In any case, it is a curious doctrine that, in order to prepare a child for great evils to come, we should, as it were, vaccinate him with a few evils now. Aren't there enough unavoidable frustrations to give any child ample training in meeting them? Why go out of our way to provide extras?

QUESTIONS

1. *Psychologically* what is the difference between self-denial and ordinary privation or deprivation?
2. Elsewhere in the text we speak approvingly of frustration tolerance. How can this be taught if you merely wait for accidental frustrations?
3. Make a small list of indirect satisfactions that result from suppressed or repressed desires. Include some that are useful.
4. Search your memory for some sort of severe deprivation during childhood. Can you actually trace any sequels in your behavior? Be very careful not to read something into your experience.

Not All Privation Is Dangerous. The evidence does not indicate that we need fear the effects of every little privation or denial of a child's whim. Starting with a misinterpretation of Freud's doctrine of "repressed desires," an enormous folklore has grown up in the last thirty or forty years as to the baleful effects of suppression. Most of us joke about it, but we more than half believe, all the same, that we have to be careful about preventing a child from satisfying his desires.

How Deprivation Works

Let's keep our bearings by taking a simple example, such as the need to sneeze. It can be very powerful; and suppressing it leaves the individual feeling pretty frustrated. But it would probably never occur to us to suppose that the suppressed need to sneeze gets stored up in a sort of psychic reservoir called "The Unconscious," waiting for a chance to come out.[7]

Nor should we make such an assumption about other repressed desires or needs. A need or desire is a sort of tension generated when one of our activities or functions gets out of balance. For example, the need to sneeze is a strong tension set up when the lining of the nose is irritated. Hunger is a tension set up when the body is short of food.

Now we can't store or impound such tensions in the unconscious or anywhere else. Nor can they go on indefinitely. Either the tension is relieved or it simply subsides. We get over the tension of a suppressed sneeze quite quickly. Our hunger, too, subsides after a while even though we have not eaten. (Since, however, the tissues are still short of their usual nourishment, hunger will return.) More often when we repress or suppress a need, we seek and find some indirect satisfaction.[8] When hungry, we chew gum, smoke a cigarette, or take a drink, and for a time the tension is relieved. Somehow or other the

---

[7] I am criticizing here the popular version of The Unconscious, not the concept as employed by responsible psychoanalysts. Our understanding of motives obviously owes a great debt to Freud, even when, as in this case, the vigor of his metaphors invites popular misunderstanding.

[8] It is now pretty generally agreed that it is when repression is complicated by anxiety that it leads to neurosis or serious problem behavior. Here I am trying to show what happens in the simpler case of plain suppression.

organism gets back into some sort of balance—though the balance may not last.

What is true of organic needs like hunger seems to be true of all our needs or desires. They, too, are "tensions." As such they cannot be "stored." Repression, since it keeps us from satisfaction of the needs or desires, may keep the tension going for a while. But eventually the tension is somehow reduced.

Tension Reduction

I may as well confess that there's a lot we don't know about the basic processes underlying the reduction of tension. But if we look at the observable facts we can understand a great deal. Take a simple case where a child's motive or need is blocked. Any case. Younger brother wants to play with the "disintegration gun" that older brother got with cereal box tops. He is denied this privilege—his desire or need is frustrated or repressed. Maybe he whines a bit but soon he wanders off and finds something else to do, and the tension is reduced. If this happens often enough, the gun will cease to be a source of frustrated need.

This is typical. We can nearly always find a diversion that is, at least partially and for the time being, satisfactory. If the deprivation is prolonged, and if the same substitute satisfaction is repeatedly sought, it is learned like any other habit. To take the most obvious of all examples, the babe is hungry and wants milk—and nothing but milk. You, however, withhold the milk and give him grated carrots and spinach. Sometimes it is quite a struggle, but eventually you get him to accept, even to demand, the substitute satisfaction.

If only all cases of repression of motive were like that! But many substitute satisfactions aren't so wholesome. Many of them are socially inacceptable. If you chastise Billy, you will generally set up a tension in him for which the *direct* satisfaction would be a counterattack on you. (Please don't think he wouldn't like to!) Since he doesn't dare do that, he can get some *indirect* satisfaction by lording it over his young sister; and, if you don't watch out, that's what he will do. He may even acquire a regular habit of this sort. Quite often, also, substitute satisfaction, good as far as it goes, interferes with the child's satisfying other motives and thus begets inner conflicts. Maslow (296) believes that it is only when deprivation is "a threat to . . . his self-esteem or to his feeling of security that it has the multitude of effects . . . commonly attributed to frustration in general."

To sum up, suppression (or deprivation or frustration) is bad because it so often leads the child *to learn inadequate and objectionable ways of finding satisfaction.*

Past repression, then, may have been the *initiating* cause of a present "problem behavior." But we can put too much effort into a fruitless poking around to discover what that initial frustration or repression was. A child's *present* "problem behavior" is his way—a bad way—of meeting his *present* needs; it is not a direct response to old repression. Your task is to help him find more useful and more acceptable ways of gaining satisfaction of his *current* needs than those ways he has learned as a result of *former* deprivation or repression (134).

This may sound too commonplace. Certainly it is not so dramatic as the picture of repressed desires writhing like so many monstrous snakes in the cellar of "the Unconscious," ready to sneak out and strike if any opening is provided. But the dramatic isn't always the most useful explanation. When you look at repression in terms of what the child *learns* because of repression, you are ready for the question of what to do about it.

Let's take a concrete example. There is a popular view that thumb-sucking is due to too early weaning. Every child, the theory goes, has to satisfy a sucking need. Deprive him in infancy of the normal amount of "oral exercise" and he will seek it in some other form.

Let's grant that this explains—at least in some cases—why a child *begins* to suck his thumb.[9] But any thumb-sucker of five or six has had, by then, far more "oral exercise" than the child who is breast-fed for thirteen months and then weaned. So the continuation of the sucking habit can scarcely be due to an attempt, conscious or unconscious, to make up for an earlier deprivation, since over the whole period involved, this child has not been deprived of sucking. The *persistence* of thumb-sucking is clearly not due to a long-ago frustration but *to a need now present.*

Correction therefore requires that we help the child learn better ways of meeting his current need. Your basic problem is, What need is he

[9] There is some evidence, however, that thumb-sucking is more apt to be found in children who spend a lot of time sucking at the breast or the bottle, rather than in those deprived.

now satisfying by sucking his thumb? How does sucking satisfy it? And then—most important—what can you do to satisfy this present need in a better way? Clinical studies generally find that the thumb-sucker lacks security. Just why sucking his thumb quiets the security need is not clear, but it does.

Anxiety and Repression

There are, of course, a few very difficult cases. When needs go long unsatisfied, when motives are permanently blocked, tension may take the form of or be complicated by anxiety; and when the deprivations are seen as due to personal agents—that is, when frustration is involved—the anxiety is apt to be colored by hostility. *Prolonged* deprivation, therefore, tends to develop a personality that is habitually anxious, insecure, and unfriendly.

When of long standing, such cases are peculiarly difficult to deal with, for anxiety tends to prevent the child from solving or even attempting to solve his difficulties. It makes him, as the psychiatrist Harry S. Sullivan (431) has pointed out, less alert to the factors that might alleviate the tension, less effective in taking the necessary steps that would bring relief. Or perhaps worst of all, it prevents him from a simple acceptance of satisfaction.

Consider the case of the pitiful children in the rescue camps described above. Prolonged deprivation—of nearly every human need—had generated in them a basic insecurity and an anxiety-ridden attitude toward life. Thus even when they had food they were anxious about food, even when treated kindly they did not know how long all these good things would last; and so at bottom they were still unsatisfied. The simple satisfaction of a full belly could not be theirs. "You have all you want," says the stomach. "Yes," says the voice of their anxiety, "but will I have food tomorrow?" And so the tension is ever renewed. The ancient hunger, even if remembered, is over and done with; the need that must now be satisfied is not that of a hunger long ago left unsatisfied and therefore still in action, but the need that springs from neurotic anxiety.

Obviously the child with an anxiety neurosis needs specialized professional treatment. But anxiety can also be reduced by exposure to affectionate security; hostility can be lessened by persistent friendliness. You can seize the moments when the child's guard of anxious hostility is down and see to it that he finds—preferably by his own efforts—satisfaction and success. Little by little you can help him to replace the personality habits generated by need-deprivation with those of need-gratification. And better yet, by these same attitudes you can prevent anxiety from arising.

The distortions of behavior due to ordinary deprivation, frustration, or repression are real, of course, but they are not usually so terrifying as they have often been pictured. To repeat, repression is bad chiefly because it tends to teach the child inadequate techniques for obtaining satisfaction. But if we are alert, we can usually prevent him from learning such techniques, or we can guide him in unlearning them.

And it is surely a fortunate thing that this is so. Man, the Bible tells us, is born to trouble as the sparks fly upward. Birth itself is a frustrating experience, and from that moment on disappointment and obstruction are the lot of every child born of woman. Life in a community with one's fellows imposes upon every one of us countless moral and prudential restraints.

Thus, as we have seen in Chapter 2, on discipline and response to authority, the child's immaturity inevitably leads him to seek goals of which you cannot approve. You feel compelled to restrain him. However wise that is and however good your motives, it is apt to be frustrating to the child. Living chiefly in the present, moreover, children cannot find compensation for present loss by the thought of future gains. Few adults realize how often a child's impulses are thwarted. Childhood is full of joys and pleasures, but it is also full of frustration and sorrow.

I draw from this no pessimistic conclusion about life. I suppose that on net balance most children are fairly happy. I do find here a challenge to your best efforts to see to it that the inevitable frustrations of childhood are not allowed to interfere with wholesome development. I do find here a challenge to see to it that the child has not only frustrations but gratifications.

Asceticism vs. Self-Actualization

Are we, then, to think of need-fulfillment as good? Why, yes!

The satisfaction of needs—of any needs—is fundamentally healthy and intrinsically good. Consider such needs as these: the need for food, for warmth, for safety; the need to love and to be loved, to have a group to belong to, to be respected, to respect oneself; the need to achieve worthily according to one's talents, to understand the world about one, to understand oneself, to be free to be oneself—all these, which are the truly human needs, ought to be satisfied.[10] Need-fulfillment, as Goldstein (170) observes, is self-fulfillment, self-actualization. To live is to satisfy one's needs, to live more abundantly is to satisfy them more completely. Robert Louis Stevenson has put the case for us in "The Celestial Surgeon":

> If I have faltered more or less
> In my great task of happiness . . .
> If beams from happy human eyes
> Have moved me not; if morning skies,
> Books, and my food, and summer rain
> Knocked on my sullen heart in vain:—
> Lord, Thy most pointed pleasure take,
> And stab my spirit broad awake . . .

It is a curious comment on the culture of our times that this obvious truth needs to be asserted. What is it that makes us so afraid of joy and happiness and self-expression? Even those who see the folly of this fear cannot wholly escape it. Purely sensual delights seem somehow childish, if not downright indecent—except of course when they can be translated into art or music or poetry, which somehow makes them respectable. And too much laughter is vulgar and common.

There are historical roots for this fear, no doubt, but they can hardly account for its strength and persistence. It must somehow be sustained by the kind of civilization we have created and live in. At any rate, this fear borders on the neurotic.

Need-fulfillment is not mainly a matter of having the right kind

[10] The list is borrowed from Maslow (298); it could be much expanded. The few truly "bad" impulses that bedevil us—hatred and cruelty chiefly—seem to spring from the frustration of needs, not from gratification.

of physical conditions. These, yes, but more important are the social gratifications. It is for this reason that there is nowadays so much stress on the value of reassurance, support, permissiveness, approval, and acceptance. These are all ways of satisfying deep-lying needs of the child.

There is, of course, danger in teaching the child that he has only to voice his desires to have them satisfied. More and more as he grows older he must learn that the greatest satisfactions come from his own

Figure 6-8. "Me do, me do myself!"

efforts. If conditions are favorable, this is an easy lesson to learn: the desire to *achieve for oneself* is one of the dependable motives that nearly all of us learn. Think how early the child says, "Me do, me do myself!" What we, as adults, should do to promote this learning is to ensure that the child's efforts—if intelligent at his level of maturity—will usually bring success and gratification. Such an atmosphere will strengthen, not weaken, the child's tendency to vigorous striving.

Not every need can be gratified. The fulfillment of any one need must be seen in relation to other needs and impulses. The unregulated pursuit of every impulse leads not to all-round need-satisfaction but to need-conflict. This even the very young child learns. He learns, too, that his goals may conflict with those of others and cannot always be immediately achieved. Learns, if he has been properly taught, that there are greater satisfactions to be gained if immediate impulse is sometimes subordinated to more ultimate ends. This, of course, is the basic principle upon which all morality depends.

But to deny the child's satisfactions merely for the sake of denying them is to act as if the *means* of moral growth were its *end,* and to misconceive also the nature of the means. For it is only when the child *learns for himself* to balance satisfactions against each other —or better yet, so organizes his motives that he seldom needs to strike a balance—that moral growth occurs.

Such healthy organization of one's motives into a sort of hierarchy of higher and lower takes place not when needs are thwarted but when they are satisfied. Continued deprivation tends to obsessive preoccupation with the unsatisfied need; gratification releases the child from this obsession. His hunger satisfied, the child is free to do something else: to sleep, to play, or even to study. His need for security and love satisfied, a child is not under compulsion to seek attention or to demand a constant show of love. *Only when our "lower" needs are satisfied are we really free to seek the satisfaction of "higher" or more idealistic motives.*

And when the child's environment is thus free from undue frustration and privation, when he finds that if he works at it he can usually satisfy his needs, there is a generalization of the emotional attitude that goes with success in satisfying needs. The child becomes more optimistic, free from anxiety, friendly.[11] It seems probable that many traits characteristic of the healthy adult are positive consequences of gratification of the child's need for love—such traits as the ability to allow independence to the loved one, and the ability to love without giving up one's independence. Need-fulfillment tends to develop a specific kind of character in children, just as does need-deprivation.[12]

---

[11] This point has been cogently developed by Maslow (297).

[12] Most of the evidence on this point comes from the studies of what happens when children are not deprived. What we should have is more research on what happens when needs are *met.* But consider, e.g., the Updegraff and Keister experiment (452) earlier referred to. It was set up to see how to cure the ill effects of failure, a sort of deprivation. What the investigators did was to show the positive *good* effects on character of experiencing success—i.e., of need-satisfaction. (See also Levy [268, 269, 270] and Maslow [297].)

Summary

A motive is to be thought of less as a distinct act than as the dynamic aspect of every behavior, as that which gives direction to behavior. Although the infant has a considerable repertory of needs that motivate him, these are rapidly modified. All motivation must be regarded as the resultant of *both* heredity *and* acquisition. Human experience rather than human nature determines what it is that will satisfy human needs.

Frustration of motivated behavior leads to an increase in tension directed in the first instance against the frustrating barrier but spreading to other persons or objects in the environment and leading to many forms of substitute behaviors. Too often these are socially inacceptable or do not, in the long run, well serve the individual's purposes. Nonetheless, they may serve the immediate purpose of reducing tension and so become habitual. It should be our purpose to teach children constructive ways of reacting to frustration. And whenever possible it should be our purpose not to frustrate them. Need-fulfillment is self-fulfillment. The need-gratified child is free to organize his motives for "higher" ends and tends to develop a friendlier, more secure personality.

7

Influencing Children's Motives

Are there dependable motives that can be appealed to in order to get children to do or to want to do what we want them to? The answer is "Yes!" But to influence children's behavior in this way requires sensitivity to the highly individual character of each child's motives and an ability to get beneath the surface to hidden motives.

To see to it that children learn what is good for them sounds like an old-fashioned idea and one that is at some variance with the spontaneity stressed in previous chapters. Yet it is an unavoidable duty of both parent and teacher. It is necessary, then, that we make effective use of motives and incentives. That is what this chapter is about.

The Nature of Incentives

You will remember that every action can be thought of as motivated. But some actions, your own or a child's, are too weakly motivated to get under way. Some means has to be found to strengthen the motivation. In other cases, there are goals and purposes that *you* think a child should pursue but about which he thinks otherwise—or just plain doesn't see what you mean. You have to find some

Figure 7-1. Incentives as Supplementary Goals

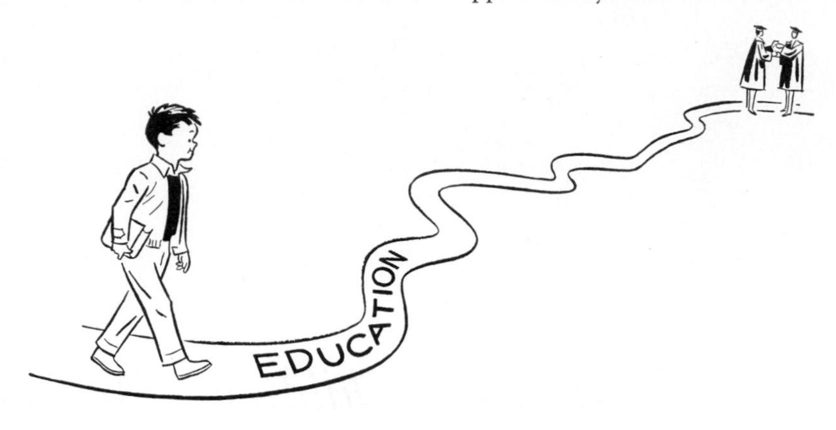

motive that will get him moving toward the goal. Such supplementary motives are called incentives.[1]

If the road to a chosen goal is long and arduous, we may have to strengthen our wavering purpose by supplying ourselves with a

[1] I have here described incentives as incitements to action. Others (e.g., Hilgard and Russell [202]) speak of them as satisfiers of a motive—the incentive of candy satisfies a need. But the incentive of candy also stirs the child to pick up his toys. The two descriptions merely emphasize two aspects of the same phenomenon. Rewards, including negative rewards or punishments, are incentives—supplemental motives. (Except when we speak of virtue as its own reward.)

supplementary motive. Or, like a cold motor that needs a rich mixture at first, we may need a "shot in the arm" to get us started.

I have often overheard a child apply the same philosophy. "That will take an awful long time," he tells himself, "but maybe if I give myself a coke for every two hours I work at it, I can get it done."

More often it is you who must provide the supplemental goals. You promise the child a treat if he does what you ask him to, or you "promise" a deprivation if he does not. You remind Jimmy how pleased his father will be if he writes a nice letter to Grandpa, or you tell Cecilia you will take away her dolls if she leaves them strewn around on the floor. You promise a class a visit to the art museum when a certain unit of study is finished; or you threaten it with detention if certain work is not done. In all these cases, you throw in an extra motive in order to get the child moving toward some goal you regard as important.

Intrinsic versus Extrinsic Motives

Such incentives are sometimes called extrinsic motives and are contrasted somewhat unfavorably with intrinsic motives—that is, with doing something for its own sake. For example, it is clearly better for a child to practice the piano because he enjoys himself than because he is to be rewarded ("bribed") if he puts in his time. If a child just plain wants to do what is good for him, you have no problem. But what are you to do if—or rather when—he doesn't?

The advocates of intrinsic motives have an answer. Weak intrinsic motivation, they tell us, in generally the result of poor understanding. The child fails to see the true advantages of the goal you hold before him; you should try to get these across. It is certainly true that a formidable amount of "lack of effort" (and consequent "misbehavior") is due to the fact that children don't understand what is wanted of them. The child who is urged to pick up toys to make a room "tidy" may not know—or care!—what "tidy" means.

In school, children, being a little older, may understand *what* they are supposed to learn—"the chief exports of Brazil"—but they don't know why. It is the function of the teacher, so the argument runs, to link this sort of knowledge to the child's own goals. Then he will be intrinsically motivated to learn.

But it is unrealistic to hope that the teacher can effect such a linkage for each and every one of the forty-seven pupils whom she must instruct this week—it says here in the course of study—in the economic geography of South America. Perhaps she can seriously interest a dozen. Perhaps another dozen or more will try to learn because others do. (But *that's* extrinsic motivation.) The rest? Later, perhaps. Not now. Many of these children are simply not mature enough to see any value in such stuff.

Maturation and Motivation

Should we, then, postpone our effort to modify the child's behavior until he has matured a little more? That would certainly be the easy way out, and in many cases would be the right way as well. It *is* necessary to respect the child's level of maturity; and it is surprising, if we but wait, how many problems of motivation simply evaporate. The child who drives his grandmother to distraction by banging a spoon on his tray will drop the practice of his own accord after a few weeks; the preadolescent boy who feels compelled to be rude to every female will, in time, find other ways to assert his masculinity.

There are reasons, however, why we cannot go all out in a program of merely waiting for the child to develop. In the first place, there are some learnings that *cannot* be postponed. A young child can seldom understand—certainly not fully—the need for certain health or safety precautions; yet if these precautions are not somehow imposed on him, tragedy may result. Almost any sort of motivation that teaches the toddler to keep off the street is justified. Another example: if a child is to become even a fair musician he has to do a lot of practicing before he is mature enough to understand *fully* why it is necessary. In school the teacher is often under pressure to adhere to a course of study despite her doubts that some of the pupils are quite ready for certain prescribed experiences. Waiting for maturation may be a theoretically sounder procedure but it isn't permitted.

Inducing Readiness

The doctrine of maturation has contributed to a fatalistic attitude that is wholly unnecessary. It may be true that "you can lead a horse to water but you can't make him drink." But usually a little exercise will quickly change the horse's motivation (even though water must then be denied him until he has thoroughly cooled off).

If a child is unresponsive to a certain kind of motive, instead of waiting for some mysterious sort of maturation, why not provide him with experiences that will increase his responsiveness? Children come to school, for example, with very great differences in their motivation for reading. Some have never seen a person reading for enjoyment—virtually have never seen anyone read. They have no yearning for it; it means nothing to them. Others see their parents or older siblings with noses always in a book or newspaper; for them reading is an evidently fascinating business.

Obviously the first-grade teacher cannot ignore such differences in children's acquired motivations; but neither should she sit with folded hands waiting for "reading readiness" to mature. Her job is to *create* a motivation toward reading, not by bribing the child nor by telling him how wonderful reading is, but by supplying experiences that will remedy his deficiencies in background so that he will want to read. The role of the parent and teacher is that of actively stimulating the acquisition of motives through experience.

When literacy teachers first tried to get Mexican villagers to read they met the objection: "But, señor, here in our village is nothing to read. Why should I learn?" So street signs were put up on all the corners, though everyone knew all the streets without them. But now it became a matter of pride to be able to read the signs. The motive was created.

Toilet control admirably illustrates both the possibilities and the limitations of the effort to speed up the process of maturing. There is a certain urgency in our culture about this. ("You just can't let the child go on that way forever!") There is, however, no technique of training yet conceived that will do any good until a certain ill-defined level of maturation, party physiological, has been attained. Harassed mothers simply have to resign themselves for some months to the necessary complications.

Even after training begins to take hold, the child's lack of full comprehension makes things difficult. No more than a puppy can a sixteen-month-old toddler understand why toilet cleanliness is so important. Accordingly, many mothers try to train the child the same way they try to train a puppy—chiefly by punishment, an extrinsic motive if there ever was one.

But the child isn't merely a puppy, and what he learns as a result of the punishment often extends far beyond the toilet-training situation. There are enough cases in which drastic toilet training is associated with neurosis in later childhood to give us pause. Rewards are perhaps less dangerous in this situation than punishment; but if given in an atmosphere of tense emotionalism, they too can lead to some bizarre learnings. The expressions used by some mothers in urging a child to defecate give him the idea that the feces are something valuable which he is being urged to give up. The result may be a stubborn attempt to retain the feces or, in other cases, a rather messy attempt to find out what makes them so precious. In some cases, the whole later personality development is affected. Learning without understanding, or rather learning with very imperfect understanding—for there is probably no learning without some understanding—can be dangerous.

Nonetheless, the time comes when, with physical and intellectual maturation, the child can be induced to adopt customary toilet practices, though still without fully understanding the adult goals of cleanliness and privacy. This is usually accomplished by the use of such extrinsic motivations or incentives as praise or rebuke. If the incentives are not too forcibly applied, toilet control is finally achieved without any real strain on either mother or child.[2]

Incentives in the School

The situation is closely parallel in school learnings. A large proportion of children in the first grade, for example, have no real sense of what a number is. Even the simplest arithmetic operation, therefore, is a complete mystery. If, as is too often the

[2] You may ask whether toilet control is not always, even in the adult, externally motivated—that is, the control is never itself directly satisfying, however its effects may be. Should not this fact impress those who insist so sharply that we should never use extrinsic motives?

case, they are induced by extraneous motivation to "learn" such operations as $2 + 2 = 4$, they get the idea that arithmetic is merely a bunch of purely mechanical processes—meaningless tricks. And as Brownell and his associates have shown (78), many such children as late as the fifth or sixth grades still show the ill effects of such extraneous motivation for merely rote learning of arithmetic at a time when they were too immature for meaningful learning. Jerome Bruner (80) has shown that if we make the child's learning seem too important, if we make a grim business out of learning, with great rewards and fearful punishments attached, the child is very likely to develop anxiety about the whole learning process and become "blocked" or functionally stupid. Pushing too hard upon the child's readiness to learn, whether it is bladder control or formal arithmetic, clearly leads to distortions of the learning process.

So far we go with the critics of extraneous motivation. But suppose you know that the children in a certain class *are* ready for a certain kind of learning. For example, any child who really belongs in the first grade is mature enough to be taught, not, indeed, arithmetical *operations* of a formal sort, but certain basic number facts. So you set about teaching them. You use entirely appropriate procedures.

It ought to work. Children like to learn; the mere activity of learning, of understanding something that is within their range, is fascinating. It is such learning we speak of as intrinsically motivated.

Nevertheless, if we are realistic we know that not all the pupils in the class will be thrilled at the same time by the task set by the teacher. Suppose she employs the standard introduction to arithmetic which consists of putting matches into groups of two and three and counting them. Bobby would rather pound nails. Davy would rather finger-paint. Nothing wrong with either, but how is a teacher to make sure that all the children attain the necessary arithmetic skills? Is there any reason, then, why the teacher should not enhance the attractiveness of that goal by supplementary motives or incentives?

None at all, provided that the extrinsic incentives lead to the real goal, in this case that of understanding "two-ness" and "three-ness." Extrinsic incentives, however, too often miss the target—or worse, hit the wrong target. If the incentive of competition merely leads Davy to see whether he can arrange matches in two's and three's faster than Susy can, he would be better occupied at finger painting. If we give a child some trifle for every little service, we have to be careful that he doesn't develop the "gimmes." We must be perpetually vigilant to be sure that the reward does not usurp the place of the real educational goal, that a *supplementary means*—such as teacher-approval, beating the other fellow, getting good marks—does not become for the child the main end. Subject to this limitation, however, external incentives have a worthy and necessary place in guiding the child's activities.

Sedative and Stimulative Rewards

The promise of a Scout uniform if a boy keeps his room tidy for two months may stimulate him for about that long. But when he gets the uniform, what's to prevent his slipping back into his old sloppy habits? Many a mother will testify sadly, "Nothing at all!" Is it different with many of the rewards used to stimulate school learning? Most artificial incentives wear off pretty fast and cannot be repeated too often. Morgan (320) speaks of these as sedative rewards.

The successive ranks in the Scouts and similar organizations represent a valiant, though not always effective, effort at more continuously stimulating rewards or progressive goal setting. Wherever possible we should utilize incentives that can be repeated again and again if they lead to the desired conduct, or incentives that are progressively replaced by others that carry the child forward toward more mature activity.

Extrinsic Motives and Learning

All along we have spoken of extrinsic motives or incentives as a means of controlling or guiding a child's actions. That is necessary, no doubt, but as teachers (and parents) we are also interested in getting them to learn. Are extrinsic motives effective for learning? If so, are they as effective as intrinsic motives?

To the first question the answer is "Yes." Experiments in learning are unanimous on this point. Indeed, practically all animals and most human experiments are based on incentives. Animal training is almost entirely obtained by extrinsic motivation.

It used to be thought that learning is proportional to the strength of motive. It is now known that the connection between the two is much less direct. The function of motivation is to get the organism to *act*. And learning is contingent upon action.

Of course the motive may be too weak to get us to act at all; or too weak to get us to act in the face of contrary and stronger motives. To that extent a stronger motive begets more learning. But it is now fairly sure, from experimental evidence, that a weakly motivated action—provided it occurs at all—leads to as much learning as a strongly motivated one.

This is a consoling finding for teachers when they consider how weak are the extrinsic motives—or for that matter, the intrinsic ones —with which they have to work most of the time. As to the issue of the relative effectiveness of extrinsic and intrinsic motives, it would seem to indicate that there is no fundamental difference.

Except—and it is a big "except"—the difference already dwelt on. Intrinsic motivation by definition is motivation toward its own goal. Extrinsic motivation is a supplement designed to further another goal —but often failing to do what it is designed to do. Prizes and awards too often are incentives to actions quite at variance with the learning activity desired. An incident in *Tom Sawyer* admirably illustrates the difficulty. A prize Bible was to be awarded to any child who presented a certain number of tickets, each showing that he had memorized a Bible verse. Tom had hardly progressed beyond the stage of memorizing such verses as "Jesus wept." He wanted that prize; but instead of exposing himself to the wisdom of Holy Writ by memorizing the required verses, he engaged in an extensive commercial traffic, swapping various articles of value for the precious tickets which the others had fairly won.

Everyone was astonished when Tom presented the "evidence" of learning and Tom was full of pride. But who was cheated?

Fortunately, there is another side to all this. Properly managed, incentives can lead a child step by step to the real goal. Judicious praise does actually help children to learn grammar. And best of all, incentives sometimes lead to the right kind of activity for its own sake—i.e., to intrinsically motivated and self-starting learning. The child who needs many accessory motivations to get him to wash his face and hands may in time actually come to take pride in looking clean and spruce. (Both the *may* and the *in time* must be emphasized.) The child who is inveigled by various incentives to study geography may find that maps are fascinating things. The child who has to be prodded into practicing at the piano sometimes comes to love music and spends hours at it of his own accord; such miracles happen.

Even compulsion may lead to the "interiorization of motives." Rules of conduct grudgingly obeyed at first are in time accepted as one's own. Sometimes, that is! We need much more investigation to learn under what conditions compulsion leads, on the one hand, to resistance and conflict; on the other, to acceptance and even joy in the activity. At any rate, once we get started on a task, the sense of progress keeps us going.[3] Interest grows by what it feeds on.

QUESTIONS

1. Can an extraneous motive ever be intrinsic, too?
2. Try, without looking it up in some reference, to distinguish between extrinsic and intrinsic motives. Is the distinction merely one of degree?
3. Many educators are very loud in their opposition to extrinsic motives. Why? Are there other objections than those implied above?

Dependable Incentives

As we saw in the previous chapter, we must surrender the hope of finding a universal pattern of motives that is due to heredity alone. But among persons who grow up in similar circumstances there develop many broad uniformities. Despite the acquisition of numerous quite individual motivations, it is probable that as we grow older the number of motives we share with others of similar status and experience grows greater. It is these uniformities which give coherence to societies and social groups and which make predictions of behavior possible. We may speak of these as *dependable motives*.[4]

What are some of the motivations upon which we can usually

[3] H. F. Wright (485) has an interesting theoretical treatment.

[4] Klineberg (252), who apparently introduced this term, seems to imply that relative dependability depends only on organismic factors; we stress that it may come from either environmental or organismic influences.

depend in our society? And—of particular interest—what are the incentives we can use in getting a child to do the things he should or must do? (By which it is to be feared we usually mean, What incentives can we use in getting the child to do what we want him to do?)

Some Common Incentives

Commands, Requests, and Suggestions

A somewhat special form of this problem concerns the verbal forms used in giving commands or suggestions. Obviously our words operate on the child to stir up incentives of one sort or another. The food that no longer sufficiently attracts the infant by its taste or smell is made more attractive by being praised. In school, the teacher's words touch off motives that cooperate with whatever intrinsic motivation to learn is present. And the glowing words of salesman or orator stir us to actions for which our motivations were otherwise too weak.

Not all words, however, are equally effective. Hence, scattered through manuals of rhetoric and of public speech and in instructions for salesmen and for army officers, even in books for teachers, there is a considerable mass of information based on everyday experience about the proper forms of command. Now it is one of the tasks of psychology to tease out the common principle or principles that run through everyday rules of thumb, even though they are drawn from very diverse experiences and are intended for very specialized applications. Generalization, however, is difficult. For this reason it is often desirable to set up experiments, not to prove, as some wag has said, what everyone knows, but to isolate the general principle that enables us to cope with a wide range of everyday events.

For example, it may be clear enough that Miss Clark and Miss Brackett direct their pupils very effectively, and we note that both of them make much use of direct, positive command. It is not clear, however, that it is their use of direct command which makes their leadership outstanding; it might be something else we haven't noticed. We can find out if we set up an experiment in which other possible factors are ruled out and the form of verbal incentive is the determinant.

This was the plan in Johnson's investigation (233). In each experiment two contrasting forms of verbal incentive were employed: specific versus general or vague command; definite versus indefinite suggestion; positive versus negative; encouraging versus discouraging suggestion; calming versus pressuring command. The exact verbal forms used and the results achieved are shown in Figure 7-2.

"These experiments show that *positive, unhurried, specific,* and *encouraging* types of direction secure more performance from others than *negative, hurried, general,* and *discouraging* types of directions" (14, pp. 251ff.). The conclusion seems plausible even to the point of being rather obvious. Yet the mother or the teacher, eager for quick results and faced with the child's fumbling efforts, is apt to be in too great a hurry to formulate suggestions either specifically or positively. Too much criticism of the child's efforts, however constructive its intent in the correction of errors, is likely to seem

Figure 7-2. Effect of Various Methods of Giving Commands and Suggestions

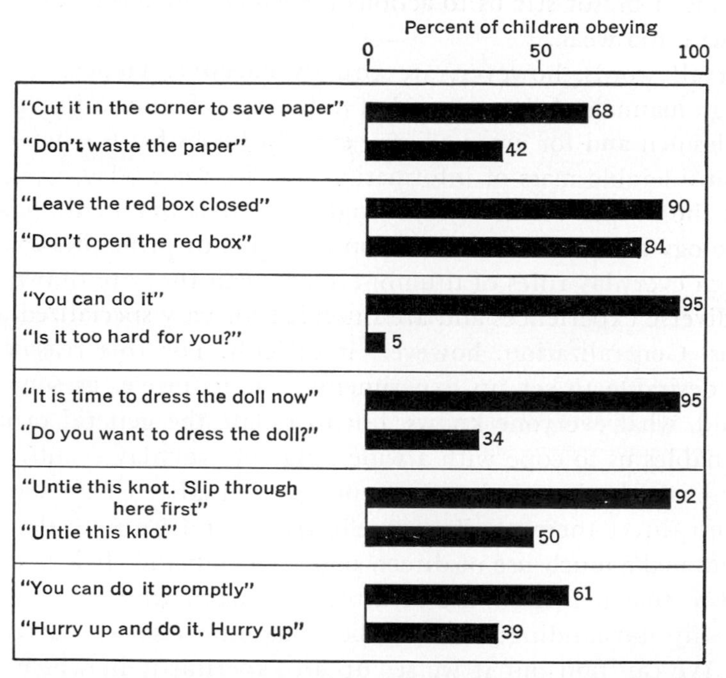

Reproduced from J. E. Anderson, *The psychology of development and personal adjustment,* 1949, Holt, Rinehart and Winston. Drawn by permission from data of M. W. Johnson (233).

merely a form of nagging; it either depresses him or leads to resistance. McClure (302) and Belogianis *et al.* (51) obtained generally confirming results. Meyers (312) found that negative commands reduced the maturity as well as the amount of activity. And Klein's study (251) shows the same general pattern prevailing in Germany. Gesell and Ilg (166) recommend a list of key words for phrasing requests in such a way as to avoid arousing resistance: "You forgot," "Guess what," "Different," "Surprise," "Secret." These invite to a pleasant future. For effective action, particularly for action that is supposed to lead to learning, a relaxed atmosphere must be provided.

Interest and Interests as Incentives

A vast and confusing literature has grown up in education concerning the role of interest. Part of the difficulty comes from confusing objective interests with the feeling of interest. Strictly speaking, the feeling of interest should not be regarded as a motive at all. The child does not do something because he feels interest (though we often say so); rather the child does something and feels interest because he is active.

There is, however, a more concrete meaning of the term "interest," especially when used in the plural. A child's interests are those objects and objective situations that observably stir him to action. In this latter concrete and objective sense, the term is merely a specialized name for motive or goal. Consequently, there is no question that we can control a child's actions by appeal to his interests. We do it all the time, particularly when we want to divert him from some undesirable conduct. The real problem concerns the use of these interests as supplementary motives—that is, incentives—in getting children to learn.

Which are the interests that have wide appeal to children? An enormous amount of research has been devoted to this apparently straightforward investigation. Carefully verified lists of the interests favored by children of different age, social status, sex, residence areas, and so on, have been drawn up. These lists are of considerable use to curriculum builders and textbook or story writers.

Unfortunately, interests change with bewildering rapidity—consider the interest in the hula hoop—and the effort to get below the surface to a list of "basic" interests has not so far been very successful. Moreover, the effective interests vary enormously from individual to individual, from one class to another. Rosamund likes fairy tale romances, Harriet likes rather broad humor. Ernest is a rock collector, Dave is crazy about basketball.

A few years ago, when the neighborhood store was a chummy personal enterprise, "playing store" was a widespread interest that could be and was often used to get children to learn a little arithmetic. One wonders whether the more impersonal supermarkets generate the same interest. In any case, neither playing store nor any other similar interest will work for all pupils or for very long. The teacher must therefore make intelligent use of what Ernest Hilgard calls the "provisional try." If one interest does not cause the children—or some of the children, or a particular child—to come to life, try another interest. There is no scientific substitute for the teacher's alertness to each child's interests.[5]

Without such use of pupil interests, very much less would be learned in school. Nonetheless, the doctrine of interest has led to some very shallow teaching. It is one thing to enlist the support of a child's already established interest in collecting coins as a means of helping him learn geography; it is quite another thing to aim at interesting the pupil, at keeping him interested. That is too much like sugar-coating a bitter pill to get it down. Telling funny stories may make the class interesting but does not guarantee that pupils will learn. The teacher who is always trying to dress things up in an interesting garb is missing the real task, which is to help the child discover in the learning activity—not in the sugar-coating that surrounds it—those aspects that are for him significant and important.[6]

Knowledge of Results

Research on how children learn has also yielded valuable clues about effective and dependable incentives. It has been

---

[5] But surely by now my readers will have seen that the findings of scientific investigation serve to sensitize persons to the problems and to indicate where such alertness is called for.

[6] In the main this is what John Dewey meant in championing the role of interest in education. The fact that he seems to have been misunderstood both by opponents and by many would-be followers shows how tricky the term "interest" is. The plural form "interests" seems less ambiguous.

established that information about how well a child is doing acts as a keen spur to his further effort. This motivation is effective in proportion as it is *prompt* and *specific*. To say "You did well yesterday" is much less valuable than to say to a child immediately after he has done something: "That is very much better—your paper is very neat and there is only one mistake—here." [7]

Habitual Situations

Popular psychology has long recognized that familiar surroundings are a big help. A child who refuses to sleep in a strange bed (though apparently not at all afraid) will drop off instantly in his familiar crib. A regular place and time for study helps the high school student to get down to work. The motivating effect of the familiar is an argument for at least some degree of regularity in school scheduling.

There is a negative side to this motive, however. Children, perhaps more than adults, are disturbed by any deviation from the habitual. Many children, e.g., won't eat when away from home. We need to see to it that children are exposed to enough variety that they do not become slaves of the habitual.

Novelty

Little need be said about the familiar incentive of novelty. Every teacher, experienced or inexperienced, does what she can to bring out novel aspects in what she teaches. It is an excellent incentive and has few bad side effects. The chief trouble is that novelty is difficult to sustain. It serves to start children going but something else must keep them at it.

The Desire to Achieve

Other dependable motives are closely related to the child's image of himself. Thus the desire to achieve cannot even be sensibly discussed without asking what achievement means to a

[7] The extensive experimental literature has been briefly summarized by English (138) and by Stroud (429).

given child. The infinite variety, not to say uniqueness, found in the development of each self makes somewhat artificial any attempt to find achievement motives common to all children. Yet there is a sense in which selves are alike as well as different, and thus it is true that everyone (or virtually everyone) responds to the challenge to achieve if only we can find what achievement looks like to that individual.

In our culture we begin very early to instill this motive in our children, especially in middle- and upper-class families. We reward the struggle to do things well, we rebuke the refusal to struggle. Everyone is expected to have high ambitions. In fact, in the famous study of the typical city of Middletown (290), it was found that ambition outruns any prospect of success in a formidable proportion of young people.[8] Such ambitions soon lose their potency as motives. A child will not long desire what he no longer really hopes to achieve. An adjustment between the aspiration level and relevant abilities and opportunities eventually has to be made.

Moreover, as implied just above, achievement has to be thought of in terms of a child's own goals, not those someone else dreams up for him. A specific goal or a level of achievement which to one child spells success to another spells failure. Much research has accordingly been directed at finding out what determines the child's *level of aspiration.*

As might be expected, the evidence is that success nearly always raises the child's level of aspiration. We seldom weary of success; each victory spurs us on to attempt more difficult goals, to gain a greater success.[9] Failure usually has the opposite effect of depressing the level of aspiration, but the effect is less consistent; quite often, indeed, failure results in raising the level (104, 239, 380).

This last finding might seem to confirm the view of those educational theorizers who esteem themselves "hardheaded realists." They hold that education has been made too easy, that children need to experience failure as well as success. Occasional failure, perhaps. Certainly every child inevitably does have a taste of this bitter medicine. But Keister's (242) study shows that toleration of failure is

---

[8] See also the summary of research data on vocational interests in Horrocks (212).

[9] Too easy a success is not, of course, really success. It is only this kind of effortless accomplishment that becomes boring.

learned *only when it is temporary and is linked with the expectation of ultimate success.*

There is no evidence that repeated bludgeoning by failure is useful. On the contrary, there are found in the research two sorts of effect—both unfortunate (380). Some children are beaten down to the point where they no longer aspire to succeed. Great ingenuity is required if we are to find for such children a goal which seems to them at the same time possible of attainment and worth achieving. Other children after exposure to continued failure seem to get hardened to it, but their behavior is not improved thereby. Instead, their attitude seems to be a careless and half-defiant, "If anybody can do it, I can." So they try again and again. They continue therefore to be motivated but to be motivated by unrealistic and unrealizable goals (380).[10] Gruen's (182) results suggest that there may be personality factors determining whether a child becomes apathetic or overoptimistic and unrealistic. In both cases, the effect of prolonged failure must be judged unwholesome.[11]

Success and failure are not the only determinants of the level of aspiration. Even when open rivalry with others is avoided, the level is affected by knowledge of one's relative standing in a group of one's peers (11, 99, 203), and even by the child's knowledge of what others in the group expect (200). The child's self-confidence, or lack of it, also makes a difference in the kind of target he sets up to shoot at (181, 277); and this is influenced by previous success (in relation to his own aspirations) but also by social encouragement and discouragement. Teachers who say to a child, "You can do it if you try" may actually get him to raise his level of aspiration; but if he raises it too high and fails, the effect of discouragement will be all the greater.

On the other hand, tasks must be really challenging if they are to get the child started. At a fairly early age, in fact, the child will give himself certain handicaps if the task seems too easy—just as the golf course architects impose bunkers and sand traps. In school, however, there are always enough real difficulties to make such artificial barriers unnecessary. The problem is to find the kind and

[10] Rats punished for nonperformance of very difficult tasks show a similar objective lack of realism (142). We aren't just sure whether it is their level of aspiration that is affected!

[11] Compare also the experimental findings concerning frustration and deprivation cited in the preceding chapter.

degree of difficulty that for a particular child constitutes a challenge.

We began by saying that the desire to achieve is a very dependable incentive. It is. All children do desire to achieve and that is a motive that will actually set them in motion. But the above discussion indicates that the incentive is itself a very complex thing, that to get a child to desire to achieve is by no means so simple as it sounds. Certainly it is most unsafe to expect a child to rise to the bait when the task is formulated for him by someone else. Only those tasks that lie within *his* level of aspiration and that have for other reasons been accepted as *his own* represent a challenge. When, however, the goal is thus accepted, the desire to achieve may act as a powerful additional motive or incentive to pursue it with vigor.[12]

Rivalry and Competition

Children seldom respond to the motive of rivalry or competition until about age two; from then on, as seen in experiments in which there are artfully arranged competitive situations, the motive becomes more and more effective—at least to age seven (179, 265, 307). At age six as high as 86 percent of the children show competitiveness when urged to see whether they can build with blocks better than another child. Yet even at these ages Wolf (480) found very considerable individual differences in the children's responsiveness to this incentive. Maller (295) found that school children work harder and more effectively when seeking rewards for themselves than when working for a group. But group competition was also effective, especially if the group was a natural one of the children's own choosing. (Not unnaturally, children are not particularly enchanted when the teacher tries to get the front rows to compete with the back rows!)

The relative effectiveness of competition (and I believe of all incentives) is in part determined by the task to be performed. Thus in Wolf's experiments, competition was more effective in tasks involving large-muscle activity than in tasks of a precise and finely coordinated character. Still more important is the fact that compe-

[12] In Chapter 14 we shall discuss the importance of the motive for achievement in the total organization of a life plan. McClelland (301) devotes a whole book to showing the theoretical and practical implications of this protean motive.

tition is seldom, if ever, the sole motive; other motives reinforce or oppose it, and the relative motivating strength of competition varies accordingly.

Logically, competition and cooperation are opposites; psychologically this is not necessarily so. The same sort of activities may serve either or both; and it is frequently impossible to determine, especially from a single act, whether the motive is competitive or cooperative. Indeed, children may compete in seeing how cooperative they can be! And finally, as Jersild (226, p. 161) points out, "the child who is not actively competing may in actuality be highly competitive in his attitude; his own standing may mean so much to him that he will not join in group activity for fear that he won't make a good showing."

All in all, however, probably the most common motive appealed to in the culture of the Western world—and apparently in this matter we must also include the Soviet Empire—is that of rivalry and competition. For one thing it is so easily manipulated. Any reader with the least bit of imagination can find a way to stir up rivalry.[13] In many ways competitiveness is the dominant note of our civilization.

Many sensitive students of the contemporary scene believe, however, that competitiveness has grown beyond useful bounds. The situation suggests a parallel with the history of the saber-toothed tiger. This species of the great cats, as is well known, started to develop enormous canine teeth, and for a time these fangs proved very useful in rending the creature's prey. But in successive generations the fangs grew ever longer and heavier, and in time they so interfered with other functions that the saber-toothed tiger became extinct. In the same way, competitiveness has certainly been a major factor in bringing our civilization to its present height; but signs are multiplying that it is now so strong a motive in so many people that it is destructive of other values and may endanger the very civilization it helped to create. Modern technology has invented "playthings" too dangerous to be put in the hands of men imbued with the desire to triumph over others at any cost or by any means. In industrial as well as in international relations, the fangs of ruthless competitiveness seem to be hypertrophied beyond a useful size, if not to the point of acute danger.

[13] But not always to control it! It so easily gets out of bounds. At its best, it requires "policing," as Lewin (274) points out, lest the pupils take undesirable short cuts.

If this be even measurably true, teachers and parents have a serious responsibility when they appeal so constantly to the motive of competition. For it must be emphasized again that *motives strengthen as they are successfully appealed to*. We do not, of course, suggest that the competitive motive be left wholly undeveloped. To continue the parallel with the saber-toothed tiger, a child needs *some* competitiveness just as a tiger needs canine teeth. It must be obvious to everyone that ours is, and for a long time will continue to be, a society in which the competitive spirit is helpful, even necessary, *for the attainment of other values.*

Here is a good place for us to remember individual differences. As a matter of rather apparent fact, many children fail to develop enough competitiveness to enable them to achieve as worthily as they otherwise can. On the other hand, many children develop far too much competitiveness (151). The clear implication is that we should play up this trait for the former, play it down for the latter. Both kinds of children—and society as a whole—will gain by an individualization of our use of this potent incentive.

How does this work in the classroom? Some parts of her work the teacher can individualize. Most of the time, however, though her *goal* may be to meet the needs of individuals, she has to do this by *means* of group activities. How, then, is she to handle that incentive of competition and rivalry?

Undoubtedly by using it she can often get immediate results. More children can actually learn more arithmetic if they are trying to excel each other. It is tempting, then, to stir up a little good-natured rivalry, especially since, as we have been saying, some of the children need competition anyway.

Unfortunately, competition usually works best on the very pupils who need it least. Hank, who is already full of "the old fighting spirit," rises to the challenge and becomes even more aggressive, while meek little Billy withdraws psychologically, if not physically, from the contest. Furthermore, competition acts as a spur to learning for those who already have made the most progress and who would continue to progress without the added incentive. The child who finds a particular kind of learning difficult is very likely to believe that there is no use in competing. A group appeal to competitiveness works on the wrong people.

The upshot of it all is, therefore, that we should do well to use this incentive rarely in group situations. The markedly noncompetitive child can be helped to develop more of this attitude by judicious *individualized* encouragement. The others will get more than enough of it from the whole temper of our culture; we don't need to add fuel to their flame.

The Need for Approval

Obviously the need for approval considerably overlaps competition; clearly we often compete to gain approval. Equally clearly we may seek approval through other means. An overlap with the need to achieve is also apparent. The desire to be approved is more or less deliberately encouraged by parents and very early becomes a strong motive. It can be fairly easily manipulated and is therefore one of the chief incentives used in schools. But again we must be sure that the approval is the kind of approval that a given child wants. Many pupils, for example, react negatively to the teacher's openly expressed approval. A Japanese investigator (253) reports that children who are rather introverted improve when praised but worsen when rebuked. For the extravert there was no difference. The experimental findings concerning the effects of praise and reproof are almost hopelessly divergent because of a failure to realize that praise is not always praise and that a rebuke may sometimes be more valued than high praise.

The Need to Belong

We have discussed one aspect of this motive in Chapter 2, where we saw the child's need to belong growing out of infantile dependence. The need is satisfied at first within the family; later it is transferred to other persons and groups, particularly of one's age-mates or "peers." Occasionally the need to affiliate with others is weak, and the child becomes an "isolate." Such cases are so far out of line with our culture that we rightly view them with grave concern.

For most children, however, the desire to belong and to be accepted in some group—generally of peers—is so strong that it greatly affects what they will learn. If a boy wants to become a Scout, he will work hard to learn whatever is needed to become a member. Less formalized groups may be even more effective.

Unfortunately, the need to belong often acts as a negative incentive. If "tough" language is the password for becoming a member of a certain gang, Jimmie will learn to talk tough. The proper language that you try to teach in school may be scorned by the gang—and the boy desirous of acceptance by the gang will refuse to learn it.

It should be noted that we speak of the desire to belong or to be accepted, not of the desire to join. There is a continuing effect of group membership, causing its members to conform to the group norms and standards more and more as membership continues. Together with the need for approval, belongingness is the primary social motivation.

It is not easy for teachers to make use of this incentive. Few children after the first two years have a strong sense of belonging in a school class. Something can be done by capitalizing on such group loyalties as exist, and we can influence the child to join this group rather than that—sometimes!

Conformity

It is not clear how far we can speak of a motive to conform apart from the desire to belong. For present purposes it is enough that we note how thoroughly conformist most children are and that we make judicious use of this motive.

Like competition, it is a readily available incentive. It is usually easy by verbal means to make a child aware of his departure from group standards and thus to motivate him to learn what he needs to meet the standards (e.g., a child who needs to learn to keep his person cleaner).

Easy, but not always wise. For in the first place, there is considerable danger that we stir up feelings of shame and of guilt along with the desire to conform. These motives are powerful. Perhaps they have some sort of useful place in the total economy of life; if so, that place is certainly limited. One of the last things we want to do is to saddle children with a heavy load of shame and guilt feeling. The sad effects of these feelings are evident in every child guidance clinic.

But do we want to put so much emphasis on conformity? A class of good little conformists is easy to manage, but it is rather dull. And a society of conformists is certainly not going to be very progressive. Yet if, as parents and teachers, we appeal to children to be like other children, we are training them to become conformists now and in adult life. I don't mind revealing my own sense of values at this point: I think too much conformity is pretty horrible.

Sympathy

It is still true, as it was in 1937, when Murphy, Murphy, and Newcomb (327) complained about it, that too little research has been given to sympathy as a motive. Though fairly easily aroused in young children, sympathy is rather weak and intermittent. Children do respond to the distress of comrades or of loved adults; they also very often are quite callous about it. Sympathy is not, therefore, a very effective incentive to use in guiding children's behavior.

But this is to take a too limited view of the matter. For sympathy is not only an incentive to be *used* but a valuable character trait to be encouraged and cultivated for itself. The adult's expectation of sympathetic behavior tends to evoke it; and the child who reacts sympathetically usually finds it satisfactory.

The Alleged Need for Aggression

We include the need to be aggressive with many reservations. Aggression is not an appetite like hunger; it is generated from without. If a child were never exposed to the stimuli that evoke aggression, he would never need to be aggressive. (See Scott's [378] thoughtful summary of the evidence.)

Unfortunately we just can't avoid all the situations that stir up aggression nor can we protect the child from them. That being so, the best we can do is to help a child learn to manage his aggressions and put them to good use. Guardedly, also, we can utilize this motive as an incentive to incite the child to action along desirable lines. It is hardly necessary to add that aggression as an incentive overlaps competition and rivalry. Indeed, rivalry is one of the prime instigators of aggression.

Virtues, Proprieties, and Required Behaviors

To list the common virtues and social proprieties among the *dependable* motives of childhood will seem distinctly ironic to most parents and teachers. Can't you hear the parent say: "I can depend on George's willingness to help his brother? on Alicia's courtesy? That's in some other family!"

Let us grant that the degree of dependability of virtuous conduct varies greatly from child to child and at its best falls short of perfection. But it is the goal of social education, at home, in school, and elsewhere, to see to it that these desirable motives *become* dependable; and, once they are instilled, they actually can be appealed to as supplemental motives or incentives.

If we are to make effective use of the child's motivation to be virtuous we must avoid several pitfalls. First and foremost is the trap of verbalism. It is much too easy to assume that the desire to be truthful means the same to the child that it means to us—or means what it does in some ethical treatise. It never does. Murphy, Murphy, and Newcomb (327) summarize a large number of studies of children's moral concepts. Especially interesting are those which show the progressive development with increasing age toward informed adult standards (for example, Lockhart [288], Kemper [245]).

Still more insidious is the error of thinking that because we call a certain virtue, say honesty, by one name it must be one trait. The studies of the Character Education Inquiry (100) reveal that for children there are many honesties—the honesty of the schoolroom, the honesty of the playground, the honesty of the supermarket.

And above all, there is the honesty that a child talks about and the honesty that he practices. Not unlike some adults, many a child "talks a good line."

On top of this there is a lot of individuality. A child who is generally "good" may be completely insensitive to the appeal of generosity, for example. And who of us has not known a home in which the family seems to possess all the virtues but one?

Nonetheless it is quite a mistake to underestimate the extent to which a child's conduct is motivated by *his own* pattern of mores, virtues, and standards. Delinquency and gross misbehavior are exceptional. Most children want to be good and succeed fairly well.

The Psychological Atmosphere

Finally, the total atmosphere of home, school, or group is also a sort of generalized incentive that not only increases or decreases motivation but powerfully helps to determine its direction. Thus the general morale of a school class was found by Hartshorne and May (100) to be more important as a determiner of honesty or of cooperativeness than was the teacher. (Indirectly, however, the teacher may very greatly help to determine that morale.)

In the classroom many factors contribute to the general atmosphere, often in unnoticed ways. Sarcasm may temporarily galvanize a careless pupil into paying attention, but the immediate effect is bought at too high a price in morale, not only of the victim of the attack but of the others in the class, who wonder when it will be their turn to be slashed into ribbons. Competition, especially when there is only one prize, can very easily injure group morale. Too many criticisms from the teacher stifle self-criticism.

On the other hand, an attitude of buoyant cheerful activity on the part of the teacher, when it can be sincerely manifested, helps to establish a similarly dynamic feeling in the group and thus enhances other motives.

QUESTIONS

1. How about the teacher's authority as a dependable incentive?
2. Can you think of other dependable motives that a teacher might appeal to as incentives?
3. Why is curiosity not listed as a dependable incentive? Are not children curious? Should a teacher not invoke this motive?
4. See if you can get a ten-year-old boy to tell you what it means to be a good sport. Draw him out gently but get his concept in as great detail as possible. Is this a dependable motive in this child? Why do you think so?

A Catalog of Incentives?

The foregoing discussion of some of the chief incentives is theoretically untidy, full of overlappings and obviously incomplete. Moreover, it will not satisfy certain hardheaded, practical persons who think they want a list of dependable motives, something like the list of sure-fire menus which experienced hostesses have in readiness. What is wrong with having a list suitable for children of a given age and cultural background?

We do have such lists. I have before me a list compiled by a student from just six sources. It contains over sixty different items. Such catalogs undoubtedly have their uses. In building a curriculum for the fifth grade for example, or in planning a program for the 4-H Club or the Campfire Girls, we need to know the sorts of activities that will engage the children's interest. The norms, to be sure, have to be kept up to date, since children's interests, like those of adults, are constantly altering with the changing times; but that task is not too formidable. Children's books, toys, and play equipment have been enormously improved in recent years by using just such knowledge.

When it comes to dealing with individuals, however, I doubt the value of any formal catalog of motives. If we examine the attempts to formulate such lists, perhaps we can see why. In an earlier day the basic motivations were conceived of as "instincts"; and William McDougall (303), one of the great pioneers in the study of motivation, used to hold that there were seven or eight such primary bases for motives. The list soon grew to twelve or more. By way of contrast, a well-known child psychologist of ten years ago listed only four important desires: to be active, to please others, to achieve, to overcome handicaps. Current discussion makes much of the child's need for security, and under this *one* broad heading often includes his need for love, for achievement, for status, and for self-enhancement.

Freud attempted to reduce all motivation to the libido and the death instinct. By libido Freud meant all pleasurable strivings, all attempts to incorporate within oneself some part of the world. By the death instinct he meant the "spirit that denies," all tendency to withdraw from the world, all self-surrender, good or bad.[14] Well, it

[14] Is it necessary to warn the reader that we have not, in two sentences, adequately summarized Freud's subtle treatment of these themes?

certainly seems to be possible to range almost any motive under one or other of such broadly conceived categories. But do we really have just two motives or a whole collection of motives under two headings?

The truth is that any listing of distinct motives is arbitrary. "Motivation," as Murphy puts it, "does not define a box that contains a few distinct tools for our use" (325, p. 89). The several motives are fluid and flow into each other. Take a concrete case. Billy says: "Look, mother, at the funny face I'm making! *Look!* LOOK!" You can say he wants his mother's approval of his "achievement" of a funny face (a fairly specific description); or that he wants his mother's approval (intermediate level of description); or that he wants social approval (fairly general description), or that he is seeking the enhancement of his ego (quite a general description).

Which one of these interpretations is best? Well, it depends a little, doesn't it? On you, on *your* purposes as the observer. It does not depend on the actual behavior of the actual child, Billy. The classification is external, imposed on the facts rather than growing out of them. If, then, we were making up a standard check list of dependable motives, at which level of generality should we operate?

A second objection to a fixed catalog is that motives are always more or less mixed. Even in the laboratory, where we strive to keep things as simple as possible, we find it impossible to restrict the animal to a single drive, say hunger. In the child one need presses upon others, fusing with them in compounds of great complexity. We may, if we use great ingenuity and patience, analyze the compound into its components; and for certain theoretical purposes this is valuable. But to understand what is motivating the individual child, we need to grasp the total motivation operating in the particular circumstances.

Moreover, there is always the danger that an inventory of motives found at any given time be taken as fixed and final, taken even as a standard to be attained. Because most American children are almost fiercely competitive, we tend to think that this is necessarily so, or that it is morally right and proper, and that any child who falls short of the norm is "deficient" and should be brought up to the norm, by fair means or foul. In short, the list of current motives tends to make us forget that one of our major educational purposes is to *change* the motives of children, not merely to use them to get things done.

Individual Differences in Motives

A further difficulty of cataloging dependable motives arises from the fact of great individual differences. While it is true that the motive discernible in a child's behavior may resemble one—or indeed several—of the motives listed in some catalog of "common motives," it certainly has an individual flavor all its own. You never fully understand a particular person's motive when you think of it in terms of its similarity to that of others. Effective dealing with a child's motives is not to be got by ticking them off mechanically on a prepared list, but by becoming sensitive to the manifold individuality of his whole motivational structure—and to the individual nature of the field of psychological forces in which this child is actually living. *Motives crystallize in the direction of satisfactions actually experienced,* and these may take myriad forms. Long before he comes to school, therefore, the child has developed innumerable highly individual specializations or modifications of his "original needs" according to the pattern of his personal experience.

Suppose that we do discover that Jasper and Juan are both motivated by "desire for approval." Such a statement may give us a fellow feeling with them; to that extent it is a helpful categorization. It may help us to understand some of their behavior and thus adjust ourselves to it better. But does it help us to know, for example, just how Jasper will react to praise, or that Juan will react in the same way? Not unless we know more about each of the boys. To praise for what? from whom? in whose presence? Jasper, though he wants approval, may be greatly embarrassed by *public* praise, whereas Juan "eats it up." Jasper may want recognition only for "manly" sports; Juan may be eager to have his singing acclaimed. Both may be a bit scornful of praise from a teacher.

Nor should we ignore the collateral effects of such incentives upon their development. Even though it embarrasses him, praise may help Jasper to overcome deep-seated feelings of inadequacy. On the other hand, it may serve only to increase Juan's conceit.

For concreteness, we have stated the issue in terms of two individuals, Jasper and Juan. Research findings dealing with the effect of praise and blame on many children are available. We get such findings as these: objective public reprimand (not sarcastic) caused 40 percent of junior high pupils to do better, 46 percent to do worse; private reprimand caused 83 percent to do better, 7 percent to do worse. Breckenridge and Vincent (73), after a useful summary of many studies, suggest a sort of scale of effectiveness which runs somewhat as follows:

a. *Ridicule or sarcasm* (especially in public)	gravely handicapping to learning in most pupils.
b. *Ignoring* the child's efforts	discouraging or ineffectual.
c. *Reproof* (particularly if administered in private)	occasionally effective.
d. *Praise* (for genuine effort)	likely to be more effective, and effective in more instances.
e. *Praise* for good effort *combined with constructive suggestions* for improvement	most effective of all methods.

But they conclude with the admonition:

f. *A judicious adjustment of any method to individual children*	**absolutely necessary.**

A negative point is also useful here. As adults we must always remember that children's motives differ in many ways from ours. As teachers we must realize that we have the special motivations of our vocation, which others, including children, do not fully share. As members of the middle class we must realize how different are our ambitions and ideals from those of lower-class children. The ideals and goals that seem to us both important and self-evident will often seem meaningless or actually reprehensible to children from another class with a different social background. Thus it is natural for us, both as teachers and as middle-class people, to promote the ideal of "correct speech." But in certain social contexts, "correct speech," so far from being helpful, would be a terrible handicap. A working-class child is quite justified in rejecting such a locution as "It is I." Why make himself peculiar? [15] Many a pupil has ruined his standing with

[15] Intonations are even more indicative of class membership than differences in diction. Although class distinctions in speech are less rigid in America than in Europe, it is true here also that "thy speech betrayeth thee."

Well, then, should not the teacher attempt to prepare these pupils for a "higher sta-

his peers by accepting a teacher's standards of manners and morals. Fortunately, most children simply ignore indoctrination that lies too far outside the motivational pattern of their everyday life. But the teacher who blandly assumes that children will be responsive to the virtues and ideology that seem self-evident to her is certain to run into stormy weather.

Finally, differences in motivation arise because children have not yet arranged their motives in a stable order of preference. Even less than adults do they know what they want, and what they want today they may not want tomorrow. There are, as we have seen, some "dependable incentives" upon which the teacher (or parent) can rely—up to a point. There is real truth, however, in the weary complaint: "You never can be quite sure what they will want next." We do well to ascribe motives to a child only tentatively and to be ready for the emergence, quite out of the blue, of some unexpected goal. A printed catalog of common motives is as likely to deceive as to help.

Hidden Motives

Is there anything that will help us to understand and even control these unexpected shifts in motivation? Yes, there is at least one basic principle which has innumerable practical implications: *Be sure you have identified the motive or motives actually operating.*

It is obvious that motives cannot be safely judged from a single incident. The sharp tussle with a comrade may reveal personal antagonism, possessiveness, or an outraged sense of injustice—or just "animal spirits." Only when we watch behavior for some time can we infer with any kind of safety at all which of the enduring motives are actually at work.

It is always tempting to suppose that others are so like ourselves that what motivates us must also move them. On sober reflection we know it isn't so, but we forget it. We forget that the child may not understand what it is we expect of him. An enormous amount of

tion" by teaching them better speech? This is obviously a complex problem involving the ultimate goals of education; it is not to be settled in a footnote! Our present point is that differences between the teacher and the children in social status, if not recognized, give rise to baffling problems of motivation. On this point see the oversimplified but stimulating discussion by Davis (113) in his Inglis Lecture at Harvard.

stubbornness, of inertia, and of "lack of interest" is simply due to the fact that the child doesn't *know* what it is all about. (In this connection, too, we may note that ability and effective motivation are connected; it is a waste of effort to try to motivate children to do something for which they lack the necessary ability. If the teacher gets any sort of result, it is bound to be a distorted one.)

No two persons are ever motivated in quite the same way in the same circumstances. Ordinarily the differences are small enough to be ignored—but not always. What to one person seems like an opportunity to gain money, to another looks like a chance for glory. In the same outward circumstances, one child is motivated by a desire to get a job done well, another is trying to please the teacher, a third is interested in securing applause. And every possible combination may be found, for most motives easily unite or cooperate. We need, then, to be alert to the areas and the circumstances in which the child comes alive with enthusiasm. If we watch thoughtfully, we can usually find certain patterns that reveal the underlying motivation.

The situation is complicated, however, by the tendency to concealment of motives. Astonishingly early, children learn to pretend to motives that they do not have and to conceal those that actually move them. We adults have ourselves to blame for this, of course; we make it satisfactory and profitable to the child to dissimulate.

Today, every high school senior has heard about rationalization, projection, and a host of other means used to fool not only others but ourselves. All of them may be classed together as "defense mechanisms" against "painful" or disturbing recognition of our true motives.

Defense mechanisms are probably not wholly bad; we should think twice before we rob a person of defenses against a too-painful self-knowledge. To understand a child's conduct, however, we must be able to get behind his defenses to the real motive. This is easier to say than to do, although fortunately the child—or the adult—more easily deceives himself than he does a sensitive observer.

Often the clue is found if we look, not for the concealed motive but for the concealed problem. Look at the twisted figure in the accompanying sketch (Fig. 7-3). Seen in isolation, the child looks like a cripple. Suppose, however, we see this child in relation to his environment, as in the detailed sketch on page 236 (Fig. 7-4). The

Figure 7-3. Concealed Motive or Concealed Problem?

twisted posture is now seen as a compensatory reaction to the heavy weight he was carrying up a steep incline.[16] Wherever the motive is obscure, we should try to find what kind of "weight" the child is carrying and over what sort of "terrain."

To put the matter in another way, whenever the child persists stubbornly in obviously unreasonable behavior, we should look for the *persistent stimuli which he can neither ignore nor yet adjust himself to.* As a clue to these hidden stimuli, we may consider what sort of end the unreasonable act would serve, if only it were reasonable. Suppose that a child, usually friendly and affectionate with his teacher, begins, quite without occasion, to be impudent and recalcitrant. The teacher is sure that she has done nothing to merit such behavior—it is therefore "unreasonable." But to what sort of situation would impudence be a "reasonable" response? Quite a few, perhaps, but we may sum them all up under the heading of "affronts to his sense of worth." In short, we may suspect that someone has been "picking on him."

Going a step farther, we note that the impudence is directed at the teacher—an authority-figure. We suspect therefore that the person who is really the cause of the impudence is likewise someone in authority, probably a parent. We may generalize the point by saying that there is a persistent stimulus which the child cannot ignore but cannot do anything about. Here, then, may be the source of his hidden motives.

Is it necessary to add that the clues suggested give no more than a vague notion of the direction in which to search for hidden motives? Popularization of the doctrine of "repressed desires" often gives the impression that there is a fixed relation between certain "symbolic responses" and the "unconscious motives." It is not quite that easy. No principle of understanding is a substitute for the patient search for facts. Nowhere more than when we are dealing with motives is it necessary to be alert to the individual nuances that distinguish one child from another.

---

16 It may be well to note that there are two kinds of "compensation." In one the reactions are designed to overcome the original difficulty; in the other the reactions are designed to obtain a substitute satisfaction. Either, however, may lead to behavior that looks "unreasonable" to the observer who is unaware of the problem the child is trying to solve.

Summary

An incentive is a sort of accessory motive used to get a person to do something for which he would otherwise be inadequately motivated. To be effective, the incentive should not merely arouse a need but point the way at least vaguely toward need-satisfaction.

By the artful use of incentives we may get the child to experience the satisfaction of attaining desirable goals; a prize for geography may help the child discover that maps are fun. The danger is that the incentive itself may take the place of the real goal.

Figure 7-4. The Concealed Problem

There are many motives sufficiently common in our culture to be dependable; we can appeal to them as incentive motives. We can also change them, and we should not forget that a major objective of education is to modify, not merely use, the child's motives and purposes.

Although in larger outline we speak of dependable motives, the fact of individual differences remains. No two persons are ever motivated in quite the same way in the same circumstances.

The situation is further complicated by the fact that children as well as adults often have hidden motives—motives hidden even from themselves. This may lead to "unreasonable" or problem behavior. Uncalled-for aggression, for example, is usually a response to some hidden thwarting of the child's goal-seeking. The clue is to look for persistent stimuli that the child cannot adjust himself to but also cannot ignore. No fixed relationship between "symbolic responses" and hidden motives or "unconscious desires" can be relied on; we must patiently unravel the relationships as they exist for each individual child. If you jump to conclusions you may land on a stony contradiction and break a leg.

8

The Psychology of Physical Development

Growing up physically is the chief business of a child. In what terms is physical growth to be assessed? What is the relation between various physical traits? How do these traits affect the child's social development?

"When I Get Big!"

As soon as he learns to talk, if not before, every child has impressed upon him how much he is "cabin'd, crib'd, confined" by being small and young. To "get big" is a tremendously important affair. This is vividly illustrated in the following monolog of a five-year-old kindergartener "resting" after lunch. (He was talking half to himself, half to the student-observer, who took down in shorthand exactly what he said.) Though few children can express themselves as well as this astonishing young philosopher, he verbalizes the usually wordless feelings and aspirations of other, less fluent children.

Today I'm not going to be big. I'm going to be a little baby and you must take care of me. I can't do *anything* for myself. I can just lie in your lap. I'm tired of being a big boy for a while.

It's awful the way you go on being big. Of course you want to grow big, but you couldn't help it if you *didn't* want to. You just keep on growing. It would be awful if you didn't like it 'cause it would just go on anyhow and how sad that would be.

But being big is the best, best thing, isn't it? When you're big everything happens, instead of just waiting to be big. When you get big you can do what you want to do and nobody tells you and you don't have to ask. You just go ahead and do what you want. And you can tell other people. That's a good thing.

When I get big I'm not going to be afraid of anything and I'm not going to cry *ever!* People who cry when they are big are silly. When my mommy cries she says it's because she loves my sister and me and things make her sad. I guess I won't love anybody. I'll take care of mommy and my sister but I won't love them to make me cry. I will be very big and very strong and I'll kill a lot of people, and I'll take care of people if they want me to, but still be all by myself.

But not now. Today *you* must take care of me. I am a little baby. Only don't tell anyone that. . . .

It would be funny if I was big and you were little. I wouldn't pay any attention to you, and I'd make you do things you didn't like to. But I guess I won't ever be able to do that to you 'cause I won't ever be able to catch up to you. I won't ever be able to be the same as you at the same time. It would be funny if when you were born you were grown up, wouldn't it? And then instead of getting older you got younger and littler till you were a baby. That would be funny.

What if that happened now? It would mix people up a lot, wouldn't it? I wish you were a baby so I could take care of you. . . .

Some day if I grow up, and I guess I will, I'll have to shoot too. [This was wartime.] Sometimes I wish I didn't have to grow big. That's why you must take care of me and we will pretend I'm a little baby and have a long time to wait till I grow big.[1]

Here we find expression of one of the child's earliest concerns—which is to grow up. And here, too, we see how even this early the concern is ambivalent—that is, mingled of two feelings. Growing up is wonderful ("the best, best thing") but, as our young philosopher perceives, it brings with it terrifying experiences and sometimes insoluble problems. No wonder that there is in every one of us—in the young as well as in nostalgic elders—a little of Peter Pan, the child who didn't want to grow up. We all have our moments when we want, as the psychoanalysts have taught us to say, to regress to the safety and securities of early infancy. ("Backward, turn backward, O Time, in your flight,/ Make me a child again just for tonight!") But usually such desire for regression is transient, and the contrary desire

[1] Clara S. Littledale, A long time growing up. *Parents' Magazine,* Feb., 1943, p. 15. Reprinted by permission of the publisher.

prevails. *To grow up is one of the child's earliest, most important, and most persistent tasks and ambitions.*

And rightly enough. As the child early learns, there are things you can't do, and many, many more things you mustn't do, because you are "too little." Partly this is because the parents' attitude is also ambivalent—they want a child to stay small, yet also to grow up. A child who cries when told he is too little to have a sharp knife is admonished not to be a baby. To which he might reasonably reply:

"Why can't I cry if I am little?
And if I'm big, why can't I whittle?"

As one grows in size and strength, however, the range of experiences—possible and permitted—increases enormously. What a change there is when one is first deemed big enough to visit a neighbor playmate, to go to school, to go to the store to make purchases, to stay out after dark, to drive a car, to have a date. For the child, the new situations which open up are exciting, and sometimes rather terrifying. He does not quite know how to act—various elements in the situation both attract and repel him. Most important, however, is the fact that with each of these new experiences come opportunities to learn, and this in turn opens the way to further experiences. Mobility—literally moving around, going places—is one of the biggest factors in the development not only of intelligence but, particularly, of social behavior and personality.

From the standpoint of the teacher, the range of possible and permissible skills and activities related to growth is also very important. In the kindergarten just such things as the mere ability—or rather inability—to put on overshoes or snowpants become a really major determiner of the day's program. In the early grades motor coordination plays its part in determining how much reading and writing should be introduced. And throughout the elementary school the sorts of games played, in the classroom or on the playground, are governed in large part by the stage of physical growth which characterizes the group.

QUESTIONS

1. Does physical growth matter so much *in the classroom* from grade 3 to grade 6? Why?

2. If anyone can do much about the child's physical condition, it is the pediatrician. What can teachers do? Answer this question now but keep it in mind as you read what follows.

Individual Differences

It is relatively easy for the teacher to adjust her procedures to the *average* developmental level of the group. Curriculums, textbooks, lesson plans, and numerous teaching aids are nowadays scientifically adjusted to the physical as well as the intellectual level of the several grades. Even without such helps only a very insensitive person would expect first-graders to play baseball or eighth-graders to be more than passingly interested in "Farmer in the Dell." (In fact, when eighth-graders play such a childish game they usually do so because it gives them a chance to mingle on easy terms and have pleasurable bodily contacts with the other sex without being obliged to admit a dawning heterosexual interest.) It is not so easy, however, to recognize and fully adapt one's program to the differences between the *individuals* in the group.

There is little need to emphasize that children differ enormously from each other in rate of physical growth (see Fig. 8-1), and that averages or so-called norms are only a highly artificial way of representing trends for a group, the individual members of which grow according to their own "personal style" (46). As *Newsweek* once put it,

> One thing that every mother knows is that age does not always tell the size of a boy's breeches. . . . After measuring 147,088 American children between the ages of 7 and 14 in fifteen states, it was found that there was as much difference in the sizes of the boys as between Maine and Georgia accents [334].

Moreover, relative differences in size are apt to remain pretty much the same throughout childhood (47). We are interested, however, less in the fact that such differences exist than in their consequences. For differences in physique have, for young children, even more important consequences than differences in intelligence, interest, or character.

> Early in September some third-graders were engaged in the typical unorganized activity of their age when a bright youngster devised a new

Figure 8-1. The Range in Height

If the size range commonly found in Grade III prevailed in adult life, then of every 30 or 40 men, one or more would be about this short or about this tall.

game. Folding his arms across his chest he charged into the back of one playmate after another, chanting a little song: "He who gets in my way is sure to get bumped." Each child, as he was vigorously spun around by the bump, registered first anger and surprise, then dawning comprehension and a desire to imitate the innovator. Soon all the boys were chanting the little song and looking for the opportunity to catch one of the others from the rear. All, except one boy. This child, larger than the rest, received his bumps from comrade after comrade with visible lack of understanding and mounting dismay. At length, however, he came to realize that this seemingly uncalled-for personal attack on him was a charming game which he too could play. And because he was larger and heavier than the rest, when he bumped, he *bumped.* In a very short time by virtue merely of his size and strength—certainly not by virtue of superior intelligence or social adaptability!—he was dominating the play of the whole group.

Any kind of physical superiority or inferiority may thus influence the child's relations with his fellows. "Vim, vigor, and vitality" are as important as size, and the range of differences is probably as great. Motor coordination and skills play an important part, especially in later childhood and adolescence. So does sheer strength. And, of course, special physical handicaps such as deafness, very poor vision, being crippled, or the like, may have a decisive role.

Interrelationships

The relation of these various physical traits to each other and to the child's total make-up is an intricate problem. Two rival doctrines, each seizing upon part of the truth, have been put forward: the doctrine of compensation, and the doctrine of correlation.

Compensation

"Common sense" usually votes for compensation. It picks up the obvious fact that a person who is lacking in one trait or quality frequently has a compensating strength in some other trait. Thus the blind sometimes have astonishing sensitivity in their finger tips, are guided in their walking about by almost imperceptible sounds, can even avoid obstacles because they "feel" their imminence by air pressure. Emerson seemed to think there is a sort of Law of

Nature that gives us such compensations for deficiencies. A little observation shows instead that our compensations are acquired. The blind gain the ability to discriminate with their finger tips by patient and prolonged attention to the messages their fingers convey.[2] The one-armed man develops strength in the remaining member by exercise.

The handicapped person also learns less obvious ways of compensating. He learns to act in such a way as to *conceal* his deficiency, learns to put his best foot forward by emphasizing activities in which he is not handicapped, learns to seek, and to be happy with, other kinds of satisfactions. In the "sour-grapes" mechanism he, like anyone else, even goes so far as to deny that he ever really wanted the other kind of success.

Compensation of this sort is well illustrated by the child who makes up for his weakness in games by working very hard at his studies—sometimes scorning games as too rude and rowdy. The teacher is more likely to be plagued by the boy who compensates for his weakness in intellectual pursuits (which he calls "sissy") by all sorts of vigorous physical activities, ruly or unruly. Alfred Adler (3) has built a whole system of psychology about the idea that nearly everything we do is an effort to compensate for some weakness or other.

Compensation is undoubtedly an intriguing concept; and there is no question that it helps us to understand many otherwise rather mysterious behaviors. We shall need to watch for it in the conduct of children. Let us beware, however, of overworking it as an explanation. Not all strenuous exertion is an indirect or devious attempt to attain a substitute satisfaction. Sometimes a child simply works hard to overcome the original weakness—think of the preadolescent boy who exercises daily with chest weights and dumbbells to build up his spindly muscles. Perhaps that, too, should be called compensation, though it is not the common usage. Less dramatic than the indirect forms, these direct measures, whether called compensation or not, are more numerous and more important.

---

[2] The blind do not, however, learn such discrimination more easily than is *possible* for the normally sighted. Indeed, investigations make it seem probable that the loss of the visual sense lessens rather than increases the acuity of the other senses (23, 180).

QUESTIONS

1. If a child is physically somewhat below the average and does well in class, is this always because he is compensating? How can you tell?
2. What can you do to help a child who is *over*compensating? For example, the boy with a "Little Napoleon complex" who struts and acts big to compensate for his actual physical inferiority? Do you want to deprive him of the comfort this behavior gives him?

Correlation

The evidence for the rival position of correlation among physical traits is less dramatic and personal; essentially it depends upon statistical study. Such study shows that, *in general,* excellence in one physical characteristic tends to be accompanied by excellence in others. The child who is slightly taller than average is likely to be slightly stronger, to be able to run a little faster, or to throw a little straighter—and even to be a little more intelligent.

Such facts as these have a bearing on administrative procedures for dealing with groups of children—for example, in grade classification. Too much should not be made of them, however, especially when we think of individuals. It would, for instance, be very unsafe to predict from Mabel's clear skin that she will be a good runner. The mathematically determined correlations between one physical trait and another are positive, but they are very low. Moreover, such correlations tell only what the general rule is. The exceptions to the general rule are numerous and individually important. We do indeed have children of almost uniformly good physical development, and we have the poor unfortunates whose development is almost uniformly inferior. But these are extremes; in between lies the great mass of children with a somewhat irregular "profile" of development—a bit below average here, a bit above there, perhaps average in most things but strikingly above or below in one or two. Marked individual differences prevail, both in separate physical traits and in their combination or totality.

Organismic Integration

This leads us to a point of view, not quite so often considered in popular discussion concerning the interrelations of physical characteristics. It lays emphasis upon the *total pattern* of growth or development. It recognizes that there are specific functions of special organs; the childish definitions, "eyes are to see with," "ears to hear with," really hit upon a big part of the truth. Yet, in a broader sense, eyes and ears are not just to see or to hear with; they are parts of a whole organism which functions as a unit in relation to its world. As Anne Morrow Lindbergh writes, when you have to see the clouds through a glass window, they aren't real. "This is just movie weather. . . . To see, one must feel also. . . . One sees with the whole body, not just with the eyes" (283). It is, then, no mere verbal quibble to insist that eyes are not merely to see with; eyes are to enable the whole person to make appropriate adjustments to what is going on in his surroundings. What we really want to know about a child is how effectively he operates as a "going concern" in his own world. The interrelations—the integration of physical traits—become the salient fact, not the effectiveness of any one of them.

I have here given concrete expression in the realm of physical traits to what is known as the "organismic" or "holistic" point of view. This view stresses the unique "wholeness" or unity of every act and, as well, the unique wholeness or unity of the organism or person. Accordingly, it tends to disparage or even to reject any attempt to analyze behavior into simple and separate "elements." Indeed, some adherents of this view react to what they call "atomistic analysis" with a cultlike antipathy.

I urge a pragmatic attitude here. A theory is of value only when it helps us solve a problem. If it helps us to understand a problem better when we take into account the relation between a certain characteristic and the total nature of the person, let's look at it that way. But if we can explain a certain behavior better by treating it *as if* it were *independent* of other behaviors and of the whole personality, why, then, let us do that. Take our present problem. Most of the problems of physical growth, especially most of the psychological problems involved, are better understood when we consider the organism as a *total* going concern, with interacting parts. If a child has defective vision, we need to think about him in all manner of activities at home, at school, on the playground. He isn't just "Poor Eyes" or the person who can't read the third line of the Snellen visual acuity chart. He is Henry Burton, bricklayer's son, in Grade IV at Hawthorne School.

And yet, when it comes to getting the right kind of glasses, the ophthalmologist or optometrist is quite right to center his attention on how Henry's eyes work, paying only a minimum of attention to his total personality. If this be "atomism," let who will make the most of it. The organismic point of view serves as a reminder, however, that the entire story is not told when the proper minus-sphere correction has been ground into spectacles. If nothing else, there is the question whether this is the kind of personality who will refuse to wear his glasses unless coerced. It does make a difference what kind of person it is who has the poor eyes; and the poor eyes—*and* the glasses—are going to help determine what sort of person we have to deal with.[3] I have never yet met a problem where the analytic and the organismic approaches seemed in genuine conflict; they supplement each other.

QUESTION

Many persons (especially many educational theorists) find the notion of "wholeness" peculiarly attractive. Can you suggest why?

Growth Rhythms

It should be added that while the several physical traits *function* together more or less as a single unit in the economy of the organism, they do not grow or develop as a unit (441). Instead, each of the several traits seems to have its own rhythm of growth. There is a time when the long bones grow relatively fast, another when the short bones speed up; and it is primarily such differences in the rhythm of growth that give rise to the characteristic differences in proportion between a child of three and one of six or nine or twelve. (See Fig. 8-2.)

---

[3] Consider what is implied in the very title of the book, *Motivation and visual factors* (53).

Figure 8-2. Characteristic Differences in Proportion

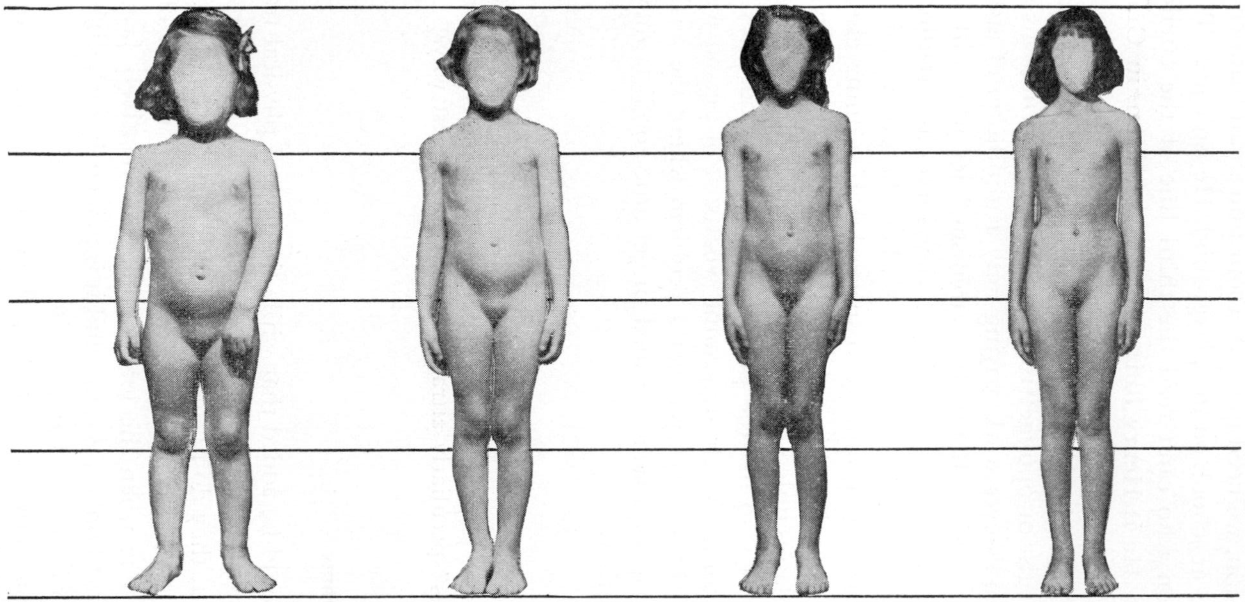

The same child pictured at ages 3, 6, 9, and 12.

There is a time for the growth of one gland, another for the growth of others, still another when the bones lengthen rapidly, another when muscles increase. Growth thus proceeds along several rather independent fronts, each of which may push ahead rapidly for a time, then relapse into relative quiet. The over-all picture of growth rhythms is set forth in Figure 8-3.

Figure 8-3. Differing Rates of Growth in Various Tissues

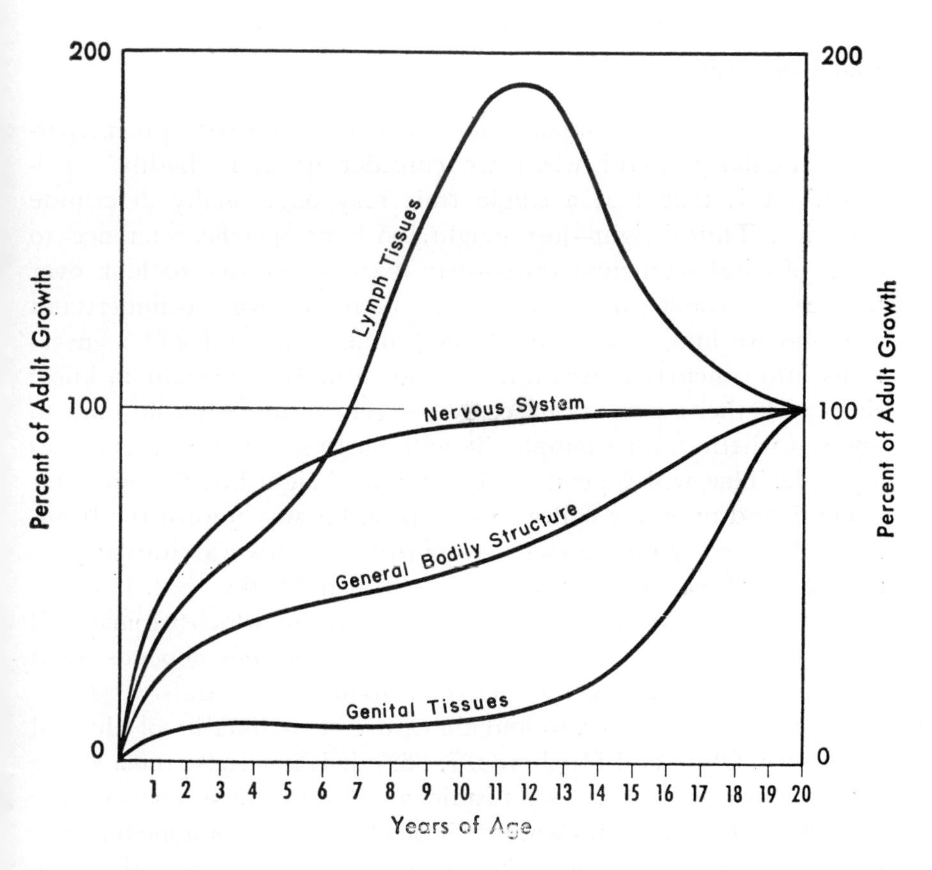

Growth is portrayed schematically in terms of a percentage of the final stage at about age 20. Thus the lymph tissues grow most rapidly at first, and just before puberty are almost double their adult size.

Redrawn from J. A. Harris and others, *The measurement of man.* Minneapolis: Univ. of Minn. Press, 1930. By permission of the publishers.

QUESTIONS

1. Does it ever help to grow markedly faster or slower in some one function than in the rest?
2. How about all-round proportionate growth much in advance of the normal? Would you feel happy about a child who in every respect you can think of was three years ahead of his age?

Bodily Excellence

The notion of organismic interaction, however, proves particularly useful when we consider general "bodily excellence." It is true that a single trait may occasionally determine behavior. Thus height—just height, without specific reference to other physical or mental traits—may make it possible to look over the heads of others in a crowd. More often, however, to understand a person we find it necessary to take other "physical and mental" traits into concurrent account. It is not usually important to know simply whether a person can see over others' heads; what we want to know is whether, for example, he will get to see such a spectacle as a parade. That will depend partly upon his height but also upon his strength and upon his willingness to push his way toward the front. Not infrequently the shorter person will work his way into a more advantageous position for seeing than will his lanky rival. It therefore seems necessary to introduce a new concept which we may call *total bodily excellence.* A person's physical efficiency depends upon the total bodily excellence rather than upon any one trait.

It is not easy, however, to find a measure of the totality of physical excellence. Olson and Hughes (337, 339), it is true, propose a single index which they call "organismic age." They first convert any measure of development—whether it be of a physical or a mental trait—into an "age value" computed on the same principle as the now-familiar mental age. Thus, forty-six inches, being the average height for six-year-old boys, would be given the "height age" value of six years. A similar procedure yields "age" measures for maturity of bony development, dental development, muscular strength, reading age, and so on. "Organismic age" is by definition the average of all such age-scale measures of development. Olson and Hughes have commonly used ten variables, the average of which is held to be a workable approximation to a "true" organismic age.[4]

The Olson-Hughes organismic-age concept combines both physical and mental modes of development; it is truly an attempt to measure the "whole child." There is no reason, however, why we cannot use an analogous procedure in obtaining a picture of a more limited aspect of development, say, of physical growth. Indeed, I believe that the time is coming when teachers will have available a single figure representing a child's physical development as a whole.[5]

Such a combined index will have to be made and interpreted with great care. Merely averaging various measurements of the child's growth won't do. One cannot assume that any one measurement is as significant as any other, and one cannot ignore the way one kind of growth interacts with another. It is good to have a broad chest—and we can measure that. And it is good to have long legs—which we also can measure. But just how broad should a seven-year-old's chest be in relation to legs of a certain length? How many plus points in a total score should one allow for a big ratio between chest and leg length? How many points should one deduct for a "pigeon breast"? No one really knows. The height-weight tables do not give an adequate picture of the relation between these two familiar dimensions, let alone of total physical growth. Moreover, as pointed out above, we must take into account the way a child sometimes compensates for relative deficiency in one area by greater activity in another. And finally we must take account of the fact that different traits play different parts at different stages of development.

Thus, in the nursery school run-about, a kind of flashy energy output is very significant; it "sticks out" like a salient angle. Endurance the child of this age can do without, since the characteristic activities of this age have a short time-span anyway. By the age of eight or nine, however, it becomes more important to be able to sustain one's energy output. At six, mere size and strength are probably more important, more salient, than motor skill; by nine or ten, motor skills become a more significant factor in bodily excellence. At all stages comeliness is not entirely to be neglected as a factor, but certainly at

[4] Some recent work (22, pp. 109 ff., 63, 64, 250, 450) throws doubt upon the adequacy of the procedure in obtaining organismic age, even upon the soundness of the basic theory.

[5] This despite the many difficulties in obtaining significant measures. For an excellent review, see Jenss and Souther (225).

some ages it is more important than at others. We must, moreover, at every stage of development and for each trait, compare the individual with the average or standard; and we must also consider how important *at that stage* is deviation from the standard. At six to be much taller than other girls may be a matter of little account or even an asset; at puberty it may seem a minor tragedy.

No standardized scales exist that enable us to take account of all these variables and arrive at an assessment of total bodily excellence. Yet the attentive observer of children can directly observe and estimate this quality with some success. You notice and somehow combine impressions (or better yet, you combine impressions and actual measures, when you can get them, of height + weight + strength + energy output + motor skill + appearance of health + vision + hearing). Out of these and other observations emerges a sort of total judgment of the child's physical quality. (Recording the ratings and measurements on a Profile Graph helps to make each of them fill out the picture.)

Does the concept of total physical excellence apply to adults too? Decidedly; but again we must consider age and the development level. In adolescence and the middle years the grosser skills so important in childhood must share their importance with the subtler "skills" which constitute expressiveness and grace of bodily movement and which give the impression of controlled dynamic energy. As old age draws near, postural tone and energy output again loom large; and at an advanced age, sheer eye-motor coordination becomes dominant in defining bodily excellence.

Although the concept of "total bodily excellence" as a *unit trait* has not hitherto been explicitly set forth, the notion is latent in most discussions. It will be noted that it raises some very knotty theoretical problems. We shall not be able to find a unit trait in this area unless we give attention to the three complicating factors briefly discussed above: the developmental level, the salience of various components of the trait, and the environmental field in reference to which the trait must be defined.

Moreover, the trait elements directly measured are anthropometric, but the *criterion* defining the trait itself as a unity is that of social status. If we seek a unity in these measurements merely as physical facts, it seems unlikely to be found. Total bodily excellence is a *social* trait *determined* by physical factors. Careful experimental exploration of this concept is urgently needed.

Most of us are accustomed to forming such total judgments about others all the time, though we usually find it difficult to make the judgment very explicit. Most of us, moreover, with experience and deliberate practice, improve in ability to judge. Teachers need really to *look at* the individual child and learn really to *see* him as well as to think about him.

Psychologists have been rather loath to encourage such "total-impression" judgments, especially when they are based on appearance. There is plenty of research to show that such judgments are fallible; but the research also shows that they are better than nothing, and that one's judgment improves with practice. As rapidly as we can, we must substitute precise measurement for impressionistic subtlety, just as in medicine laboratory findings are more and more supplementing and even replacing the diagnostic skill of the practitioner. As indicated above, however, we simply don't know yet how to *measure* total bodily excellence and must, for the present, rely on impressional judgment. It is my opinion that teachers should develop greater attentiveness to the sort of total bodily excellence children display. If they learn nothing else, they learn how an individual *appears* to others, which is, by any criterion, an important part of his total social effectiveness.

Physique and Social Development

More than anything else it is total bodily excellence which determines what, and especially how well, a child plays. Excellence at play is, in its turn, of major importance in companionship and friendship and in all the child's social relationships. It is chiefly in play that a child interacts with his fellows and learns to get along. The physically excellent child—often just the merely big child—has opportunity to lead in games, and thus to learn the vitally important techniques of leadership and cooperation. The child's social development—indeed, his whole personality development—is thus from the first in large part dependent upon the facts of his physical development.[6]

[6] Just to keep our perspective, let's note that whether one owns a bat and ball may also be of tremendous importance in determining one's status in the gang. Or whether Mother allows one to go out at the "right" time, dressed in the "right" clothes. Or whether—shame to us adults for instilling such ideas!—one is of the "right" color or racial ancestry or "family." In short, a child's social relationships, like an adult's, depend on a whole range of factors. Physique is only one, but it is perhaps more often than any other the *chief* factor in determining how a child develops socially.

Probably no one will be inclined to dispute the fact of a relationship between the kind of body one has and one's personality. But scientists have been very busy working out the details. The first finding is that there is virtually no truth at all in phrenology, physiognomy, and all the sorts of "character analyses" which diagnose personality from the size and shape of eyes, ears, hands, or other bodily parts.

It is true there have been a few studies which seemed to find a relationship between the total bodily type and personality. Some of these studies have been conducted by honest and competent scientists, e.g., Sheldon (388), but I must add that many of them have been made by men who were neither. When the studies were cross-checked in the careful fashion required in science, the findings were disproved or rendered doubtful at best. I feel very safe in saying that you will be misled if you attempt to classify children as endomorphs or mesomorphs or dysplastics and try to deduce anything from it. Whatever validity there is in the "body type" theory, it won't be worked out in time to help you with the children you will be dealing with.

And yet we began by saying that bodily physique does affect personality—and there are many scientific studies which spell this out (e.g., Sanford *et al.* [372]). The relation, however, is indirect. Furfey (159) showed that physical development has a larger correlation with companionship than has intelligence. Wellman (471) found that boys selected companions from those of about the same height.[7] Jones and Bayley (237), basing their conclusion upon an intensive study of a group of young adolescents in a natural setting, write that children larger than average are "accepted and treated by adults and other children as more mature." As a result, they have more self-confidence, are less inclined to join the hectic struggle for status. "In contrast,—because others tend to treat them as the little boys they appear to be—physically retarded boys exhibit many forms of relatively immature behavior." In general, differences in size and strength and health are more important determiners of social adjustment than are moderate differences in intelligence.

The relationship of physique to the specifically social trait of lead-

[7] Nonetheless, in junior high school you may observe a large number of Mutt-and-Jeff pairs. Many are doubtless due to a sudden spurt in height in one but not in the other member of a pair. But often you suspect that at this age a compensatory mechanism is at work: the larger and physically superior lad is pairing up with a smaller friend who has superior scholastic or social abilities.

ership is especially close. In pre-Nazi Germany, Lieb (282) found that both boys and girls mentioned physical superiority most frequently as the basis of leadership. Even at the Lincoln School (Teachers College, Columbia), where athletics were "de-emphasized" by the authorities, Caldwell and Wellman (85) found that class presidents and similar leaders were usually taller than the average. Terman (437), in his ground-breaking study of leadership, found that the boys who actually took the initiative were usually the larger boys, even though the experimental situation did not put a premium on bigness. Jones and Bayley (237), in the study referred to above, found that the outstanding leaders of the student body were usually drawn from the physically accelerated. And Cabot (83), in a very extensive study of the relation of body build to personality, found that boys of the athletic type of physique are more likely to be "ascendant"—that is, to take the lead in social situations. Stogdill's summary of leadership research (422) found height, weight, energy and health, and especially athletic prowess all associated with leadership.

It is true that the correlations are rather low. This should not surprise us. Physique is only one trait among many that may influence leadership (or any other social behavior). Moreover, as Barker, Wright, and Gonick (38) point out, physique is not measured in *psychologically* meaningful units. The reasoning here is simply that embodied in the popular expression: "An inch makes a lot of difference on the end of a man's nose." If you are an adult female of 5 feet, 6 inches, even a whole inch more or less in height would not make much difference. If you are 4 feet, 10 inches, or 5 feet, 11 inches, an inch less or an inch more, respectively, would probably seem nothing short of calamitous. An inch is not a psychological unit.

Perhaps Figure 8-4 will give you one clue to how these correlations came about. The fat child learns to be genial because active aggression is too difficult. I hate to spoil a good cartoon, but at least one study found that most fat children are less good natured than the average (157). But this study does not controvert the idea that the good nature or surliness is learned—as a result of different experiences some fat children learn one way of acting, some the other, but in both cases their experiences are related to their physiques. In the same way, superior initiative and leadership qualities are not innately correlated with bigness or with athletic build; they are acquired, but they are usually acquired more readily by the person of good physique because he has more opportunities to acquire them in the social play of childhood.

There is, of course, another partial explanation of certain relations between visible physical traits and personality. It works on the same principle as making a dog bad by giving him a bad name. If most of us believe that redheads are hot-tempered, we are likely to treat them in just the ways that will make them so. (This is an instance of what is called a self-fulfilling prophecy.) And there is a great deal of such folklore about physique and personality. Stockily built boys are expected to be daring leaders—real boys; slender lads are supposed to be bashful, submissive, unhappy (188).

Figure 8-4. Anatomy and Personality

"Us fat kids has got to be good natured. We can't fight and we can't run."

Finally, in our culture a child's physical vigor and his ability in games and sports are likely to influence markedly his attitude toward himself. Thus, in a diary which I recently analyzed, a distinctly intellectual adolescent devoted over 20 percent of his space to his somewhat meager athletic achievements and status. His superiority over his fellows in intellectual pursuits he obviously took for granted; but he wanted "to prove that a fellow with some brains isn't necessarily such a dub in sports." The emphasis on sports and physical prowess would probably be even greater in the diaries of less intellectual youths.

During childhood the desire for physical excellence may be less self-conscious than in adolescence, but it is nonetheless influential. In nearly every classroom is found the frail child who, wittingly or unwittingly, strives to compensate for his inadequacies in the world of physical activity by superiority in study. Perhaps less common, certainly less often noticed, is the child so satisfied with his physical prowess and leadership that he feels no need for scholastic achievement. The child whose inferiority feeling, generated by physical inferiority, makes him so miserable that he cannot try, in class or elsewhere, stands out clearly enough; but too often his inferiority is attributed to lack of effort instead of the other way around.

As if the complexities of differing rates of physical growth were not enough, we must add certain social factors. The physical excellence of a child is not to be judged by some absolute standard; it must be judged in relation to the degree of excellence found among his peers or in his family, and in relation to family and social expectancy. Thus the smallish boy whose father was a varsity tackle faces a more difficult problem than does the similarly small son of a frail intellectual. The somewhat hoydenish big girl in a family of older brothers is in a different situation from that of a similarly developed girl who has genteel sisters to criticize her unseemly ways. The rather dull lad who has been kept back for a year in school may be of only average or even of slightly inferior physical development; but he looks very big among children one or two years younger than he.

The relationships between physical growth and personality above set forth may seem merely common sense, and not half so dramatic as some of the mumbo jumbo of so-called character analysis. What we have said can indeed be summed up in a sentence: Physical growth is an important factor in the development of the whole personality. This scarcely any one would deny. Not in theory, that is. Yet our school practices are full of concrete denials. To take but a single example, little attention is given to grouping children according to their physical development. Instead, they have traditionally been grouped in school according to the number of seconds and minutes that have ticked off on the clock since they were born. The purely chronological grouping is then altered a little to take some account of scholastic achievement—primarily by refusing promotion to those of lesser accomplishment. This plan—if we can call it a plan—brings together children of enormously differing physical development and leaves to the hurried and distracted teacher the problem of adjusting procedures to these differences.

The doctrine of interaction between physique and personality here presented is not at all a fatalistic one. If you believe what some physiognomists tell you, that one has to have large ears to be musical, there's nothing you can do about the child with small ears. But if you perceive that Bill's rather frail physique is making it hard for him to play with his fellows, there *is* something you can do. Remember Theodore Roosevelt's struggle with just that problem and his successful, or more than successful, solution of it? The truly important relationships between physique and personality development are of the "that depends" variety. They depend upon how the child learns to react to his physique, and how he learns depends on the learning situations he encounters. The big boy or girl can learn either to be a bully, or a protector of the weak. It depends—depends pretty much on the parents, but with a big assist from teachers. The growth of personality depends greatly on learning how to react to one's physical capacities. Both the physical structure and the learning are important.

Summary

The truly enormous differences among children in physical development play an important part in the psychology of childhood. Single traits by themselves are less important, however, than is the interaction between them. Particularly important is the effect of differences in general physical excellence upon the social and personality development of the child.

9

The Psychology of Illness and Physical Handicaps

How do illness and special physical handicaps affect the child's psychological development? What can parents and teachers do to help children with physical difficulties attain a normal development?

When Zarathustra went one day over the great bridge, the cripples and beggars surrounded him. In profound dejection he turned to his disciples and spoke, saying:

"Verily, my friends, I walk amongst men as amongst the fragments and limbs of human beings!

"This is the terrible thing to mine eye, that I find man broken up, and scattered about, as on a battle-and-butcher-ground.

"And when mine eye fleeth from the present to the bygone, it findeth ever the same: fragments and limbs and fearful chances—but no men! and I should not know how to live if I were not a seer of what is to come.[1]

If "normal" physical development is as significant for the psychology of childhood as it was pictured in the preceding chapter, the temporary interruptions of normality that we call illnesses, and those enduring departures from normality that we call physical handicaps, must be judged as even more serious. Yet the first book in America to deal directly with the health of the school child appeared as late as

[1] From Friedrich Nietzsche, *Thus spake Zarathustra* (trans. Thomas Commons). Modern Library ed.; New York: Boni and Liveright, n.d., pp. 147, 149.

1914.[2] Students may still be graduated from teacher-education programs and be certified to teach without ever once having come to grips with the notion that the child is a *biological organism*. Education, we still seem to believe, is concerned primarily with the mind and book learning; physical development is secondary and a thing apart. Apparently we continue to think that a child has a *mind* to be *educated* and a distinct *body* to be *trained*.

In part this is due to traditional thinking about the mind and body. Way back in man's hoary past—before the days of written records—the notion grew up that a person was composed of two distinct parts: a sort of "ghost-mind" and a "body." Whole systems of philosophy grew up in the effort to make sense of this distinction.

With this philosophic dispute psychology as a science has no proper concern; the attitude is—or should be—one of stout neutrality. Psychology is not a study of more or less disembodied minds, nor of mind-free bodily processes, nor of some sort of combination of these. Psychology is one way of studying the *complete human being* (or other organism) as a going concern. It starts with certain observable events (how a person or other animal acts) and seeks to relate these events to other observable activities of the organism (the work of the hand or the tongue or the thyroid gland) as well as to events lying outside the organism.

The difficulty in maintaining neutrality is that the words used in referring to these observable events, "mental" and "bodily," are also used in the philosophical controversy. Thus issues belonging to the latter get illicitly dragged into what started out to be a factual inquiry.[3]

I rather doubt the present possibility of clearing up the resulting confusions, rooted as they are in everyday vocabulary. But at least I shall try in my use of the terms "mental" and "bodily" not to increase the confusion. By "bodily" or "physical" I shall mean the structures and functions studied in anatomy and physiology (including medicine). This chapter is devoted to a survey of how their soundness or unsoundness affects the child's behavior.

---

[2] That book, written by a psychologist, Lewis M. Terman, is *The hygiene of the school child* (438). A revised edition, published in 1929, contains suggestions which are still in advance of much current practice.

[3] I have dealt more fully with this issue in "The Ghostly Tradition and the Categories of Psychology" (133).

Physical ailments are more common than is generally realized. The number of men rejected in World War II as unfit for military service shocked the nation. According to the Office of Vocational Rehabilitation, more than sixteen million people suffer from *chronic* disease or physical impairment. To this must be added all those temporarily sick. And let us note that to be in what is called "normal health" is not necessarily to be truly healthy and happy self-fulfilling human beings. Truly, as Zarathustra says in the quotation with which the chapter opens, we find cripples and fragments but few *whole* men.

Children, too? Unfortunately, yes. Approximately a third of American children have major physical difficulties, and another third have minor handicaps. Not all of the handicaps are easily recognized nor is their importance, when recognized, always understood. Thus in a typical midwestern county the combined judgment of teachers and pupils identified only one child in ten as sufficiently handicapped to hinder his participation in important activities (33).

Yet any physical defect, even if it is fairly slight, may interfere with a child's psychological adjustment. In order to compensate for his physical defects, he may exhibit excessive activity and attention-getting (237). More troublesome are those children who, instead of seeking to compensate, merely withdraw from social situations. If it does nothing else a handicap affects the vitally important image that a child has of himself—a crucial factor in his whole development (309).

This image of himself is largely a reflection of how others react to him—or at least of how the child thinks they react. If others are repelled by or are scornful of his physical handicap or deficiency, the child is likely to react "with feelings of self-depreciation, hypersensitivity, self-consciousness, and anxiety in facing new or competitive situations" (Ausubel [22], summarizing the findings of Carter and Chess [91], Cruickshank [112], Mohr [317]).

It surely does not need to be emphasized that these psychological correlates do not afflict every child having physical difficulties. They are more frequently associated with *severe* handicaps (38), especially when the handicap directly interferes with social participation. The psychological difficulties may be lessened or even prevented when there are compensatory personality qualities, good social and economic status, and similar factors. Especially important is the attitude shown by parents, who can increase or greatly decrease the impact on the child's psychological development of unavoidable physical handicaps (91).

We should not, moreover, expect to find any specific kind of maladjustment as a result of some physical deficiency. The physically handicapped have the same failures in psychological adjustment as those of better physique; but their failures are apt to be more severe as well as more frequent. Timidity, shyness, and self-consciousness are found in many otherwise thoroughly healthy children. But such maladjustments are far more likely to be found in association with chronic ill-health or physical handicap (37).

All in all, the teacher will not be far wrong who assumes that every child is potentially a health problem, and that this may involve psychological problems. On the other hand, teacher, parent, and pupil should beware of the tendency to make ill-health an alibi for poor schoolwork or for social and personal ineffectiveness; it is seldom the sole factor. This may be seen from the fact that from a third to a half of those with considerable physical handicap have been free of personality problems (38). Excellent surveys of the whole problem may be found in Barker, Wright, and Gonick (38), in Garrett (163), and in Wright (483).

QUESTIONS

1. How many psychological effects of ill-health can you think of?
2. Is there any psychological effect that is attributable solely to some organic defect?
3. The mother of a child who had a small but clearly visible "hump" on her back early took pains to assure the child that the hump was "nothing special." She wanted her girl to grow up thinking she was "just like other people." What do you think of this tactic?
4. Is the sort of relation between physical defects and behavior just discussed the same as that involved in what is called psychosomatic disorder?
5. As you read the following pages ask yourself whether any of the disorders are "psychosomatic" as the term is usually used or whether they all are.

The Nervous System

Organic conditions can have both direct and indirect effects on behavior; particularly any sort of injury to the brain and nervous system must be given first place.

Apparently brain injuries at a very early stage of development have particularly harmful effects. Thus it has long been known that birth injuries may lead to spastic paralysis (in which the patient is subject to jerky or spasmodic movements). But only recently was it found that a milder damage to the brain during childbirth, one which may pass unnoticed, sometimes results in persistent "clumsiness" and motor incoordination. Many a child has thus become the butt of cruel jest or contemptuous pity when he should have been receiving highly specialized motor training. (Such training, while it seldom wholly eliminates the difficulty, often makes enormous differences in motor coordination.[4]) As high as one fourth of "problem children" referred to a clinic by the courts were found to have had brain damage.

Failure of the brain to receive adequate oxygen from the blood during prolonged labor seems in some cases to cause widespread impairment of the brain tissue with consequent feeblemindedness. And evidence has recently been put forward which seems to show that similar oxygen deprivation and resulting feeblemindedness is *sometimes* a consequence of the incompatibility of the Rh blood factors of the parents.[5] It should be noted, however, that we are speaking only of oxygen deprivation severe enough to damage brain tissue. Prolonged labor does not ordinarily result in such impairment of brain tissue. There seems to be no correlation between the amount of oxygen in the blood of the newborn and the development of intelligence as measured at age four (18).

Striking changes in the whole behavior pattern, mostly for the worse, sometimes follow *encephalitis lethargica* or epidemic "sleeping sickness." Cases so mild in the outward physical symptoms as nearly to escape diagnosis sometimes lead to an almost complete transformation of personality. Epilepsy, also, sometimes leads to mental deterioration; in addition, the convulsive seizures or "fits" which characterize this disorder put a severe strain on a child's social development. Other severe illnesses (for example, whooping cough), particularly in infancy or early childhood, may have direct effects on the nervous system and thus upon behavior. Both rickets and calcium

4 There is a fascinating account of the triumph over such obstacles in the life story of Earl R. Carlson, *Born that way* (88).

5 The incompatibility—which is relatively rare—does not affect the first-born child and not all of those born later (404, 405).

deficiency cause widespread and probably permanent damage to the nervous tissue. A summary of present knowledge of so-called organic or brain-damaged behavior problems is given in Bradley (71). The relation between brain pathology and mental subnormality is summarized by Benda and Farrell (52).

Apparently a revolution in medical thinking is under way. A few years ago medical men reacted against the old wives' view that any behavior difficulty was due to a fever in infancy—or to being "dropped on his head." Certainly in most cases that was a too-easy explanation. Yet there is now sufficient evidence to show that injury or disease of the brain is responsible for many forms of behavior disorder.

Direct treatment is, of course, primarily a medical problem. In many cases much can be accomplished, especially by *early* medical treatment. But whether the physical condition is or is not improved, *behavior training* is possible and necessary. Every resource of medical science should, of course, be utilized, but the role of the applied psychologist and that of the teacher remain of fundamental importance.

QUESTIONS

1. Aren't *all* behavior disorders due to brain deficiency or disorder? Why make a special category?
2. Are all cases of feeblemindedness due to oxygen deprivation?
3. Why is not feeblemindedness dealt with in this section? Surely it is a disorder of the nervous system.
4. How about the psychoses? Do they not belong in this section?

Glandular Disturbances and Behavior

So much nonsense has been written about the "glands regulating personality" that one hesitates to deal with the topic at all. Yet there are well-established facts of the greatest importance in this field. Particularly important in influencing children's behavior are the thyroid, adrenal, and pituitary glands. However, the whole body chemistry, which the glands so largely control, has both direct and indirect effects on conduct.

Roscoe was a thief—caught in the act and admitting many previous delinquencies. A fat, pleasant, healthy-looking boy in the fifth grade, nothing seemed more remote than a physical cause for his misdemeanors. Little by little, however, in conference with the boy, his parents, and later his physician, the story began to take shape. Some two and a half years earlier Roscoe's parents became alarmed over his obesity. On the physician's advice they cut down on his sugar intake. When Roscoe raided the pantry for sweets, they locked it up. He was forbidden to use any spending money on candy and was required to account for every penny.

Roscoe's weight did show a small decrease. But he *had* to have sweets. His craving for it—due to a glandular disorder—amounted to a burning passion. Presently he discovered that he could get money for candy at the "tuck shop" by robbing the cloakroom where many children kept lunch and spending money.

One noon Roscoe appeared on the playground, happily eating. "Whatcha got, Fatso; gimme some." "Yeah, gimme some." "Me, too."

Now Roscoe was not used to being the center of favorable attention. He was absolutely no good at games—too fat for anything but spectatorship. He now found to his great delight that attention and "friendship" could be bought. How far Roscoe was intrigued by the thought that he was buying the other boys' acclaim with their own money was never clearly discovered. At any rate, his thefts became bolder for he now had to supply others besides himself. Of course detection followed.

Glandular therapy was instituted and Roscoe's weight and his craving for sweets were simultaneously reduced. It is obvious, however, that his problems were not all thus easily solved. The distorted point of view with regard to others' property, though in its origin related to hormone defect, was not to be removed by feeding hormone capsules. Nor did glandular therapy wipe out from Roscoe's mind the discovery that "popularity"—of a sort—can be purchased. More important still, the glandular treatment could not supply the physical and social skills which Roscoe had failed to learn during his years of obese isolation from the world of childhood play. A constructive psychological and educational program—a rather prolonged program—was necessary to make up for Roscoe's deficiencies.

Finally we should note that it was only when Roscoe was caught in delinquency that parents and teachers were stimulated to the constructive medical and psychological measures which—quite independent of delinquency—were long overdue. A child so fat that he is seriously handicapped in play is a medical problem, no matter how much the physician may judge, as Roscoe's did, that "his overweight is not doing him any serious physical harm." The harm was psychological, not physical; but the treatment had to proceed along both lines.

QUESTION

What are some of the behavior consequences of milder glandular disorders?

Nutrition

Resentment of current attempts on the radio and television and at the drugstore to exploit scientific findings about nutrition, especially vitamins and minerals, should not blind us to their very real importance. Probably most readers of this book get all the vitamins and minerals they need, and in the best possible way, as part of a reasonably adequate diet. But there are obscure physical conditions in which extra supplies are critically needed.

More important for us is the fact that a really large number of school children simply do not have a diet anywhere near adequate as to either vitamins or total calories. To the undernourished by reason of poverty must be added those children of the well-to-do who are improperly and unwisely fed. The assertion that one third of our people are chronically "ill housed, ill clothed, and ill fed" turns out to be an understatement.

Lethargy, dullness, inability to put forth effort, and irritability and misconduct are the concomitants of malnutrition; susceptibility to all manner of other diseases is its sequel. If we spend little space on the topic here, it is because it is too important for merely incidental treatment in connection with child psychology. An extended and special treatment of the problems of nutrition should be part of the curriculum for all teachers.[6]

Invalidism

Prolonged illness and convalescence are obviously important influences on a child's total development. True, the relation between bodily well-being and general mental effectiveness is still obscure. While most of us find our efficiency reduced by illness, there are many examples of high, even permanently great, achievement despite

[6] For a review of pertinent investigations, see Shock, Physiological factors in mental development (397).

continuing sickness and invalidism. If the illness is such that you are not forbidden to exert yourself physically, it is often surprising what you *can* do. But one of the commonest effects of sickness is to raise the threshold of motivation—that is, to make a person less sensitive to ordinary motives and incentives. Thus most of us have experienced the distaste for serious reading, almost for any reading, during the early stages of convalescence. One *can* do things but doing them is so much less attractive than is customary; and as fatigue or lassitude increases, the attraction quickly becomes still less. The child—or adult—who is ill or half ill is a distinct problem in motivation. The relative incidence of illnesses at different ages is shown in Figure 9-1 (43).

Figure 9-1. Relative Incidence of Various Categories of Illness

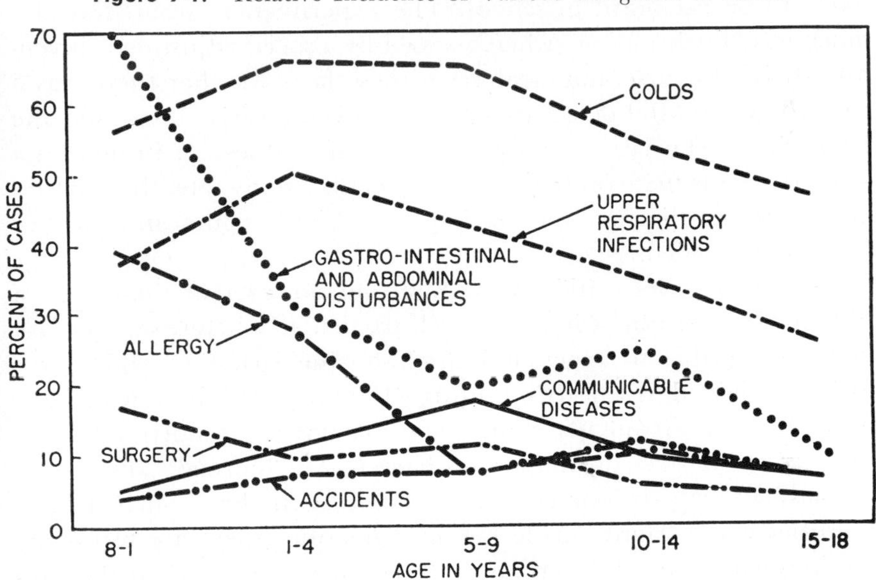

From L. M. Bayer and M. M. Snyder, Illness experience of a group of normal children. *Child Develpm.*, 1950, **21**, 93-120. Used by permission.

Surgical operations, illness, convalescence, and invalidism also contribute to personality difficulties. Here the attitude of parents is very important. If parents react to illness as a family calamity, or maintain an attitude of guilt for not preventing it, or blame the child, the child's reaction will be poor (234, 351). It is natural and indeed entirely proper to give special consideration and attention to the child who is sick, but this must be done with unusual delicacy and finesse if it is not to "spoil" him. Selfishness, self-centeredness, and expectation of attention are extremely common sequels of illness, especially long illness.

Yet the tendency to baby the child who is ill can hardly be the whole story. Stott (424) undertook to study the long-time effect of hospital illness of children under two years. A representative sample of such children was found in schools seven to eleven years later and compared with a control group. Of the illness group, 27.5 percent were found to be definitely backward in reading as compared with 11.3 percent of the controls. For the early pneumonia cases the percentage of reading backwardness rises to 57.1. Children who had had multiple illnesses (still before age two) were strikingly more likely to be backward in school. The experimental group was also much less "forthcoming" when assessed by a social adjustment inventory. It is, of course, not clear from these facts whether there was a common congenital defect that led to both the early illness and the later school retardation, or whether the early illness set in motion a series of events unfavorable to development. At any rate, the relation of early illness to school retardation seems highly significant. Further research is needed.

A study of college students by Stratton showed that those with a history of much illness in childhood, particularly before age six, are more susceptible to anger and unreasonable irritation (427). Less easily explained is Hardy's finding (190) that children who have never been ill frequently show somewhat greater tendency to personality twists than do those who have had a "normal" amount of sickness. Perhaps in our culture—or at least in the suburban communities where Hardy made her investigation—there are too many families where the children never experience, except when they are sick, the warmth of affection they need. Perhaps also a little sickness increases one's sensitivity to others, helps to prevent a sort of bumptious, energetic, extraversion which can be greatly trying. These are speculations. The fact seems to be that wholesome personality development is most often found in those whose health history shows a few, but only a few, minor illnesses.

The loss of normal experience due to long illness must also be considered. Teachers are apt to stress the loss of school time, though it has been shown that average or better-than-average pupils can make up for quite long absences in a very short time (336). The loss of social experience and the simple matter of losing one's place in the society of one's peers are probably more serious issues, particularly in later childhood and early adolescence.

When I was six, I returned to school from an attack of measles to find that the one subject of conversation was the performing bear who had just visited our village. For a whole week I was psychologically as much excluded from the life of my comrades as if I were still home with measles, and I felt it keenly. (I still wish I could have seen that bear!)

That was only one and relatively brief episode. But there are children who over a period of years are "out of circulation" one fifth to one half of the time because of illness. They can seldom be anything but outsiders in any group of children. They cannot share the current interests, for these are based on past experiences in which they had no part. They are deprived of the chance to learn many of the usual social skills and techniques of child social life. From overlong association with adults—parents, nurses, doctors—and overlong periods of solitude, they are apt to seem reserved and too grown up. And, of course, they are apt to expect attention.

Now none of these consequences of invalidism is inevitable. But if we think about them as probable consequences we can see what, as parents and teachers, we should be doing to ensure that invalidism does not damage the child's development.

QUESTION

Can you see any relation between your own health history and your present behavior? (Note how difficult it is to be sure of the causal connection.) If the effects are unfortunate, what might have been done to avert them?

Special Handicaps

Vision

Perhaps we can best understand the psychological implications of a physical defect if we consider one type in some detail.[7] Take the most common and perhaps the most important:

[7] If we were dealing only with vision, this section would be disproportionately long, despite the great importance of this sense in the child's development. But in consid-

defective vision. Nearly 40 percent of school children have some visual defect. One in 500 must be considered as "partially seeing" (490). The most frequent defects are defective discrimination of distant objects (nearsightedness or myopia), defective discrimination or strain in seeing near objects (hyperopia—often miscalled farsightedness), distortion of the image due to irregularity in the curvature of the cornea or lens of the eye (astigmatism). Apparently every eye has a little astigmatism, and most eyes have, in addition, either some myopia or some hyperopia. Small children generally have what would be called mild hyperopia in an adult—that is, they have difficulty in adjusting their eyes to seeing objects close up—a point with obvious implications for schoolwork. (The orthodox theory—not accepted by all specialists—is that their eyeball is too short at first, but gradually lengthens throughout the period of childhood.) But more severe or abnormal hyperopia, as well as severe myopia, is fairly prevalent. These three difficulties—astigmatism, hyperopia, myopia—can usually be "corrected" by glasses, and a very considerable number of children, perhaps as many as 15 percent, really need correction. This is a far larger percentage of children than actually wear glasses. It must be clearly understood, however, that glasses never give a person "normal" vision; a fixed lens system is always a compromise.[8]

Strabismus or squint (which include both cross-eyes and walleyes) is not only very disfiguring; unless corrected it may lead to the loss of the use of one eye. Some degree of it is found in about 1 percent of all children. Other defects in the muscles controlling eye movements set up strain and fatigue and hinder the efficient use of the eyes. Failure to use the images from the two eyes—whether due to muscular difficulties or to other obscure causes—makes for low visual acuity, distorts the "space world" of the child, and in extreme cases causes double vision. No one knows just how numerous these disorders are, since they are hard to detect unless quite extreme. The child performs the necessary visual tasks but does so inefficiently and at the expense of discomfort, a discomfort which may be vaguely referred to the eyes or may be unlocalized. Special examination techniques are thus required to detect these difficulties.

---

ering defective vision we are really discussing it as typical of all kinds of handicaps. Moreover, as was pointed out in the previous chapter, we cannot consider one sort of behavior—in this case, seeing—without relating it to other facets of living.

[8] This will be apparent if you consider that opera glasses or binoculars need an adjustment for different distances. Spectacles are fixed-focus binoculars.

And the detection of visual defects is by no means as far advanced as people commonly think. True, many schools now have a routine physical examination which includes a check on eyes. It is a question, however, whether this superficial test, by creating unfounded confidence, does not do more harm than good. The Snellen Test Charts, headed by the big E, are now known to be unsatisfactory diagnostic instruments, especially for children, even in the hands of skilled examiners. A routine examination by means of these charts is likely to reveal only the very worst cases of farsightedness and the medium and severe cases of nearsightedness. These are the children that the observant teacher is almost certain to detect without the test! Most other cases of farsightedness and nearly every other kind of visual disorder remain undetected. Yet these may be the very cases most in need of expert care.

Whether or not, then, there is a school examination, teachers (and parents!) have a responsibility to watch the child's *behavior* for signs of visual discomfort or defect. Persistent or excessive squinting or frowning, forehead wrinkles, rubbing the eyes, irritated lids, bloodshot eyes, holding a book too close or too far away, excessive head movements while reading, frequent closing of the eyes or holding the hand over them, tilting the head, poor sitting posture during visual work, thrusting the head forward, report of seeing double or of eyes hurting in bright light, body rigidity while looking at distant objects, headaches—any of these should excite suspicion that the child's eyes are giving trouble, especially when they are accompanied by general "nervousness" or irritability.

And if you do entertain such a suspicion how can you help the child? Here we leave the field of child psychology for the more general realm of the teacher's relation to parents and to various social agencies. Certainly the parents should be encouraged—strongly—to see that the child is taken to a competent specialist for examination. This sounds simple; often it is not. A few parents refuse any sort of medical attention on sectarian grounds; with these we can usually do nothing. More common is the parent who intends to have the matter looked into "sometime"—but never gets around to it. Common also is the parent who takes the child to the incompetent and the quack—the former may fail to find a real defect, the latter is almost sure to find one whether it exists or not, and bleed the family for "treatments." All a teacher's tact may be required to see that the child reaches the really skillful specialist, and sometimes even to see that the specialist makes more than a perfunctory examination. Routine creeps up easily on everyone, and the unusual case is too often dismissed with the verdict "nothing wrong." Many eye-muscle conditions "hide" themselves in the doctor's office only to reveal themselves a few hours later. It takes patience as well as special knowledge to stalk such conditions—and the busy practitioner is, perhaps, to be forgiven for not taking all that time on ordinary cases. But if we are convinced that *something* is wrong, we are justified in insisting that this is not an ordinary case.

Finally there is the perpetual problem of the child from a poverty-stricken family. Examinations and glasses cost money—a great deal of money. Sometimes there are charitable agencies which will help. The best specialists almost always do a certain amount of charity work. Often the school administration has ways of having needy cases taken care of. The solution thus varies from community to community. The only general rule which can be laid down is that the teacher must use both tact and persistence until the child's needs are met.

So much by way of *preliminary* to the psychological problems consequent upon visual deficiency. Let us now turn to those problems themselves. The teacher is perhaps likely to think first of the effect of poor eyes upon school learning. We ought not to make too much of this effect, however, or rather we ought not to interpret it in the

Figure 9-2. Visual Defects of School Children

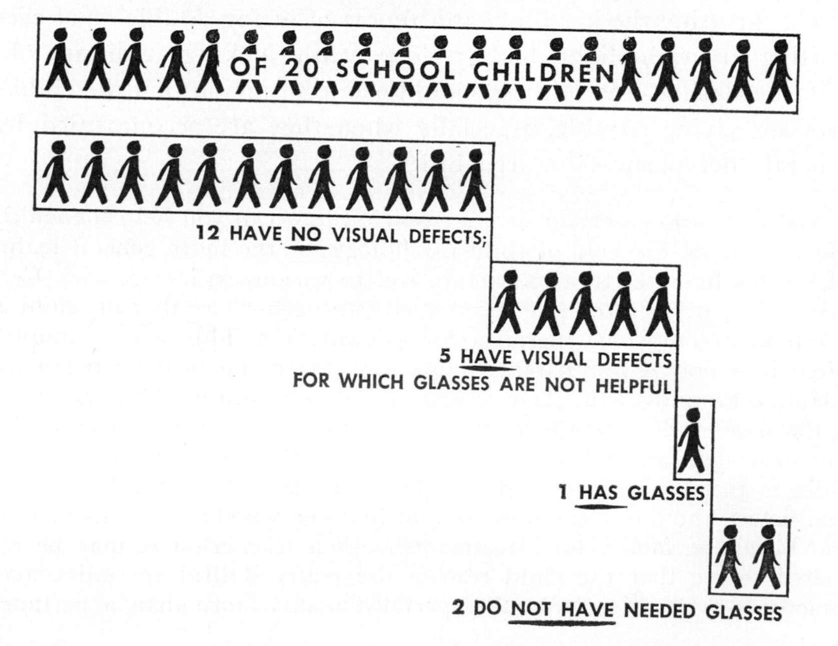

wrong way. The direct evidence is surprisingly negative.[9] Nonetheless there are important effects.

The effects of hyperopia and of various kinds of eye-muscle difficulties upon school learning are quite straightforward. They make reading, or any kind of close discrimination, just plain uncomfortable. Now if they did nothing but thus make the child unhappy and uneasy they should be of great concern to us. But from this uneasiness and discomfort flow other results. Irritability, peevishness, and bad temper, or a cry-baby dependency on adults follows naturally, though of course not inevitably, from the strain, the headache, and the general discomfort.

Moreover, the unpleasantness is apt to be associated in the child's mind with the place and activities which cause it. He does not always know that his eyes are troubling him; he just feels bad at school or when he is reading. Thus school becomes a hateful place and everything connected with books becomes distasteful. Undoubtedly a considerable amount of anti-intellectualism has its beginnings in the discomfort of hyperopia in the school years.[10] To motivate away from learning certain things is certainly to affect learning, even though sheer "ability to learn" may be unaffected.

A different sort of influence on personality development affects the myope. It doesn't seem to be uncomfortable for the nearsighted person to use his eyes; he just can't see things so well, especially at any distance.[11] From this proceeds, or may proceed, a number of serious limitations on experience and thus on the development of wholesome personality.

It is probably true that children with moderate myopia *can* learn to read and *can* learn all that goes with reading about as well as those with normal sight. Indeed, many of them obviously do. A person only moderately nearsighted can see letters well enough by getting

---

[9] See, for example, Clark (106) and Edson *et al.* (130). On the other hand, Park and Burri (344) did find a fairly direct relationship between *certain kinds* of eye difficulties and reading.

[10] The "normal" hyperopia of the early years usually becomes less, and may be entirely overcome, by the time of puberty; but the distaste for school and the aversion to all intellectual activities may continue long after the original cause has disappeared.

[11] It is still disputed whether close visual work, as in reading, if kept to a normal amount, increases myopia in childhood. The issue is highly technical, but this much is clear: long-continued close visual work is fatiguing to the young child and causes "nervousness." Whether for protection of the eye or for protection of personality development, close visual work should therefore be restricted to a few minutes at a time.

close to them—especially the commendably large and clear letters of modern children's books. He can usually see well enough for most other school tasks—that is, he can if his teacher has noticed his defect and *helped him* to get around it. Unfortunately, teachers do not always detect defects or pay attention to them if they do. I once saw a child scolded for walking up to the board without permission, though the thick glasses he wore should have made it obvious to anyone that only so could he hope to see what the teacher was writing there. And this was an experienced teacher; indeed, one with something of a national reputation.

When the myopia is very severe the problem is intensified. I once had occasion to sit in on the intelligence examination of a three-year-old with about 5 percent vision. (Such vision is just at the borderland between the ability to carry on as a sighted person and the necessity for training as a blind person.) Elaine's achievement on form boards—a test in which the subject must fit fairly large geometrically shaped blocks into correspondingly shaped slots—was conspicuously below her performance with tests involving language. The examiner, who was apparently not too well grounded in her understanding of children, was greatly puzzled to explain the discrepancy. "It can't be her eyes," she said. "Bad as they are, she can see these shapes all right." It seemed never to have occurred to her to consider what sorts of experience this child had had in her three short years of life and how these influence achievement.

Elaine's world had been a world of sounds; of the feeling of her bodily movements; of colors, perhaps, but only when these were in great splashes. She was sensitive to masses of light and shadow; already she had learned that "danger" of injury might lurk in shadows. But from her earliest years she had been denied that happy preoccupation with small visual *shapes* which is so characteristic of an infant's quieter moments. Never had she watched the lazy flight of horsefly or bumblebee; probably she had never been close enough to either to see their differences even as to size. Never had she seen the swooping flight of a swallow or the labored flapping of a crow. How should she be interested in the identification of birds, she who had never seen them save as flashing blurs? How should she be interested in circles and triangles and rectangles, even if she could *see* them, when in her daily life visual forms played so subordinate a role? She could be *taught* these forms as readily, perhaps, as any other child; but the normal course of daily experience (which is the base upon which intelligence testing rests) had left a great gap in her learning.

If this sort of deficiency of experience continues throughout the preschool years, the child is apt to be, even more than most children, uninterested in the queer little shapes called letters upon which we adults lay such mysterious stress, likely to be at first very slow in "catching on" to reading and writing. With our schools dominated as they are by these basic skills, the whole academic career of such a child may get off to a very bad start.[12]

Elaine, however, had intelligently cooperative parents. When the decision was made to bring her up in the world of the sighted, a careful analysis of probable deficiencies was undertaken and an effort made to supply them. Elaine thus came to school understanding the "looks" of right- and left-sided things like gloves—and like *p* and *q*—with a developed interest in geometrical figures, and with a desire to get close enough to things to examine them and see what they look like. Her reading met with no unusual difficulty. She quickly became a "total impression" reader—or rather was never anything else—and gained fair speed, despite the fact that with the book at four inches from the end of her nose she could see at most two words at a time. But other half-blind children, without the intelligent and explicitly planned training she had had, might, by the age of six or seven, be as good as blind when it came to making visual discriminations.

Two effects of severe myopia may thus be noted in the early school years. There is, first, a definite and irremediable slowing up of the reading because the myopic eye can see only a small part of the line at a time. And there is a direction of interest away from visual discriminations, a sort of negative preparation for the learning of reading that tends greatly to slow down the process in the first years in school.[13]

Second, and more important still, is the effect on nonacademic pursuits. For the myope the physical world is full of hidden dangers. Missiles (balls and the like), people, and vehicles appear suddenly from nowhere to threaten one. Obstacles in the way of hurrying feet are unseen; wire fences and brush and low-hanging limbs catch one unaware. Even chairs and footstools have a perverse way of getting in one's road. If he is even to keep on living, the nearsighted child must

[12] Note that a mere shift to an "activity program" would not by any means meet the needs of such a handicapped child. Most activity projects are just as baffling to a half-blind child as is reading. Nor are the needs of all the handicapped alike, even when they have the same *physical defect.* Psychologically, a handicap is only one aspect of a total personality.

[13] Many of the studies on reading ability and visual defect fall into a statistical trap by taking pupils matched in intelligence and comparing their reading scores. But the child who, despite poor eyes, equals another in intelligence-test scores is intrinsically a *better* learner. "Matching" thus, instead of ensuring equality, ensures inequality in "learning ability." Matching is an inappropriate method of experimental control when the matching factor correlates with *both* the performances to be compared.

learn more caution and vigilance in his movements than is entirely consistent with the carefree and possibly reckless play of normal childhood.

Then, too, the games that can be played successfully—or at all—are limited. Ball games particularly require a speedier or more accurate eye-motor coordination than the myope can easily manage—and from marbles to football, it is astonishing how many games depend on some kind of "ball." Games and play involving bodily contact are dangerous for the child who wears glasses. Boxing or fighting, when you can't see your opponent's arms, can barely make out his face as a vague blur, is apt to be a pretty sanguinary business. And so it goes through nearly all the activities of boys and a fair proportion of those of girls.

Now play in childhood, as we have suggested, is the chief determiner of a child's social status; and it is the chief schoolmaster of social intelligence and personality. It is in play that the child first learns to give and take, the most essential of social virtues. It is in play that one best earns the applause of one's fellows. It is in play that the child can most easily explore his own capacities, including his emotional capacities. And it is chiefly in play that one learns that easy control of the body which is the basis for poise and grace and for the appearance of dynamic energy which is so important in social relations. It is no small matter for the child when all of this is sharply curtailed by poor eyes and the necessity for wearing glasses.

Small wonder, then, in view of all the difficulties and perplexities of the active world, that so many myopes retreat to the world of books and become "bookworms." Here no missiles rise up unexpectedly to strike them, no cruel playmates taunt them because of a failure to "smack it on the nose" or to catch an easy fly. Almost we dare to say that children don't wear glasses because they read too much; they read too much because they have to wear glasses.

QUESTION

How, specifically, can a teacher help to minimize these consequences?

Another limitation on social learning affects even the moderately nearsighted. Far more than we are likely to realize, we are guided in our social intercourse by the play of expression on a person's face, by the little shifts in posture, by almost imperceptible gestures. Now these guides to the other fellow's feelings are not natural endowments; they have to be learned. It is difficult, however, to learn them when you can't see them, and most of these cues are very fine and fleeting. Even when they lie within the limit of what the myope can *see,* they often lie below the level of what he is apt to *notice.* There is thus likely to develop an insensitivity to social stimuli, and a tendency to tediousness in conversation—which simply means a failure on the part of the speaker to recognize that what he is saying is boring his auditor. In later life not to have learned these social cues may be one of the most calamitous of all the effects of poor vision.

Add to all these, the self-consciousness of the handicapped due to the taunts of playmates ("Old four eyes"), the disfigurement of strong glasses ("Men seldom make passes at gals who wear glasses"), the judgment that one is high-hat or peculiar because of failure to recognize friends or acquaintances—put all these together and you have a complex set of problems facing the visually handicapped child. They are clearly too many and too difficult for him to solve unaided.

In strabismus the chief problem is disfigurement. Even a small amount causes a person to look "funny" to other children. The strain this imposes on his personality development should be obvious. Correction (whether by surgery, orthoptic exercises, or just by glasses) has been found to improve very greatly the child's personal and social adjustment.

What Can Teachers Do?

This brings us to the role of the teacher in helping the handicapped child. A little can be done by direct action in the classroom. We can ensure that window shades are properly adjusted to avoid glare, we can try to have adequate artificial light—something that too few classrooms have. Then there is the problem of correct posture and the proper holding of books. The myopic child must carefully guard against reading with his head bowed as this tends to increase the myopia. We can be sure that the children read from large type, that they do not read too much or too long at a time. These are sound hygienic measures for any child, and they are particularly necessary for the handicapped.

It will have been noted, however, that we laid most stress upon the effects of poor vision on personality and social development; and it is here that the teacher's responsibility is greatest. *Scarcely one of the dire effects listed is an inevitable result of visual handicaps.* They are merely what will happen *unless someone does something about the situation.*[14]

Suppose we look back a moment and review the effects discussed. We find the visually handicapped child limited in his play life and therefore in his opportunities to learn effective social behavior. Clearly, then, what the teacher should do is to set the stage for play activities and other opportunities for social behavior in which the child will be at less of a disadvantage. That sounds easier than it is. We do not dare build our entire class program simply to help the handicapped; that would be unfair to the normal children. We need, therefore, to develop our insights into the present weaknesses and strengths of the handicapped child, need to watch for every opportunity to adjust both his strengths and his weaknesses to the play and social life of the whole group. We need also to plan programs sound for all but giving opportunity and scope for full participation by the child with special deficiencies.

Related to this program of helping the child to make external adjustment is the problem of helping his internal adjustment. The handicapped person must face reality. He must realize his limitations, must accept them with courage; yet he must not get into the habit of making his handicap an "alibi" for failure. The balance between these two is a delicate affair; we should not expect the child to keep it without a great deal of help.

The trend of thinking today is against segregation of handicapped children in institutions and special classes unless the deficiencies are very grave. It is held, and rightly so, that the handicapped need to learn to live in the world as it is, need to learn to associate with normal people. We should remember, however, that an ordinary or "normal" situation for most children is not "normal" for one who is handicapped; the world is designed for the normal person. Only in a "supranormal" environment can we expect normal behavior from a person with subnormal physical equipment.

---

[14] And an extended study of the problem (38) shows that not enough is done; psychological maladjustment is more frequent among the physically handicapped than among those of normal physique.

In a "sheltered environment," such as a sight conservation class, we *limit* a person's living space. It is too easily forgotten that we may thereby *increase* his freedom of action. A road certainly restricts where one goes but it gives far greater freedom of motion than does rough ground. A child is made free to walk when fenced in from the perils of traffic—and gains success experiences in this limited area (37). To *give the handicapped—that is, the subnormal—child a* normal *chance to develop requires special pains and special consideration.* For some, the special treatment can be best given in institutions or special classes. In that case, the goal should be the development as fast as possible of the most nearly normal behavior and social adjustment that circumstances permit. For the majority of the handicapped, the special consideration should be given in regular classes. (For a more extended treatment, see Pelone [348].) Perhaps no better index of the teacher's sensitivity to the individual needs of children can be found than the provision she makes for the social development of handicapped and deviating children.

Other Special Handicaps

We can deal more briefly with other handicaps. The essential problems are the same. Defects of hearing are much less frequent than those of vision; also, they are more frequently overlooked. From 5 to 10 percent of all pupils need special attention, medical and pedagogical, because of auditory defect.

The discomfort associated with poor vision seldom occurs in auditory impairment, but the social consequences are similar. Many children are unwilling to admit auditory impairment and sometimes make themselves quite foolish in their attempt to conceal the handicap. They often pretend to hear what is said when in fact they understand almost nothing. Such behavior not only is exasperating to the teacher but is very unfavorable to good schoolwork.

Somewhat similar difficulties arise when the child genuinely does not realize that he is handicapped. A few hard-of-hearing pupils indulge in misbehavior as a conscious or unconscious way to conceal their deficiency. Occasionally a deaf child gets the idea that people are talking about him behind his back, though this is more common with deaf adults. Finally, as is well known, the hard-of-hearing are often misjudged as dull or even mentally defective by both teachers and fellow pupils.

The social isolation of the hard-of-hearing is a little more obvious, though probably no greater, than that of the visually defective. In any case it presents us with the same challenge to alter the situation, to create opportunities whereby the handicapped child may develop his personality and learn the necessary social adjustments.

QUESTION

Which of the specific psychological problems of the visually handicapped are met in the hard-of-hearing?

Unlike the partially sighted and the hard-of-hearing, children with severe motor or orthopedic handicaps are seldom neglected in school. Their handicap is visible and understandable to teacher and fellow pupils, and usually appeals to sympathy. But our help needs to be judicious. The environment *has* to be simplified for the handicapped; but this may restrict his chances to learn. It has been suggested that those who deal with crippled children may even have to be ready to let them suffer minor mishaps in order to learn independence.

In one study, children with motor handicaps were found less able than normal children to use the knowledge or skills they actually had in an integrative solution of certain problems. The details might be all right but they were not welded together (472, II). In another study they were found to lack realism in setting goals for themselves (472, I, II, III).

One of the most insistent problems is to keep the handicapped from self-pity on the one hand; and on the other hand from a bitter resentment of pity or even of sympathy. Especially is this true of conditions which are markedly disfiguring. While full participation in games is generally impossible for most of the handicapped, such a child may be given roles which permit him to take part in the activities and feel himself one of the group. The problem is most acute in out-of-class activities.

Harold Russell, in his autobiographical story *Victory in my hands* (370), records the lift that came to his spirit when a wise surgeon reminded him that he was not crippled, merely handicapped, though he had lost both hands. A cripple, he learned, is one "incapable of proper or effective action"; a handicapped person, on the other hand, is one who has a "disadvantage or hindrance making success in an undertaking more difficult." The particular verbal distinction is not really important; children, at any rate, usually become quite used to being referred to as crippled. But the difference in attitude which Russell points to is of tremendous value. When we think in terms of a person as a going concern—eating, digesting, hoping, breathing, planning for the future, loving—we see that there are many who are indeed handicapped by loss of limb or sight or hearing but who *as persons* are not crippled at all and are gloriously alive and whole. Many of us on the contrary, though our bodily members seem sound, are, with our petty aches and pains, our anxieties and our fears, our jealousies and our hates—and our indigestions—really crippled persons (136). (See also 37.)

Finally, as Barker (34) has pointed out, "the parent may feel guilty, resentful, or socially stigmatized for having produced a defective child, and this may cause him to push the child aside. Or, the parent may, either from genuine sympathy or from reaction to his own guilt, do everything in his power to recompense the child for his misfortunes." Or, worst of all, he may vacillate between these attitudes.

In short, the problems of the handicapped are seen to be those of the normal child, somewhat intensified; and the responsibility of the teacher to understand the individual and to deal with him on the basis of his particular needs is, once more, the same in kind, but greater.

Summary

Two thirds of all children have health problems sufficiently serious that they may affect psychological development. Defective health or physical development restricts activity and thus the opportunity to learn the things that children usually learn. Especially important are the restrictions upon play—the major vocation of a child, and the occupation in which the child learns both physical and social effectiveness.

The adult can help the handicapped child both by providing opportunities to learn the things he is deprived of by his handicap and by assisting him to make realistic adjustment to his deficiencies.

10

Intelligence in Childhood

Intelligence is the ability to perform the intellectual tasks that are usual and expected of one's age. Does a child have a stable amount of such intelligence? Can his intelligence be improved by individual or social effort? What are the factors favorable to intellectual growth?

It has become fashionable to be a little disparaging of "mere intellectual development." I think it will not be denied, however, that the country and the world in general could use a little more intelligence. Moreover, as the previous chapters have shown, intelligence plays a determining part in emotional, social, and personality development. To deal effectively with children is to give constant consideration to the intellectual side of their natures.

Intelligence is not the whole of this intellectual side of life, any more than "emotion" is the whole of the emotional life. Intelligence, however, is the hard core of understanding, rationality, and wisdom; and most research has been centered about this core. Let us begin there.

The Nature of Intelligence

Psychology has made spectacular advances in the field of measuring intellectual growth; yet in no other area is there more controversy among experts—or more confusion among laymen. We can clear up some of the confusion by a careful definition of intelligence.[1]

In advanced scientific circles it is popular nowadays to talk about the need for "operational definitions." In plain English what this means is really quite simple: If you want others to know what you are talking about, appeal to *facts of observation;* and facts are best made clear when you show how you got them, that is, what operations you carry out in observing. So if you want to know what intelligence is, you look at how one goes about observing it.

QUESTIONS

1. Don't you already have a pretty fair idea as to what intelligence is? How does it differ from zero intelligence?
2. How did your grandfathers before the days of intelligence tests observe and estimate intelligence?
3. Has progress in psychological knowledge made any other improvement over grandfather's methods, except to introduce tests?

Take an ordinary case, a neighbor's child, Doris, aged seven and a half years. Suppose there were no tests or testers available. What would you do to find out how intelligent she is? You would, I am sure, pick out a few intellectual tasks which any child of her age should be able to manage, put her to performing them, and then see how well she does.

But what is an intellectual task? Well, thinking. Remembering. Putting two and two together. Solving problems. Making generalizations—simple ones at age seven and a half, of course—getting to the heart of an issue if the issue is a proper one for young children.

Something like that would emerge if you asked any thoughtful person to list the earmarks of intelligence. It is not a perfect list but it serves to indicate the domain within which intelligence performs.

The psychologist, in constructing tests of intelligence, does the self-same thing. He, too, seeks tasks that show how well the child is

[1] What to do about citing research and critical interpretations is a real perplexity in this field. There is just too much of it! A mere listing of titles fills a whole book. Moreover, a text on child psychology is no place for an extended discussion of tests and measurements. Yet the testing movement has so revolutionized our thinking about children that we must give it a place. Fortunately two recent books, Tyler (451) and Anastasi (7), have excellently summarized the field. This makes it less important to cite supporting evidence all the time, but it does make what follows sound dogmatic. I shall try, however, to warn the reader whenever any statement is not thoroughly substantiated by research.

able to perform the intellectual activities that are usual and expected at his age. We may take this as a definition of intelligence.

The definition of intelligence as the ability to perform the intellectual tasks that are usual and expected in a given population is not just something dreamed up by psychologists. I must take the responsibility for *formulating* the definition; but all I have done is to extract the common element that is found in the everyday use of the term. When you—and the other fellow—say that Jill is more intelligent than Jack, you mean that Jill can do more of the usual and expected things than can Jack. At least that's the evidence you offer when asked how you know.

While the definition of intelligence is thus a matter of just plain everyday usage, theories about intelligence are not. A valid theory of intelligence must rest on facts. Many of the popular theories flagrantly contradict facts. It is the virtue of a good definition that it helps us to find out which facts are relevant.

To get tasks that are reliable indicators of how well a person can perform the usual and expected intellectual activities of his age takes a lot of careful and highly technical work. Thus it is impossible to ask a child to perform for you all the "usual and expected" activities of his age. Hence samples have to be used, and we have to prove by actual trial with thousands of children that the sample is representative. (This is called "validation.") A valid and, if possible, foolproof scoring must be provided. Many such sample tasks, called "test items" when used in this way, are then combined in a test scale.

QUESTION

What are some behaviors other than those referred to above that might reasonably be taken as indicators of intelligence?

The Varieties of Intelligence Tests

You will recall that we spoke of the "usual intellectual tasks." The term *intellectual* must not be given a "high-hat" or an "academic" interpretation. To rid his fingers of a sticky feather is, for an infant, a real intellectual task. (It would not make a good "test" because luck plays too great a part in success.) In our culture, being able to fit a triangular block of wood into a slot of corresponding shape and size is as much an intellectual task as being able to name the days of the week. (Both these tasks have been used as tests.)

A casual inspection of various tests permits classification into two types: *verbal tests* in which the response demanded is made in words; and *performance* or *nonverbal tests,* in which the response is made in some other way. To test intelligence we need a representative sample of all the "usual and expected" behaviors, and it is obvious that a sample restricted just to verbal responses would be quite unrepresentative. In certain special circumstances, the verbal tests may give us the information we need; even then *they do not measure the whole range of a child's intelligence.* Both verbal and performance tests measure intelligence, and both kinds are needed for any thorough assessment of a child's intelligence.

Figure 10-1. A Kent-Shakow Formboard

The most frequently used "scales of intelligence" for children—especially the Stanford-Binet (S-B), and the Wechsler Intelligence Scale for Children (WISC)—incorporate both verbal and performance tests, but they are more heavily loaded with the former. Various scales composed exclusively of performance tests as above defined are therefore used as supplementary measures.

It should be added, however, that calling the two kinds of tests "verbal" and "performance" is misleading if we take the two terms too literally. A verbal test requires the child to perform—to name the days of the week is surely a performance. And you have only to watch (and listen!) while a child works at the sort of tests illustrated in Figure 10-1 to see that he often uses his verbal skills in a "performance" test. The classification is useful chiefly to remind us of the variety of intellectual tasks that are "usual and expected" of children of various ages. It is not a clue to the nature of intelligence.

The Component Theory

That clue must come from a more detailed examination of the development of children. The "usual and expected" obviously differs from year to year; it changes not only in amount but in kind. Intelligence does not show itself as a single entity that grows by accretion. Instead, there is a dynamic succession of functions, the later ones depending greatly on the maturing of the earlier, yet having an independent growth curve of their own (45).

Hofstaetter's statistical analysis of the data from the Berkeley growth study (206) finds three basic factors that account for most of the differences in intelligence. During infancy and early childhood, differences in what is "usual and expected" depend chiefly on a sort of sensorimotor alertness. Sensorimotor alertness continues to increase until well past childhood, so that a youth or a young adult is generally a great deal superior to an infant in sensorimotor functions.

But the *relative* contribution of these sensorimotor functions to intelligence decreases rapidly after two years of age. By about age six differences in sensorimotor functions play comparatively little part in the total of the behavior that we judge to be intelligent. (This is true except for cases of extreme defect in sensorimotor function.) Our tests merely reflect that fact.

From the close of infancy to about age ten differences in intelligence seem to be controlled chiefly by a factor that is rather hard to characterize; Hofstaetter suggests that we call it persistence. The children that we call intelligent at this age are those who get things done by staying with it. (Parents do well to remember that this major factor in the intelligence of a seven-year-old often looks like stubbornness to them.)

During this period of childhood another determiner also begins to make itself felt. This determiner is the ability to use symbols, especially the verbal symbols that stand for abstract concepts. This component of intelligence begins quite early. Indeed, McCarthy

(299) finds that even in infancy the development of speech is predictive of intelligence in later years. It plays a steadily increasing part in making a person's behavior intelligent. From about age ten onward throughout life most of the differences between the intelligent and the less intelligent seem to reside in this ability to use abstract symbols. A highly schematic picture of this development is given in Figure 10-2. It does not show the dynamic influences of these factors upon each other but only the outcome in the development of intelligence.

The practical implications of this Component Theory of Intelligence bring us back to examining the actual operations of measure-

Figure 10-2. The Components of Child Intelligence

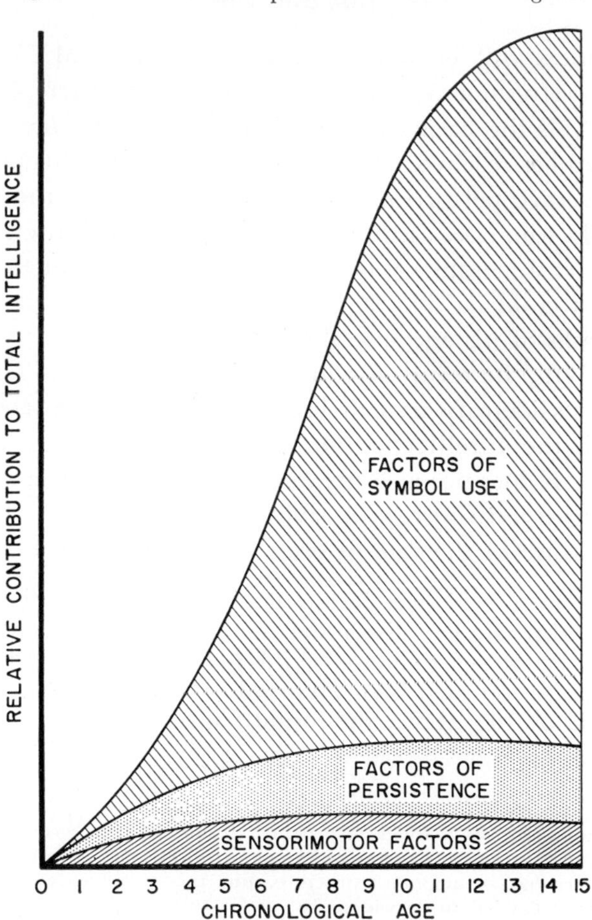

ment—i.e., to testing. We may conclude that to find out how able a person is, it is necessary to sample a considerable number of different kinds of task-performances. If we select this sample carefully, we get a combined score that is a useful predictor of very many sorts of intellectual ability—so many that we are entitled to speak of it as an index of abilities in general.[2]

As a child grows older, however, new abilities become "usual and expected," and prediction from one stage of development to another becomes hazardous. We shall present some of the facts about prediction in later sections.

The MA and the IQ

Most readers will be familiar with the terms "MA" and "IQ," but a brief refreshment of memory may be in order. The *Mental Age,* or MA, is the basic measure; it designates the *level* of intelligence a child has reached, and does so by comparing his performance with the average performance made by children of the stated age. Thus a child who does as well on the tests as a typical eight-year-old is said to have a mental age of eight years. If you want to know how intelligent a child is—that is, how well he can meet the usual and expected tasks of his age—use the MA.

Not the IQ! The term "Intelligence Quotient" is so familiar that many persons identify it with intelligence testing. Surprising as it may sound, the Intelligence Quotient is not really a measure of intelligence. It does not measure *how much* intelligence a child has—for that, as we have just been saying, we use the MA. Instead, the IQ is a measure of the rate of growth in intelligence.

To get a measure of rate—in any field—always divide the amount by the time: in this case you divide the "amount" of intelligence or mental age by the length of time the child has lived—his chronological or calendar age (abbreviated CA). To avoid decimals the resulting quotient is multiplied by 100. Hence the formula is

$$\frac{MA}{CA} \times 100 = IQ.$$

[2] Note that we speak of "abilities in general" rather than of "general ability." The latter term seems to imply a single entity that is intelligence, whereas we have seen that intelligence has a compound structure. But the convenience of the expression "general ability" has led to its widespread use.

Thus, if a child has a mental age of 8 years, 2 months (or 98 months) and a chronological age of 7 years, 1 month (or 85 months), his IQ will be $^{98}/_{85} \times 100 = 115$. (There is a refinement of the formula for the Revised Stanford-Binet after the child reaches age thirteen. The computation of MA and IQ on the WISC is a little different, but the interpretation of the two scores is roughly the same.)

But doesn't this IQ show "how smart a child is"? Not directly. It shows, if you will, how smart he is *for his age*. That is quite different from showing what a child can do.

Take an actual comparison. George is 9 years old, his MA is 12, his IQ is 133. Benny is 6, his MA is 8. He too has an IQ of 133.

Both children have developed rather rapidly—approximately one third faster than the average. But George has been at it three years longer and, as his MA shows, can do a lot of things that Benny won't be able to do for some time. The same IQ stands for very different actually realized abilities.

Conversely, different IQ's may represent about the same level of ability. Jim and Gail both register MA 7.2. This means that on the test, and in everyday life too, they perform at about the same level intellectually; but their respective IQ's are 60 and 120, for Jim is 12 and Gail is only 6.

QUESTIONS

1. Even psychologists sometimes use IQ and MA interchangeably. Under what circumstances is this permissible? When does knowing the IQ tell you how intelligent a child is?
2. Are there any intellectual differences that you would expect to find in two children of the same MA and widely different IQ?

The child who develops in mental age at the normal rate has, of course, an IQ rating of 100. (This is simply arithmetic; look at the way the score is calculated.) Even "average children," however, are seldom exactly average. It is usual, therefore, to regard IQ's anywhere between 90 and 110 as representing average rate of development in intelligence. On the Stanford-Binet about half of all American children fall within these limits. (On other tests somewhat more or somewhat fewer are within the 90–110 limits.)

As you move up from IQ 110 or down from IQ 90 the percentage of children who make a given score diminishes rapidly. Only about 2 percent attain an IQ rating of 140 or above. It is conventional to speak of these as "gifted children," but the division at 140 is arbitrary; we could, if we chose, call the additional 2 percent who fall between 135 and 140 IQ gifted, too. All of them are children of exceptionally rapid intellectual growth.

At the other end, about 2 percent or a little more test below IQ 65. These children are seriously retarded in their intellectual development; few of them can ever be helped to the point where they can carry on the normal work of the school for children of their age (though, as we shall see later, there are exceptions). Nearly all of them, therefore, belong in some sort of special class. It is now recognized, however, that it is wholly improper to characterize a child as "feebleminded" on the basis of low intelligence test ratings *alone.*

So numerous are the misconceptions which have attached themselves to the term "IQ" that many psychologists would gladly see it abandoned. We could state all the essential facts in other ways. But it's not quite that simple. When every person in the land who has finished the sixth grade is talking about the IQ, our only recourse is to get as many as possible to use the term properly.

Let us remember, then, that an IQ is only a number and, at that, a number that doesn't stand for a single concrete fact. It stands for a ratio or relation between two other numbers: the number that represents calendar age and the number that represents how well a child can do the things that others of his age can do. Neither in theory nor in fact does an IQ represent some permanent endowment.

It follows that the practice of labeling a child as "having such and such an IQ" as if it were some enduring personal trait is seriously misleading. A child's IQ is not like blue eyes or a humpback or one short leg; it is more like an index of health—something that may be difficult to change but subject just the same to modification. All in the world that an IQ tells us is how fast a child has developed in intelligence up to this time and in comparison with other children. That's a handy thing to know. But if we want to know what a child is capable of doing or of learning to do *now,* the basic datum is the MA and not the IQ.

I strongly urge that teachers do not tell parents—or the children! —either the MA or the IQ of any pupils. Tell parents what the score *means* if that seems indicated, not what the score is. Say that the tests show that Marylyn seems capable of intellectual work at about the level of a nine-year-old. If the parent presses you to say what IQ that is, say that you don't believe in that kind of score;

you prefer to work with test scores that get down to concrete facts about what a child can be expected to do. Marylyn, for example, is intellectually ready for fourth-grade work. This statement will not enable Mrs. Pusher to gloat over her sister-in-law—as she might if she were given the respective IQ's of Marylyn and her cousin. But this sort of statement tells the mother what she needs to know and can do something about. More serves no good purpose.

If, however, we are careful not to attribute to the IQ score meanings it cannot support, it can be a useful index of the *rate* of intellectual development. It will be so used in what follows.

QUESTIONS

1. Tests for college students are often called IQ tests. Why is this a serious mislabeling?
2. How much special education and experience does one need to give an intelligence test?

Testing for intellectual growth looks deceptively simple—there is little of the shining chrome or the purring machinery that makes testing in some other scientific fields so impressive. And indeed, as we have repeatedly said, it does rest on just the commonplace tasks and operations of everyday life. Testing is only common-sense judgment refined; but the refinement is all-important. Moreover, in making these refinements it is necessary to introduce assumptions—perfectly proper assumptions, but assumptions that limit the way in which the measurements can be used. (For example, averaging of IQ's is improper.) *Thus professional judgment is needed in utilizing or interpreting test results.*

Many tests, and on the whole they are the most searching and valid ones, cannot be given at all except by professional testers. Not infrequently a principal will say to some teacher: "You've had a little psychology; 'bone up' on the Binet tests tonight, and you and I will test some of the children tomorrow." It cannot be too strongly stated that this is professional malpractice. The so-called tests thus administered are not the Binet tests; they are not even "reasonable facsimiles thereof." Binet testing is an art that must not be practiced by the unqualified. Serious harm has been done to children through such malpractice.

On the other hand, some tests of intelligence are designed to be administered by any adult willing to follow the simple but very precise directions given with the test. (Apparently, however, a good many adults, not seeing the why of the directions, just won't follow them all the way. Yet if the test is not given as directed, it loses all meaning and value.) Properly administered and scored, tests yield information that helps enormously to understand the child's intellectual growth.

Moreover, they enable us to define what intelligence is, and to do so in conformity with the demand of modern scientific logic that the definition be in terms of definite and measurable operations. *A person's general intelligence is his ability to perform the usual and expected intellectual activities of his age and his culture;* it is measured by taking a representative sample of those performances.

QUESTIONS

1. Does the definition of intelligence given above imply that there is a different kind of intelligence in, let us say, Tibet and in Oregon?
2. Should we not have a different test for Oregon and New York?
3. If intelligence is to be defined by the tests used to measure it, what is to prevent any screwball from inventing his own kind of test?
4. Has your intelligence changed since you were sixteen?

How Dependable a Quality Is Intelligence?

Granted that we have tests of reasonable validity and reliability (and this has been demonstrated to be the case), it is still pertinent to ask whether intelligence is a stable characteristic in childhood. If Jenny stands at the head of her class in intelligence when she enters school at age six, is she likely to have the same relative position six months later? or twenty years later, for that matter? When the question is thus phrased, most people, in my experience, answer "Yes." Jenny, they believe, may not hold exactly the same standing, but she will not be far from it.

Now if Jenny maintains the same relative position in intelligence, not merely with her classmates but with her age-mates in general, her IQ will remain the same. (This is a matter merely of the arithmetic by which IQ is computed. When we say the IQ remains the same we mean that the child has kept his or her *relative* position in intelligence as tested.) Thus the question as to her holding the same relative standing has usually been asked in the form, "Does the IQ remain constant?" [3]

The Constancy of the IQ

The issue of the "constancy of the IQ" has led to some furious controversy. Yet I cannot find that any psychologist has ever believed in an absolutely constant IQ. The real question is not "Is the IQ constant?" but "How nearly constant is the IQ?" Or better, "How nearly constant is a child's rate of intellectual growth?" How many shifts in relative rank do we get with the mere passage of years? How much shift do we get under certain stated conditions? How dependable a quality, in fact, is intelligence? That sort of question calls for a resort to facts, not to speculative charge and counter-charge. And enough facts are in to give an answer.

Not quite a simple answer, however. Let's begin with intelligence in infancy. Here we have the so-called developmental tests which are commonly regarded as a sort of intelligence test. It turns out that an IQ obtained from one testing will often differ quite markedly from the next. Moreover, an IQ after age four will often be considerably higher or lower than the IQ a child had on infant tests. Thus the IQ in a child's earliest years is decidedly not very constant.

Is not this merely a sign that the developmental tests for infants do not really measure intelligence? The theoretical question thus raised is too involved to be discussed here, but the answer seems rather to be that (as was pointed out on page 286 ff.) there is a change in the *composition* of intelligence as we pass from infancy to childhood. What is "usual and expected" of an infant differs in kind as well as in quantity from what is expected from a three-year-old. The practical conclusion, in any case, is that "infant intelligence" is not a dependable predictor of child or adolescent intelligence. This fact should be known to parents who may be either too hopeful or too distressed by an infant's scores on the developmental tests.

---

[3] It has been pointed out that the issue would be more sharply defined if stated in terms of what the statisticians call *z* scores rather than IQ (208). But the final conclusions and the interpretations are the same.

After the child passes about the age of three, however, the constancy of relative position—and so of IQ—becomes fairly high. From one year to the next there is seldom a big change; on the other hand, no change at all is also unusual. Between six and fourteen, *the average change from one year to the next is about 4 or 5 points in IQ*, and it may be in either direction. Where tests are more than a year apart, the change may be slightly greater. Indeed, in a third of all the cases the highest and the lowest IQ attained will differ by 20 or more points (208). *But on the whole, most children keep their relative positions.* The children who developed rapidly at first continue at that rate, and the slow ones remain slow. It is a plain matter of fact—abundant, recorded fact—that, knowing a child's age and his MA, you can predict his mental age for a year or two ahead with a fair amount of accuracy and safety.

If only this were the whole story! Unfortunately, it is not. First, there are some cases of really considerable changes in IQ—changes of more than 20 points. In many of these cases the changes cannot be attributed to poor testing, or to any sort of "accident." Although most people evidently grow in intelligence at a fairly constant rate, be it fast, slow, or average, a few people set us a knotty theoretical problem by growing now slowly, now fast. The Harvard Growth Study (117) showed, moreover, that there are individual patterns of growth; it is not merely a matter of being fast or slow in general, but of being now slow, now fast.

The recent monograph from the Fels Foundation gives evidence that irregular growers may be more numerous among slightly superior children from above-average homes than among the children who find their way into the behavior clinics (408). These irregular growers are few; but we should keep our testing eyes open for them since they may need special educational opportunities.

Obviously, then, the IQ is not constant. But it is not highly inconstant either. The important thing is to note that the changes which do take place—even the big ones—nearly always take place slowly, gradually. A child who in September is suitably placed in school for his level of intelligence will seldom get out of step within a year. (Not, at any rate, because of rapid or slow development in intelligence; other things can, of course, happen.) Intelligence must therefore be regarded as a fairly *stable* and *dependable* quality—

a fact with important implications which will have our attention a little later.

QUESTIONS

1. Have you ever known a person whose IQ showed rapid change?
2. What do you think is the explanation of big changes in IQ?
3. Do these changes in IQ reflect changes in real intelligence? What is *real* intelligence?

Can Intelligence Be Improved by Deliberate Effort?

Important from every angle is the question whether we can intentionally set up the conditions that will foster or hinder the growth of intelligence. Note first that this question is again couched in terms of the *rate* of growth. All children, without exception unless it be the lowest idiots, make gains in intelligence. The question is, Can we *increase the rate of gain* and thus perhaps the final level reached?

To this the only answer must be a resounding Yes! But how much can we change it and by what sorts of changes in environment? That is the proper scientific form of the question; it is also much harder to answer.

There is a story of a Greek from the "provinces" who came to Athens when Pericles was at the height of his glory and somehow got audience with the great man. "Well, Pericles," he said, "No doubt you are the greatest statesman in the world. But you were born of noble family in Athens, the light of the world. Now I was born a peasant in the backwoods of Crete. What do you think would have happened if we had been exchanged in our cradles?" The story goes that Pericles replied, "Doubtless the world would never have heard of either of us." Achievement requires both opportunity and the basic capacity to profit from it.

In all cases, the rate of intellectual development can be changed—much or little, for better or for worse, by altering life circumstances. How *much* you can change the rate of growth, however, depends only in part on the environmental influences you bring to bear on the child; it also depends upon what sort of a child you have, upon the nature of the child you seek to change.

Upon the inherited nature of the child? I did not say that. At any given age, a child will have a potentiality for intellectual growth —that is his "nature." Logically, no doubt, that nature depends in part upon the kind of organism which was formed at conception by the union of two infinitely complex cells. But that is only the starting point. Continuously the individual develops and changes as new experiences are confronted, continuously he puts on a new "nature," and each new "nature" helps to determine how he will further profit from still further experience. The accompanying chart (Fig. 10-3) sets forth this relationship in a schematic form; it will clarify your thinking if you study it carefully.

We conclude that for practical purposes, at any rate, we need not speculate about the relative contributions of previous experience and of innate capacity; we just recognize that we have a child who, at age three or six or eight, has a certain present potentiality for growing in intelligence.

Now as we said above, that potentiality can be altered—be it much, or be it little—by favorable or unfavorable circumstances. In other words, the IQ can be raised or lowered. The enormous mass of detailed fact which proves this is analyzed in a readily available form by Harold Jones (235) as well as by Tyler (451) and Anastasi (7). As to the main conclusion, there is hardly room any longer for controversy.

The limitations of this conclusion must, however, be recognized. It is easy to speak of a good or a bad environment; but any given environment is a fantastically complex affair. A given environment may have just what one child needs, and fail to have what another needs to help in the development of intelligence. For example, one child may find a certain rather coldly intellectual teacher inspiring; another child's home life has made him so dependent on affection that he cannot respond to the ideas which that teacher presents. The "same" environment just isn't the same.

A certain vaguely defined minimum of environmental opportunity is necessary for ordinary growth in intelligence. Beyond that minimum, however, improvement in conditions is only irregularly related to faster growth in intelligence. There is significant parallel here with physical growth. Long ago it was recognized that a man cannot "by taking thought add a cubit to his stature." You can stunt his growth, though, by poor food and unhygienic conditions.

Figure 10-3. Schematic Representation of "Nature" in Interaction with Environment

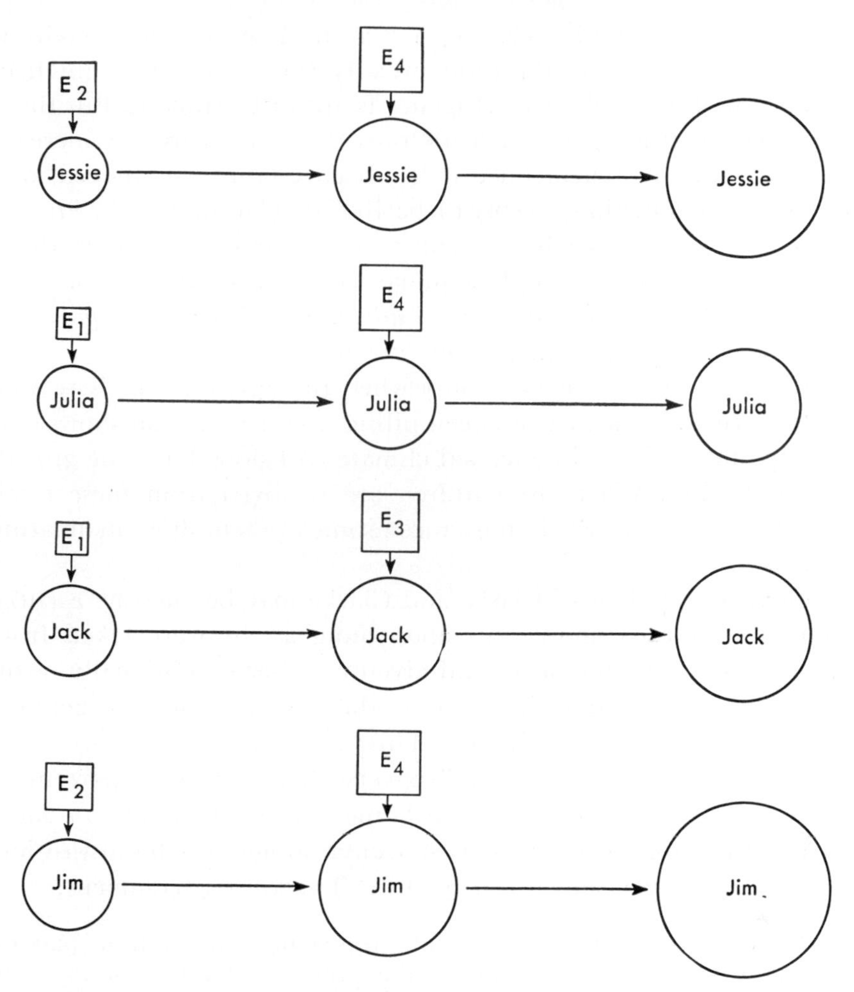

Circles represent the child's "nature" or capacity to improve at a given stage of development. The squares represent the environment which acts on the "natures."

Jessie and Julia are identical twins, who thus start with identical "natures"; so are Jack and Jim.

E_2 is a more favorable environment than E_1 (the box is larger). Thus Jessie develops further than Julia, Jim than Jack, as represented in the second column of circles.

Jessie, Julia, and Jim are now all exposed to the same environment, E_4. Julia, however, is unable to profit very greatly from E_4. The problems of E_4 are too much for her, and she shows only a minimal gain. Jessie and Jim gain greatly, Jim the faster because he had the greater capacity at the second level. Jack is exposed to a different environment, one as little stimulating to him as E_4 was to Julia; he makes little gain.

Note that it is not necessary to know whether it is heredity or environment that has made Julia (in the second column) relatively less capable of responding to E_4 than is Jim or Jessie.

Not all the possibilities have been pictured; moreover, the entire diagram greatly oversimplifies the complex relations which actually exist.

So it is with intelligence. Deprive a child of favorable environmental conditions—of education broadly conceived, or of intellectual stimulation—and his intelligence is apt to be stunted. But these favorable conditions, even if richly provided, do not usually increase the rate of development once it has been established. Indeed, our predicament sometimes seems to be like that of Alice in *Through the Looking-Glass;* she had to run as fast as possible to stay where she was. As a far too simple summary this must suffice: *If a child has had ordinary home and school advantages, it is very difficult to alter his rate of intellectual development very much.*

All of this holds, however, only when the environment is reasonably "normal." Evidence has been piling up for years that shows that a sadly impoverished intellectual climate will slow down the growth of intelligence. When the children are removed from these intellectually impoverished circumstances, some of them show an amazing increase in IQ.

The investigations of Clarke and Clarke may be cited here (107). Mentally retarded adolescents and young adults were taken from adverse home circumstances and given a rather exceptionally favorable environment in an institution. Many of them showed genuine gains in measured intelligence. Thus after three years, about 23 percent of those from "mildly" adverse homes and 56 percent of those from exceptionally adverse homes gained 10 points or more in IQ after three years in the richer environment of the institution. Such gains are very much worth while. The authors comment:

> Our data suggest that these results represent recovery from past experiences rather than response to the present. And they seem to be paralleled by change in other aspects of personality. We believe that exceptionally adverse experiences in childhood prolong the immaturity of the organism, and that Hebb's work [198] is particularly relevant. Many years are needed for learning . . . the experiences missed or disrupted. There is no way of knowing what these persons would have been like if brought up under good conditions—all we do know is that a very different prognostic picture is presented at 25 than at 15 (unless of course the social history is taken into account at the earlier age). This, then, is further evidence that very severe deprivation effects can fade.

Other evidence suggests that even more striking improvement may be found in children removed early from the adverse environment. In some of them! Unfortunately not all of the children taken from impoverished homes make great gains. In the Clarkes' data, for example, about half of the cases gained 10 points but half did not. Nearly all, however, do respond a little.

Figure 10-4. Gains in Relative Intelligence when Environment Is Improved

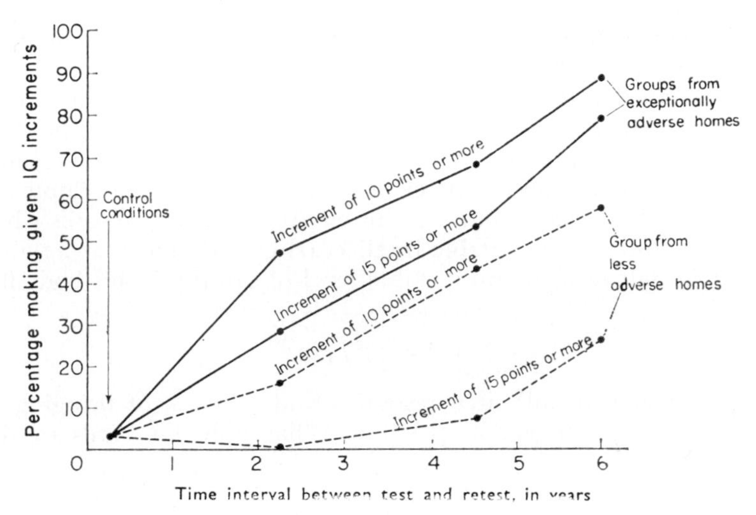

From A. D. B. Clarke and Ann M. Clarke, Some recent advances in the study of early deprivation. *J. Child Psychol. and Psychiat.*, 1960, 1, 26-36. Used by permission.

But the fact that some children taken from appalling circumstances have shown great improvement is no justification for implying that mentally defective and dull children from ordinary good homes can be brought up to the average. To say this, or even to allow this to be inferred by distressed parents, is to arouse tragically false hopes.

QUESTION

Can you suggest why, of two children of equal MA and CA, one will profit greatly from an improvement in his circumstances and the other will not?

The Early Stabilization of Intellectual Growth Rate

There is much evidence—it is not quite conclusive—that favorable or unfavorable conditions are more influential, if experienced very early in the child's life (during the years when he is learning to speak and to react to his world as a social being) than they will be later. A few cases are on record of startling improvements due to a radical change in life circumstances after the age of six or seven; more often, the change after that age is moderate or even too small to measure.

At the cost of being repetitious we must say again that it is the *rate of growth* which is thus somewhat intractable after about age six. This does *not* mean that the child ceases growing in intelligence (i.e., in MA). On the contrary, it means he *does* continue to grow, but that he does so *at about the same rate as before,* largely uninfluenced by differing environmental circumstances. After a certain stage of development is reached, the child reaches out into his environment and absorbs what he needs to *continue* a fairly stable intellectual growth, much as he absorbs just enough salt to maintain a stable level of salinity in his body fluids.

QUESTION

Suppose you had unlimited resources and the task of bringing up a child to be as intelligent as possible. What different kinds of things would you do?

Factors of Advantage

It is not true that we know nothing about how to foster the growth of intelligence. We know too little, but what little we know is important. And there *is* something to do.

Socioeconomic Status

Investigations going clear back to the early years of the century consistently show that the higher the socioeconomic status, the higher the *average* intelligence of the children. For a long time there was much controversy over which was cause and which effect. Does the higher socioeconomic position help to raise the level of intelligence, or is it merely that more intelligent people rise in the social scale and beget more intelligent offspring? Today you will find few who doubt that it works both ways. It is not possible, however, to say whether heredity or social conditions are the more influential.

For the teacher does it matter? Here are Ralph, the son of a lawyer, and Bill, the son of a casual laborer. Both are in the third grade. Ralph is age 8 chronologically, age 9 mentally. Bill is age 9 chronologically and age 7.5 mentally. Now we can speculate all we want about how much better Bill might have been had he grown up in a better environment. Here he is. Our task is to do the best by him that we can—"as is." And that goes for Ralph also; no matter how much we think he has already had the best of it, we still want him to have "every advantage" that will help the further development of his intelligence and its proper utilization in the total growth process.

So the practical thing is to start with each lad where he is and give him every opportunity we can provide for intellectual growth. Ordinarily that does not mean we can take Bill out of a rather unstimulating home; and there's nothing to be gained by complaining about his home. It does mean recognizing that Bill is going to have a rather rough time in doing the work of the third grade, and it means being prepared, therefore, to give him some special attention —which may well include an attempt to make up for some of the deficiencies of his poor home.

It means also that Ralph needs some special attention. For him, third grade is a little easy. He needs to have special projects unobtrusively given him, opportunities to work at his own level of ability and at his own pace.

It means that the teacher also has a problem of motivation, of helping the two boys to find a realistic level of aspiration so that each may have a sense of accomplishment. And in most such cases, it means that the Ralphs and the Bills will continue to be together in the same class. One asks again, Just precisely what difference does it make whether Bill's low IQ is due to poor heredity or to poor socioeconomic circumstances?

It does matter, however, if we are thinking broadly in terms of social remediation. Is it worth while to help the underprivileged? Is it not true that they are by heredity too unintelligent really to improve? There is a very large mass of evidence on this point and the answer is fairly clear-cut: embedded somewhere in the total complex of factors that make up social status are some of the factors that influence the growth of intelligence. More particularly, embedded in *low* social status are some of the factors *hostile* to growth.

You *can,* therefore, raise the level of intelligence of underprivileged children by improving their socioeconomic conditions, especially if you begin early enough. Not of every child, of course, and not a big gain in every case, but enough to count. A larger number of "mute inglorious Miltons," waiting to have unsuspected talents developed, are to be found among the underprivileged than among those who have had superior advantages. (A larger number, be it noted, who are undiscovered, not necessarily more in absolute numbers.)

There is another problem, however. Low intelligence is not the chief evil associated with inferior social status. Much more important are superstition and ignorance, bad habits and bad customs, low morals and a low level of aspiration. We are sometimes told that the underprivileged —most of them—are too unintelligent ever to be educated out of these vices. This is utterly untrue. While there is a small percentage of the too-dull-to-educate among them, the *overwhelming majority* of the children in every socioeconomic group have quite enough intelligence to profit by a properly conceived program of education, even at the level of secondary education. When it is found that secondary education does not work, the fault must be found elsewhere than in low intelligence of the children. When morals remain corrupt, it is not because they are too dull to learn.

The widespread opinion that "these people are too dumb to be helped —you can't make a silk purse out of sows' ears, you know" rests upon one solid factual base, but also upon other bases less solid and less respectable. The solid fact is that we do often fail; nothing we can do seems to help in some cases. As a result people of good will who attack the problem of helping the underprivileged in the hope of effecting miracles are apt to become pessimistic when miracles turn out to be scarce. But a further reason for the opinion quoted is that most of us are just a little unctuous and self-satisfied with our own superiority— and are not unwilling that others should remain inferior. Also it might cost us something to do anything about it; better to close our eyes to the facts. The facts show that we can help enough of the underprivileged, if we try, for the effort to be very much worth while.

QUESTIONS

1. Just what is it that happens to children in privileged homes to make them more intelligent? More baths? Better food?
2. What in the environment of the underprivileged retards intellectual growth? Be specific.

Race and Intelligence

Nearly the same things need to be said about race that were said about economic status. In fact, here in America, race is far more a matter of socioeconomic status than of biology. Colored people—whether Negro or Mexican—are almost invariably "underprivileged," if not economically, at least psychologically, and in ways which tend to depress the growth of intelligence. Indeed, the study of the differences in the way of life of Negro and white children promises to throw light on the subtle psychological factors making for or against intellectual development and may thus lead to the improvement of both races.

Meanwhile it must be stated as unambiguously as possible that there is no great difference between Negroes and whites in the numbers of the bright, the average, and the dull—not nearly so great as the difference in money, for example. (If wealth were to be distributed according to intelligence, the Negro community would nearly double its share.) At the extremes of the scale there is virtually no difference: there are about equal numbers of feebleminded and of gifted in the two "races." The highest IQ on record is that of a Negro girl. The chief difference is in the slightly greater number of Negroes falling just a little below the average. It is clear from very many researches that much, and possibly all, of the difference is due to the environmental handicaps which the Negro suffers in our culture.

Being of white ancestry is therefore not an important factor of advantage for intelligence; living as a white child in the white culture is a fairly considerable, though not decisive, advantage as compared with living as a Negro in the Negro culture.

Health and Intelligence

Most bright children are also of better-than-average health and general physical excellence, yet some are not. Moreover, although the feebleminded are, as a group, rather an unhealthy lot, we do occasionally find cases of the "strong back and weak mind." Evidently, then, the relation of health to intelligence is not simple.

What happens when health is radically improved? Before we answer that, let us ask what happens to a child of five, previously healthy and of normal life circumstances, who suffers a prolonged illness. Would you expect his IQ to decline? It very seldom does. Why, then, should we expect the improvement of health to raise the IQ?

Yet someone is always announcing a new physical treatment that will raise the rate of intellectual growth. Adenoids and tonsils had their day as barriers to intellectual growth, but careful studies showed no considerable change in intelligence as a result of their surgical removal. Nowadays we are more apt to hear of vitamin or glandular deficiences or of certain "miracle drugs." But again it is very hard to get evidence for a causal relationship.

There are indications, as we saw in Chapter 9, that *very early* and *severe* damage to the brain may permanently interfere with the normal capacity for development. It is altogether possible, indeed rather probable, that there is a small cumulative effect of continued ill-health upon intellectual growth, but the experimental evidence makes it very clear that healthiness of body is not a major determiner of growth in intelligence. The important relation lies elsewhere; ill-health is a serious handicap to the effective *utilization* of intelligence, not to its development.

The Effect of Education

A considerable number of investigations have been concerned with the effect of schooling upon the rate of intellectual growth. The effects found are smaller than were expected. As a rule, amount of schooling seems to be but a minor influence if a certain minimum is provided; and there is little gain in IQ when children are transferred from schools of average quality to distinctly superior schools.

On the other hand, where schooling is sharply curtailed, there does seem to be a drop in IQ, though not in all individuals. This last fact suggests that schooling is not the whole of education and that there can be compensations for lack of schooling. What, for example? Books. Not books as such, however. Books have to be used if they are to affect growth. Not instruction, either; that may go in one ear and out the other. What, then, can we do to children that helps them to grow in intelligence?

Intellectual Stimulation

To say that we provide the child with intellectual stimulation is obvious enough—or just plain circular reasoning. It is surprising, however, how little attention has been given to what makes a situation stimulating. We have such studies as Van Alstyne's (455), which showed that "opportunity to use constructive play materials" was quite highly correlated with intelligence in urban three-year-olds, whereas the "number of hours the father spends reading to the child" had very little influence on IQ. That is fairly explicit; we need more such evidence. What we have adds up to this: The environment must provide the child with a wide range of problems at a level of difficulty suited to his achieved ability; and it must provide him with the necessary means to solve the problems.

QUESTIONS

1. Take a look at your own upbringing in the light of these two principles. Did your parents set you appropriate problems?
2. How about Abe Lincoln's upbringing?

Problems are presented to the child in a number of ways; the "constructive play materials" spoken of above is one way. The whole way of life of the home makes a difference. At one extreme we have the "coddling" home in which the child is overprotected, has too much done for him out of misdirected affection. At another extreme we have the harried and hurried mother who does things for the child because she can't wait for him to do them for himself. (This mother has her counterpart in many a classroom.) Some homes out of sheer neglect fail to give the child problems he can solve. A few force upon him problems that are too much for him. A little later, the parents' own lack of broad intellectual interests may act to restrict the range of problems presented to the child; there is a big difference between homes in which intellectual problems are envisaged and discussed, and those in which such discussion is unusual. (Lest this seem too high-brow, let's remember that why Bill Tucker is in a batting slump, or why Nellie should wear yellow rather than purple may both be treated as intellectual problems.) A fair part of the advantage in homes of superior economic status probably comes from the fact that more things in life are treated as problems to be solved rather than as something to be settled by traditional dictum. A problem-raising and problem-solving orientation is tremendously important (80).

The means to the solution of problems again take many forms. In part they are physical. Tools—hammers, screw drivers, saws, scissors, needles, pencils, and spades—are a big help in solving problems, and in leading a child on to tackle more complex problems. But the chief means to the solution of problems are the "intellectual tools," most of which are verbal in nature. It is not without significance that children who are talked to a great deal have an advantage in IQ. The growth of intelligence depends *pre-eminently upon the acquisition of the verbal tools for problem solving.*

It will be noted that we do not say that intelligence and linguistic ability are the same thing. That is an oversimplification. On the one hand, language serves many other functions than that of problem solving. On the other, by the "tools" of problem solving, we mean something more than language, though these tools certainly involve language; we mean concepts, ideas, and techniques and habits of thinking.

Does that sound too formidable for an eighteen-month-old or even a three-year-old child? But that is precisely when children are learning to use simple concepts. They get almost no direct or systematic instruction, of course; they have to pick up their concepts from the conversations of their elders. (Often, of course, they get seriously muddled and are a long time in getting straightened out.) Probably nothing else makes so great a difference in the child's ultimate intellectual growth as the habit, acquired along with his speech, of using abstractions, of comparing, inferring, making generalizations. Here is one of the richest fields of psychological exploration, and it's not overcrowded.[4]

---

[4] As we shall see presently, we are not entirely without research. We know about when certain kinds of thinking appear, about the relative ease or difficulty of certain kinds of problems. Enough is known, in short, to make us aware of how much more there is to discover.

Motivation to Intellectual Growth

More subtle but perhaps even more important are the emotional and motivational factors.

In one study (459), rather typical of a great number, it was found that children who do badly in school seem to have a defective concept of themselves. They cannot express themselves freely either in overt action or in feeling; and they take small slights as criticism or rejection. Their whole intellectual growth seems hampered by a lack of self-confidence.

The motivational factors are often associated with socioeconomic status. Only those who have experienced the emotional drag of an inferior status are likely to appreciate fully how it can depress intellectual effort. Of course it does not work that way in all cases; some people never accept their inferior status, but they are exceptional. Moreover, the total culture of certain groups in our society tends to push children toward intellectual pursuits; in other groups it tends to pull them away.

There is, furthermore, at this point a decided difference in individual homes. First Champney (97) and then Baldwin, Kalhorn, and Breese (29) found that children reared in an atmosphere of *freedom,* of *emotional warmth,* and of *expectation of achievement* made statistically significant gains in IQ—that is, they not only increased in intelligence, as all children do, but they increased faster than others. The rather casual and indulgent home also provides an atmosphere favorable to intellectual growth (it is not so favorable for some other aspects of personality). Indulgence by itself, on the other hand, is not particularly favorable. Warmly indulgent parents tend to protect and coddle the child too much to allow his intellectual development to proceed unhampered (415). Children whose parents are rejectant, restrictive, cold, and autocratic tended to have rather stable IQ's. The investigators suggest that there might be a real decrease in IQ where the rejection is severe.

Other aspects of intellectual development round out the picture in an interesting way. The [children from *democratic* homes are] significantly high on the variable of *originality, planfulness, patience, curiosity,* and *fancifulness.* This array of high ratings suggests a group of children who are genuinely interested in intellectual matters. They seem to have not only the IQ but the creativity and imagination to reinforce it and put it to use. The *democratic-indulgent* group on the other hand shows none of this superiority on the other variables. This may indicate a shallow sort of intellectual development or it may indicate a different set of interests. . . .

The *indulgent* group seems to be quite low on a number of intellectual variables, *originality, tenacity, curiosity,* and *fancifulness,* although of these only originality is significantly low. This is much the same pattern as shown by the *actively rejectant* group. These two groups seem to be alike in that they are surrounded by restricting influences. In one case these influences are babying and protective, in the other they are autocratic and domineering, but in each case freedom is curtailed. Perhaps this pressure and lack of freedom constricts the intellectual growth of the child so that he cannot be original, planful, curious, and fanciful.

In summary, it would appear that the democratic environment is the most conducive to mental development; when it is non-indulgent, it is conducive to intellectual growth in all its aspects. The least stimulating sorts of environment seem to be the highly indulgent or the highly restrictive ones [29, p. 66; by permission of the American Psychological Association.]

It seems likely that the same elements account for the rather startling facts presented by Skodak and Skeels (400). Foster children adopted into homes offering emotional warmth and security as well as superior educational and social position have higher IQ's than might be predicted from the intelligence of their own parents. Furthermore, they have higher IQ's than children brought up by their own parents in homes similar in social and educational status to the foster homes of this study. It is not suggested, of course, that children would be better off if there were a general swapping of parents! Rather we are suggesting that those married couples who adopt children are likely to be especially affectionate and also intelligent in their child-rearing behavior.

Differential Birth Rate and Heredity

I have all along insisted that intelligence—actual, real intelligence as manifested in everyday life as well as in tests—simply does not exist apart from learning. All intelligent behavior is learned. I have not denied, however—indeed, I have directly asserted it—that heredity plays a part in helping us learn to be intelligent.

Thus one of the factors of advantage is to be well born, not in the traditional sense of being born into an "old" family but in the sense of having good genes. And of course it works the other way, too; an individual can be at a great disadvantage in acquiring intelligence if he has poor genes.

Of course you get your genes from your parents; and the chances of getting genes somewhat like those of your parents are excellent. Now it is well known that "the birth rate among families from which the duller children were drawn was about twice as high as among those supplying the brighter. . . . Even within the same social and economic class, fully significant correlations were found" (82, p. 56). The obvious conclusion is that we are likely to get a larger number of stupid people in successive generations. From the known facts of the differential birth rate, Sir Cyril Burt calculated that, "if no counteracting factors were operative, the intelligence quotient would drop at the rate of about 1½ points per generation (82)." Such a loss would have most serious social implications.

However, as Burt pointed out, in comment on his own prediction, "an armchair calculation is no safe substitute for direct evidence." The evidence is now available in the results of the Scottish Survey (444). An unusually careful and nation-wide testing program of all eleven-year-old Scottish children was made in 1932 and repeated in 1947. Instead of the expected drop in the national level of intelligence, there was a gain in IQ from 101.6 to 102.5. "Thus the child of today is not duller but brighter than his predecessor of fifteen years ago."

A number of other elements have undoubtedly contributed to this change, but the chief fact is almost certainly the improvement in the total environmental conditions over this fifteen-year period. It is perhaps particularly relevant to note that the years preceding the 1932 survey were years of black depression, economically.

QUESTIONS

1. What bearing do the facts brought out above have on the proposal to improve intelligence—and other qualities—by eugenics?
2. Before reading the next section ask yourself what you might do to bring up the level of intelligence in a group of children—assuming reasonable freedom of action but not unlimited funds.

A Formula for Creating Intelligence

These, then, seem to be the things that promote the development of intelligence: The child should be presented with intellectual problems so adjusted to his attained level of ability that he is challenged to solve them. The child should be encouraged to solve the problems by a person who believes in him and who is on friendly, affectionate terms with him. Only such help should be given as will prevent a sense of failure or frustration, but that help should be available. Especially is it necessary to provide the child with the means whereby the problems can be attacked; such means may be tools and materials, or they may be intellectual tools and information. Particularly valuable is the habit of critical generalization of experiences. The child's zest for achievement should be sustained by having his achievements recognized, especially by those with whom he identifies himself emotionally.

Now all this sounds suspiciously like merely a formula for good teaching. And so it is! In the child's more formative preschool years, the teaching is somewhat more informal, and the results are registered in the development of intelligence—as measured by the gain in mental age—as well as in the acquisition of the skills and knowledge with which intelligence may be said to work. During the school years the latter effect of teaching—that is, the acquisition of skills and knowledge—becomes of greater significance; we can do less and less to affect the *growth* of intelligence as such, but good teaching is as necessary as ever to the effective *utilization* of intelligence.

It is possible, then, to increase the average level of intelligence of a community or a nation. The level can be raised by procedures which take aim with a "shotgun"—merely in the general direction of the factors that specifically increase intelligence, hoping that some of the shot will actually reach the mark. Such "shotgun" techniques include efforts to raise the economic level, particularly of the submerged tenth, to improve the health of the children, and to improve the educational level of prospective parents. These procedures, justifiable on other grounds also, do actually tend to raise the level of intelligence. Results, however, are both slow and "spotty." It is clear that we need a more direct attack upon the *specific* factors which directly foster the development of intelligence. As noted above, a beginning has been made toward discovering the nature of these specific factors.

To sum it up: I have been making the point that, whatever may be the contribution of one's innate capacity, *intelligence must be learned.* The effective conditions for learning to be intelligent are the conditions for any kind of learning. Perhaps I have overemphasized the importance of the emotional factors as compared with the patient acquisition of skills—both motor and intellectual—and of knowledge. The latter, however, is obvious and hence does not need so much emphasis. Research on the emotional-motivational conditions of learning, on the other hand, calls attention to factors that are more in danger of being neglected.

More is needed, however, than knowledge of what the favorable circumstances are. We must create them. And the chief limitation lies in ourselves. Read again the description of what needs to be done to help the child acquire intelligence; and read it with an eye to the sort of person who can thus help. Does it sound like an easy task for a person such as you? Or will you have to do a good deal to reconstruct your patterns of behavior before you can adequately fulfill your role? Generalizing the problem, does it not look as if we shall need to re-educate both teachers and parents for this task? That takes time—a whole generation, perhaps.

But a shift in the right direction has been going on in America in the past twenty-five years. Beginning with Haggerty's (184) pioneering work in 1925, successive investigations reveal a slow but fairly steady growth in teacher and parent understanding of the child's needs for democratic freedom (243, 420). We inch forward; but psychologically, as well as economically and educationally, the child of today has a little better atmosphere in which to acquire intelligence.

The gain, however, is not a biological one; it cannot be passed on automatically through the germ plasm. Only through constant vigilance can we maintain and improve the conditions that foster intellectual growth. Each of us, with all his limitations of background and personality, has a role to play; each of us, by an effort to understand and by firm intent, can help to provide children with the conditions for further progress. And if another war brings in its train throughout the world not only economic and hygienic disaster but an upsurge of totalitarianism with all its restrictions upon intellectual growth, we shall simply have to start over again on the slow, uphill path.

Summary

Intelligence is measured by finding out how well a child can perform the tasks that are usual and expected of his age. In this procedure, testing is merely a refinement of common-sense judgment. But the refinement is necessary if the judgment is to be reliable and accurate.

No informed person supposes that this ability is acquired at a perfectly constant rate. During childhood, however, the rate of intellectual growth seems fairly stable. Such changes as there are take place slowly, and prediction is therefore practicable; the child who is very bright today will still be very bright a year from now, and the dull will still be dull, though in both cases there may be some change in relative position.

Changes in environment affect the rate of growth in intelligence, but large improvement is to be found chiefly where environment has been conspicuously lacking in the conditions for intellectual growth. Thus, contrary to a widely held prejudice, though not all these children are capable of responding to the improved environment, most is to be accomplished by improving the lot of the underprivileged.

Two specific conditions make for development in intelligence: providing the child with appropriate intellectual problems, and providing him with social motivation to attack and solve the problems. Both of these depend mainly on the pattern of behavior of the parents and of teachers in early childhood.

11

Intellectual Achievement

Intellectual achievement comes about by learning. What is learning? Not merely memorizing or otherwise just getting information. Learning is a process of reorganizing one's ways of thinking, feeling, and acting for what we hope will be more effective living.

What we measure by our tests is often only the information *by means of which* a person learns rather than the learning. It is, however, important to discover whether a child has acquired the necessary means for learning. Knowledge is such a means. How is knowledge related to intelligence?

Should bright children and dull ones be exposed to knowledge in the same classes?

Throughout the whole discussion so far a constant theme has been that a child becomes what he is by learning.[1] New ways of acting, new motives, even new emotions were said to be learned. Health and ill-health, though of course important in their own right, were discussed chiefly as affecting how and what a child learns. In the last chapter we saw that intelligence is also learned.

---

[1] For a discussion of the relation of the psychology of learning to the psychology of development, see John E. Anderson (15, pp. 37 ff.).

The Nature of Learning

In all of this it has been assumed that everyone knows what learning is. Unfortunately they don't. Do you? What do you think the expression "to learn" means?

Well, children go to school to learn—correction, children are *sent* to school to learn. Every reader of this page has spent many years in school. What happens there?

Doesn't what follows describe most of what goes on? The teacher tells the pupils something or has them read it in a book. Then later the children must repeat to the teacher, orally or in writing, what was earlier told them. What happens in between is "learning." That may not be quite a fair summary of schooling but neither is it a gross caricature.

Turn to studies of "learning" in psychological laboratories. A rat is caused to run a maze until he takes the "correct" path without error. Or a pigeon learns that he will be fed a pellet of food if he pecks at a yellow disk but not at a red one. Or a college sophomore reads off a series of nonsense syllables on a memory drum until he can repeat them without error. The implication is the same as in the school situation: learning is the acquisition of information or knowledge. (Many psychologists generalize this in the statement that learning is the acquisition of stimulus-response bonds or connections.)

I hope this account has made you a little uneasy. For this conception of learning, though very widely held by teachers, pupils, and even psychologists, is a great oversimplification. What I have described above may indeed be a *part* of learning, perhaps an essential part, but it is a meaningless part when considered out of relation to the rest of the process. To think of learning as the getting of information only is like trying to study the running of an automobile by concentrating on the mechanism whereby fuel is brought from the tank to the carburetor.

To apprehend a fact—that is, as the root of the word suggests, to grasp it—is not enough; to learn, you must *com*prehend—that is, grasp *with*. New information must be related to, integrated with, your previous knowledge—and with your previous attitudes, too, and with your established patterns of acting.

In this process, both your previous knowledge and the new information are somewhat transformed. The information that you "take in" alters your previous stock of ideas, but your previous knowledge also modifies what you take in. Learning, according to this view, is a *reorganization* for more effective living of one's ways of thinking, feeling, and acting. New information is seen not as something to be stored up in the mind but as a dynamic force that modifies the person. Information is not *what* you learn but what you learn *with*. It is the means whereby, to great or small degree, the learner becomes.

This altogether too brief statement of what learning is is nothing new. You have certainly heard teachers say, "Now I don't want you just to memorize this; you must understand it." To understand means to relate the new knowledge with your established ways of thinking and acting. Over a century ago the great psychologist and educator, Herbart, was pressing this very point.

But it is not easy for anyone to be consistent about it. Many of the very teachers who emphasize the need of understanding give examinations which measure a pupil's memory instead. I confess to have been in this numerous but inglorious company more often than I like to admit. It is relatively easy to measure memory, difficult to measure comprehension and the degree to which information has been worked into the pattern of one's way of living so that it constitutes real knowledge.

Yet it is only this last which constitutes the intellectual achievement which is the major topic of this chapter. This imposes a nice little problem of interpretation. A great deal of the evidence about achievement concerns only the acquisition of information, or at least is stated as if that were the only concern. Since, however, information is usually a necessary part of true knowledge, it is far from useless to discover what information children have and how they get it.

QUESTION

(May I remind you that these questions are not merely rhetorical? You really ought to see what answer you can make.)

How can we tell when a child has progressed from the state of mere information to that of real knowledge?

The Acquisition of Knowledge

It is natural to think first of schoolwork: of reading, spelling, woodworking, or whatever else the curriculum includes. Fortunately, intellectual achievement is not limited to what we learn in school. Everyone learns a tremendous lot outside school.

When the four-year-old learns about "The Little Train That Could" he has achieved something just as genuine as the high school freshman who memorizes—under pressure—the plot of *Ivanhoe*. Indeed, the child is likely to learn *from* "The Little Train That Could" more than the freshman does from *Ivanhoe*. (What *does* the average freshman learn *from Ivanhoe?* Have you ever known a teacher to measure these real changes in boys and girls from studying such a book? And are the changes that are actually achieved the ones we really want?)

Nor is verbal knowledge the only kind of achievement. Skills, also, are achievements—usually intellectual achievements, at that. No one would question that language skills are intellectual; but dancing, playing hopscotch, spinning a Yo-yo, throwing and catching a ball, cooking and sewing, and caring for the baby—these, although they include a nonintellectual element, also include a large intellectual component. Musical, artistic, mechanical, and other so-called special abilities are likewise predominantly intellectual in a broad sense of the word and are definitely achievements. In the broad perspective of a child's development they are not to be ignored.

There is another area of specialized intellectual development, peculiarly difficult to measure but of great importance: the ability that we call wisdom. Though wisdom is clearly related to intelligence it is—alas!—not part of the "usual and expected"; it must therefore be classed as a special ability. The same must be said of "practicality" and "sagacity" (both of which overlap wisdom). About all we can say of these is that they often seem to be acquired by associating with others who manifest these traits.

QUESTIONS

1. How would you justify the assertion that musical ability is predominantly intellectual?

2. If you were intensively studying a foreign language under a private tutor, how many words would you learn a day? How does this compare with a child's learning of his own language?

Achievement in Language

Of all a child's achievements, that of speech is most amazing.

At one year unable to utter a single true word and able to understand at most but a score or so, by age six the average child can recognize about 24,000 words—from a tenth to a fifth of all he will ever know (401).

At the base of this development is a prodigious amount of practice. Anderson (13) points out that a child may utter from 10,000 to 12,000 words a day. Many mothers find this estimate ultraconservative. None the less, such rapid growth in vocabulary in five short years is most impressive. And it is mostly self-taught! The vocabulary doubles again in the next five years; thereafter the growth is slower, though it continues throughout life. The average high school graduate can recognize in the neighborhood of 80,000 words.

The rate of growth in vocabulary *is* impressive. Yet let us do some computing. At age eleven a child has spent about ten years learning to speak—for easy figures call it 4,000 days. If he learns 48,000 words that comes to 12 a day, average. Now if you were this year making a real effort to learn a foreign language, could you not exceed that rate? Or if a teacher got sixth-graders really interested in increasing vocabulary, could they add, say, 10 more words a day to the average of 12?

But understanding words is only a part of the total growth of language. The child must master the delicate and complex skills of articulation and of intonation with coordination of lips, larynx, diaphragm, tongue, and throat. And then the fantastic grammer and syntax of his native tongue! We have only to remember that the French or German we struggle with so ingloriously is the everyday speech of Paris or Berlin urchins—even of the French or German morons—to realize how tremendous an achievement it is to learn to speak one's native language. And, on top of that, reading, spelling, and writing it. The judicious assessment of these many kinds of language achievement is much more difficult than at first it seems. Vocabulary achievement is probably the simplest. But consider, just what is a word? Are "play," "playing," and "player" three words or one? [2] Are we interested in the child's "active" vocabulary or in his "passive" or recognition vocabulary? A word has many meanings, and these shade into each other like colors in the rainbow. Is each such shade of meaning a distinct unit? How accurate must the child's comprehension of a word be to receive credit? In measuring his active vocabulary, how much credit do we give for readiness or fluency? How much do we count off for errors? And since we cannot try out the child on every word in an unabridged dictionary, how shall we go about making a sample?

Other aspects of language achievement present parallel and even greater difficulties. In measuring language, moreover, we have not unnaturally tended to classify gains in linguistic rather than psychological terms—gains in the use of nouns versus verbs, for example, or gains in the length or the complexity of the sentence. Clearly, however, these are rather arbitrary indexes of the *changes taking place in the child*—it is quite conceivable, for instance, that the identical change in the child would lead him to increase both the ratio of nouns to verbs in his speech and the length of the sentences. Efforts to find psychological rather than merely linguistic measures of language growth in the child have so far not met with much success. A beginning has indeed been made; we have found that the *extent* of vocabulary and the *fluency* with which one uses that vocabulary do not depend upon each other but may develop independently. For the present, however, we have a very inadequate understanding of the developmental changes in the child which are mirrored in the growth of his language.[3]

This is not to say that the measures of language achievement we now have are not useful. The fact that few fourth-graders understand the word "cooperate" is full of significance for the teacher who values this virtue as a mode of behavior; she will not be tempted to try to promote the behavior by praising "cooperation" to children who don't know what the word means. The fact that a given pupil has a weak understanding of sentence structure points to needed educational practices. Knowing that a fourth-grader misuses the comma

---

[2] In the estimate of a child's vocabulary cited above, such derivatives as "playing" are counted separately from "play."

[3] For a fuller discussion, see McCarthy (300).

may tell us little about his intellectual development, but it indicates an area in need of attention.

Helping Children Learn Language

Since most language is learned by intentional or unintentional imitation, the presence in a child's environment of good models is of prime importance. "Good models," to be sure, must not be taken to mean models of accuracy and purity of diction as defined by most specialists in English. A "good model" is one that the child will actually copy to his own advantage.

Now to begin with, there is always the question whether so-called pure diction is correct. "Highfalutin" oral speech is actually incorrect—or at least improper. The rounded oratorical periods of the eighteenth century, if they were ever part of anyone's everyday speech, certainly were never part of the speech of young children. The model of good speech for children must be simple enough to be grasped by the child.

By the time the child comes to school, and increasingly thereafter, speech is primarily a medium of communication with his *peers*. Stilted formalism of speech is not only not indicated, it is highly contraindicated. Parents and teachers should recognize that a certain roughness and toughness of speech is a necessity. It is a substitute form of aggression which might otherwise take more overt form, and is a necessary weapon in the give-and-take tumble of child life. Much of a child's language must be modeled on that of other children—distressing as that fact is to many parents and nearly all teachers.

Finally, the good model must make language seem satisfying to the child. Intrinsically and naturally it is. The infant spends hours babbling, later spends hours in talking and crooning to himself with no specific purpose beyond the verbal activity itself. Language is obviously fun.

But what happens? Understandably enough, after a while we adults think the time has come for him to "put away childish things." Where the struggle of the infant to master a new word had been greeted with cries of loving delight (even though the "word" is barely recognizable), the bumbling effort of a six- or an eight-year-old to master a complex sentence form is met with jeers or at best with a critical comment. We correct and criticize the child's errors and insist upon his speaking more correctly, until the mechanics of pronunciation, of proper diction, and of writing get in the way of free expression. It is probably not mere coincidence that most stutterers begin to stutter at about age three or six. The first is the period when we quit treating the infant like a delightful doll, and begin to expect him to behave—verbally and otherwise—like a responsible human being. The second is the period when he meets the pressures of school and its requirements that he talk like a "big boy."

Less and less, especially after school entrance, does the child feel that language is fun. It becomes a mere tool for immediately practical and pedestrian uses—a blunt tool at that, and to use it is hard and unrewarding work. Only a stalwart few manage to keep alive to the end of their school days something of the joy in language with which speech begins. Home and school must share responsibility for thus weakening the motivation toward language achievement. By all means, then, let us foster first of all the love of language. Let us encourage all kinds of fun and play with language. Let us subordinate correctness or good taste to enjoyment. The child who loves language will in due time purge himself of most of his errors; the child who hates or dreads it will never speak or write well, no matter how meticulously he is instructed.

Obviously, however, I do not mean that teachers should forgo all effort to correct faulty speech. I do mean that the emphasis should shift to helping the child succeed in communicating both his ideas and his feelings and with the glow of satisfaction that comes with success.[4]

QUESTION

Both in Chapter 7 and here I have been rather severe on formal correctness in speech. What defense can you make of teaching children to speak correctly? (Be sure you take account of child development.)

[4] See also the discussion of language in the development of emotions on page 131 ff.

Speech Correction

What, however, about the child with definite speech defects?

That, clearly, depends upon the nature of the defects. Those with organic impairment of the speech mechanism (tongue-tied, imperfect palate, and so on) need surgical attention. Children with baby talk, lisping, and similar habits should be encouraged and helped to learn to speak more clearly; they can. Stuttering, however, presents a more difficult problem.

Stuttering has a very complex causation and both reflects and causes very real emotional difficulties. The layman's efforts to cure stuttering are all too likely to do more harm than good. *The classroom teacher must, therefore, make no effort at all to treat stuttering.*

We do not say, however, that the teacher should not do anything for a *stutterer,* if she has one in her class. It is the disorder of stuttering speech she must let alone, not the stuttering child. Her role is more like that of the nurse who makes the patient comfortable than that of the physician who prescribes treatment.

There are, however, several things she can do. First, she should try to persuade the parents to call in expert help, though, if the case seems mild, they usually won't.

Second, she should treat the whole social situation which stuttering creates among the others in the class. No easy task, that. Little children are not notable for their sympathy and understanding and are apt to react to stuttering with amazement, disgust, or ridicule or all three. To prevent this without increasing the stutterer's already excessive self-consciousness takes tact and understanding on the teacher's part.

Third, she needs to lessen any strain on the stutterer that may be contributing to his disorder. Whether to call on such a child to contribute to class discussion depends on circumstances. Some stutterers feel neglected and hurt if they are passed over; others get into a terrible dither if asked to speak. You should not, of course, discuss the child's malady publicly, and you should almost never intervene to finish a word for the child. Wait quietly, and be yourself at ease. The basic principle for you is to avoid everything that will increase the stutterer's emotional strain. (That is good mental hygiene for all pupils, of course.)

And finally, the teacher can train the stutterer (as she should all the children) in better techniques of social adjustment. Such training will help him to feel more at ease with others and thus lessen the tendency to stutter.

No, the stutterer won't recover as a result of such friendly and common-sense treatment; he needs more than this. But, I must repeat, to attempt anything more is dangerous. The treatment of stuttering is strictly for the specialist.

The Achievement of Concepts

Among animals only the most rudimentary concepts are ever attained; concepts are man's most distinctive achievement. *A concept is a general meaning, usually embodied in a word or phrase.* To achieve such a general meaning, the child must somehow be aware of the similarities between objects.

Mammals, and probably most animals, react to "functionally equivalent" objects. Thus a monkey, having been taught to find food under a square-shaped lid, will try a triangular lid in preference to a circular one. In effect, the monkey has generalized the similarity of angular objects versus curved ones.

But the child carries the process considerably beyond such simple generalization. Welch observed that a child who has learned to recognize a folding chair as a chair and has seen one half-opened can recognize the completely folded chair. If this seems a small achievement to you, reflect that the folded chair cannot be sat on (and that is important, for children think of things in terms of use), and the folded chair certainly looks very different from others.

Impressed by this and kindred observations, Welch designed experiments to throw light on the development of generalization in infancy (467, 468, 469, 470). Suppose we have six blocks shaped like those in Figure 11-1. If you teach the child that the large equilateral triangle is a VIC and that the square is a DAX, he quickly generalizes that the other two triangles are also VIC's and the other rectangles DAX's. The generalization is what Welch calls "horizontal"—from one member of a class to another of the same class. Generalization of this sort is made by the higher animals all the time and can be demonstrated in infants as young as eighteen months.

But suppose you give the three triangles their specific names of MEF, TOV, and KUK, and the three rectangles their specific names of YOP, ZIL, and BEZ and get the children to know which is which; the problem now is to learn that MEF, TOV, and KUK are all VIC's and that YOP, ZIL, and BEZ are DAX's. The next step is to learn that both VIC's and DAX's are XIP's so that MEF, TOV, ZIL, and BEZ may all be called XIP. With appropriate teaching, children from 42 to 83 months learned to solve such a problem as this:

> "Put XIP on the table." (All the blocks)
> "Now take away DAX." (All the rectangles)
> "Now take away TOV."

This involves a hierarchical or "vertical" classification. Probably only the ape among the animals can master even so simple a set of categories as those of Figure 11-1. Yet this "vertical" classification is very important for clear thinking.

The fact that children tend to form concepts on the "horizontal" level often leads them to make what seem like peculiar errors to those who have their eye fixed on a "vertical" grouping of concepts. Suppose you showed a child the KUK and asked him to pick out a piece like it. He might perfectly well pick out BEZ. Now obviously

Figure 11-1. Generalization

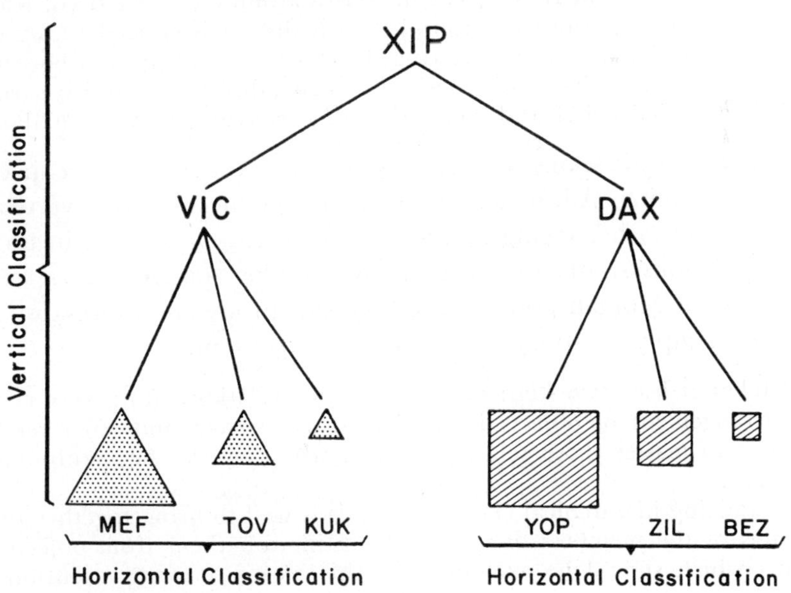

there is nothing fundamentally wrong with this classification. KUK and BEZ *are* alike in being "small," and if the problem is to find the pieces which will slip through a small hole, it is the best classification.

We adults, however, are apt to be a little rigid. Long ago we learned to think of such objects in terms of rectangularity and triangularity; that's a very useful classification, of course, which fits many situations. When the child follows a different scheme, we charge him with grouping objects on the basis of trivial or even fantastic similarities. Indeed, the celebrated Swiss psychologist Piaget (350) has postulated a special kind of thinking in children which he calls "syncretism" to account for the "odd" way they react to certain intellectual problems. Morgan quotes an example:

A child was given the proverb: "When the cat's away the mice can play," and was asked to select from a number of statements the one which expressed the same meaning. The child selected: "Some people get very excited but never do anything." Asked why the two statements meant the same thing, the child said: "Because the words are about the same. It means that some people get very excited, but afterwards they do nothing, they are too tired. It's like when cats run after hens or chicks. They come and rest in the shade and go to sleep. There are lots of people who run about a great deal, who get too excited. Then afterwards they are worn out, and go to bed."

Here is a simple justification of selection based on superficial resemblance. When the cat is near, the mice run around and get tired, which is the same as men running around. When the cat is gone the mice can rest, which is the same as men resting. Because the child was not bothered by any need for analysis, this conclusion was a direct one; and it carried with it a settled belief and conviction of correctness [320, p. 403].

Nonetheless, it seems unnecessary to suppose that this is a special kind of thinking. Adults also find the abstractness of the "vertical" classification rather trying and are prone at times to think in terms of the obvious similarities which give us the "horizontal" system. Children, as Morgan points out, often fail to use the more abstract concepts simply because they haven't learned them.

It takes at least two steps to learn abstract relations: (a) a very clean-cut arrangement of objects in a hierarchical system and (b) intensive practice to master those relationships so that they can be manipulated easily. . . .

In teaching hierarchical classifications it is well to bring together illustrations of the members of the class; distinguish them from objects or events which should be excluded, by this means drawing attention to the characteristics which determine inclusion in or rejection from the class in question; and finally attempt to formulate a definition which will provide a basis for any future judgment as to inclusion or exclusion. For example, if it is desired to teach a child what a triangle is, show him some triangles with other figures; distinguish the triangle from the others while pointing out the factors which determine the distinctions made; and by this means draw finer and finer lines until a definition is reached. If, in the process, a faulty definition is formulated, show the child by further examples where the flaw is. It is poor technique to begin such instruction by giving the child a ready-made definition. Let the child learn to evolve his own differentiations and he will be in a position to reason clearly [320, p. 404]. [The conclusion is based in part on research by Smoke (403).]

To Morgan's advice on how to train children in the use of vertical concepts, let me add the caution that they also be permitted great freedom in the use of the horizontal ones. This simpler and easier grouping has its uses. Perhaps not "useful" when a child says in rapid succession that a broomstick is a gun, a horsie, a man. But decidedly useful when he sees that a broomstick is a poker, a rake, a lever, a hammer—or a convenient club for use on an adversary. Such use of simple resemblances gives flexibility to one's thinking. It is the essence of figurative or poetic speech, and of practical inventiveness. Adults, to the great loss of originality, tend to stereotype their concepts, to think of a thing only in the one approved way. To lessen this tendency we might even find a place in our teaching for the encouragement of all sorts of bizarre classifications, for having fun with imaginative groupings and combinations. In short, for a little "brainstorming." Certainly we must be tolerant if not approving when the child conceptualizes the facts in a way that differs from our own predetermined pattern.

Of course the more abstract vertical system of concepts is also a necessity and must be carefully taught. Practice in finding the *appropriate* classification of objects (or ideas) is of highest importance for intellectual development. A poetic classification of animals ill serves the purposes of zoology, and an imaginative horizontal categorizing would play hob with an office filing system.

Like their elders, however, children often learn words better than they do concepts. Thus they often use abstract terms without true understanding of the higher-order concepts to which the words ostensibly refer. The resulting haziness of ideas is a very different thing from the fluid and imaginative freedom of association of which we were speaking just above.

Much has been written about the danger of "empty" concepts; such concepts are the bane of sound thinking at every level of devel-

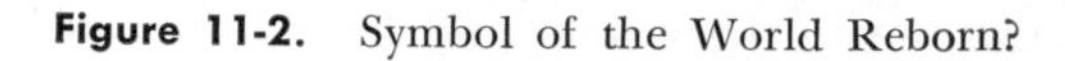

Figure 11-2. Symbol of the World Reborn?

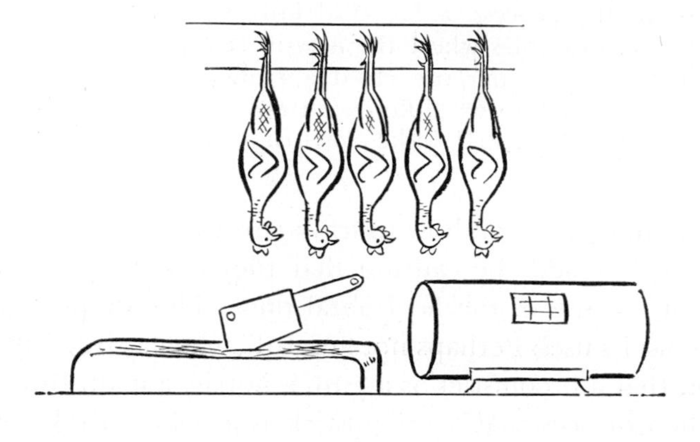

opment. It is evident that pushing abstraction too fast is a major cause of this fault. The teacher who is engaged in teaching a certain classification of objects (or ideas) seldom realizes the wealth of concrete detail upon which her own thinking rests and is very apt to forget that her pupils may not have had what she regards as ordinary experiences. A third-grade teacher in a metropolitan area tried to develop the idea of the Easter chick as a symbol of the world reborn in spring. When the children were then asked to make drawings, many of them drew pictures of dressed chickens hanging in meat markets. They had never seen any other chicken. They lacked the wealth and variety of concrete experience which must underlie abstract conceptual thinking.

Two cautions, however, are in order. Experience alone cannot be trusted to generate concepts, or, rather, cannot be trusted to generate the most useful ones. Guidance of the process is essential—the sort described in the quotation from Morgan.

It is, in the second place, a mistake to underestimate the wealth of conceptual thinking of which the child is capable. For the sake of concreteness we have elaborated a little on just one aspect of the development of ability to conceptualize. There are many others. Studies of children's concepts of time, space, causality, religion, and the rest have, however, overemphasized the blank spots in the child's knowledge—the funny mistakes he makes. We should rather note (and marvel at!) how much he *has* learned. Quite elaborate space and time concepts are learned very early. Many of the basic logical principles are also operative, even though the child cannot formulate them (108). And even such a difficult concept as that of causality is used part of the time, often in a very scientific way (120). In fact, the growth in intelligence during the years from three to fourteen is chiefly a growth in the richness and complexity of concepts; and this growth is so nearly complete by fourteen that it was once thought that intelligence did not develop beyond that mental age.

Certainly it is true that there are concepts at once too complex and too abstract for seven- or for ten-year-olds; it is virtually impossible for them to have the requisite experience. But at every age there is a level of abstract thinking which children can learn.

Scholastic Achievements

A text on the psychology of children is no place to review the voluminous material on scholastic achievement and its measurement. Yet in every culture, and particularly in ours, school achievement plays too important a part to be wholly ignored. For us the important issues revolve around the relation of scholastic achievement to other aspects of child development.

The Relation of Achievement to Intelligence

At first sight it is not easy to see how achievement and intelligence are to be distinguished. Both refer to activities or performances, both are acquired or learned, both are in the broad sense intellectual (in contrast with emotional). If, however, we consider how achievement and intelligence are measured, certain practical operating differences appear.

It will be recalled that we measure intelligence in terms of the child's ability to do the things "usual and expected" of his age. Now I do not see how it can be denied that this includes many things which are "achievements." For example, to be able to distinguish between two sounds one musical tone apart is, in childhood, a part of the "usual and expected," and a test of this sort may therefore be legitimately a part of a comprehensive testing program. But to have very much greater ability along this line would be a sign not of intelligence but of musical ability or achievement.

Similarly with other school achievements. Simple addition problems occur in many intelligence tests; in our culture the tasks are definitely part of the universally "expected." But we do not expect of all children facility at square root or even long division; these, we realize, are too contingent upon the amount and quality of schooling. We make, that is, a distinction between being unintelligent (unable to do the "usual and expected") and being uneducated (unable to do the specific things which have to be taught beyond the "usual" level).

Put in another way, we see that achievement tests *look backward;* they ask whether a child has learned certain specific things. In contrast, the intelligence test, although it certainly consists of items which have been learned, *looks* forward and helps us predict how well the child is likely to learn in the future. The distinction is by no means hard and fast, but it is a workable one. *You use an achievement test to find out the specific things a child still needs to learn; you use the intelligence test to discover his learning potentiality.*

The last statement, though a fairly accurate statement of actual practice, needs certain qualifications. An intelligence-test score is the *best* single measure of learning ability, not the only one. A child's ability early begins to show a stable differentiation in certain preferred directions. We need not at this point press the issue as to how far such special ability is the product of nature or of nurture; the point is, it tends to be fairly stable. If, over a period of four or five years, Harriet excels in reading and spelling and the linguistic subjects while Loraine excels in numerical work, the difference is unlikely to change a great deal as the years continue to roll by. Future excellence can be fairly well predicted from already established preference and ability.

Fairly well. For there are vast differences in background to be considered. An example is the enormous difference in background between two children, both of good intelligence, in the sixth grade. Tom is a lawyer's son. Already his reading has been directed toward simple biographies and historical fiction. At the dinner table he is accustomed to hearing lively, even heated, discussion of current events, not infrequently with references to historical parallels. Tony is the son of a bricklayer. His father came to America at twelve and left school at fifteen with only about fourth-grade schooling, chiefly because of language handicap. His mother finished the eighth grade. Tony's father is skillful and shrewd—a success—but he is certainly not an intellectual.

No one, I suggest, would expect Tony to take to social studies as easily as Tom does. In the initial stages of their work in this field, Tom has a great advantage. But he may not hold it long. His interest may lag while Tony's may increase. Such shifts in motivation have their causes, of course, and sometimes we can find them; the point here is that they exist and that they exert a very real effect on achievement and on achievement-test scores.

Moreover, the achievement test is much more sensitive than an intelligence test to differences in opportunity to learn—indeed, it is designed for that. Consider two typical cases. Grace, at eleven, comes in to a centralized school from an isolated outlying district. The one-room school she attended was poorly taught, and Grace's attendance was highly irregular. On achievement tests she makes irregular scores, somewhat higher in reading than in spelling or arithmetic and quite low in language skills. At best she rates placement in the fourth grade. Yet her mental age is nearly twelve, equal to that of most sixth-graders. In such a case, the intelligence test is a better index of future learning than are the achievement tests. With a little encouragement and special help, Grace can easily catch up with at least the fifth- and probably with the sixth-grade pupils.

Contrast with this the case of Louise, also eleven. She has attended the centralized school from the start and has had the usual instruction. There is nothing noteworthy about her home background. Her achievement tests place her nearly a year in advance of Grace. When, however, we learn that Louise has a mental age of just under ten years, we see that her achievement in school—about a year behind in most subjects—is about what would be expected. Unlike Grace, Louise is unlikely to catch up in school achievement with those of her own chronological age. The practical conclusion then is that, *for the prediction of future achievement, we need both achievement and intelligence tests.*

It remains to add that some kinds of achievement are less closely related to intelligence than others: "manual arts" and artistic achievements, particularly. Some have held that this is the result of an artificial definition of intelligence. I prefer to say merely that it is because achievement in these fields is always a little unusual or specialized in our culture, hence, naturally, it is not well measured in terms of mere intelligence. At any rate, the fact is that we cannot so well predict these special abilities from intelligence tests.

QUESTION

Is it conceivable that artistic achievement can become "usual and expected" in our culture and hence part of what we mean by "intelligence"? Has it in any other culture?

The use of achievement tests in guiding pupil-learning is too important to remain unmentioned, though the details of that use belong to the psychology of learning and instruction rather than to the psychology of the child. Any achievement test is diagnostic—that is, it indicates the areas wherein pupil-learning has not taken place. The diagnosis may be coarse—the child is weak in arithmetic—or very detailed—the child does not know how to add 6 and 7. In some fields we have pushed diagnosis to the point where weaknesses in underlying processes are revealed—for example, we may find that a third-grader does not have the basic idea of the "decade cycle" of number formation, or that he does not know how to "borrow." Teaching and learning are enormously more efficient when effort is directed at the specifics that are to be learned, whether the specific be a detailed fact or a broad and general principle. Modern testing gives to teachers a diagnostic skill that they otherwise gain only after years of experience.

Individual Intellectual Differences and the School

The problems raised by the existence of great individual differences in intellectual development are dealt with in texts in educational psychology and educational administration rather than in a text on child development. Yet how the problems are actually met must be considered here because these practices materially influence the course of development in children. Our discussion is necessarily only an overview. It emphasizes primarily the implications that the facts of development have for a point of view in school practice rather than for specific methods and practices.

Let us begin with an area of agreement. Most children, we agree, will be better educated if they are schooled with other children. Even if we could we would not want a private tutor for every child. Learning is too social an experience for that.

Thus we face the problem of forming groups of children for school purposes. From the very beginning these groups have been formed of children who were thought to be of about *equal readiness to learn* whatever it was they were to be taught: how to string a bow, how to distinguish different animal footprints, how to sing the rain prayer—or how to read, or how to solve long-division problems. As the number of children to be taught increased, they were formed into larger groups (called classes) but still presumably they were of about the same readiness to learn. As a first approximation this could be judged fairly well from the child's age.

Fairly well! Not well enough, of course. Some children were obviously unready at age six to learn what other children of that age were being taught; some had already learned most of it. When intelligence tests were devised as a rough measure of ability to learn, it was suggested that children be graded and assigned to classes according to mental rather than mere chronological age.

This was, of course, a rather myopic proposal. The "mental age" is not what the name implies, a measure of the child's total intellectual development; it is a measure of his development in respect to the central core of tasks which are "usual and expected" in our culture. It takes little account of the individuality of intellectual development, of relatively high ability in this respect and low ability in that, and almost no account at all of other aspects of development. There was, then, good reason to reject the proposal to group children just by mental age.

Moreover, "homogeneous grouping," as it was called, began to be advocated and practiced at the very time when thoughtful educators were rediscovering the nonintellectual aspects of development as prime objectives of schooling. Just when we were beginning to think of the "whole child," here were people who sought to assign children to class merely on the basis of intellect! Almost a whole generation of educators has been traumatized by the ensuing controversy to the point where they cannot think calmly of any suggestion that a test score be used to place a child in school. "The *whole* child goes to school. Social and emotional development is more important than intellectual development [That one is a little inconsistent with the whole-child thesis; it should be read "is just as important as"]; and a child should learn in his natural group."

The Child's Natural Group

Agreed! But what is the "natural group"? Pete is the son of a mill hand of foreign extraction. He is large and strong, a trifle below average intelligence, rather uncouth in his social behavior, and not very popular. Is it not obvious that he might best learn certain physical activities such as football in a group of older boys, might learn school subjects with a different group, and social behavior with still a third? The one best "natural group" for learning is evidently not easy to attain.

Well, then, should we not have many "natural" groups? Yes, we should. There are a great many adaptations of this sort; the classroom group or "grade" should not be a fixed unit for all the child's activities. On the other hand, children need a great deal of stability in their social groups. Hence the almost universal policy of assigning elementary school children to a single class for *most* of their activities is a sensible adaptation to this need.

The "natural group," therefore, needs to be envisaged as a sort of compromise. It is that group in which, on the whole, the child himself learns best whatever he has to learn, and contributes best to the learning of the other children. It is obvious that this implies that we know as much as possible about the children.

School Experiences and the Natural Group

Before we elaborate on that, let us consider the kinds of experience the school offers and what these imply if the children are to profit fully from the experience. A school is—or should be—an experience in healthy living. This implies that the children be free from communicable diseases. A few children need highly special health experiences; tuberculous children are sent, nowadays, to "open-air schools." But within very wide limits differences in personal health do not prevent children from profiting from the same kind of health experiences in the school.

How about physical development? Clearly it is desirable that children be at *about* the same level of physical development in order to form a "natural group." Six-footers and three-footers would make a difficult combination in the fourth grade. But just what are the limits of permissible difference in physical growth? Those who advocate age-grouping evidently believe that the tolerance limit is very great, for there is a great variation in size and weight and physical maturity at every age. Differences of two feet in height in a single classroom are not unusual in our elementary schools today. Clearly, physical development all by itself is seldom the decisive factor in grade placement.

A school is—or should be—an experience in social living. This demands, in sharp contrast to the foregoing, a considerable degree of similarity within the group. Best results are obtained when the children have reached about the *same general level* of social maturity. Nonetheless, there can be large qualitative differences in all sorts of things from manners to morals, not only without loss but with great profit to social experience.

QUESTIONS

1. Can you justify having children of greatly different social maturity in the same school class?
2. Does your argument hold for intellectual differences? Why or why not?

A school is also an experience in intellectual growth. Indeed, this is now, as it has always been, central in the whole educative process —central because *intellectual processes play an essential part in other modes of growth* as well as having a development of their own. We emphatically do not say that intellectual development is a more important *goal* than social or emotional or character development. We do say that intellectual development plays a larger part than any other factor in attaining these other goals.

A group composed of children at greatly different levels of intellectual development is not a good group for learning anything, whether morals or manners, sports or sportsmanship. Even when they are said to be "learning the same thing," their ways of learning are quite different. On the playground, differences in interest and outlook (both chiefly intellectual) cut across differences in strength or skill. Two lads, respectively MA 8 and MA 12, may jump equally badly, but the wise teacher would not try to teach them by the same methods or with the same incentives.

Or take such social learnings as those of leadership and followership. Leadership does not correlate highly with intellectual level, but there is bound to be trouble in a group when many of the members find the leadership "dumb"; nor is it much better when the leaders are contemptuous of less intelligent followers. When experiences are to be shared in a cooperative enterprise, the intellectually more mature may sometimes serve as "teachers" of those less mature and may benefit thereby. But it is more valuable to be in a group of true peers—that is, equals—where there can be a constant *shifting* of roles—each member having his turn as leader and as led.

Finally, where the differences in intellectual level are too great, the children cannot profitably work together upon what may seem common problems. For example, both bright and dull preadolescents have the problem of learning to get along with the other sex; but they need different kinds of heterosexual activities in order to learn this adjustment.

From all these considerations it appears that *the most important single criterion of the child's ability to profit from the experiences offered by the school—and hence of what constitutes his "natural group" in school—is his level of intellectual development.* We repeat: this is so not because intellectual development is more valuable than social and emotional or physical development but because intellectual activity plays so determinative a part in *all* educative processes, including those which promote social, emotional, or physical development.

How Do We Usually Group Children for Learning?

The answer to this question is obvious. We group children primarily according to the number of seconds which have ticked off on the clock since they were born. Fortunately, this mechanical classification has a certain workability. It is designed for the average, and most children are by definition rather average. Then, too, most children are fairly adaptable. And, above all, children learn so much, no matter how poor the opportunities we provide them, that we are inclined to be complacent. In other words, we can do a bad job of grouping children for learning and get away with it. And that is just what we have been doing!

The Effects of Chronological Grouping

As we have said, chronological grouping works fairly well with children of more or less all-round average development. If we are generous in our interpretation of "more or less," this includes a fair proportion of all pupils. But the deviants from average development must be considered. At least 5 percent of the children are sufficiently above and an equal percentage is sufficiently below the average in intellectual development to constitute a serious problem of grade placement. This problem is not solved by "letting nature take its course." *Prolonged association with others of very different ability under conditions of presumed equality distorts the situation not only for intellectual growth but for personal and social growth as well.*

In the case of the dull this has long been recognized. Inability to meet the intellectual demands of the situation tends to frustrate the child, subjects him to the ridicule of his fellows, deprives him of the proper intellectual stimuli for growth, and drives him to other means of obtaining satisfaction—"mischief," and other "disciplinary" activities.

Curiously enough, the effect of poor school placement is much the same for the bright child. He too is apt to be frustrated (by the dullness of the tasks); he too gets into jams with his fellows (for one thing, because he has not learned to be properly tolerant of their inability to learn as fast as he does); he too is deprived of intellectual stimulation; and he too becomes something of a disciplinary problem (partly for want of enough to do).

In my own first survey of a school in 1913, Byron, who by our tests was of outstanding intelligence, was found to be doing very mediocre schoolwork. Neither the principal nor the teacher (both competent) had recognized his ability. He was lazy, indifferent, and "troublesome." Moved to a higher class, however, he dug in and not only maintained himself in the new grade but rapidly went to the head of the class. More important, his entire behavior changed for the better: he was more alert, more responsive, more friendly. So far from being socially maladjusted, he was a more acceptable member of the new class than of the old one.

Linda was just over five when she brought her father directions for coloring a picture and read to him: "After you have finished coloring it, you may wish to show it to your schoolteacher." "Isn't that a joke, daddy!" she giggled. "That lady who sent me the picture book doesn't know I'm not old enough to go to school." Somehow it seemed to her parents that she *was* and accordingly she was presently enrolled in pre-first-grade summer school. When, at her parents' request, I visited the school to observe her adjustment, I found the class engaged in reading a "book" they had dictated to the teacher. Each child was to read the page he or she had composed. Linda was first and rattled off her page easily. George faltered at a word and Linda supplied it. Ken couldn't read his page and Linda immediately volunteered to read it for him. Gwen got through her page without Linda's help, but when Arlene got stuck Linda again tried to take over. At this point, however, the teacher intervened and got someone else to help Arlene. But the whole lesson was one long struggle to keep this bright little child from "hogging the show." There was no exhibitionism apparent—indeed, nothing was wrong except that she knew how to read so much better than the others that their bumbling efforts led her to eager but tactless efforts to help.

Nothing was wrong—*yet!* But how long could Linda go on this way without "getting ideas" and feelings of superiority verging on arrogance? How long without arousing the resentment of the other children? It wasn't her intellectual development that was being retarded by associating with her "inferiors"—she was making excellent intellectual progress. The difficulty was that her intellectual superiority was leading her almost inevitably into decidedly unfortunate social behavior.

QUESTIONS

1. What would you advise for Linda if you object to any kind of acceleration?
2. Suppose that the only second grade available had been made up of unusually mature children. Would you put Linda in with them?
3. If she is accelerated, isn't Linda going to be at a disadvantage in high school, e.g., in dating, since she will be younger than her classmates?

A Formula for Grade Placement

No single administrative expedient will solve all the problems arising from individual differences, but there is a *formula* which will cover all cases: grade placement should be made in the light of *all* that we know of the individual child's development in physique and of his social, emotional, and intellectual development—all these in relation to the developmental level of the other children.

Consider Linda's case once more. She had taught herself to read by pointing to a word and asking her mother or her brothers, "What does that word say?" She was, of course, a very bright child, though her Binet IQ of 140 was not extraordinary. She came from a home of high intellectuality, and she was the youngest of a family of six, all fairly close in age and a rather compact social unit. Her fund of social techniques was, for her age, unusual. When, therefore, she was skipped past the first grade, she made an excellent all-round adjustment in the second. Explaining her selection *by the other children* as the leader in a certain school activity, Linda herself said: "Well, last summer I just watched how Mac [her brother] did things like that, so I knew how and none of the other kids did. But," she added, "I just wish the other kids would tend to business and quit fooling around so much." Linda at six and a half was already, you see, exhibiting the desire for structured teamwork, which is seldom shown before nine or ten. Even though she was rather slight and short for her own chronological age, she was fully able to hold her own in a group of children averaging about a year and a half older. Had she been assigned to the first grade, she would have been decidedly *out* of her "natural group." This judgment, be it noted, is based not merely on her intellectual but also on her social maturity.

It should be obvious, however, that the existing group structure also has to be considered. Had the children in the available second grade been unusually large and socially mature, Linda probably would not have belonged with them. Successful placement also requires that we consider neighborhood relationships, the existence of cliques, even such unfortunate circumstances as social status. A child moved into a strange and hostile group, whether as a result of non-promotion or of double promotion, may be so unhappy that learning is virtually impossible—any kind of learning. Willard Olson (338) describes a typical case of a child of superior development who was nonetheless unready for an extra promotion.

Though again it lies outside the specific province of child psychology, I must add that little is gained by grouping children in proper natural groups only to teach differing groups in the same way. Studies of the gifted show that they are seldom treated differently enough (1). We do better in this respect for slow learners. Children of different intellectual abilities need different teaching methods, different sorts of experience—including different social experiences. And one inevitable consequence of such differential treatment is that for some children there will be school acceleration or retardation.

Educational Acceleration

Retardation of the dull is an old story and nearly everyone accepts it—in general, too complacently unless the child happens to be his own. But acceleration is one of those ideas that arouses deep feeling.

First, let us be clear what educational acceleration is. It is not limited to grade skipping; that is merely the commonest and also the clumsiest method. By acceleration we mean any method—including "enrichment" of educational content—whereby a child is allowed or helped to make educational progress at faster than the average or lock-step rate. There are several such methods.

Opponents accuse advocates of acceleration of thinking only in terms of intellectual development. Proponents of acceleration, on the other hand, insist that they seek in behalf of every child the opportunity to achieve his best all-round development; but they do not believe this possible if parents and teachers are so afraid of superior intellectual development that they *artificially* hold back the child's progress in that area. It is granted that lopsided emphasis upon intellectual achievement—or upon any other kind—is unfortunate;[5] but it is held that a child may be *allowed* to develop more rapidly in the intellectual sphere than his less gifted age-mates without necessarily interfering with other aspects of personality. Indeed, they contend that allowing a child to develop *at his own rate* intellectually is a precondition for wholesome personality.

The Personality Development of the Gifted

The evidence for this view is conclusive. Under the leadership of L. M. Terman a careful study was undertaken of over 1,500 gifted boys and girls. Begun in 1925 and still in progress, the study has followed these children into their forties. No amount of speculation can stand up against the solid volume of facts thus accumulated.[6] At all stages of their lives, these intellectually gifted persons have shown far richer and more varied interests than the average.

True enough, at age eight, the child whose mental age is about twelve finds it difficult to play the "silly" games of other eight-year-

---

[5] "Our preliminary data suggest that there is a great deal of irrational overrating by teachers and parents of *physical* characteristics during childhood" (227).

[6] The five fat volumes of *The genetic study of genius* (439) are a veritable treasure house of information. Both Volume IV, *The gifted child grows up,* and Volume V, *The gifted group at mid-life,* have a convenient résumé of the earlier findings. The gifted, we should add, are somewhat arbitrarily defined as the best 2 percent of the total child population—138 IQ and above on the Stanford-Binet tests. With proper allowances what is true of the top 2 percent is true of the top 5 percent, who, we noted, are also too bright to be treated as average.

olds. But he relishes games adapted to his intellectual *and social* maturity. By actual test, the gifted child knows as much about games as the average child three years older. Usually he plays them with the skill and sportsmanship of older children. When we find the gifted child retreating unwisely into mere bookishness, it is because the environment provides him with too little else of a satisfying sort.

The Terman studies—and many others—show that the gifted child is about 5 percent above the average in height, is more than that above the average in other indexes of physical excellence (313). In general, children superior in intelligence have been found emotionally stable and well adjusted in childhood, and follow-up studies have shown them continuing so in adult life (357, pp. 39 f.). See Figure 11-3.

The Bugaboo of Maladjustment

Granted, however, the essential healthy-mindedness of the superior and the gifted, it is still held that allowing them to push through the school grades faster than their fellows tends to make them maladjusted. This belief is based in part upon the sad outcome when an overambitious *parent* pushes a child toward a level of school achievement for which he is unfitted. There is no defense of such exploitation, but this, of course, is not what advocates of appropriate acceleration are after.

Short shrift can also be given to the argument that acceleration makes pupils conceited. When you accelerate a child, you do in effect tell him and others that he is "smarter" than the rest. Do you think you have told him anything he doesn't already know? Superior children are, indeed, likely to be conceited; but it suffices to inquire which child is most likely to be conceited: the child who finds himself invariably ahead of his duller classmates, or the child who is placed in a grade with children approximately his intellectual equals?

We may add, parenthetically, that the same reasoning applies to the duller child. He, too, in school is building a picture of himself. When he is literally outclassed in most school activities, what sort of picture is being formed? Assignment to a slow-learning class may bring some slight initial disturbance—research has shown that most of the duller children don't mind—but it is much less troubling than the daily humiliation of being surpassed at every turn by one's brighter classmates. The real danger for duller children is an apathetic acceptance of inability that prevents them from doing what they would otherwise be capable of doing—and this is much greater when they face constant comparison with abler children.

A more important objection to acceleration is that the child will become socially maladjusted. This is a hard one to deal with for a number of reasons. Accelerated pupils themselves sometimes make this complaint, though the majority of them do not. (For instance, in one study [248], 17 percent rated their personal relations as unsatisfactory, compared with 6 percent among equally gifted non-accelerates.) The truth is, of course, that all of us have a sneaking feeling that we aren't liked as much as we want to be, aren't wholly successful in our interpersonal relations. If we can only blame it on our being accelerated!

Figure 11-3. Traits of Four Intellectually Superior Children

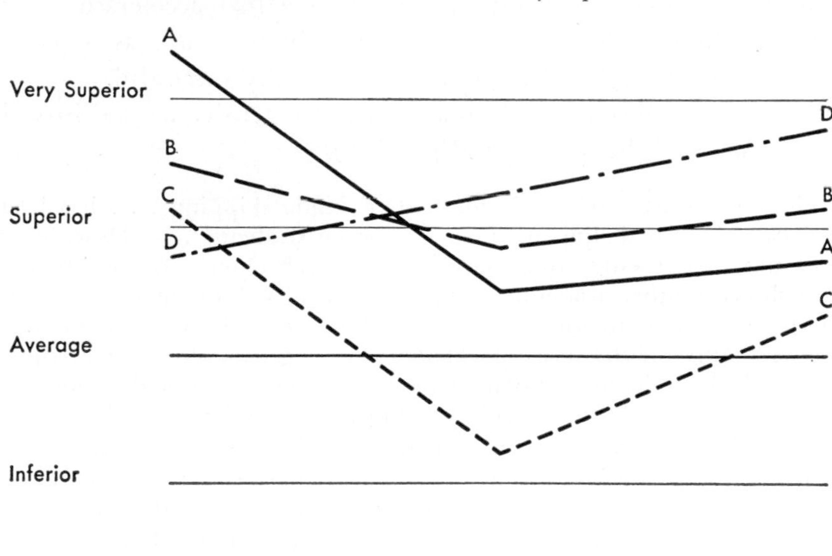

A and *B* represent instances where the child is superior in all three groups of traits but is most superior intellectually. *D* is also a common pattern. The pattern shown in *C* is somewhat unusual and reflects distorting factors in the background.

Despite such doubts as these, however, the pupils who have themselves had the experience of special classes for the gifted strongly approve. (In Barbe's study [32], more than 94 percent.) The social adjustment can't have made them too unhappy.

We must remember, moreover, that nonaccelerated bright pupils have their social problems, too. The true comparison we should make is between two children, equally bright, one accelerated, one not. Moreover, we should follow through to the high school, the college, and the afterschool life. This has been done. For example, Keys matched forty-six accelerated high school graduates with pupils of equal IQ's who were not accelerated. "With respect to participation in student activities, the underage group equals or surpasses the equally gifted controls [i.e., those not accelerated in school placement] on virtually all comparisons"—including even athletic participation (248).

Pressey (357) has brought together data from the Terman studies of gifted children already referred to. These are set forth in Table 4, page 343. They show rather conclusively that accelerates, even those finishing college at eighteen and nineteen, are as a group healthy, socially well adjusted, and vocationally successful.

Pressey's conclusion based on a survey of extensive factual investigations may well be quoted and pondered:

> The commonly used crude method of grade skipping . . . has been responsible for maladjustment . . . in some students. . . . However, a large majority, even of those advanced by such clumsy means, seem to have shown neither academic nor social difficulty. [On the other hand,] not to accelerate superior students—to hold them back with less able fellows simply on the basis of chronological age—may *cause* maladjustment. When accelerated students have been carefully selected as not only intellectually superior but also in good health and initially well adjusted, and have been given some guidance and help in acceleration, maladjustment has been minimal. When public schools accelerate not simply scattered individuals but groups moving forward together in rapid-progress sections . . . much less difficulty of adjustment is found.

In short, it appears that acceleration has caused much less social maladjustment than has ordinarily been supposed. A little care in selection and guidance of accelerated students should make difficulties even less common. Increases in the number of accelerated individuals should decrease difficulties even more. It is not putting it too strongly to say that the risk of social maladjustment in any adequate program of acceleration

Table 4

Relationships of Age of Graduation from High School to Later Educational Career, Social Adjustment, Health, Marriage, and Vocational Success

	Age of Graduation from High School [a]		
	13–6 to 15–5	15–6 to 16–5	16–6 and older
	Test scores		
General Ability:			
Childhood Binet (Intelligence Quotient)	158	154	149
Concept mastery score (1940)	112	98	95
	Percentage record		
Educational Record:			
Graduated from college	83	74	67
Average mark B or better	77	82	74
One or more graduation honors	43	38	35
One or more years of graduate work	58	48	39
Social Adjustment:			
Rated "satisfactory" by field worker (1928)	80	79	85
Activities "several" to "outstanding" (college)	28	37	38
Satisfactory—composite all-round data (1940)	77	83	81
Health:			
Parents' rating of health as good (1928)	100	89	85
Self-rating on health as good (1940)	91	81	86
Marriage:			
Men	73	68	70
Women	60	74	71
Separated or divorced	5	12	12
Vocational Success:			
Men in highest group	42	22	19
	Mean age		
Graduation from High School	14.9	16.0	17.3
Graduation from College	19.9	20.9	21.9
Puberty: Men	14.2	14.5	14.8
Women	12.7	12.8	13.1
Marriage: Men	24.8	25.5	26.1
Women	22.8	23.5	24.1

[a] Total number 1,392 persons: 785 men and 607 women. Numbers in the age groups were:
13 years 6 months to 15 years 5 months .... 62 Persons
15 years 6 months to 16 years 5 months .... 332 "
16 years 6 months and older .... 998 "

From Sidney L. Pressey, *Educational acceleration—appraisals and basic problems.* Columbus, Ohio State Univ., 1949. Adapted from Terman and Oden, *The gifted child grows up* (439).

has been exaggerated to such a degree that it can be labeled a bugaboo [357, p. 138].

Gallagher [161] has a summary written for classroom teachers.

Summary

The idea that intellectual achievement is solely or even mainly a matter of how much one has memorized is challenged. Learning and hence achievement are conceived as a reorganizing of one's capacities for more effective living.

This chapter has not attempted the impossible task of surveying intellectual achievement in all its manifold varieties. Three major kinds of achievement only have been considered.

Undoubtedly the achievement of language is one of the most important as well as the most interesting accomplishments of childhood. The extraordinary rapidity of the child's spontaneous development in language, the joy that language affords him in these early years, is in striking contrast to the apathy or dislike for language which sets in after formal language training begins. This suggests that there should be greater emphasis in language training upon expressiveness and less upon correctness.

The achievement of concepts is closely related to the development of speech. Children need ample concrete experience as the basis for abstract concepts, but they also need explicit guidance in their formation. Two dangers lurk behind the teacher's desk: that a too-rigid abstract pattern of concepts be insisted upon at the expense of originality, and that abstraction be pushed so fast that the children acquire only empty words instead of concepts.

Scholastic achievement is a major aspect of a child's total development. It undoubtedly overlaps the achievement of intelligence dealt with in the previous chapter, but if we look to the methods of measurement used in testing, a difference emerges. Achievement tests differ from intelligence tests in construction and use. The former measure whether a child *has* learned certain things, whereas intelligence tests utilize certain selected achievements as an index to whether the child *can* learn at a given level of difficulty. Scholastic-achievement tests are of great value in showing exactly what a child has yet to learn and in helping to predict proper placement in school.

Reasons are advanced for having children move through the stages of formal education at their own rate, not in lock step. This rate is a function of the child's total level of development. The intellectual aspect of development is necessarily of great importance in determining rate of progress; but social, emotional, and physical development must also be properly weighed in this connection.

12

Social Behavior in Childhood

Children are social animals. The needs for affiliation and dominance are basic to social behavior, but they do not automatically determine it. Children have to learn how to act in the varied social situations in which they find themselves. Adults can do much to promote such learning.

When the difference between poetry and prose was explained to the social-climbing *Bourgeois Gentilhomme* of Molière's play, he was astonished to learn that he had been "speaking prose all his life." In like fashion we have been studying the social behavior of children in every chapter of this book. Nonetheless, there are phases of social development which remain for specific consideration in this chapter.

The Need for Affiliation

Basic to all social behavior is man's need for affiliation or belongingness. Every human being has this need, even the frustrated misanthrope or the hermit. No person is a whole person who is isolated from his kind. No animal, unless it be the dog, so needs affiliation as does man. As we saw in an earlier chapter, almost the first differentiated behavior displayed by an infant is a reaching out toward the attending mother. As the child grows older, the need for affiliation takes many forms: the need to love and be loved, the craving to be accepted, the desire for prestige.

In the adult, the tendency to form close relations with others is obviously in part a manifestation of sex. Is this also true of children? "No," says a certain kind of prudery. "Not of normal children! In the days of childish innocence, sex is absent or at most very rudimentary." The psychoanalysts, however, have presented convincing evidence that even infants have something that looks very much like sexual experience. Indeed, orthodox Freudians hold that sex

Figure 12-1. Reaching Out to Mother Is an Early Response

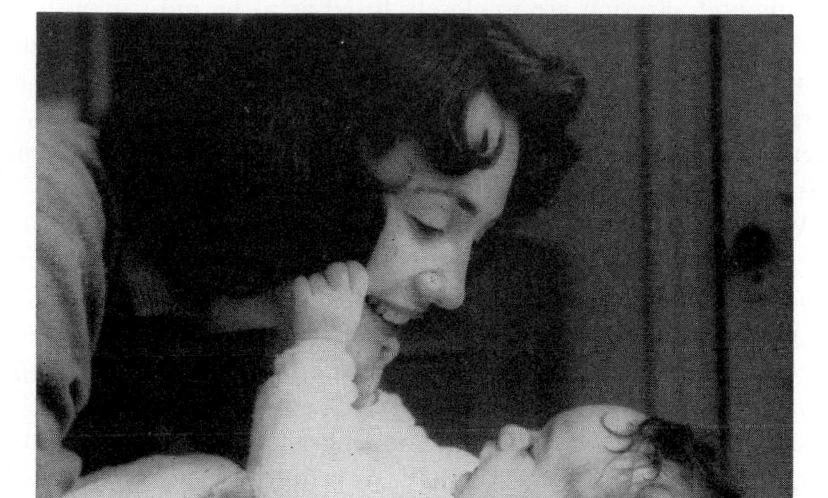

is the *primary* social tendency and that all affectional behavior springs from it.

This is not merely an ivory-tower theory. A whole generation of parents was led astray in the twenties and early thirties into believing that any manifestation of affection for an infant or child would arouse sexuality, and sexuality bordering on the perverse, at that. Few parents *fully* accepted this belief and fewer still acted consistently in accord with its implications. But it did affect their treatment of the children, and it especially affected their satisfaction in living with them. It may be hard for the present generation to imagine that mothers could have a guilty conscience if they cuddled their babies "more than necessary." But so it was.

Of course this theory—which opponents call pansexualism—did not remain unchallenged. In fact, there has been quite a furious controversy—a controversy not made simpler by a confusion as to what is meant by "sex" and by "love."

I think we can stay pretty clear of the heat of this battle. Let's look at it this way. Whether or not sex and affection are different in nature and origin—and numerous facts make that probable—it is clear that they early form a sort of partnership. They find (generally) the same object, and they work together (generally). Often sexual feeling and affection are so closely fused as to be indistinguishable.

The partnership results from learning, but it is a learning made nearly inevitable by almost universal human experience. Even universal experiences, however, have their individual characteristics. Hence the linkage of sex and affection, though universal in man, has all the variety of human experience.

What is the implication of this way of looking at the relationship? First of all, even though sex and love are closely linked, they retain much independence. Qualitative and quantitative changes in the one do not always entail similar changes in the other. *You can increase a child's sexuality without a corresponding increase in his affectionateness, and vice versa.*

On the other hand, although showing affection for a child need not, and generally does not, have much direct influence on his sexuality during childhood, it does influence the manifestations of sexuality later in life when sexuality and affection are more closely intertwined. Ordinary affection shown to the child does not increase his present sexuality or give it a possibly perverse direction. On the contrary, it helps to ensure that mature sexuality and mature affection shall not be divorced. So far from being "dangerous," overt expressions of affection in childhood seem to be necessary for normal adult sexual development.

Whatever happens in the development of an infant's or a child's affection and affiliation thus influences, generally very greatly, the whole texture of his adolescent and adult psychosexual life. And just as genuinely, the incidents of a child's sexual development affect how he relates himself in his later years to his fellows. It is not their common origin that makes the relation of affiliation and sex so important; it is their common fate.

The Need for Dominance

Almost as important in human life as our need for affiliation is the need for control, dominance, or ascendance over others. Small infants make imperious demands for "service." As the child grows older, the ways in which he is brought up create enormous differences in the strength and direction in this tendency. Probably nothing else so largely affects a person's social effectiveness as the ways in which he learns how to control others and, as a sort of corollary, to submit to the control of others.

Are affiliation and dominance manifestations of one or of two basic underlying needs? The problem is much the same as it was for sex and affiliation. In a comprehensive study, Schutz (377) has recently concluded that there are two separate needs which he calls affection and control. Analysis of his own facts, however, shows much overlapping. In childhood it looks as if there is but a single tendency that slowly differentiates into two. Affiliation and dominance in the infant can scarcely be distinguished; as the child grows up the distinction in behavior becomes greater. Yet affiliation and dominance continue throughout life to show a high degree of interaction and mutual influence.

Man's tendency to relate himself to others thus has a complex origin and development. In all its manifestations and throughout life, the need to be closely related to others is one of man's most insistent needs. As Spinoza long ago recognized, man is a social animal.

The Requirements of Social Adjustment

Although a human being is inherently social, he does not come into the world equipped with the necessary traits and techniques for social living. He has to learn how to be social, and this learning is one of the most difficult things he has to master. We may follow Morgan (320) in distinguishing four important *levels* of social development:

1. The child must learn not to get into undue trouble with others. He must learn not to hurt others, to respect their rights, to refrain from interfering with them and thwarting them. "This is the negative aspect of social adjustments; yet, in many instances, it embraces all that children are specifically taught about social dealings."

2. The passive type of adjustment is a little higher in the scale and is learned a little later. The child is taught to be docile, to obey authority, to conform. This form of social adjustment is convenient for the adult in charge of children: obedient children seldom make much trouble. But as we noted in Chapter 2, obedience and docility, though they have their place, are of very limited value in the child's social development.

3. The third level is that of full social interaction, of cooperative give-and-take. We shall say more about this shortly.

4. Understanding the other person is the highest level of social adjustment, Morgan tells us—a simple statement, easily made—but to gain this understanding takes a lot of learning.

The Social Code

To attain any of these levels, moreover, the child must learn the appropriate social codes. The social code includes not only the moral code and the code of manners and etiquette, but the whole vast apparatus which defines the way people act toward each other. Not one tenth of all this is explicitly verbalized as rules, still less written out. Yet we all learn, more or less successfully, to live within the framework of this code.

QUESTIONS

1. What are some of the things ordained by the social code that are not moral, not legal, or not etiquette?
2. What is meant by a social role?

Particularly important in the code is the definition of the child's own social roles. There is a role for small children and a different one for older children, a role for girls and a different one for boys. From birth to two or three the infant is expected to be "cute," the idol of the family; from six on he is expected to sit quietly at school. From six to twelve, moreover, the boy is expected to be male, and independent of grownups; the girl is expected to be "feminine" and, in most circles, to be more docile and dependent on adults than are boys (Murphy, Murphy, and Newcomb [327]). There are prescribed and proscribed methods of aggression, prescribed and proscribed methods of submission, both changing with advancing age. As we all recognize and as our British friends say, there are things that "just aren't done"; equally important, there are things that have to be done. And woe betide the child who does not play his proper role!

The code also defines the roles of other persons and tells us what we should think about them. There is much inconsistency at this point, even downright hypocrisy. It is part of the code of religion and of political democracy to recognize the supreme value of the individual person; but other parts of our code gnaw great chunks out of this precept.

We must value the individual—yes; but, we tell children, of course there are people of inferior race or class, people who don't count, servants who have an inferior place, and people whom one's parents just don't like. There are naughty children and nice children (children with whom you may play and children with whom "you don't want to play"), children you may taunt or pity, children you must be careful not to offend, children to be afraid of. Jersild (227) has evidence that there is much irrational overvaluation of physical characteristics in both childhood and adolescence.

The social code—or rather the many different social codes, for each culture and each subculture has its own—is far from a perfect instrument. We have all felt the sting of its harshness and injustice. With Omar Khayyám we would gladly "shatter it to bits—and then/ Re-mould it nearer to the Heart's Desire." Yet we must help children learn what the code is. We need not strive to make them perfect little conformists—as they grow in understanding we can help them to see both good and bad in the code, and can teach them how to *evade* its more onerous precepts. But awareness of the code is an essential for social growth. And there is, further, the necessity to make habitual and automatic many of the prescribed behaviors.

QUESTIONS

1. Are you satisfied with the answer about conformity? Can we in fact effectively teach the code without making conformists?
2. Are there any aspects of social living not touched by social codes?

Kinds of Social Participation

Parten (345), from a study of preschool children, was able to distinguish six forms of social participation—or rather four, for the first and third are forms of nonparticipation:

1. *Unoccupied behavior,* in which the child watches anything of momentary interest, or makes idle movements.
2. *Onlooker behavior,* in which the child watches other children at play. He often talks to the children at play or offers suggestions but does not overtly enter into the play.
3. *Solitary independent play,* in which the child plays alone and independently with toys different from those of the other children within speaking distance and without reference to what they are doing.
4. *Parallel activity,* in which the child plays with toys like those used by the other children but plays beside rather than with them. He is not overtly influenced by their actions and does not try to influence them.
5. *Associative play,* in which the child plays with others. In this play, all other children in the group engage in similar if not identical activity. There is no division of labor, but there is borrowing of material, imitation of each other.
6. *Cooperative or organized play,* in which the child plays in a group organized to make some material product or to play some game. The group is controlled by one or two members who direct the activity of the others, and there is other distinction of roles.

Figure 12-2 pictures the frequency of occurrence found by Parten at five different age levels. Although the number of cases is small, there is no reason to think them atypical. Of course, all sorts of temporary conditions may affect the frequency of any given activity. Sickness, e.g., often introduces much unoccupied behavior at any age. Proper training, moreover, can induce more cooperative behavior even in quite young children (9). All these six forms of social activity continue into the later years.

Figure 12-2. Types of Social Participation for Ages 2 to 4½

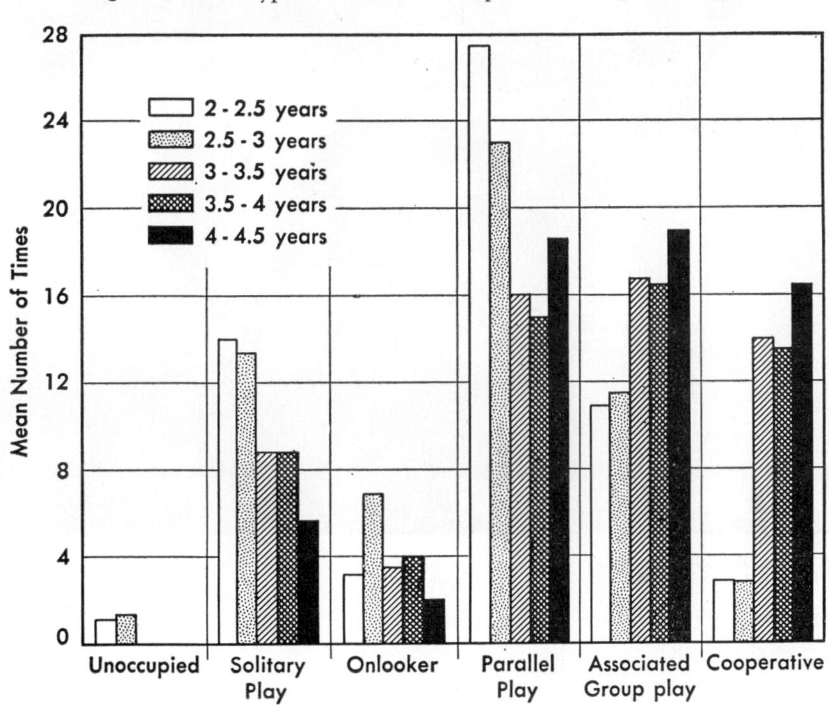

The different bars show the mean number of times each activity was engaged in at different ages. (Six children at each age level, sixty observations on each child.

Adapted by M. L. Parten, Social participation among pre-school children. *J. abn. soc. Psychol.,* 1932, **27,** 260. By permission of the American Psychological Association.

Another way of classifying social behavior, and perhaps a more useful one, is to speak of social participation (a) in casual interactions, (b) in organized groups, and (c) in intimate personal relations of love or close friendship. Casual interactions are so familiar to us all that they need no elaborate description: chatting with people one meets on the train, conversation with slight acquaintances, and—at the early-childhood level—onlooker behavior and parallel play. This relatively simple and undemanding sort of social behavior, however, plays a comparatively small part in childhood. Children have the courage to ally themselves with others in organized groups whereas adolescents and adults keep the relation casual until they know each other better.

Onlooker behavior (The Buckley Schools)

Figure 12-3. Stages i

Parallel activity (The Buckley Sch

ciative play (The Buckley Schools)

ocial Participation

Cooperative or organized play (Virginia Babcock)

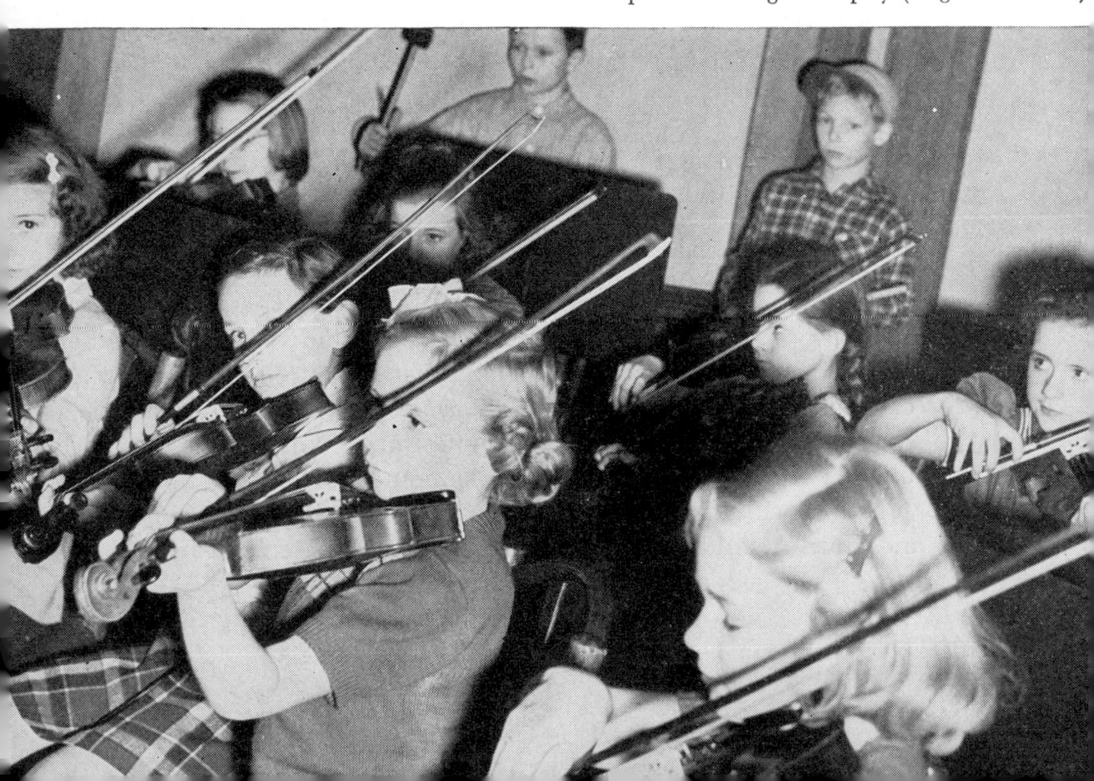

On the other hand, the organized group in childhood is impermanent and the structure is rather loose. That is characteristically the case in early childhood. Each child, nonetheless, has a place, a function of his own. Even in Pom-pom Pullaway there is an "It."

Elaborate rules, teamwork, and the playing of special roles come later. The characteristic social unit in the first grade is a group of two or three, at most four; a child leader rarely holds together a larger group for even a short time. Gradually the group grows larger and at the same time gains in cohesiveness, until in late childhood we reach "gangs," clubs, and cliques with rigid membership and carefully defined regulations for each member.

QUESTIONS

1. To what extent should the teacher encourage pupils to more mature play? In other words, to play games having a higher form of organization?
2. Did you ever belong to a "gang"? What harm or what good do you think it did to you?

Gangs. A great deal has been written about "gangs" and the "gang age." There is no question that, at least in Western culture, there is a tendency in late childhood for the sexes to separate and for the children to form tight little groups of from four to eight or ten. These used to be called gangs—and still are by their members. But "gang" and, of course, "gangster" have taken on unpleasant meanings. In French and German the English words have been taken over with exclusively derogatory implications (sometimes with the implication that "les gangs" are an American invention, now threatening other countries). But gangs as such are neither bad nor good. It does sometimes seem as if they are more often antisocial than not; but this is just part of the general fact that it is easier to be "bad" than "good." Properly led and guided by an adult—and that means not too closely guided—a gang provides a wonderful opportunity for social learning. Here above all a child has a chance to try out his social skills and techniques and *learn what is effective.* Here also is a chance to associate on terms of close intimacy with equals, a chance to carry love into a circle outside the home.

Not all children get into a gang, however. There may be none available. A child may not be accepted. Or his parents, fearful of unwholesome associates (or unwittingly reluctant to share their authority with the child's peers), may forbid the child to join. Moreover, a child who does join a gang or club may belong for only a short time. On the whole, this is unfortunate. I hesitate to declare gang membership an essential phase of development, but it is a valuable one. If no suitable ganglike groups are available, we should be at some pains to see that they are formed.

But these groups are not the only manifestations of organized social life, even during the "gang age." There are family cooperative activities, there are many less highly stylized work and play activities, and, not to forget, there is the school classroom. The last is an experience in group relations of very great value; and more than we realize, it is a social organism in which the children themselves make many of the rules. In fact, one of the chief obstacles to the introduction of more modern methods lies in the stubborn traditionalism, not of teachers but of children. Even kindergartners come to school with rather fixed ideas of the respective roles of teacher and pupil. Many are quite frustrated when the teacher refuses to behave in the expected traditional fashion.

Discussion of the third form of social participation, that of close friendship and love, we shall postpone to Chapter 14.

Play. In the preceding discussion of the forms of social participation I have made no distinct place for play. It should be obvious by now that this is not because play is unimportant. Play, however, is not a special kind of behavior but an attitude toward any kind of activity. Play is what you do when you are free to do what you want to do. It is thus very close to being the same thing as the intrinsically motivated behavior discussed in Chapter 6. Much that is sometimes called play—especially the "play" of adolescents and adults—is rather grim work, not play according to this concept; but fortunately a great deal of what is called work is genuinely playful.

I do not, moreover, retract from the position, repeatedly taken in this book, that play is a great educator. The spontaneous activities of children, though without, on their part, any thought of utility, provide much the largest part of the child's learning. Constrained and guided learning, in contrast, has but a minor role. Particularly is this true in the development of social behavior.

Different Sorts of Social Behavior

Manners and Social Skills

An old proverb has it that "manners myketh a manne." If we take the term broadly enough, there is considerable truth in this observation. For I have in mind not merely conventional rules of politeness and the like but the whole range of behaviors with which we respond to others or cause them to respond to us. Posture, bearing, facial expressions, gestures, manner of speaking, ease and poise, self-confidence (or a reasonable facsimile thereof), the know-how of meeting people, graciousness, heartiness, joviality, a quick attentiveness to the other person, alertness, quietness or loudness, dignity—these and a thousand others are included. Many of these behaviors do not seem to send deep roots into the personality; they are in that sense relatively superficial. They are not, on that account, unimportant. They are indeed the "small change" of social life, yet the person who is short of this change is greatly handicapped. However great one's other merits, one simply cannot get along without knowing "how to act."

The Learning of Manners and Social Skills

Manners, even in this broad sense, are much more susceptible to direct instruction by precept than are most other social behaviors. They can, moreover, be learned by assiduous practice; and they are enormously influenced by example, especially consistent example.

It ought to be remembered, however, that even manners may spring from much deeper sources in the personality. Every one of us has what Alfred Adler calls a "Style of Life" that alters only slowly. We cannot expect the chronically unhappy child to grow up with a "bright and smiling face." Friendliness of manner is seldom found unless the child feels secure. Part of the task in educating for habitual good manners is to help the child develop the sort of personality of which good manners are the natural outcome.

QUESTIONS

1. What about the control of manners by direct injunction? What are the values? The limitations?
2. Is it possible to control manners by controlling the situation?
3. Is it ever too late to learn good manners?

It is often said that manners must be learned early in life. The popular view is vividly stated by William James:

> The period below twenty is . . . important . . . for the fixing of personal habits, properly so called, such as vocalization and pronunciation, gesture, motion, and address. Hardly ever is a language learned after twenty spoken without a foreign accent; hardly ever can a youth transferred to the society of his betters unlearn the nasality and other vices of speech bred in him by the associations of his growing years. Hardly ever, indeed, no matter how much money there be in his pocket, can he even learn to *dress* like a gentleman-born. The merchants offer their wares as eagerly to him as to the veriest "swell," but he simply *cannot* buy the right things. An invisible law, as strong as gravitation, keeps him within his orbit, arrayed this year as he was the last; and how his better-bred acquaintances contrive to get the things they wear will be for him a mystery till his dying day [222, I, 122].

The point is undoubtedly well taken; but there is also a good deal of picturesque exaggeration. James neglected to notice, moreover, that many of these behaviors are foreign to child conduct, correspond to no contemporary need of the child, and seem to him meaningless and arbitrary. We thus face a small dilemma: Shall we let the child grow past the stage of his development wherein he can most readily make these manners automatic and smooth; or shall we force him for his own good to learn something that makes so little sense for him at the time?

One solution is to make the learning of "manners" more interesting by means of dramatic games and like contrivances. Even a rational approach has some merit; most children can be helped to see *some* sense in "doing things the right way." Usually, however, we endeavor to inculcate these behaviors by main force. We dingdong away—"No, give Mrs. Purcell your right hand, Herbert; your *right* hand!"—at the expense of strain, anxiety, and resentment. It isn't worth it. After all, despite what James said, manners *can* be learned later when needed—at least well enough.

Moreover, we should ask ourselves whether the manners we are so exercised about are really those the child will need in the sort of social life in which he is actually going to move. Certain old ladies to the contrary notwithstanding, "good manners" can sometimes be out of place; and "good manners" that are out of place are bad manners.

QUESTION

What do you think of the ethics of teaching children the kind of manners appropriate to their social class?

Yet, for success in life and for pleasant and comfortable living, it would be hard to exaggerate the importance of having the social skills that are valued in the society in which one is actually to live and work. Teaching children *how* to act is almost as important as teaching them *what* to do.

Ascendancy

Ascendancy is defined as the tendency to direct the behavior of others and to persist in one's own purposes against social obstacles. A very large number of behaviors seem to be covered by this definition. In the nursery school period we list the following as evidence of ascendant behavior: possessiveness with playthings (attempts to get them from others by force, words, or guile, or to retrieve them when lost to others); attempts to guide and direct the behavior of others; and criticisms and reproof of others. In older children we may have overt aggression, coercive leadership, bullying, rivalry and jealousy, competitiveness, criticism and verbal disparagement of others, and the same struggle for possessions (in slightly more sophisticated form) as found in younger children.

The names of these behaviors, it will be noted, are all slightly disapproving. But ascendancy can be described in more favorable terms. Instead of aggression we can speak of courage, independence, initiative; we can speak of persistence; we can speak of leadership by persuasion and diplomacy. Ascendant behavior, as defined, it is clear, is intrinsically neither good nor bad.[1]

[1] Are all these varied behaviors manifestations of a single trait of ascendance? There is much evidence that they are. This means that there are some principles which apply to them all. Of course there are also differences: gaining your ends by diplomacy may be somewhat (it is clearly not wholly) like fighting for them.

Modifying Ascendant Behavior

Even at a very early age children differ enormously in their tendency to be ascendant. There is indication that bodily constitution plays some part; healthy, energetic infants seem to be more ascendant. In nursery school it is certainly the mobile child, the child who gets around, who displays this trait (329). Thompson (440) found that a warm, responsive teacher-child relation brings out more ascendance. Jack (219) and Page (343) have shown that young children low in ascendancy can be directly trained to be more ascendant, and Chittenden (105) showed that children high in aggression can be helped to be less so. Clearly, then, the degree of ascendancy can be influenced by the child's experience. Moreover, the particular ways in which it is expressed is even more subject to control by the kinds of experience to which the child is exposed.

Reducing Aggression

Although we harbor a sort of sneaking admiration for many of its manifestations, most of us profess a desire to lessen aggression, at least in "aggressive children." It can be done. In the first place, we must lessen the amount of aggression to which the child himself is exposed. In childhood as in later years, aggression begets aggression. And in this connection we note that repressive adult discipline in the child's eyes is aggression; whatever our rationalizations, valid or invalid, he usually sees it in no other light. The literature is full of evidence that the children from repressive homes are likely to be quarrelsome or sneakily aggressive. (See, for example, Meyer [310].) When the child cannot work off his aggression upon the adult who arouses it, he is likely to displace it upon the most convenient and available victim among his associates—or upon his pets.

Teachers and parents, moreover, generally have simply no idea of the number of times they interfere with and block the child's activities. (See, for example, Murphy [329], and Dawe, *et al.* [116].) When faced with an objective record of their own behavior, they usually refuse to believe the record is fair or typical. The cumulative effect of these interferences certainly is to induce overt or covert aggression. The overanxious parent or teacher may create aggression almost as effectively as the authoritarian parent discussed in Chapters 2 and 3. And other things being equal, the more a child practices aggression, the more aggressive he becomes.

Of course some fighting is hardly aggression at all. It is just fun—more like the fighting play of two puppies than anything else. Moreover, much fighting and quarreling is due to ignorance and lack of understanding of how to get things done without fighting. Jersild and Fite (228) found, for instance, that quarreling reaches a sort of peak at age three; the children are old enough to get about and to have many contacts with others but haven't yet learned how to manage them. That is why it is possible with nursery school children to lessen the tendency to be bossy and domineering by helping the child, as Chittenden (105) did, to understand the social situation and why the other children were acting as they were. When children get a firmer grip on the techniques of social adjustment they have less need of fighting. Guidance in less violent techniques can be of great help here.

The heavy reliance upon rivalry and competition in our schools certainly does nothing to lessen undue aggressiveness. We must remember, furthermore, that in any competitive situation there is always a loser—usually many losers to one winner—and that the frustration of losing tends to build up aggression.

But do we really want to eliminate or even greatly reduce a child's aggressiveness? Basically aggressiveness is just wanting to see one's own purposes fulfilled. Wanting that enough to do something about it, even if others stand in the road. Of course there's the rub. What we are really concerned about is that aggression shall not be so all-prevailing that the child cannot recognize the rights of others to carry out *their* purposes. It is more important that the child be taught awareness of the rights and feelings of others than that he be taught to suppress his aggressiveness.

There often develops, however, a love of aggression for its own sake, a pleasure in dominating others just for the sake of dominating. It may appear very early in childhood. Such love of being the boss is rather dangerous. Aggression needs to be demoted from the position of being an end to that of a means to the end. Children should learn to utilize aggression and other ascendant behaviors in order to reach objective goals.

Moreover, they must learn the acceptable and effective ways in which aggression may be shown. Note that I state the case positively in terms of learning acceptable modes rather than in terms of learning to avoid unacceptable ones. We are much too prone merely to forbid "bad" aggression and leave it at that. "Good" aggressiveness differs greatly in various cultures and social classes and at different ages. (The child may actually have a better idea of what is acceptable in his peer group than the teacher, especially if the latter comes from a different social class.) All in all, the proper use of aggression presents many problems, but they are all learning problems—learning problems where we can be of much greater help to children than we commonly are. McNeil's review of the literature brings together facts about the manifold forms taken by the tendency to aggression (306).

Leadership

As we have implied, there is a positive side to ascendant behavior. We no longer think in terms of "born leaders." Any child has the potentialities for some sort of leadership.

The Desire to Lead

There have been many attempts to discover and describe the qualities of successful child leaders. Probably the most important qualification for leadership is the desire to lead. Many children seem perfectly content to sit back in a spectator or follower role. This, however, is almost certainly a learned response, just as eagerness to take over leadership is learned. The child needs satisfying experience in leading if he is to acquire the desire to lead.

But note the inevitable semicontradiction here in our thinking. Only four paragraphs ago we were condemning the desire for domination; now we are praising the desire to lead. Is there really any difference? Inherently, probably not. It depends, does it not, on the total pattern of behavior, and on ethical values? "Bossiness" for its own sake and "selfish leadership" are condemned, but leadership as such is "all right" or even commendable. As inconsistent as this sounds, it is probably quite reasonable. *Every kind of human behavior may be either "good" or "bad," "useful" or "harmful," "wise" or "foolish," depending upon the relations this behavior has with other behavior and with the total human situation.* The difficulty in guiding the development of children is to keep this wider context in mind. In promoting the desire to take the lead, we have to be careful that we do not promote "bossiness." It is probably very much the same trait; only the context makes it different.

Visibility

If the desire to lead is to bear any fruit, the leader must first of all manifest a certain "visibility," must somehow stand out from the group. Almost any quality, sometimes even rather disagreeable ones, can contribute to visibility.

Superiority

Once visibility is gained, the leader must be able to manifest useful superiority. He may be the child who knows the rules of the game, he may be able to think of interesting things to do, he may inspire confidence in his fairness; he may be able to play the games better than the others; he may simply be bigger and stronger. At any rate, in some way or other, he is superior in doing the things that the group wants to do.

Child leaders, like their elders, often have their own axes to grind; but they early learn that they can gain their ends only as they make the group feel the *usefulness* of their superiority. Thus the successful leader will seldom interrupt an ongoing activity—he joins it. Only later will he attempt to divert the group to some other activity.

Self-confidence

Sheer superiority, however, is not enough. The leader has sufficient self-confidence so that he puts his superiority to work. Leadership which is thrust upon a child (because he is thought to be able) is seldom held very long, unless the child responds by doing something to hold his leadership (224).

Social Sensitivity

Finally the successful leader is "socially sensitive." He is quick to sense the needs of his followers, quick to perceive their reactions to him and to adjust his behavior accordingly. This is especially true in later childhood; in early childhood the leader is more likely to just "bull it through."

Leadership Training

We said above that leadership may be acquired; more than that, it can be taught. Thus Jack (219), in a widely quoted experiment, took those children whose ascendance scores were in the bottom third of their nursery school group and trained them to come pretty close to the top in ascendancy, particularly in the matter of directing the activities of others. She did this by putting them into a situation where they were confident of a special skill and where they were almost compelled to take the lead and show the other child how to play. Apparently they found this an agreeable experience, for their ascendance spread to many other situations.

There clearly are implications here for the classroom. As Breckenridge and Vincent say: "Much more than is ordinarily done can be done to train the less prominent and less skilled children in some special capacity which will be useful to the group and which will give them status in the group" (73, p. 410).

The training for useful superiority should, moreover, precede the child's attempt to assume leadership. You can't just throw the socially nonascendant child into a group in the hope that he will find his own level. He will—at the bottom. If a child is to learn to lead, he must, as it were, have aces or at least kings and queens to lead with.

There are no comparable experiments dealing with the second main requirement of leadership, social sensitivity. We know, however, that social sensitivity depends on the perception of minimal cues (which we discussed briefly on pages 147-155) and on facility in emotional communication. Unfortunately, we do not seem to know very much about how to increase it.

QUESTION

What are some things to do that at least *might* help the development of social sensitivity?

We make a brave beginning in the nursery school by specifically calling attention to the manifest feelings of the other child—particularly in cases where feelings have been hurt. We say, "See, Jane is hurt. She is crying." Or to a child whose approach to a timid newcomer is too vigorous, we say, "He's afraid of you. See how he pulls back. You must be more gentle." We specifically direct attention to the behavior and guide the child in interpreting it.

But as the children grow older, we do less and less of this. Surely the need is not less. On the contrary. The indicative behaviors become actually less visible, a slight movement replaces the overt gesture; the interpretation also is more subtle. Why, then, do we let the child learn this much more difficult task by sheer trial and error?

Because we feel so insecure about it, for one thing. And particularly because it is very difficult to translate our own social perceptions into verbal terms. How do we know that Mrs. Brown is a bit bored by the conversation? We know it all right, but how? We have a total impression from her facial expression and from little restless movements but we can't put our finger on it. Indeed, if we try to analyze our impression and put it into words, we are practically certain to overemphasize parts of the total complex of expression and thus distort it. The little wayward frown on Mrs. Brown's face helps to tell us she is bored; but the same frown on Mrs. Smith's face means attention, and on Mrs. Jones's that she is myopic and needs better glasses. Thus, even if we are fairly skillful at social interpretation, we are unable to transmit our skill to others.

But you can challenge the child to learn, even if you cannot instruct him. You can direct his attention to the little behavioral signs that have such important social meaning, can check the cocksure extrovert in his certainty that everyone feels as he does, can encourage greater awareness of others' reactions. Here's a boy who is too insistent upon his own plan. Ask him (preferably in private) to notice the expressions of the other children; he probably hasn't been aware of the extent to which he is offending them. Equally important is learning to detect approval. Thus, the child who scores a hit may also be encouraged to observe people's reactions. The classroom can and should be a wonderful laboratory in human relations.

Within limits! In the nursery, you can say to Billy that Gwen is afraid of his vigorous friendliness—say it in Gwen's hearing, and point out the signs. But if Gwen is six and still shy, you don't dare publicly to dissect her behavior or even to direct attention to it. By six years, children have developed far too much self-consciousness to be made the public object of such scrutiny. While some attention can still be directed to the behavior signs of feeling and attitude, tact and consideration impose strict limits.

In many cases we need recourse to literary and, particularly, to dramatic presentations. Stories are full of first-rate descriptions of the way children behave—the descriptions are usually not too subtle; in the early years of childhood, they can't be. But the lesson is there to be reinforced by the teacher. (It often does need reinforcement. Take any story you like and ask the children to interpret the behavior depicted. You will be enlightened as to how deficient is their ability to interpret.) Drama—suitable to the child's level—is even better because the presentation of behavior, though artistically simplified and thus made more intelligible, is still concrete. Plays written by the children themselves are, of course, excellent for this purpose.

Good teachers have always striven to increase children's sensitivity to social stimuli. I am suggesting nothing new but rather a more explicit awareness of the problem and a more conscious effort to develop in all children one of the essential qualities needed if one is to act as a leader.

Compliant and Submissive Behavior

We have already discussed compliance with the directions of adults in Chapter 2. Child leaders quite as much as adults seek and gain the compliance of their fellows. It is important to notice that the compliant behavior need not be in the slightest degree burdensome. Indeed, if the leadership is good, there is real joy in following it.

This holds for those capable of being leaders no less than for others; in the nursery school Murphy found that those who are most ascendant are more likely also to be submissive when the occasion requires (329). Good leaders do not necessarily make poor followers; it is likely to be just the opposite.

Cooperative Behavior

Organized interaction between children makes somewhat higher demands upon the children's maturity. In Parten's study of nursery school activity, cooperative behavior was the slowest to develop. (Compare Figure 12-2 on page 353.) Wolfle and Wolfle (481) believe that only the most rudimentary kind of cooperation is possible without speech. Thus monkeys, and children who had not learned to talk, were unable to solve the simple problem of helping each other which is diagrammed in Figure 12-4, whereas equally young children who could direct each other by words were able to solve this cooperative problem quite readily.

Cooperative activity incorporates a great deal of leading, and of compliance with leadership; but it is more than that. It involves the ability to perceive the goals of others and the willingness to help forward them. The social awareness of which we spoke earlier under the heading of leadership is thus fully implied. Undoubtedly, also, intellectual maturity plays a big part. The children must be able to understand what others are doing and how their own efforts can be coordinated with it. Man has developed such a large body of rules for effective social interaction that just to learn them is an intellectual undertaking.

In its most developed expression, cooperation merges into what Harold Anderson (8, 9) calls integrative behavior. In integrative behavior, neither child dominates the other. Nor is there mere compromise—that is, each child giving up part of his purposes in order to salvage the rest. Instead, a way of acting is found whereby both children find better satisfaction than would either pursuing his ends in dominating fashion.

Does this sound too elaborate and difficult for young children? But even so simple an activity as teeter-totter is an illustration of integrative activity. Here the physical requirements of the situation compel it. Where they do not, it is the function of the adult leader to help the children discover activities in which all find greater satisfaction just because others are likewise achieving their purposes.

Figure 12-4. A Pictorial Diagram of Apparatus Used to Test Cooperation in Children

The boy gets the "prize" only if the girl pulls the string. At the back of the cages, the boy must pull the string for the girl.

Cooperation and teamwork are a fairly slow development, though the beginnings are laid in early childhood. Childhood play is here the great educator, closely followed by the massive structure of childhood traditions—a structure whose educative function in all directions we tend grossly to underestimate.

Sympathetic Behavior

Writing in 1937, Murphy, Murphy and Newcomb complain that "sympathy, humor, enthusiasm, and other subtler aspects of a warmly human personality receive little or no mention" in works on child psychology and development (327, p. 369). Lois Murphy's monograph (329) the same year was a strong corrective, but it still remains true that sympathy receives scanty research investigation and is too little understood.

She found reason to believe that, viewed from the standpoint of origin, there are really four kinds of sympathetic behavior. First, there are specific habits of sympathy learned from others by imitation or by direct instruction. Second, there is the sympathy that comes from identification with someone, from making his feelings yours because of your love for him. Third, sympathy may be a reflection of a "basic, warm attitude or feeling toward others in general." Fourth, sympathy may be a spontaneous response to perceived distress.

There is also great diversity in the forms of sympathetic behavior; they range from mere inquiry about the nature of the difficulty, through anxiety and protest, to punishment of the attacker or help to relieve the situation.

> Functionally, however, we do find . . . that *all* sympathetic responses may be distinguished from all unsympathetic responses in the following respects: first, the need of another person gets the attention of the sympathizing child; . . . second, there is some response directed *toward* the other person; third, the response is positive, in the sense that it is an effort to share intellectually or emotionally, to relieve or to compensate for the distress. The common ground, then, lies in seeing and feeling the distress as the other person sees and feels it, and in doing something about it which he would want done [329, p. 285].

Logically, sympathy would seem to be the very opposite of aggression. Yet in careful studies we find a fairly strong tendency toward correlation: the child who is aggressive is rather likely to be sympathetic. Lois Murphy and others have suggested that both forms of behavior rest upon a basic "outgoing response." It is the socially active child who bumps into others and receives and gives aggression and who also runs into distress and learns to be sympathetic.

Two-year-olds occasionally react with sympathetic wails to the crying of another child; they do not often respond to the objective causes of distress in another—cuts, bumps, and the like. By three, many children have begun to learn, and by four nearly all have learned, to recognize such signs of distress. They also will sometimes respond sympathetically when another child is being punished, or is attacked by a third child, or is entangled in playthings, or is locked up in a playpen or yard, or is obviously failing in some undertaking. Gradually, as social maturity increases, more and more situations are perceived as distressing and may give rise to sympathetic response. The ability to recognize the facial and postural expressions of distress in their more subtle manifestations is, as we have noted, a slow development. Individual differences are very great both in ability to recognize the distress of another and in the tendency to respond to it in some sympathetic manner. At first no sex differences are apparent, but later, society demands that girls be more sympathetic than boys—so, of course, they are. It is interesting to note that between nursery school children there were approximately eight times as many instances of conflict as of sympathetic behavior (Murphy [329]). As

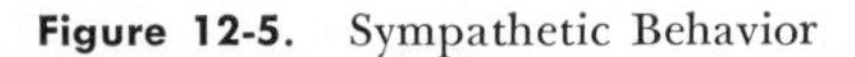

Figure 12-5. Sympathetic Behavior

Patrick takes Joyce's purse from Seth, who had rudely snatched it

Patrick returns the purse to Joyce

This is characteristic behavior of Patrick, although it is the same Patrick who, unadjusted in his group the year before, appeared to be one of the consistently unsympathetic children at that time.

From Lois B. Murphy, *Social behavior and child personality*. New York: Columbia Univ. Press, 1937. By permission of the author and Columbia University Press.

Figure 12-6. Individual Differences in Sympathetic Behavior
Reinhardt ⑯, 48 months, and Patrick ⑮, 50 months

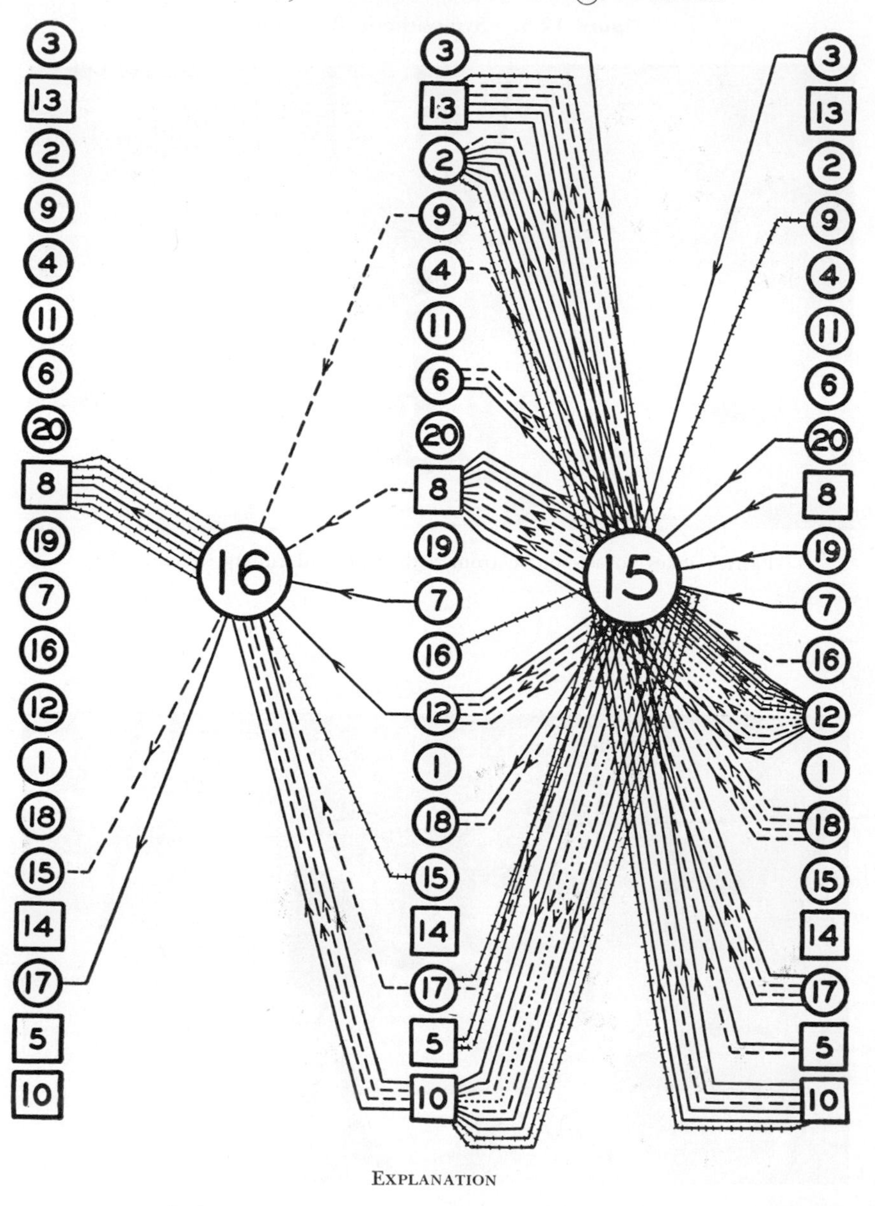

EXPLANATION

———	Active
- - - -	Verbal
. . . . . .	Miscellaneous
⊣⊣⊣	Unsympathetic

Arrows indicate the direction of the behavior. Girls are numbered in squares, boys in circles, from youngest at the top to oldest at the bottom.

Reinhardt's few contacts included a majority of unsympathetic ones; Patrick, who was unhappy and unsympathetic the year before, is more happily placed in his group and is both recipient and giver of many responses.

From Murphy, *Social behavior and child personality,* p. 142. By permission of Columbia University Press.

children grow older, however, they are more *capable* of sympathy, and thus the proportion of sympathy rises.

Sympathy gradually merges into altruism in older children. But where in the early years sympathy shows a fairly consistent increase with age (both chronological and intellectual), altruism apparently does not. At least Turner (449) failed to find any consistent gain with age in the group of boys from nine to sixteen. This should not be too discouraging. It merely indicates that we have to do with a learned form of behavior and one which is not always well taught. What is the remedy? We have already discussed the problem of teaching social sensitivity; it is difficult but not impossible. We know, unfortunately, very little about how to make children really *care* about the distress of others, even if they notice it. It is reasonable to hope that experiencing satisfaction from both giving and receiving sympathy will help.

Summary

Running like a silver thread through the discussion of social behavior is the theme that such behavior must be learned and that adults do entirely too little to assist in this development, either by direct teaching or by intentionally providing the social situations in which effective social behavior can develop. We do teach parts of the social code—the vast body of rules that define the way people act toward one another—but even at this point we often hinder more than we help by teaching an inapplicable or unrealistic code. Much of our teaching of the code is unwitting and by example.

Manners and social skills, also, though open to direct instruction, are more often learned from example and from the traditional lore of parents and peers.

The personality traits that play a part in social effectiveness are less easily taught, less affected by precept. They are nonetheless learned, and the conditions for learning may to a great extent be controlled.

13

The Growth of Personality

The development of personality consists chiefly in a change from motives that work independently of each other to motives that are organized in complex patterns. The sentiment of a child for his mother is an example of such a complex. In this sentiment many feelings and motives are subordinated to the controlling attitude of affection, pride, and gratitude. Of the same nature are what we commonly call ambitions, ideals, values, and standards of conduct; they are sentiments organized around an abstract idea. The total organization of these dynamic patterns is what we mean by personality. The proper guidance of such sentiments during their slow formation in childhood is of highest consequence.

From Tissue Needs to Lifelong Ideals

The life of an infant is largely, though not entirely, dominated by direct tissue needs; his motives are those of hunger, thirst, the escape from pain; and each of these operates more or less independently of the others. The young child, though his motives are less obviously organic, also lives only for the present moment. In joy and sorrow, in quick-changing affection and anger, his behavior is spasmodic and disconnected. Little by little, however, there emerge enduring consistencies of behavior. Out of sight is no longer out of mind. Motives persist longer, take in more territory. Even the infant hunts purposefully for the missing rattle; an older child plans an elaborate project and doggedly carries it into execution over a period of many weeks. Emotional behavior is related not merely to the circumstances of the moment but to longer-range purposes and goals.[1]

Purposes and goals, furthermore, reveal more and more organization or system, with lesser goals being subordinated to more inclusive ones. Consider your own present activity. Perhaps you have just left an unfinished rubber of bridge because you had determined to get down to work by eight o'clock. The game was exciting, the company pleasant. Certainly you would have preferred the game to reading this book. You are resolute in your purpose, however, because it serves more inclusive ends: perhaps the goal of getting good marks, which in turn is a means to getting a job—or, more idealistically, of learning about children in order better to serve humanity. (Here, as is often the case, the "realistic" and the "idealistic" motives lead to the same end; they are by no means always in conflict.)

You have your counterpart in the small child who gives up the attractive dawdling over breakfast in order to accompany mother to the grocery for the day's shopping: or in the older child who gives up his recess periods to work on a stage setting for the class play. Very early in life, then, motives begin to be arranged in a sort of *hierarchy* of control—like the chain of command in a corporation or the military—with superior or inclusive motives regulating lesser ones.

Sooner or later in any discussion of personality we must face the distinction between what actually happens in behavior, the behavioral *event,* and the *disposition* or tendency that accounts for the event. It is very much like the distinction between the performance and the structure of the machine. The behavioral events are such activities as taking a stroll, biffing Joe on the nose when he called you a stinker, or wanting an ice-cream cone. They are observable facts. They take place and are over and done. The disposition is not observed but, like gravitation or electricity, is inferred to account for the facts. A habit is an example of a disposition. A child may be disposed to pop his thumb into his mouth whenever he is not otherwise occupied. We also speak of a good or a stormy disposition. Quite generally, a disposition is a set of arrangements within a person, a sort

[1] From this point of view, the distinction between motive and emotion becomes somewhat artificial. Motives are emotional; emotions are motivating.

of structure or mechanism, that is inferred to account for the fact that behavior shows consistency of strength and direction.

Most of the terms referring to motivation have such a double reference. Thus, "need for food" refers to an actual "event," to a certain inner commotion, chiefly vigorous churning movements in the stomach. But it also refers to the fact that this person is so constituted or "disposed" that the need recurs rather regularly.

Or take the desire for praise. Desiring praise is an event in time, a way of acting (no less real for being mostly "inside"), and, like any action, may have a dynamic effect on our conduct. Such a desire, as an event, can be naturally and easily displaced by some other desire. Even those most avid of praise can be distracted. A lad who, originally to win praise, takes up the making of model ships may become so imbued with the true spirit of craftsmanship that he will even introduce features in his model that win him dispraise from some of his critics: he knows these features are what the boat needs to be "right." The desire for praise in his case is largely elbowed aside. No problem for theory here. The *event* of desiring praise is prevented and the *disposition* to seek praise is inactive; under other circumstances the event of desiring praise will recur.

But suppose that you inhibit the boy's love of praise by making him feel that it is shameful and ignoble. Not so simple now, is it? The desire for praise is not merely crowded out; it is repressed. In both instances the event of desiring praise is kept from occurring. But in the first case, the disposition merely becomes temporarily inactive; in the second, the disposition continues in action but manifests itself indirectly: there may be self-disparagement of one's work. Whole books have been written about such indirect effects of repression. We can sum it up by saying that the repressed disposition, though it does not lead to its normal manifestation, continues to have a very dynamic effect on behavior.

QUESTIONS

1. Children are often kept from doing what they want to do, but does this amount to real repression? Aren't repressions abnormal?
2. The indirect effect of a repressed disposition is a behavior. How can you distinguish it from a direct effect of a disposition?

A great deal of confusion has arisen from the failure to make clear the distinction between the desiring (as a specific event in time) and the enduring desire (which is a disposition). Things true only of desiring as event are attributed to the disposition, and sometimes vice versa.

I wish it were possible to avoid the resulting shabby thinking by working out a consistent terminology. I'm afraid it can't be done. One might, indeed, use nouns such as "wish," "need," "desire" for the disposition, and the gerunds "wishing," "needing," and "desiring" for the actual behaving. It is unlikely, however, that either writer or reader would stick to the distinction with enough consistency. But if we keep in mind the distinction between the structure and the operation of the "machine," we can tell whether, in a given context, an author means the observed behavior or the inferred disposition that accounts for it.

In this chapter we shall be primarily concerned with the dispositions, rather than directly with the actions. We shall see how relatively simple motive-dispositions become connected so that they function as larger units. Just as an automobile is a complex machine made up of smaller machines (carburetor, water pump, generator, and so on), so the larger motive systems are made up of smaller ones.

The Organization of Motives

The idealized or "logical" picture of the organization of motives is that of a perfect pyramid with each having a fixed place subordinate only to the one next above it in the system; at the peak is the master motive or life ideal (see Fig. 13-1). Such a hierarchy of motives, as it is called, is altogether too neat a pattern for so complex a creature as man. Cattell (95, pp. 157 f.) therefore pictures the relationships in the form of a complex latticework. But even that does not fully do justice to the complexity of the situation. As another writer (349) puts it, motives "ramify as do trees, converge as do streams, interconnect as do canals, divide as do nuclei."

Any single motive plays its part in many relationships. The desire to find social acceptance is one reason for dieting for a trim figure; yet at a dinner party it may lead to caloric indiscretions. A child's desire to please his mother may lead him to tell the manly truth; but the very same desire may also lead him to lie. Such imperfect harmonization of motives provides the novelist and dramatist with their richest material.

Figure 13-1. The Hierarchy of Motives

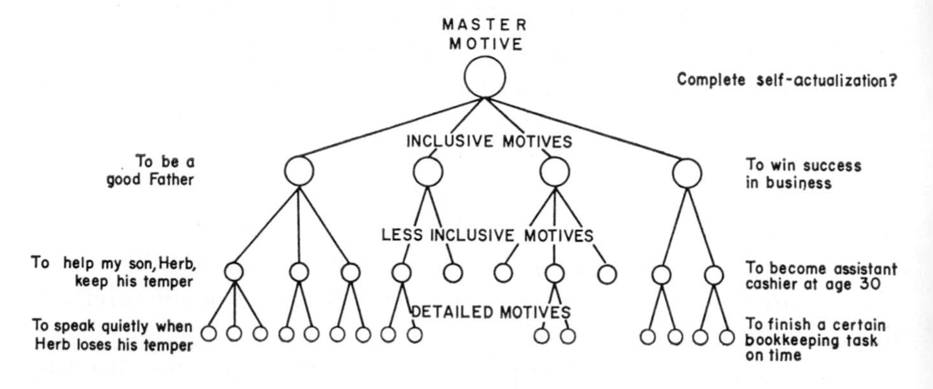

QUESTIONS

1. Can you supply other examples of motives arranged in a hierarchy?
2. Consider that a man's desire to become a success in business stems in part from a desire to be a good father, but that working nights to win this success interferes with being a good father. Can you diagram these relationships?

Although the perfect harmony of motives symbolized by the hierarchy diagram is never achieved, it is not just an empty logical schema. Each of us, often in a stumbling, half-blind fashion, is pushing toward such organization of our lives. There is no surer measure of maturity than the degree to which we achieve an enduring order and system in our emotions and motives. Without it, the child of high intelligence remains but a precocious child, whereas many a duller person who has achieved a certain organization is judged mature.[2]

[2] Too great an intellectual deficiency, however, makes it impossible to develop a rich and complex life pattern. It is not without significance that in the institutions for the feebleminded the patients are almost invariably called "boys" and "girls," though they may be thirty or forty years old. An imbecile, as Thorndike (446) suggests, is only part of a person; a child is in the process of becoming a person.

The Role of Learning

How is this mature organization of motives achieved? The basic principle has been repeatedly stated: *Whenever a need or motive is satisfied, the child becomes* (a) *more sensitive to the sort of stimuli that led to satisfying behavior, and* (b) *more likely to respond with that behavior.*

Thus, in the course of experience, a large variety of life circumstances, originally neutral, become potential instigators of a particular motive, directors of behavior toward this or that satisfaction. The nursing bottle becomes associated with hunger satisfaction, so that its appearance stimulates the hunger motive and leads to agitated clamor. The odor of frying bacon reminds an older child of how hungry he is—that is, it really sets the hunger motive in action. The first flash of a Mickey Mouse "short" galvanizes all the small fry into agonized anticipation. The repetition of a certain phrase in the "Liebestod" from *Tristan* sets up an almost intolerable "hunger" for its resolution. All these situations are able to stir or move us in specific ways because of earlier satisfactions.

The direct effect of experience, then, is to increase the variety of life circumstances that arouse our interest or engage our strivings and, as well, to increase the ease with which a need can be aroused by a familiar stimulus. The world of the child, as Robert Louis Stevenson says, is "so full of a number of things," but the life of an adult is even more full. While unfortunately we soon lose the child's freshness of interest in the commonplace, we constantly acquire interest in much that the child cannot even conceive. *It is a sign of maturity to be interested in and motivated by an ever-wider range of objects and situations.*[3]

Paralleling this expansion in the number and variety of objects leading to action is the somewhat opposed process of *specialization or canalization of response,* which is well described by Gardner Murphy:

---

[3] It is true that Lehman and Witty (263) in their classic study found that play interests decrease with age. They reach this conclusion by counting teeter-totter (at age 4) and basketball (at age 10) each as one interest. Valid as such units may be for other purposes, they give a false impression of the wealth and range of interests at different ages.

Needs tend to become more specific in consequence of being satisfied in specific ways. Children all over the world are hungry; their hunger may be satisfied by bread, by ice cream, by peanuts, by raw eggs, by rice, or by whale blubber. Eventually they develop, when hungry, not a demand for food in general, but a demand for what they are used to; in one part of the world peanuts are good food, whale blubber disgusting, and vice versa. So, too, over the face of the earth, children enjoy rhythms; the need is satisfied by different kinds of rhythms, different games, different types of music. Soon they find the ones which they are "used to" natural and satisfying; others seem awkward, difficult, unsatisfying.

If a person is hungry . . . he may nevertheless be more hungry for bread than for corn, for beef than for mutton . . . but specific attitudes are defined within the general, and within the specific there are some still more specific, so that one wants not only currant buns but the one with the darkest crust. Tastes have become specific.

The restlessness or muscular distress which in the infant freed of his blankets appears in active writhing soon becomes a regular roll-over or push-and-pull game. Activity has become specific. The muscles develop specifically as differentiated responses appear, and to some extent in relation to specific use; those which have been exercised need still more exercise. The eye, too, tends to turn to the familiar [325, p. 161]

Nothing, we may add, is so intensely satisfying as the twice-told—nay, the hundred-times-told—tale of Peter Rabbit or of Winnie the Pooh. (Which is not to deny that novelty also has its charms.) Children's preference for their familiar toys is also well known. Particularly significant is the attachment to the familiar doll, for here the personal element enters. In all these and countless other readily recognized examples, everyday experience and learning lead to a

Figure 13-2. The Charm of the Familiar

preferential selection of some stimuli and a stabilizing of satisfactory responses. Need-satisfaction is channeled or *canalized* in specific directions.

The Beginnings of Organization

A further stage of development is reached when several such specialized satisfaction patterns become grouped about a specific object—usually a person. Even in early childhood such organization is taking place. The infant watching the kitten chasing its tail gurgles with amused delight. When the kitten scratches him, the child is angry or afraid. Yet a few moments later, he will tenderly cuddle the kitten, and when his mother puts the kitten out of the room the child will cry for its return. The kitten thus serves as a focal point for a whole series of motives and feelings, and these therefore become related.

The most constant as well as the most important object in the infant's experience is the mother. Her movements attract his attention, her visible appearance is associated with the satisfaction of food and other bodily wants. At a later time, playthings, songs and sounds, caresses, and innumerable delights—but also frustrating restraints—proceed from the same almost ever-present source. Nearly every motive capable of exciting the child is related in some fashion to the mother. Parallel, though less extensive, emotional relationships toward other persons also make their appearance.

Dominance of the Commonest Attitude toward a Person

Despite the variety of motives that any familiar person thus comes to excite, there soon emerge *dominant* relationships. With the mother, the most common relationships are those of tenderness, security, physical and social satisfactions, and submission; and this complex regulates the functioning of other motives. To paraphrase G. B. Shaw, a child's love for his mother causes him to exaggerate her differences from all other women. Thus a nursery school child may howl and refuse if his teacher offers to remove a splinter, but he may permit his mother to perform the same service. Fear is submerged in her case partly because the child is used to submitting to her ministrations and partly because, even in fearful circumstances, she is still a source of security.[4] Toward another adult, the controlling relationship may be a blend of fear and anger and resistance. In sum, for the child each familiar person (or personalized object) comes to have a sort of central emotional value about which other emotions are grouped. Such complex and enduring emotional relationships are commonly called sentiments.

The further development of a sentiment may be best understood from a concrete illustration. Tim, like many another five-year-old, had come to admire, even to idolize, his older brother. George was kind to "Bub" in an offhand way, played with him now and then, did little things for him. But over and above all this, George (at nine and a half) was so big, could do so many things to which Tim could only aspire. So it was that when the little hoodlums down the street ganged up on Tim, the arrival of George brought a special feeling of relief, as well as actual safety. When George was himself in trouble with a neighborhood gang, Tim shared his brother's anger, sorrow, hope, or shame according to the changing tide of battle, almost as if he himself were the contestant. Resentment at being teased by George was not simple anger but a peculiar blend in which the special emotional value of this older brother was incorporated. Indeed, if the teasing was not too severe, there was no anger at all but a sharing of the jest, *because it was the action of the admired and loved brother.*

Note how the picture differs when the relation between brothers is dominated by jealousy and dislike. Teasing now evokes strong and unmitigated resentment—stronger than the teasing itself warrants. When the older brother arrives to "protect" the younger in some neighborhood fracas, his help is accepted grudgingly if at all. If the older is beaten in a fight, the younger child, though restrained by a certain amount of family loyalty, is tempted to rejoice in the elder's deserved comeuppance.

Almost, we can say, the emotional tone or motivational "valence" is just reversed in these two cases. Identical situations arouse opposite emotions and motives in the two instances because the child has established opposite dominating emotional relationships with the chief actor in each: a relationship of love and admiration in the one, of jealousy and hatred in the other.

[4] Inanimate objects and situations also become the basis for such feelings. Compare the example cited on page 124 of the child who was not afraid of the slippers so long as she was in her own "safe" highchair.

Sentiments as Complex Combinations of Motives

The complexity of the sentiment of love has long engaged the attention of the poets. Thus Shakespeare writes:

PHOEBE: Good shepherd, tell this youth what 'tis to love.

SYLVIUS: It is to be all made of sighs and tears:
All made of passion, and all made of wishes;
All adoration, duty and observance;
All humbleness, all patience and impatience;
All purity, all trial, all observance.

And Chaucer—

The life of love is full contrarie,
For now the lover is joious,
Now can he plain, now making moan.

Swift—

Love why do we one passion call,
When 'tis a compound of them all?
Where hot and cold, where sharp and sweet,
In all their equipages meet;
Where pleasures mix'd with Pains appear,
Sorrow with Joy, and Hope with Fear.

Coleridge—

All thoughts, all passions, all delights,
Whatever stirs this mortal frame,
All are but ministers of love,
And feed his sacred flame.[5]

Swift's statement that love is a *compound* of all the emotions is perhaps less accurate than Coleridge's insight that all our motives are "but *ministers* of love." We are not talking of what it is like to *feel* love or affection but of the organization of the dispositions to feel and act that comes about when we feel lasting affection for a person. In terms of our earlier discussion (page 375 f.), we are dealing with the "machinery" of love.

Thus, as the child begins to love his mother, all his emotional relations with her tend to become consistent with and to advance the goals which characterize *the dominant relation or attitude*. Even as

[5] The quotations are suggested by Shand (387).

an infant he takes pleasure in her presence, is frightened or saddened at her departure. As the sentiment develops, the child rejoices in the mother's successes, is cast down by her failures, incensed at those who disparage her. Thus the sentiment of love brings within its scope even such apparently discordant emotions as anger and joy and grief. And these varied emotions no longer occur more or less at random or in response to the immediate situation alone, but when the immediate situation makes them appropriate to the dominant relationship.

Hatred, no less than love, may organize our feelings. We not only seek to avoid the object of our hatred, we seek to put him down; and, it must be confessed, we feel delight when he comes to harm or social disfavor. (While religion enjoins us to love our enemies—that is, to cease hating them—it does not ask the psychologically impossible feat of being glad at the success of those whom we have not ceased to hate.) Hate, like love, tends to bring order and consistency into our lives; it may be a dreadful consistency from an ethical standpoint, but it is nonetheless psychologically real. The *total* integration of one's life is, however, possible only with love, not with hate. For if hate be total, it includes oneself and leads to self-destruction. Hate thus seems self-limiting as love is not.

Moreover, the sentiment is not merely a matter of feelings: *action is involved.* The child tends to model his behavior on that of the beloved mother, and he also seeks through his own behavior to give her pleasure or to lessen her displeasure or pain. Not always, of course! His sentiment of love for his mother is but poorly organized and is not always brought into action. It is possible, moreover, to have partially contrary sentiments toward the same person. (Indeed we nearly always do!) Occasional behavior *not* in accord with a particular sentiment is therefore to be expected and certainly occurs; but just as clearly, in even quite young children behavior occurs that can be understood only in terms of an *organized system* of motives.

QUESTIONS

1. What are some of the most common sentiments found in the elementary school child?
2. Consider one such sentiment. What is its dominant motive?

The Varieties of Organized Motives

We must not limit our attention, however, just to the great and overarching sentiments of love and hate. In the most trifling details of everyday life essentially the same motivating mechanism is at work. Habits are not merely stimulus-response sequences but expressions of preference and directed feeling.[6] Attitudes are also simple forms of sentiment—that is, an organization of feelings and motives about a certain object. Even our opinions, despite our pretense that they are intellectual and objective, are expressions of underlying motives and operate to organize feeling and action in harmony with those motives.

And our ordinary goals and purposes, how neatly they too fit into the same formula! Consider not just a rat running in a maze toward the goal of a food box, or a child attracted by the relatively immediate goal of a piece of candy held out to him. Consider, rather, a child busily at work upon some goal of his own choosing. Let him be building a house of blocks, or let him be writing the club constitution for the "Secret Four." Note how feelings and actions are integrated into a harmonious pattern directed toward the goal; interruptions annoy or anger him, dispraise of the marvel being created arouses scorn, and anything, material or social, that is seen as helping toward the goal is invested with urgency and value. The goals of childhood do not last long but they organize and systematize feeling and action temporarily, just as the purposes, the ideals, the lifelong ambitions give more enduring direction and organization to adult life.

There is a somewhat embarrassing wealth of names for motive systems: sentiments, attitudes, ambitions, complexes, goals, purposes, prejudices, tastes, values, ideals, and doubtless others. I propose to use "sentiment" or "value system" as general terms to include them all. It is not that the terms mean exactly the same; clearly, what we mean by a purpose differs in important ways from an attitude. But when we speak of a firm purpose to be honorable, or of a favorable

[6] It is tempting to think of inflexible and robotlike movement sequences (which we do sometimes find) as the type and, as it were, the goal of habit formation. It is not so. Habit is an adaptive, preferential readiness to respond; when readiness passes over into rigidity, we have the degeneration of habit, not its perfection. The role of habits in human life is misconceived when we think of all habits as rigid movement sequences.

attitude toward the United Nations, we are referring to something that might also be called a sentiment of honor or a favorable sentiment toward the United Nations. The distinctions in usage between the several terms are for the most part those of common speech; I shall observe but not emphasize them.[7] What I do want to emphasize is that beneath the diversity there is a basic similarity. All these terms refer to the fact that a person's behavior shows an *organized consistency.* It is this consistency that gives at once individuality and maturity to the developing self of the child.

Sentiments and Values as Guides of Conduct

To see how sentiments give direction and consistency to life and conduct, consider the matter of sex. If sex were not incorporated in an enduring sentiment of love, it would display all the vagaries of appetite, changing with the physical appearance of the object and with one's own glandular condition. In contrast, as Shakespeare reminds us,

> . . . Love is not love
> Which alters when it alteration finds,
> . . . it is an ever-fixed mark,
> That looks on tempests and is never shaken; . . .
> Love's not Time's fool, though rosy lips and cheeks
> Within his bending sickle's compass come; . . .
> . . . If this be error and upon me proved,
> I never writ, nor no man ever loved.[8]

We need not limit ourselves to such high-flown examples. In our everyday life, there are many sentiments that give an inner consistency to our conduct. When I regard the noise of my own children as a mere sign of animal spirits but that of my neighbor's children as an infernal racket, I may seem inconsistent; yet in terms of my sentiments both judgments make sense. When a certain labor leader an-

[7] Only the term "complex" seems in need of special definition. It is a sort of "abnormal" sentiment, an arrangement of motives into a pattern which is internally consistent but inconsistent with the rest of the self and with reality.

The terminological problem for systematic psychology is dealt with by Cattell (93) and by Murray and Morgan (332), who also have a useful theoretical discussion of the nature of sentiment. See also French (152).

[8] Sonnet CXVI. Example and quotation suggested by Cattell (94).

noys his fellow citizens by his arrogance, a unionist, though admitting the indictment, seeks to find extenuating circumstances.

In childhood, the sentiment for fairness may serve as an example. Children often become positively fanatical in their demand that fairness be adhered to. Especially, of course, by others! But by themselves, too. They will often voluntarily forgo other satisfactions for the sake of fairness. A regulating principle is clearly at work; character begins to be formed.

A host of such regulating principles is assiduously inculcated in the infant and particularly in the child: promptness, neatness and orderliness, cleanliness, nondestructiveness, and, at a little more inclusive level, obedience—all the virtues and required behaviors. Indeed, a virtue may be defined as a simple sentiment organized in relation to an abstract idea as to what is "right."

In the young child, sentiments are imperfectly organized, hence deviations from consistency are many. The child who is punctual at school may dawdle and be late at home. The boy who loves his puppy will occasionally lose his temper and kick him. But he will also clean up after him, will tolerate a considerable amount of discomfort while playing with him or while training him, will even go without his own food, if necessary, in order to feed his dog. None of this is understandable except in terms of the child's sentiment for the beloved pet. When we know what a child admires or scorns, his behavior becomes more predictable. If for his every moment we had to postulate a distinct motive and figure out how to strengthen or weaken it, I'm afraid we would have to give up the idea of any sort of control of the child's behavior. But as his motives become organized into larger patterns they can be dealt with as a whole.

QUESTIONS

1. Sentiment refers to feelings of liking and disliking; virtue to what one *ought* to do. How, then, can virtue be said to be a sentiment?
2. The formation of sentiments has been described as a matter of development. Can we do anything to facilitate or guide the process?

The Danger of Verbalism in the Teaching of Values

Mankind has always recognized the very central role of language in any kind of teaching. We simply cannot do without it. Thus verbal instruction, at times almost pure rote instruction, has been standard practice in the effort to modify conduct, not only in schools but in the home. Is it putting it too strongly to say that the results are not entirely satisfactory? Why is this?

Well, let us take what I am afraid is a rather typical procedure in trying to teach virtue—say, honesty. First of all, we begin with the *idea* of honesty. We explain to the child—"in very simple words, of course"—what honesty means. And then we praise the virtue and try to make the child see how "nice" it would be if he practiced it. Such an ideal, however, generally "fails to draw blood in action." The whole thing is just a matter of words.

Contrast this with the *natural* growth of a sentiment, e.g., the gradual acquisition of love for animals. The child begins with his own pet kitten or puppy. He plays with it, experiences varied delights with it, gradually learns that love means that one must sometimes put up with dissatisfactions and disappointments. But through all this there is a concrete, vital relation to an actual beloved pet. Beginning with this the child may progress—and should be helped to progress—to love of other pets and finally to love of all innocent and helpless creatures. As the terminus of this development the child may have acquired a sentiment that seems as abstract and as verbal as the sentiment of honesty. He learns, quite in the absence of any specific pet animal, to react to the abstract *idea* of protecting the helpless and builds a complex pattern of motives and feelings around this idea.

But this sentiment, though it focuses upon an abstract idea, still rests upon a definite basis of concrete experience. About the *idea* of protecting the helpless there is "a pungent sense of effective reality" which naturally leads over into action. In contrast, the sentiment for honesty, when it has been set up by an almost purely verbal process, tends to remain empty, devoid of real implication for practice.

It is not that words have no value in building up such sentiments. It is a question of timing. "First the deed, then the word." You cannot get a child to be motivated by an ideal such as "fair play" until

Virginia Babcock

Figure 13-3. A Love for Animals May Begin with Love for One's Own Pet you find him actually manifesting some form of fairness. (Or perhaps seeing someone else acting fairly, but that is less likely to register.) *Then* language comes into play. Tell him, "Now that's being fair; that's good." You thus simultaneously reward him (by your approval) and give him a verbal tag for the approved behavior. The next time he acts fairly, tell him: "That's being fair. That's another way of showing fair play. Like when you let Jimmy have a turn on your trike." Thus you help him acquire a generalized idea or concept of fairness. But it is a generalized idea of the way he himself is acting or can act to get social approval.

Most of our attempts to teach morality and other required behaviors make the mistake of skipping the first step—that of concrete behavior.

If you want your child to be generous, arrange things so that he will *act* generously—and experience satisfaction from doing so. If you want him to grow up with prejudice against Negroes (such prejudice is a kind of sentiment, of course), you should ensure that he is put into the position of discriminating against Negroes. If, on the contrary, you want him to be free of prejudice, put him in the position of actually dealing with Negroes upon their merit as individuals. The superiority of the playground for character education over the traditional "fixed-seat" classroom, with its primarily verbal program, lies precisely in this: the playground gives opportunity for the actual practice of many important virtues. But many modern schools have so loosened their program that they can encourage properly motivated *action* instead of merely exposing the child to moral precept.[9]

QUESTIONS

1. If a Sunday school wanted to follow the injunction, "First, the deed, then the word," how would it ever get started? Can you just sit around waiting till a child displays a primitive sort of generosity?
2. Give an account of how you once resolved an important conflict of motives in your own experience.

---

9 Much the same point is made in our discussion of emotional maturing on page 131 ff.

Conflict of Motives in Childhood

Conflict of motives arises when a child is pushed or pulled in two directions at once. Sometimes it is because he is attracted to two objects but can't have both. Who has not seen a small child poised irresolute between a scooter and the jungle gym or alternately starting first toward one, then toward the other? [10] Play and even food must compete with Captain Kangaroo, though here the conflict is usually resolved in favor of the latter as a momentarily more potent motive; food can wait. (But parental insistence when added to hunger may outweigh TV.) The desire to please the teacher is often in flagrant opposition to the desire to stand in well with the gang.

Conflict also arises when a single object in the environment excites opposed tendencies to action. The bipolar relation of the child to authority, which we discussed in Chapter 3, means that parents are often the focus of conflicting motives. To obey but also to resist are almost equally a means to gaining satisfaction. Bill most certainly loves his mother and wants to make her happy; "but doggone it, a fellow doesn't want to be shoved around all the time, even by his mother." He also thinks his baby sister is "cute," but it is hard not to become pretty irritated when she messes up his chemistry set.

Internalization of External Obstacles

During early infancy, however, there are probably no true conflicts of motives. The hindrances to the satisfaction of needs are the infant's own incapacities and certain physical barriers; and, of course, throughout the life span, such external obstacles continue to play their part. As the child grows up, however, the more important stumbling blocks to full satisfaction come from within, from the clash of his own needs, motives, and purposes.

Ask yourself how often in the last few months some external force or barrier has quite literally made it impossible for you to do some-

---

[10] Later we learn to suppress these overt yearnings toward the rejected alternative, but they often persist as little symbolic movements that can be perceived by sensitive observers. Thus we often give away our dislike of a person despite the effusive cordiality of our greeting. In childhood the suppression is much less complete, the signs of conflict are more obvious.

thing you wanted. Lack of money? That is external, all right, and quite a hindrance to the satisfaction of desires. Yet it is not really lack of money which keeps you from ordering a fancy dinner you can't pay for; it is the fear of what will happen to you if you don't pay. Even fairly young children have to struggle with barriers which are thus only half external. The child hungrily eyeing the candy behind the store window is deterred as much by his fear of punishment as by the physical barrier. An external obstacle is important chiefly because it is a sign, a representation of some positive or negative motive. The external barrier is internalized.

Socialization

Social barriers, also, become internalized. At first the conflict between the peremptory demands of hunger, thirst, excretion, or pain avoidance on the one hand and the social regulation of these functions on the other is a conflict between inner and outer demands. Soon, however, the child becomes sensitive to the motives of approval and disapproval and begins the long, long process of *socialization*—that is, the process of adopting as his own the motives imposed by society. Thus, sometime toward the end of the second year, toilet control becomes not merely something mother insists upon but one of the child's own goals. The inner need of prompt excretion is now in conflict not with an external command but with another inner need.

A somewhat similar development often, but quite needlessly, invests the child's external sex organs with ambivalence. The child's curious and mildly pleasurable exploration of these parts is apt to be rather severely punished. Thus they become, even more than before, the object of curiosity and of pleasure, but also now of dread. It should be realized by all concerned that pleasure from the sex zones is entirely natural in children, that a certain amount of handling of the sex organs does no harm and certainly cannot be prevented. Severe measures merely make it more attractive, and lead to furtiveness and a conflict of motives—in some instances to a very damaging conflict.

In both these illustrations, we have organic urges running into what is at first an external social restraint. But the social restraint is transformed into a positive or negative motive: into a desire to conform and to be approved by others; or into a fear of punishment, of disapproval, of loss of affection. Such internalized social motives are the primary controls over organic needs and urges.

The Unruliness of Organic and Safety Needs

The control, however, is imperfect; organic motives are at best unruly members of the hierarchy, ready to break the bonds of propriety whenever aroused in strength. Conflict between organic needs and prudential restraints lies always close to the surface.

The "safety needs," as Maslow (297) calls them—flight, fighting, and disgust—are likewise too strong to be easily brought into firm subordination, and in younger children they are not. Activity needs may also be difficult to suppress to the degree required by the demands of elders or associates; although they are of less obvious biological urgency, the same is true of laughter, joy, and excitement. Since social demands come, however grudgingly, to be accepted as binding, the child soon is in conflict with himself as well as with society. Thus the child who feels fear finds himself in conflict with his own sentiment for manliness or courage; the twelve-year-old girl who wants to seem sedate and grown-up in church must fight her own activity drive ("fidgetiness").

Conflict Represents Imperfect Personality Organization

In the child as in the adult, value systems and sentiments are often in conflict. The immigrant child's love for his parents may be in sharp conflict with his shame at their being "different." A boy's desire to be "good" conflicts with his motives to be one of the gang. Interest in a TV program conflicts with the desire to finish a baseball game.

This prevalence of conflict reflects the low degree of organization of the child's needs and purposes. If the system of motives formed a perfect hierarchy, there would be little inner conflict. Every desire would be related to some higher motive, and this in turn to one still higher in the system, until at length we came to the "master motive." Each subordinate motive would find expression only as its expression was consistent with those higher in the scale. How far we adults are from attaining such perfect harmony of motives needs no discussion; in children the integration is even less complete. The organization of purpose begins in childhood, but only begins. Self-consistency is far from an achieved ideal.

Thus, Carleton, at age ten, had already developed a strong desire to be a "big shot," to dominate over others. Carleton also loved his dog. Yet in his imperious urge to surpass his fellows, he was inveigled into fighting his dog with a much bigger animal, to his pet's considerable suffering and to his own discomfiture and sorrow. Though the stronger motive prevailed, the lesser motive of love for his dog was not suppressed.

Moreover, the relations between two motives may be actually reversed. On another occasion, Carleton was observed to give in to his younger brother George—actually to take orders from him!—in order to extract concessions from the brother for the benefit of the beloved pet. Here we see that his love for the puppy prevailed over his bossiness—not, we may be sure, without some inner conflict. The dominance relations between motives are complex, shifting, and not entirely logical. Yet we repeat, as the child grows older, more and more order is introduced, more and more does the organization tend toward a hierarchy. Character in the last analysis depends upon the adequate organization of the various sentiments (or simpler motives) in relation to each other, with an inclusive master sentiment in more or less supreme control.

The Resolution of Conflict

Many and various are the ways children (and adults, too) find to rid themselves of the stress of conflicting motives. Sometimes they fling themselves into action, abandoning one course in favor of the other, though without any basis for choice; anything seems better than vacillation between alluring alternatives, both unrealized so long as nothing is done. Sometimes, on the contrary, apathy seems to solve the problem; worn down by the strain of conflict they are no longer stirred by either motive.[11]

[11] During the long depression of the 1930's whole populations manifested such defeatism. For a carefully documented study of a village in Austria, see Lazarsfeld and Zeisl (262).

Often, moreover, external conditions change and the conflict just disappears. Or a change of mood or a change in the social atmosphere so alters the whole scale of values that conflict is automatically resolved. The sobering effect of grief in a household will hush childish quarrels and bring out sympathy and tenderness toward the bereaved. In the face of a crisis, even a child changes from a careless to a serious attitude; all "light fantastic" notions, as William James puts it, lose their motive power, all solemn ones find theirs multiplied. Abandoned are the trivial projects which had seemed so attractive, accepted are the grim and earnest alternatives which until then one could not quite bring oneself to embrace.

Reinterpretation

A useful way of ridding oneself of conflict is to acquire a different outlook on the situation out of which it develops. Bruno was much the largest boy in a play group and was inclined to use his physical advantages to monopolize the play facilities. Being a properly reared boy, however, he knew this was "selfish." So he alternately "hogged" the show and felt guilty about it, or reluctantly gave way to smaller children. The playground teacher got him to see that the play apparatus was really too "kiddish" for him and he was induced to adopt the role of helper for the younger children instead of their competitor.

Occasionally reinterpretation takes place as a result of a stubborn attempt to reason things out, but more often reasoning is aided by a direct change in the way one *perceives* the situation. The very strain of conflict sometimes forces us to see the situation in a new way. A regrouping of the stimuli, even just a renaming of the facts, enables the child or adult to perceive or think about the situation without being torn by opposing motives. The child who is alarmed by a gruff manner may be relieved if he is informed that the older child is "teasing." The pupil who is afraid of tests may be relieved if he can be got to regard them, not as a threat to his security but as a means of finding out what he has learned and what remains to be learned.

Other examples are so numerous as to make choice difficult. The pain cheerfully endured by a boy playing football certainly still hurts; yet in a very real sense the pain is no longer pain—that is to say, something to flinch away from if possible. The pain is now an occasion for showing manhood and courage and loyalty; it is no longer mere pain but an element in a larger pattern.

Though I may be very hungry, it simply does not occur to me—as a rule—to snatch a piece of candy from a child. Time was when I might have! Now, however, I do not *perceive* a child eating candy as an opportunity for satisfying my hunger. The situation has been permanently reappraised.

Or consider the illustration used in Chapter 5 of the differing reactions at different maturity levels to the stimulus of a pinprick. For the infant a few weeks old the pinprick is just that and no more; it elicits only a cry of pain and some rather ill-directed defensive movements. The young child reacts with rage; he is capable of perceiving the pinprick as due to a personal agency and as an affront to his self. But a still older child, anxious to prove his "courage" in the presence of his peers or of older children, may bite his lips and hold his tongue. A teacher, reacting to a pinprick administered as part of the traditional bent-pin-on-the-chair "joke," might display injured dignity, amusement, or self-controlled stoicism; she would not, one hopes, react with the rage we expect from a four-year-old.

It is apparent that as the individual moves up the scale of behavior maturity, an ever-widening net of circumstances plays its part in determining what he does. It is not the pinprick that determines response but the pinprick as "interpreted" in the light of a complex set of circumstances. For the older child, the reactions of his peers become determinative, for the mature adult it may be the verdict of the Great Society as embodied in codes of morality and etiquette. A given stimulus becomes only the nucleus for a group of other stimuli which determine its meaning.

Note, however, that the growth in meaning which a simple stimulus takes on is in part a reflection of the organization of motives. It is because one has become sensitive to peer judgment that being stuck with a pin comes to have a different meaning. It is equally true, of course, that as objects take on new meanings, they appeal to different motives. The growth of intellect, the ability to take a wider perspective and to integrate many life circumstances into a single unified situation, develops hand in hand with the hierarchical organization of motives.

Helping the child to reappraise the situation is a very commonly used technique for changing motivation—and rightly so. Of course it doesn't always work. The child's perception of things may be too firmly structured to yield to the usual exhortations and reassurances; subtlety as well as prestige and authority may be needed.

The reappraisal is more effective, moreover, if it takes place *before* the conflict actually gets the child stirred up emotionally. If the scoutmaster waits until the hot and dusty troop arrives at the bank of a river, it will inevitably look cool and inviting; to make them see it as polluted and filthy is then quite a chore. But had he told them about its filthy condition before they actually perceived it as cool and refreshing, their initial perception would have been quite different, and the conflict avoided or at least lessened. (See also the discussion of essentially the same point on pages 134-135.)

A special form of reinterpretation is found in rationalization. The child who ignores an insult from a playmate, because, as he says, he "considers the source," is trying to view the insult in a different light. It sometimes works, too, at least temporarily. The conflict between the motives of prudence or good behavior and aggression really is reduced if you can laugh your opponent to scorn. After all, there's nothing—well, almost nothing—against which to retaliate if the insult emanates from such an unworthy person. The grapes which hang too high above our heads cause us less yearning if we can only perceive them as sour. Although the habit of rationalizing is not to be encouraged, it would be cruel to deprive children—or adults—of all their defense mechanisms. Rationalization is a bit like an air pillow; there's nothing in it but it cushions the strains due to conflict.

Dominance

A persistent conflict, however, can be resolved only when for some reason or other one motive becomes strong enough to prevail over, and inhibit, the other. Anyone who has dealt with the child who sucks his thumb knows how strong is the need or motive which supports this habit. Parents nag him, restrain him with mittens, paint his thumb with bitter aloes or quinine, punish him, coax him—all to no avail. And then one day, he just stops!

Not all at once or without lapses, to be sure; habits deeply rooted in some obscure but potent need don't disappear that easily. But there comes a time—generally at about age five or six—when the child pulls his thumb out because "big boys don't act that way." This is not a new idea, of course; probably there's not a living mother of a thumb-sucking boy who has failed to try that line. It begins to work, however, when the child's motive to be a big boy becomes powerful enough to inhibit the dreamy satisfaction of sucking one's thumb.

The development of dominance relations among motives has received too little attention in psychological theory. We have, it is true, shown that one response may, by conditioning, take the place of another and thus suppress it—the case of Peter whose fear of the rabbit was thus cured is a good example. (See page 122.) Murphy (325, p. 195 ff.) has brought together a considerable range of experimental evidence to show that the simpler sorts of dominance in everyday life can be explained in terms of principles found useful in the experimental study of conditioning—especially inhibition, substitution, summation. It is possible that these established principles may also account for the more complex manifestations wherein a dominant motive controls a whole system of submotives, determining in what circumstances and how these shall appear. Or we may find that we need supplemental principles. At any rate, the reality of dominance relations is evident whenever one says, "I'd like to but—"; and it is present in many other instances where it is not so apparent.

Integration

Solving one's conflicts by the mere dominance of one motive over another is not, however, exactly pleasant. As James says, to "resolve that of two mutually exclusive trains of future fact, both sweet and good, one shall forever become impossible [is] a desolate and acrid sort of act, an excursion into a lonesome moral wilderness" (222, II, 534). Indeed, we may question that a child has really resolved a conflict so long as he yearns for the "rich and mundane delights," drearily resigned for the sake of the motive of "austere and naked duty." So long as there is resignation, there is at least potential conflict.

Fortunately, we need not depend on dominance alone. There is the relation, spoken of earlier, in which conflicting—or rather, potentially conflicting—tendencies are swept up into some larger purpose. If we watch the intermediate phase when the child is breaking himself of thumb-sucking, we may get a clue to the manner in which conflicts are ultimately cleared away. At first the thumb goes automatically into the mouth, only to be pulled out as the child "remembers." Later the movement of thumb toward mouth acts as a signal to arouse the more powerful motive; the thumb is arrested in mid-air. Finally the tendency is checked *before it even gets under way.*

Where the hierarchy of motives is firmly integrated, the incitements or cues that formerly stirred up conflicting goals are tied in with some stronger and more inclusive motive. Stimuli that once touched off spasmodic and undisciplined emotion and thus led to conflict are now organically related to larger patterns of behavior. Almost literally the stimulus that formerly touched off a subordinate motive is short-circuited by its relation to some more enduring life purpose.

Consider the shifts in the motives and value patterns when a high school boy determines to become a great athlete. He gives up eating between meals and spends hours with chest weights and in dull jogging around the track to get into condition. Old goals, such as the building of model planes, though still "all right," now fail to have any pungent attractiveness. An invitation to a late-evening "shindig" is no longer perceived as a chance to have a good time but as dissipation or a violation of training. There is thus little or no inner conflict; indeed, there may be a triumphant feeling of dedication. What would formerly have aroused the subordinate motive (that of having a good time with the fellows) now directly stimulates instead the dominant goal; instead of regret there is a certain joy in "being strong enough" to sacrifice the lesser goal for the greater. While it lasts, the "great ambition" can almost completely reorganize an adolescent's behavior patterns.

The larger patterns more than the small, of course. The adolescent doesn't change his "Style of Life" with every passing change of goal. His handwriting, his way of walking and talking and gesticulating remain little affected. Even the posture of the would-be athlete is likely to remain the same except during the relatively few times when he remembers how an athlete should bear himself. Despite the "great change" he feels he has made in himself, his associates seldom have trouble in recognizing him for the same person! But these smaller patterns are used within different larger patterns: our would-be athletic hero employs the same speech patterns—but he uses them to decline the invitation to a party where earlier he would have used them to accept it.

An example from the teaching situation illustrates how even a very powerful motive, that of self-enhancement and self-defense, may be subordinated as a part of a *system* of motives and purposes. When a pupil ventures to challenge some statement you have made, it is natural to feel some annoyance or even anger—your ego is wounded. But if you have genuinely accepted the goal of teaching pupils to think, you will take pleasure instead in the signs of independence. Even when the child's challenge is obviously motivated by the desire to flout your authority, you will accept the challenge in good spirit and use it as an occasion to induce this pupil—and the others—to think critically about the issue. Thus instead of a somewhat unsatisfying enhancement of your ego by defensiveness, you have rewarding enhancement from properly performing your role as a teacher. (And to this ego-satisfaction you add the pleasure of seeing the children make progress both in character and in ability to think.)

The organizing goals of young children are, of course, more fleeting; yet even so, in their self-sacrifice because of affection, in their acceptance of parental guidance in the face of their own direct impulses, even in such a simple case as their subordination of hunger in order to finish building a complex block structure, we see the beginnings of such integration of motives into a larger whole or system.

The Role of Selfhood

A major role in organizing and unifying motives is played by the developing selfhood of the child. Goals and purposes are clarified by reference to the child's concept of himself. The boy who stoically endures pain in the dentist's chair does so because he thinks of himself as a big boy—or as a "man."

Now, of course, the self of a child is not very highly developed. Indeed, the infant does not at first have a self at all. His self begins with a special awareness of his own body. When he strikes his hand against the side of his crib, there is feeling just in the hand; when he strikes his hand against his own ribs, there is feeling in both hand and ribs. From many such experiences there gradually emerges a percept of his own body as a special kind of object—a percept, however, which is rich in feeling tone.

Horowitz (210) has some very interesting accounts of the different ways in which the young child localizes his self—in chest, in head, even in the lower right jaw.

That even the self of an adult is largely due to the perception of his own body is amusingly illustrated by the Mother Goose rime of the old woman who fell asleep after a long walk beside the King's Highway.

> Along came a peddler whose name was Stout
> And cut off her petticoats all round about
> He cut off her petticoats up to the knees
> Whereat the old woman did shiver and freeze.
>
> When the old woman first did wake,
> She began to shiver and she began to shake;
> She began to wonder and she began to cry,
> "Lauk a mercy on me, this cannot be I!
>
> "But if it be I as I hope it be
> I've a little dog at home, and he'll know me
> If it be I, he'll wag his leetle tail
> And if it be not I, he'll loudly bark and wail."
>
> Home went the old woman all in the dark;
> Up got the little dog and he began to bark
> He began to bark, so she began to cry,
> "Lauk a mercy on me, this is none of I."

The old lady, you see, went to sleep warm and tired, she woke up cold and rested—"feeling like a different person." Note also that her appeal to the dog's recognition shows how social our sense of selfness is.

The infant's direct experience of his own resistance to the environment, particularly to personal agents, also sets him off as a peculiar "object," a different object from the rest of the world. The child's imperious demands for attention both reflect his sense of selfness and help to develop it further. Timidity in the presence of strange persons takes on reference to the child's own self and becomes shyness. By age three, success and failure are pointed up as particular experiences related to the self.

A crucial part in the development of the self is played by the mother. Her person is a more constant visual object than the child's own and provides the child with a sort of pattern of what a self or person is in contrast with inanimate objects.[12] The emergent self of the very young child is modeled on that of the mother by a sort of direct imitation or identification.

Moreover, from a very early stage parents and other adults begin deliberately to increase the child's sense of selfhood. His name is particularly important as a focus for self-perception. We play peek-a-boo; "Where's Bobby? There's Bobby!" We exclaim when Bobby correctly identifies Bobby's nose or ears or toes. Above all we make him aware of self when we tell him that he is a "good" boy or a "bad" one.

Against this praise or blame of his self, he is peculiarly defenseless. When you praise the spoonful of homogenized vegetables you want him to eat, the child may oppose to your praise the direct testimony of his own dislike and stubbornly persist in pushing it away. But when you tell him that *he* is good or bad, he has no standard of goodness to oppose to yours. Later, of course, he does acquire other standards, notably the standards of his playmates, and little by little he evolves standards which are his own.[13]

Nonetheless, it is all compounded of social judgment: the self of the child is chiefly a mirror of the responses which others make to him, and the self continues so throughout life. But social though it is, it is also a unique self, based upon all the individual reactions experienced in social living.

QUESTION

What effect does a child's sense of self have upon the organization of motives? Describe a specific instance.

It is a great mistake to underestimate the influence of this self even in children as young as three years. Ill-defined it may be, and subject to change it certainly is; yet it is the central reference point in resolving conflicts. Throughout childhood and throughout life, the sense of self is the final arbiter in most of our conflicts.

---

[12] Indeed, Zazzo (492) finds that definite *recognition* of others precedes recognition of one's own body. The more primitive awareness of one's bodily self, however, evolves concomitantly with awareness of the mother's bodily appearance.

[13] The process whereby the child forms ideals at variance with those of the beloved parent is complex. Stoke (423) has some interesting examples and comment. The Freudians speak more or less interchangeably of the ego-ideal and the superego in referring to this aspect of self.

It would, indeed, be the top control of *all* our motives were it not that, as we noted earlier, our motives are not organized in perfectly orderly fashion. As it is, the control of conduct by the self-ideal is imperfect, vacillating, and inconsistent; and the conflict of the self divided against itself is the most poignant of all conflicts.

Yet even so, it is the self which, more than anything else, establishes the order of priority among our sentiments and ideals. It causes our values to be literally *self*-consistent. Motives and actions in accord with the self come to have the right of way. What we are, and particularly what we hope to be, comes as close as anything else to being the "master motive" of our lives.

Summary

Not even very young children act from truly simple motives. Everywhere we find combination, system, and organization at work. The degree to which lesser motives are subordinated to more inclusive ones is a measure of maturity of character and personality. Each familiar and important person or object in the child's world takes on a dominant emotional value, and this value regulates other motives. Such a system of motives is called a sentiment or a value system.

Each such system eliminates conflict among the motives subsidiary to it; but the various systems themselves are often in conflict. Conflict may be avoided or resolved by somehow managing to reappraise or reperceive the situation giving rise to it. Conflict may also be resolved by one motive's growing stronger. But the best solution of conflict lies in the integration of conflicting motives in some more inclusive whole.

Most important of the "inclusive wholes" which integrate lesser motives is the child's self-ideal. Ill-defined as this self-ideal is, it is still the central reference point in resolving conflicts and the key to the understanding of personality.

14

Achievement, Friendship, and Love in the Development of Personality

In the development of personality, there are two main groups of human values: those of personal achievement—fame, honor, success, and skill; and those of friendship and love. Nearly all our other values relate to one or both of these and come to be their servants. It is in childhood that one learns to put these values in order. From his earliest weeks, parents impress on the child how important it is to succeed. The need for love is less directly inculcated. But no part of a child's growth is more important than the friendly and affectionate relationships he forms with adults and with his peers.

Religion has long commanded that love should be the central object of man's striving. Sigmund Freud went further: Love not only ought to be, it inevitably is, the great organizing principle of all life. All other striving he characterized as either "part instincts" or as disguised manifestations of love.[1] The same idea is expressed, you will remember, in the quatrain by Coleridge quoted in the previous chapter: "Whatever stirs this mortal frame . . . are but the ministers of love." Perhaps Coleridge did not mean this too literally. Freud did.

---

1 Freud later added a "death wish," but apparently this was merely the negation of the life principle, not a positive force. See Gregory Zilborg's discussion (493).

One of his first disciples, Alfred Adler, soon broke away from the Freudian group because of a conviction that the primary organizing principle is not love but the striving for superiority or excellence. He vigorously denied that the need to be superior or to achieve is only an indirect manifestation of frustrated love. In recent years, McClelland (301) has brought forward a great deal of detailed information showing how the achievement need influences the development of personality.

Must we then choose between these two rival theories? Perhaps not. In the culture of the Western world it is generally agreed that both love and achievement are good. Study of the development of personality, moreover, clearly indicates that both play an enormous part in organizing our motives into systems. Nearly all other values seem to be subordinate to these two, and nearly all we do is a means to the satisfaction of the needs for love and for achievement.

That both are important does not tell us, however, what to do when they are in at least partial conflict. Here, as Woodruff (482) points out, the applied psychologist has an obligation. He cannot prescribe what our values should be, but he can help us attain them. Specifically, he can help children (and others) learn how to resolve the conflicts between the values of personal achievement and of love.

The Values of Personal Achievement

There has been some tendency of late to disparage the importance of achievement as an ideal. In practice it is still pursued and cherished. Early in life the child is made to feel how important his achievements are. His first tottering steps are rewarded with admiring cries. At school he gets stars for excellence of performance and report cards that periodically grade his relative superiority—or inferiority—in reading, arithmetic, and deportment. He even gets a prize for pinning the tail on a donkey at a birthday party. Almost as soon as he can talk we see the dominance of this motive to achieve expressed in the excited demand: "See me! Watch how well I can do this!" As he grows older the child becomes more discreet in his demand for praise, but throughout his life are echoes of the childish injunction: "See how well I do it."

A survey by Child and Bacon (102) shows that many societies place much less premium on achievement than we do in America. The imperious demand that everyone seek what William James called the American bitch-goddess of Success is certainly not without its complications. Defining excellence as being better than someone else—and even psychologists have been known to grade students according to the frequency curve—is particularly likely to create conflict and frustration. Only one child can win in the drive for competitive success. Even to win second place when one hoped for first can cause unhappiness and depress one's level of aspiration. Thus in the national high school scholarship contest, those placing in the second class, though virtually indistinguishable from the first-place winners in ability and personality, lost zest for the intellectual life. And the child or adolescent who too conspicuously achieves better than his peers wins hostility rather than popularity. (Think back to the discussion of competition in Chapter 7.)

Yet I believe that our final judgment must be that the motive of achieving excellence deserves to play a leading role. To achieve is important not only from the standpoint of human progress but of one's own personal self-realization. It is no coldly intellectual affair; it is a passionate search, a burning adventure into the unknown. There can be few greater joys than the sense of triumph that comes when we have reached a long-sought goal. We should cultivate this sense of triumph in our children from their earliest days.

Achievement and Affection Not Always at Cross-purposes

Let us keep in mind, however, that achievement need not be sought at the expense of affection. *In truth, there is a sense in which the fullest achievement requires love.* The first achievement of the infant is that which is greeted with the approbation of the mother, and throughout life achievement takes place in a context of social approval. The finest achievements are those that contribute most to a richer, fuller friendship and love. Indeed, the real meaning of selfhood is not to be found in the self alone. There is an expansion of selfhood when one lives in the lives of others with whom one identifies. The fullest life is that which somehow manages to be not one's own life alone.

Now this may sound like a very exalted ideal that cannot be taught to children. But what we do teach children can be *in accord* with this ideal. Unfortunately, usually it is not. We tend to evaluate achievement chiefly in competitive terms. We do not teach children to think of achievement as the handmaiden of affection; rather it is something to be gained only at the expense of someone else—thus as the enemy of love. Whittier's poem "In School Days" beautifully sets forth the dilemma: The spelling lesson, a "spelldown" (as was customary), was over. Now, after school, the ten-year-old maiden addresses the proud but crestfallen boy:

> "I'm sorry that I spelt the word,
> I hate to go above you,
> Because"—the brown eyes lower fell—
> "Because, you see, I love you."

Yes, she hated to go above him—but she did! Our culture told her she must "do her best," and the only way to do her best was to "go above" someone.

The "spelldown" has practically disappeared as a technique for teaching spelling; its equivalent has by no means disappeared as a measure of achievement in school or elsewhere in life. Whatever our fine preachments, by our *practice* we still teach children that they can achieve only by thwarting someone else. The result is that in later years many a person of eminence finds life hollow and empty because, in achieving fame, he has robbed himself of the fullness of love and affection for his fellows.

QUESTIONS

1. How is it *possible* to achieve without in fact surpassing others? If I "build a better mousetrap," will not people buy mine and not the other fellow's?
2. Isn't it actually more efficient to keep the values of love and achievement in separate compartments?

Neither in practice nor in well-considered precept do we often show children that the conflicting goals of two or more persons may be reconciled, so that both may achieve satisfaction. What, for example, do we do when two children are in conflict—each, perhaps, wanting to ride the same tricycle? Too often, we just try to see which one can be got to yield with the least clamor. Or we side with the weaker contestant. Or, with somewhat more sensitivity, we try to determine who had it first and is justly entitled to it. In any case, we limit the physical conflict by edict and compulsion, thereby using adult authority to impose frustration upon one child or the other. The effect is to encourage the child to get rid of the conflict by victory over his comrade—or, if he is submissive, to seek peace by giving in.

Only occasionally do we have the patience to see, or the imagination to find, a solution in which the clashing motives of the two children may be not merely composed but integrated—that is, made one. Just as a child may learn to unify two of his own conflicting purposes (see page 394 ff.), so he may learn to harmonize his purposes with those of another for the sake of some goal shared by both. If, for example, the two children can be led to use the tricycle in companionable play *together,* each will more fully satisfy his needs.

Anderson (8) found extensive individual differences in the degree to which children show such integrative behavior, and there is reason to think that these differences are chiefly the result of learning. Thus, the children from business and professional homes were much more likely to display integration than those from orphanages. The former, of course, were taught "sharing" and politeness (both of which conduce to integration), whereas the children in the orphanages were for the most part just pushed around by the authorities (which conduces instead to alternate submission and resistance).

There are many opportunities in school to teach children integration of interpersonal conflicts, especially in a school where the children are free to engage in a variety of activities. Even in a more conventional school, conflicts occur and the children can learn to harmonize them. In group discussion, for example, they may learn that their own "cause" can often be furthered not by batting down opposing arguments but by finding a common ground on which all or most of the group may stand. It is naïve, however, to expect the children to seize such opportunities automatically; they must be taught both the advisability and the methods of harmonizing differences.

The Values of Love and Affection

The harmonies of love and friendship have often been likened to those of music. And like those of music, they have almost infinite variety. The simple trust of the child in the goodness and sympathy of his mother might be likened to the piping of the flageolet. The comradeship of children at play is like the slightly disharmonic chirping of birds. There are friendships of silken smoothness like the harmony of two violins; there are quartets, and the full-voiced symphony orchestra. Through all these forms of love run the quality of security and the intuitive understanding and affection which the child learns from his mother's—and his father's—love.

The Basis in Infancy

The foundations of all affection are laid in infancy and early childhood. There is reason to believe that, if they are not well and firmly laid then, the child will be gravely handicapped in all his later efforts to manifest warmth and friendship. It would be difficult to exaggerate the importance for personality development of a loving interaction between the infant and those about him. From our child-guidance clinics come tragic tales of lives stunted because children were starved for love. But love is not merely a passive acceptance; it must be given as well as received. This, too, children must learn.

Affection Must Be Learned

Moreover, it is only the basic attitudes that are thus formed in the earliest years; the arts of love and friendship have still to be learned. In the words of Breckenridge and Vincent:

> There is more to friendship and love than being [a warm and affectionate] person; one must know how to find and win other persons who will respond to one's real self, and, ideally, each person should become a richer, more useful and happy personality because of friendship and love experiences.

Even elementary school children learn something of this art of revealing themselves to others, and of responding to others on a friendship basis. Kindergarten and preschool children learn less consciously, but deep layers of friendship and family-life relationships are being laid in the first years of life. How much one concedes to the people one loves, or demands of them; whether one "goes to war" in the open about differences of opinion and desire or buries one's resentments; loyalty or self-centeredness; generosity or selfishness; cheerful acceptance or glum resistance; these are all attitudes and practices in intimate living caught as patterns from the intimate living one knows best in childhood [73, pp. 441-442].

Stages in the Development of Affection

In our Western culture, the friendship and love relations of a child tend to follow a certain sequence. The first stage is the stage of parental love. In the young infant, love is perhaps merely a clinging to the mother (as manifested by Harlow's [191] charming study of monkey infants), a desire to be cuddled. By the second half of the first year, love begins to be selective (413). The infant recognizes the mother or other constant attendant, greets her presence with a smile and her departure with a cry of distress, strives to attract her attention by pulling at her dress. Already, as Baldwin (28) observes, love demands reciprocation.

There follows a period in which affection is also directed to persons of the same sex (96, 448). Next is a period in which it is nonspecific but directed to the opposite sex. Finally, at about puberty, comes the stage in which affection is specifically centered on a person of the opposite sex (474).

The Freudians distinguish a "narcissistic phase" of development in infancy in which affection is centered upon one's own body. There is no question that stimulation of the body yields great pleasure and is sought by the child and also by the adult. The stimulation of the primary and secondary sex zones is particularly gratifying. Hence this desire for bodily stimulation does get all mixed up with the direct expressions of sex, and later with affection. It does not follow, however, that because they become mixed up, they are the same thing. Nor does careful observation of infants reveal a distinct period dominated by the need for sensuous stimulation of the body. The later manifestations of narcism, i.e., love of oneself, have a social origin and are not a harking back to an infantile pleasure in bodily stimulation.

In view of certain popular misconceptions, it may need to be specifically said that as the child progresses from one stage to the next he does not have to abandon the affectional relations of the previous stage. There is nothing abnormal—rather, it is entirely normal—for a child to continue to love his parents during the stage when he also develops fast friendships with pals of his own sex. It is only when the affection of the early stage is pre-emptive, blocking progress to the later stages, that we speak of pathological "fixation."

Figure 14-1. Not by Milk Alone

The infant monkey, reared with two artificial "mothers," one providing food, the other the comfort of something to cuddle up to, tries here to have the best of both worlds. When he is afraid, however, he runs to the cuddly mother.

From Harry Harlow, The nature of love. *Am. Psychologist,* 1958, **13,** 673-685. Photo by Sponholz, Madison, Wisc.

Moreover, it should be noted that this pattern of development is chiefly determined by social experiences, very little by the direct influence of sex hormones. (This is true even at puberty.) What we have sketched is the pattern developed by the culture of Western society. Almost every conceivable variation from this sequence is found in some culture or other (87).

In our society, however, this is the customary line of development; deviations from it are apt to be somewhat uncomfortable. The ten-year-old boy who still likes to play with girls is likely to be unmercifully ribbed by his more "manly" fellows. Nonetheless, deviations and variations from the customary pattern are very numerous and most of them are not inherently unwholesome. We should especially beware of characterizing them as perverse. We should, instead, think of these various stages in sexual-social development as the appropriate periods during which, as our society is organized, the child can learn various necessary attitudes and behaviors.

The Unisexual Stage

During the preschool period, children should begin to understand something of the family and its responsibilities—here, of course, doll play and "playing house" are invaluable, and if properly guided can be made even more useful. In the early elementary grades, the fact that boys and girls play together without much distinction of sex should be utilized to teach them to get along together as equals. In the home, at this time, they should be learning how mature men and women who love each other behave toward each other, what men concede to women and women to men, how they divide work and responsibilities. And at school, particularly through literature, these lessons are reinforced or corrected.

The Sex Antagonism Stage

During the prepubertal period (ages nine to eleven or twelve), there is apt to be a fairly complete segregation of boys and girls. At first it seems to be mainly just a drawing apart because of differing play interests and activities. Many authorities believe that this is a favorable time to help them gain "a respectable, courteous attitude toward children of the opposite sex, free from undue sex-consciousness, and a definite appreciation of the values of wholesome comradeship and friends, and practice in securing them" (474).

But there presently develops a rather active antagonism, a scorning of the opposite sex. Apparently this antagonism is really genuine at first; girls really don't like boys and boys don't like girls. But little by little the real dislike begins to yield to interest, covert at first and concealed beneath a merely surface antagonism which takes the form of teasing, of razzing, of sometimes rather mean practical jokes, and of definitely scornful remarks. At this stage, too, most of the boys find

Figure 14-2. Anonymous Reactions of 700 Boys, Age 9 to 18, to a Question Concerning Their Attitude toward Girls

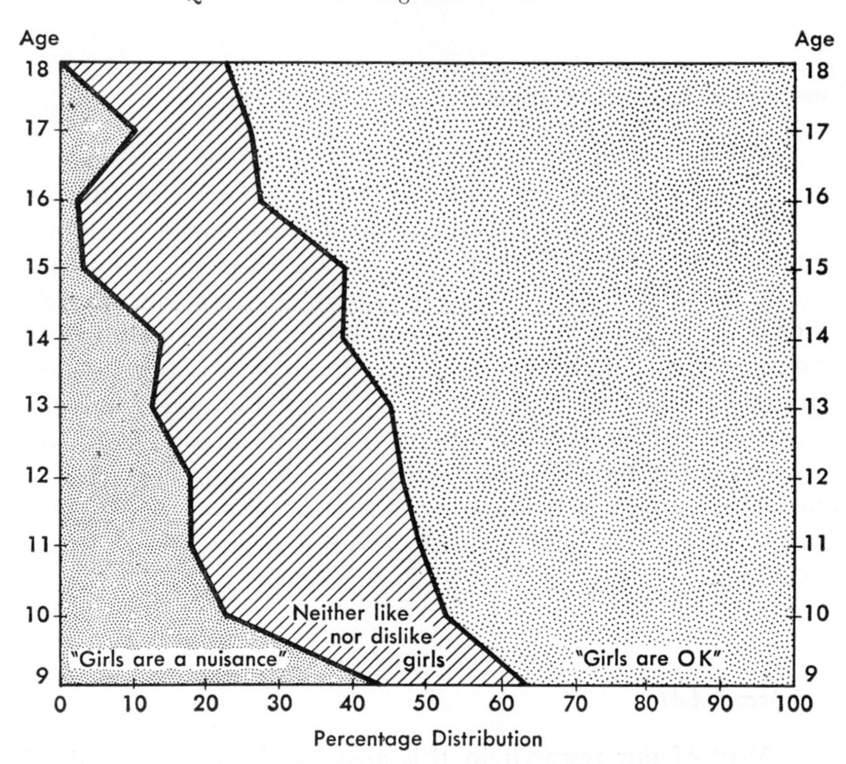

At age nine few boys will admit that they like girls—and most don't.

Based on unpublished data of R. T. Sollenberger. From F. K. Shuttleworth, The adolescent period. *Monogr. of Soc. Res. Child Develpm.*, 1938, **3**, no. 3. By permission of the Society.

it necessary to prove their manliness by intentionally rude behavior to women teachers or women generally. As this stage merges into the bisexual interests of adolescence, many a boy (it is usually a boy) finds himself so deeply committed to an antifeminine position that he just doesn't know how to extricate himself. He really desperately needs help in the form of a tactful push over the line into bisexual companionship.

QUESTIONS

1. Figure 14-2 is based on replies made a quarter of a century ago. What sort of replies would we get today? Would the "girls are OK" reply be given earlier?
2. What can we do to help a boy of ten who "likes girls"?

General and Specific Affection

An important aspect of the development of social behavior is what Miles (314) calls the "personalization of affection." Friendliness and hostility are at first chiefly products of the immediate situation: indeed, some authors would class the rudimentary friendly response as mere sympathy. Gradually, however, the child builds up more enduring sentiments toward the chief persons in his environment, as described in the preceding chapter. But before we turn to the consideration of close friendships, let us take a look at the less personalized affectional relations. It is an interesting fact that we do not have any term for the relationship of mild affection which stands between mere acquaintance and "true" friendship. Yet much of our need for giving and receiving affection is met in such friendly associations.

Social Acceptability

Most of our research in this area has been concerned with the personal qualities that make it possible for a child to find some degree of affectionate acceptance by his peers. Undoubtedly whether or not a child easily finds acceptance is partly a matter of the particular group structure to which he seeks to relate himself, partly even a matter of the nature of the activity. But there are some children who seem permanently isolated, while others make friends quickly with almost anyone. As might be expected, cheerfulness, enthusiasm, a jolly manner, good looks, ability in games, energy, help to make a child acceptable. Not quite so obvious is the finding that positive traits are more important than merely negative virtues. To be highly accepted a child must make an impact on others, even if the impact is sometimes a little unpleasant (65, 66). But he must be able and willing to fit into the ongoing situation and make himself visible therein (Lippitt [286], Hardy [189]). Interestingly enough, in view of popular opinion about the socializing value of large families, children from small familes are more frequently acceptable than those from large families.

Isolates and Fringers

It is now fashionable to be much concerned about the socially isolated child and those always on the fringe of group activity. No doubt the concern is fundamentally right, but let us not forget that a child can be too fully socialized, too dependent upon other children, not able to find satisfactions except in a whirl of peer activities. Moreover, among the less socially active we need to make distinctions (335).

There is, first of all, the *socially uninterested* child. He may be quiet and retiring and perhaps even truly shy in personal relations, but he is not a maladjusted child at all. He has interests, but they are objective rather than social interests: collecting, music, scientific experimentation, or crafts. In a popular article published under the title "Lo, the Poor Introvert," Dorothy Canfield Fisher (who is a distinguished educator as well as author) pleaded that we let this sort of child alone, not try to force him into the usual socially extravert mold. Undoubtedly she has a point. We should recognize the essential wholesomeness of this sort of adjustment and not try to make such a child over. On the other hand, by tactful management he can be induced to take a more active social role and profit from it. From the standpoint of practical success a child needs to learn how to get on with others, and even the socially uninterested child, as he goes through life, is going to find himself needing affection. The time to learn to give and receive is while still young.

The second type of unpopular child is much the most serious. He is withdrawn, ingrown, and lives too much within himself. This is the true *introvert.* (Despite Fisher's title, the child who is merely socially uninterested is not truly introverted.) Every effort should be made to draw such a child out of himself, and at the very earliest opportunity. If, as is only too likely to be the case, he does not respond to friendly treatment and social advances, professional treatment is indicated and should be instituted as early as possible.

The third type of unpopular child is the *socially ineffective.* In general, he is the opposite of the acceptable child; often his difficulties are merely those of poor social techniques which can be fairly readily overcome. More frequently, perhaps, he is a child whose insecurity causes him to overact: to be noisy, boisterous, boastful. This kind of child can usually be greatly helped to improve his social acceptability by an understanding adult.

QUESTION

What can we do to help a child who is actively disliked by his fellows?

Before age five the choice of a play companion remains fairly constant (185), but there is little true friendship. Very young children have not learned to be discriminating—almost any child will serve as playmate. Later, they recognize that one child is more pleasurable to associate with than another and more lasting companionships arise. In the elementary school, shifts in friendship are still frequent but decrease with age (211, 379).

Friendship

A very considerable amount of research has been devoted to the study of children's friendships. During the first three grades, the friend or chum is almost as likely as not to be a child of the other sex, but there follows a period of about five years during which friendships, and indeed most social relations, are restricted to one's own sex.

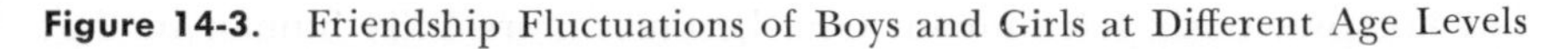

Figure 14-3. Friendship Fluctuations of Boys and Girls at Different Age Levels

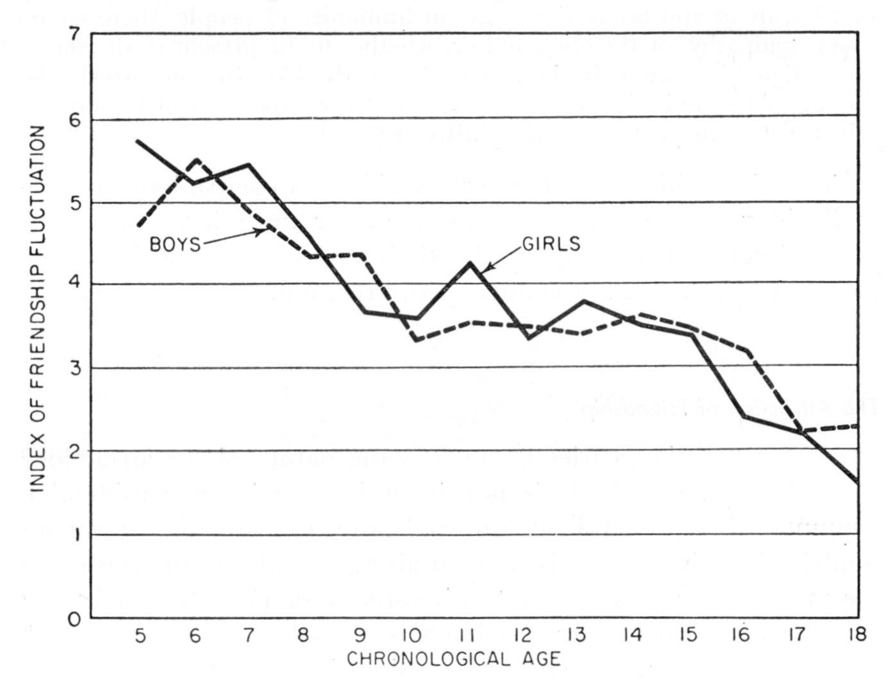

From J. E. Horrocks and M. E. Buker, A study of friendship fluctuations of preadolescents. *J. genet. Psychol.,* 1951, **78,** 131-144. Used by permission.

Around the age of eight-and-one-half, nine-and-one-half to twelve, in this culture, there comes what I once called the quiet miracle of preadolescence. . . . Now for the first time . . . there is a movement from what we might, after traditional usage, call egocentricity, toward a fully social state. . . . When the satisfaction or the security of another person becomes as significant to one as is one's own satisfaction or security, then the state of love exists.

This state of affectional rapport—generically love—ordinarily occurs under restricted circumstances. In the beginning many factors must be present. Some of these may be called obvious likeness, parallel impulse, parallel physical development. These make for situations in which boys feel at ease with boys rather than with girls. This feeling of species identity or identification influences the feeling involved in the preadolescent change. The appearance of the capacity to love ordinarily first involves a member of one's own sex. The boys find a chum who is a boy, the girls find a chum who is a girl. . . .

As soon as one finds that . . . [one's feelings,] one's thoughts, one's personality, is really open to some comparing of notes, to some checking and counter-checking, one begins to feel human in a sense in which one has not previously felt human. One becomes more fully human in that one begins to appreciate the common humanity of people—there comes a new sympathy for the other fellow, whether he be present to the senses or mediated by rumors in the geography, or the like. In other words, the feeling of humanity is one of the aspects of the expansion of personality which comes in preadolescence [Sullivan (430)].

From about thirteen or fourteen on, intersex companionship, generally in groups, reappears. Sometime after the middle of adolescence, intersex friendships make their appearance, usually to be followed by some sort of enduring love relation.

The Attraction of Friendship

What makes a friend? What is the nature of the attraction?

Whatever it is, it is not inconsistent with a considerable amount of hostility. Friends quarrel more, not less, than ordinary nonfriends—this seems to be true at all ages—and the quarrels often are marked by real anger and animosity (176, 177). No doubt the frequency of quarrels among friends is related to the fact that they are together more and have more occasions for disagreement. But for the distressed parent who sees the children engaged in seemingly endless bickering—in one study, once in every five minutes of being together (176, 177)—and for the lover who doubts his love when he finds himself angry with his beloved, the fact that the warmest attraction can be reconciled with antagonism is significant and comforting.

Propinquity

A child can hardly form a friendship with another child unless he has many opportunities to be with him. But propinquity—just plain nearness in space and time—exerts a stronger influence than would follow from this purely logical consideration (59, 159, 353). The available child is often given higher status as a chum than others with more desirable personal traits. Evidently we come to be attracted to that which is familiar.

Similarity

Popular opinion vacillates between the view that like attracts like, and that opposites attract. A good deal of evidence supports the former position (365). Certainly children, when asked why they choose their friends, usually speak of similarity of interests and of personality (21). Challman (96) for preschool children and Reader and English (361) for adolescents or young adults, found some reason to believe that this factor is emphasized too much. When actual measurements of likeness or unlikeness were made, friends were indeed slightly more similar than nonfriends, but hardly enough to account for the attraction the friends felt for each other. Similarity, they suggest, is but one manifestation of a wider principle.

We believe that the secret of friendship is to be found not in similarity of more or less fixed traits, but in the kinds of responses each person elicits from the other. Wertheimer and the Gestalt psychologists speak of the "we" character of a social relationship—the entity which is the interaction of two dynamic personalities as they meet and function together. Either person by himself is incapable of duplicating the "we" for it is a product of only these personalities in interaction under a given set of circumstances. Friendship is thus not a matter of duplication but is rather coattraction and especially of cooperation between two active-receptive dynamic persons. . . .

Friendship as Need-Fulfillment. The needs which characterize the personality of one are not necessarily similar to those that characterize the other. The primary requirement is that *the two individuals mutually satisfy one another's personality needs* [italics supplied] in a kind of psychological symbiosis. A given relationship may be yielding very different satisfactions to each of its two participants at the very same time. The authoritarian person and his timid, submissive friend are examples of the symbiotic functioning of two personalities, each of which has for the other stimulus and consummatory value attuned to it. One needs to dominate and the other desires to be dominated. But another person, no less dominant but with another pattern of personal qualities, may need someone to stand up to him. One person needs a "clinging vine"; another equally dominant, a "sparring partner." It follows that no general rule can be made by which we could identify *the* satisfying element characteristic of all friendships. At best, we can state that every relationship does satisfy certain needs in the participants. . . .

We often find that certain people "bring out the best" in us. They stimulate us in such a way as to elicit from us behavior which makes us feel pleased with ourselves. Conversely, we may truly admire someone with whom we come into contact, but feel rather inadequate, insecure, and humble in his presence. It would seem then that the more satisfying friendships are those in which each of the participants appreciates and admires his own role as well as that of his friend [361, pp. 217-219].

The reasons given by sixth-graders for choosing and changing friends bears out this view of complementary need satisfaction (21).

The Social Environment

We have been speaking, however, as if friendships existed in a social vacuum. Of course that is not so. Most close friendships in childhood begin within the larger circle of "friends" or of the gang, and all friendship relations are mightily affected by all one's social relationships—including even those with adults. It is probable, say Murphy, Murphy, and Newcomb, that "the history of one's friendships and one's areas of interest and happiness cannot be written at all without a knowledge of one's successive roles as companion, bully, scapegoat, pet, and idol in varying group structures" (327, p. 518). Perhaps, however, this is but another way of saying that in friendship one seeks fulfillment of one's needs. For, of course, the child's needs develop as he plays out his varying roles in social interactions.

The Distortions of Affection

Jealousy

For the parent one of the most perplexing and difficult aberrations of affection is jealousy. Jealousy is a direct limitation upon love. In the elementary school it is seldom manifested strongly save by those who have learned it at home. The Freudian notion that *all* children are jealous of the parent of the same sex is not confirmed by careful investigation; it is, however, somewhat more common than is generally realized. There can be little doubt, also, that most children have attacks of jealousy of brothers and sisters or that this jealousy often becomes a serious cause of maladjustment.

The basic cause of jealousy, of course, is the fear of loss of love

(457). Sibling jealousy is most likely to be found, therefore, in small families (369) and where the mother is oversolicitous (267, 386). Not unnaturally, the oldest child—the one who has been dethroned—is most likely to exhibit the trait. And it is most likely to be found where the age differences range from eighteen to forty-two months; children closer together are more apt to be companions, those further apart are less likely to be rivals (386). ?

Probably there has been too much concern over sibling jealousy. Certainly in its milder forms—in which it is better called sibling rivalry—it can be regarded as normal. Nonetheless it is unpleasant at best, and it interferes with the proper growth of affection. It cannot be combated by punishment: that only convinces the child all the more that he is not loved as he wants to be. The cure lies in attacking the root cause—the child's fear that he is not loved. He should be assured that *love is not less for being shared;* rather, that parents who love one another and who love their other children have on that account more love and understanding to give. But this assurance in words has to be backed up by concrete deeds, and that is difficult. Love may not be less for being shared, but time and attention are. Baldwin (27) and Lasko (260) found a 50 percent reduction in child-centeredness in the home following a new baby's birth. In the face of such a concrete fact of relative neglect, Mother's assurance that she loves her older boy just as much as she loves the new baby may not be believed. By displaying impartial affection for all her pupils, the teacher, whose task in this respect is simpler, can do much to teach children that love can be shared.

Hardness

In contrast is the tendency in our culture to teach children not to be too loving. Of course we disavow that intent. But, particularly here in America, we want our children to be self-reliant, we want them to learn how to "get on" in this world, and we believe that to get on one has to be a little hard. "Unselfishness" (which is a name for love in action) is encouraged within the family circle; yet even there, besting the other fellow receives plaudits and admiration. And the child who too generously shares his possessions with children outside the family circle quickly learns how strictly limited, in fact, is the unselfishness theoretically approved. Can we blame the child if implicitly he concludes that this business of loving your neighbor is not to be taken too seriously?

Disbelief in One's Affection

Two other denials of affection help to warp personality development. There is, first, the child who is somehow given to believe that he is cold and unaffectionate or, even worse, that he can neither give nor inspire affection. This happens very frequently, probably most often in homes where there are several children and where unintended but invidious comparisons are made. The warmth and demonstrativeness lavished on a sweet, cuddly little sister may convince the older child that he is not loved and that his loving behavior is not valued. If he turns to attention-getting, as many do, he is apt to be reproved in ways which still further deepen his unbelief in his own lovability. If he is a boy, he is particularly likely to turn his back on affection. (Alternative behaviors for girls—for example, play with dolls—are a little more apt to remain within the boundaries of affection.)

Repression

From almost the opposite kind of circumstances, we may get parallel results. The child who loves too openly quickly finds himself in difficulties—again the problem is more acute in our culture with boys. If he is too affectionate, he is called a sissy. If he tries to kiss all the little girls, as many a four-year-old does, people talk behind their hands about depravity and his mother has to intervene. Little by little the child's naïve warmth and outgivingness are repressed. Indeed, after a child has passed the "doll" stage, his direct manifestation of affection makes us a bit uncomfortable. Instead of encouraging him in overtly loving behavior we are apt to make the child feel that it is unnecessary, even a little queer—and in the case of a boy, a bit unmanly.

Elizabeth Hibbs

Figure 14-4. An Expression of Sibling Jealousy

The Relation of Affection to Sex

In part, the reason for the child's behavior is that he must often express his affection directly in physical terms—he hardly knows any other way. And here sex "raises its ugly head." In no area are our values and ideals more confused than in the realm of sex. We have commonly allowed the intricate problems involved to be postponed to the period of adolescence. This, of course, is a mistake. To be sure, sex motivations, though not nonexistent, are weak during childhood. But it is important that the child be prepared to meet sex problems before they descend upon him.

Most of us reject the Freudian notion that all physical affection is directly sexual; but we are uneasily aware that there is more relation than we like to admit. Thus, in most families, the cuddling phase in child rearing is followed by a period in which the child's affectionate behavior upon a direct physical plane is limited to a certain few prescribed forms; meanwhile he has not yet learned to express it on other planes. In our fear of sex, we have tended to repress any manifestation of love that seems to us in any degree "infected with sex"—which comes close to meaning all physical expressions and most verbal endearments related to them. There is "a taboo on tenderness" (432).

The result is the stifling, especially in boys, of the natural tendency to give as well as to receive affection. It isn't good form for a boy to be too fond of sisters, let alone of brothers, fathers, or persons outside the family. Only to Mother may love be frankly shown, and then only in certain conventional circumstances. Now, it is impossible thus to restrain all outward manifestations of feeling without in the end weakening it; moreover, it is not only physical demonstration of love which is restricted or repressed. Hence the growing child cannot fail to be influenced in his self-ideals by a social scene in which affection, save in such limited ways, is disparaged or scorned.

If it be thought that I exaggerate the cultural restriction upon affection, let the reader try out a simple experiment. Try describing some man as "a very loving, affectionate person in all his personal relations." Or think of the distorted picture called to mind when a man is described as "The Great Lover." What should be the description of one of mankind's finest ideals is debased by connotations of a cheap romanticism. As one of the characters in Mona Williams's novel *The Marriage* says, "Oh, love! The very word smells of buttered popcorn."

Sex Education versus Love Education

Clearly the teacher as well as the parent has a tremendous responsibility to prepare children for a normal sex adjustment. By this I do not mean primarily instruction in the anatomy and physiology of sex. Of course, that is necessary, and the question as to whether the instruction should come from an informed adult (whether parent or other teacher) or from a misinformed playmate surely answers itself. There are excellent books designed to help the adult in this task, which is neither so difficult nor so "delicate" as it is supposed to be.

Nor do I mean that there should be extensive discussion of the problems of sex ethics. This too easily degenerates into an attempt to frighten children away from something which they only vaguely understand. At its best, discussion of the ethics of chastity and of marital fidelity and all the complicated skein of problems which revolve about them is really over children's heads. What I do mean is that children should be encouraged in natural friendliness and love, that the necessary cautions be introduced quietly and as needed, without destroying or limiting the central value. Marital love can thus be envisaged as but the highest expression of a universal value. The best form of "sex education" is education in normal, healthy, warmly affectionate, and assured personal relations.

Summary

In the development of personality the values centering around success and personal achievement and those grouped about love and affection tend to be set in partial opposition. This is unnecessary and self-defeating. We can help children to harmonize these two sets of values.

In our culture the development of love and affection proceeds through fairly definite stages, during each of which the child is learning how to give and to receive affection. In each he must learn that the basis of love is to fulfill the other person's needs. Even the mild affectional relation called social acceptability depends less upon not annoying or offending people than upon making a contribution to the group. Deeper friendship even more is a secure relation in which we are free and take joy in meeting our friend's needs. Nor is the case different with adult heterosexual love.

The child's progress toward mature affection is beset with serious difficulties; the child thus needs help. At every stage of his development he needs experience in both giving and receiving love. If you wait to learn to love until you fall in love, you wait too long.

Bibliography and Author Index

Light-face numbers in parentheses following a citation refer to the pages of this book on which the reference appears.

1. Abramson, David A. The effectiveness of grouping for students of high ability. *Educ. Res. Bull.,* 1959, **38,** 169-182. (338)

2. Adler, Alfred. *The practice and theory of individual psychology* (trans. P. Radin). New York: Harcourt, 1924. (405)

3. Adler, Alfred. *Understanding human nature* (trans. W. B. Wolfe). New York: Greenberg, 1927. (244)

4. Adorno, T. W., Frenkel-Brunswik, E., Levinson, D. J., Sanford, R. N. *The authoritarian personality.* New York: Harper, 1950. (49)

Allen, L. See **208** and **292.**

5. Allport, G. W., and Odbert, H. S. Trait names: a psycho-lexical study. *Psychol. Monogr.,* 1936, **47,** no. 211. (2)

Almack, J. C. See **438.**

Ames, L. B. See **216.**

6. Ammons, C. H., and Ammons, R. B. Aggression in doll-play: interviews of two-to-six-year-old white males. *J. genet. Psychol.,* 1953, **82,** 205-213. (159)

7. Anastasi, Anne. *Differential psychology.* 3d ed. New York: Macmillan, 1958. (283, 296)

8. Anderson, Harold H. Domination and integration in the social behavior of young children in an experimental play situation. *Genet. Psychol. Monogr.,* 1937, **19,** 343-410. (368, 408)

9. Anderson, Harold H. Domination and social integration in the behavior of kindergarten children and teachers. *Genet. Psychol. Monogr.,* 1939, **21,** 287-385. (56, 352, 368)

10. Anderson, Harold H. An examination of the concepts of domination and integration in relation to dominance and ascendance. *Psychol. Rev.,* 1940, **47,** 21-37. (56)

11. Anderson, Harold H., and Brandt, H. F. Study of motivation involving self-announced goals of fifth grade children and the concept of level of aspiration. *J. soc. Psychol.,* 1939, **10,** 209-232. (219)

12. Anderson, John E. In a personal communication. (96)
13. Anderson, John E. Principles of growth and maturity in language. *Elem. Engl. Rev.,* 1941, **18,** 250-254. (317)
14. Anderson, John E. *The psychology of development and personal adjustment.* New York: Holt, Rinehart and Winston, 1949. (214)
15. Anderson, John E. Dynamics of development: system in process. In **193.** (313)
16. Anderson, John E., and others. *A survey of children's adjustment over time.* Inst. of Child Develpm. and Welf., Univ. of Minn., 1959, p. 18. (16, 119)
17. Anderson, John P. *Study of relationship between certain aspects of parental behavior and attitudes and behavior of junior high school pupils.* New York: Teach. Coll., Columbia Univ., 1940. (49)
18. Apgar, Virginia, Girdany, B. R., McIntosh, R., and Taylor, H. C. Neonatal anoxia: 1. A study of the relation of oxygenation at birth to intellectual development. *Pediatrics,* 1955, **15,** 653-662. (263)
19. Arsenian, Jean M. Young children in an insecure situation. *J. abn. soc. Psychol.,* 1943, **38,** 235-249. (133)
20. Asch, S. E. *Social psychology.* Englewood Cliffs, N. J.: Prentice-Hall, 1952. (146)
21. Austin, Mary C., and Thompson, G. G. Children's friendships: a study of the bases on which children select and reject their best friends. *J. educ. Psychol.,* 1948, **39,** 101-116. (419, 420)
22. Ausubel, David. *Theory and problems of child development.* New York: Greene & Stratton, 1958. (27, 41, 172, 251, 261)
23. Axelrod, Seymour. Effects of early blindness. *Am. Found. Blind, Res. Ser.,* no. 7. (244)
24. Ayer, Mary E., and Bernreuther, R. G. Study of relationship between discipline and personality traits in little children. *J. genet. Psychol.,* 1937, **50,** 165-170. (49)

Bacon, M. K. See **102.**
25. Bain, Winifred E. A study of the attitudes of teachers toward behavior problems. *Child Develpm.,* 1934, **5,** 19-35. (19)
Baker, C. T. See **408.**
26. Bakwin, H. The emotional status at birth. *Am. J. Dis. Children,* 1947, **74,** 373-376. (111)
27. Baldwin, Alfred L. Changes in parent behavior in pregnancy: an experiment in longitudinal analysis. *Child Develpm.,* 1947, **18,** 29-39. (421)
28. Baldwin, Alfred L. *Behavior development in childhood.* New York: Holt, Rinehart and Winston, 1955. (124, 410)
29. Baldwin, Alfred L., Kalhorn, J., and Breese, F. H. Patterns of parental behavior. *Psychol. Monogr.,* 1945, **58,** no. 3. (51, 307, 308)
30. Baldwin, J. M. Quoted in **389.** (27)
31. Bandura, A., and Walters, R. H. Relationship of child rearing antecedents to adolescent behavior disorders. Unpublished data quoted in **150.** (49)
Banker, M. H. See **321.**
32. Barbe, Walter B. Evaluation of special classes for gifted children. *Exceptional Child,* 1955, **22,** 60-62. (342)
33. Barker, L. S., Schoggen, M., Schoggen, P., and Barker, R. G. The fre-

quency of physical disability in children. *Child Develpm.,* 1952, **23,** 215-226. (261)

34. Barker, Roger G. The social psychology of physical disability. *J. soc. Issues,* 1948, **4,** 28-34. (281)

35. Barker, Roger G., Dembo, T., and Lewin, K. Frustration and regression: an experiment with young children. *Univ. of Ia. Stud. Child Welf.,* 1941, **18,** no. 1. (180)

36. Barker, Roger G., Kounin, J. S., and Wright, H. F. (eds.) *Child behavior and development.* New York: McGraw, 1943. (38)

37. Barker, Roger G., and Wright, B. A. The social psychology of adjustment to physical disability. In **163.** (262, 279, 281)

38. Barker, Roger G., Wright, B. A., and Gonick, M. Adjustment to physical handicap and illness. New York: *Soc. Sci. Res. Coun. Bull.,* 1946. (255, 261, 262, 278)

39. Barker, Roger G., and Wright, Herbert F. *Midwest and its children.* Evanston, Ill.: Row, 1954. (50)

40. Barr, A. S. Personnel-teacher. In Harriman, Philip L. (ed.), *Encyclopedia of psychology.* New York: Philosophical Library, 1946, 497-512. (15)

41. Bavelas, Alexander. Leaders can be trained. *Association Forum,* 1942, **23,** 12-16. (56)

42. Bavelas, Alexander, and Lewin, K. Training in democratic leadership. *J. abn. soc. Psychol.,* 1942, **37,** 115-119. (56)

43. Bayer, L. M., and Snyder, M. M. Illness experience of a group of normal children. *Child Develpm.,* 1950, **21,** 93-120. (267)

44. Bayley, N. The emotions of children: their development and modification. Childh. Educ., 1944, **21,** 156-160. (105, 108, 109)

45. Bayley, N. On the growth of intelligence. *Am. Psychologist,* 1955, **10,** 805-818. (286)

46. Bayley, N. Individual patterns of development. *Child Develpm.,* 1956, **27,** 45-74. (241)

47. Bayley, N., and Pinneau, S. P. Tables for predicting adult height from skeletal age. *J. Pediat.,* 1952, **40,** 423-444. (241)

Bayley, N. See **237.**

48. Beach, F. A., and Jaynes, J. Effects of early experience upon the behavior of animals. *Psychol. Bull.,* 1954, **51,** 239-263. (191)

49. Beeler, S. Angry girls—behavior control by girls in latency. *Smith Coll. Stud. Soc. Work,* 1953, **23,** 205-226. (113)

Beeman, Alan. See **250.**

50. Beller, E. K. Dependency and independence in young children. *J. genet. Psychol.,* 1955, **86,** 25-35. (23)

51. Belogianis, D., Kymer, K., Lukes, A. J., and Geisel, J. B. Positive techniques in the classroom. *Elem. Sch. J.,* 1944, **44,** 594-601. (215)

52. Benda, C. E., and Farrell, M. J. Psychopathology of mental deficiency in children. Chapter 5 in **205.** (264)

53. Bender, Irving E., and others. *Motivation and visual factors: individual studies of college students.* Hanover, N. H.: Dartmouth Coll. Publ., 1942. (247)

54. Bender, L. Mental hygiene and the child. *Am. J. Orthopsychiat.,* 1939, **9,** 574-582. (102)

55. Benedict, Agnes. Violence in the classroom. *Nation,* 1943, **156,** 51-53. (16)

56. Benedict, Ruth. *The chrysanthemum and the sword.* Boston: Houghton, 1946. (57)

57. Benne, Kenneth D. *A conception of authority: an introductory study.* New York: Teach. Coll., Columbia Univ., 1943. (27)

Berger, Harriet. See **116.**

58. Berne, E. V. C. An investigation of the wants of seven children. *Univ. of Ia. Stud. Child Welf.,* 1929, **4,** no. 2. (172)

Bernreuther, R. G. See **24.**

59. Blanchard, B. E. A social acceptance study of transported and non-transported pupils in a rural secondary school. *J. exp. Educ.,* 1947, **15,** 291-303. (418)

60. Blatz, W. E., Bott, E. A., and Millichamp, D. A. *The development of emotion in the infant.* Toronto: Univ. of Toronto Press, 1935, *Child Develpm. Ser.,* no. 4 (106, 107, 108, 109)

61. Blatz, W. E., Chant, S. N. F., and Slater, M. D. Emotional episodes in the child of school age. *Univ. of Toronto Stud. Child Develpm.,* 1937, no. 4. (146)

62. Block, Jeanne, and Martin, Barclay. Predicting the behavior of children under frustration. *J. abn. soc. Psychol.,* 1955, **51,** 281-285. (183)

63. Blommers, Paul, Knief, L., and Stroud, J. B. The organismic age concept. *J. educ. Psychol.,* 1955, **46,** 142-150. (251)

64. Blommers, Paul, and Stroud, J. B. Note on the organismic age concept. *J. educ. Psychol.,* 1958, **49,** 106-107. (251)

Bond, G. L. See **130.**

Bonham, M. A. See **160.**

65. Bonney, Merl E. Personality traits of socially successful and socially unsuccessful children. *J. educ. Psychol.,* 1943, **34,** 449-472. (415)

66. Bonney, Merl E., and Powell, Johnny. Differences in social behavior between sociometrically high and low children. *J. educ. Res.,* 1953, **46,** 481-495. (415)

Bott, E. A. See **60.**

67. Bousfield, W. A., and Orbison, W. D. Ontogenesis of emotional behavior. *Psychol. Rev.,* 1952, **59,** 1-7. (105)

68. Bowlby, John. *Maternal care and mental health.* Monogr. Series, no. 2. Geneva: World Health Organization, 1951. (27)

69. Boynton, Paul, Dugger, H., Lewis, P., and Turner, M. Emotional stability of teachers and pupils. *J. juv. Res.,* 1934, **18,** 223-232. (124)

70. Brackett, Catherine. Laughter and crying of pre-school children. *Child Develpm. Monogr.,* 1934, no. 14. (113)

71. Bradley, Charles. Organic factors in the psychopathology of childhood. Ch. 6 in **205.** (264)

72. Brambaugh, F. N. Laughter and teachers. *Educ. Meth.,* 1940, **20,** 69-70, 327. (113)

Brandt, H. F. See **11.**

73. Breckenridge, Marian E., and Vincent, E. Lee. *Child development.* Philadelphia: Saunders, 1943. (130, 149, 231, 365, 409 f.)

Breese, F. H. See **29.**

74. Bridges, Katherine M. B. A genetic theory of emotions. *J. genet. Psychol.,* 1930, **37,** 515-527. (27, 105, 110, 113)

75. Bridges, Katherine M. B. *Social and emotional development of the preschool child.* London: Kegan Paul, 1931. (110, 116)

76. Bridges, Katherine M. B. A study of social development in early infancy. *Child Develpm.*, 1933, **4**, 36-49. (106, 107, 108, 109, 113)
77. Brodbeck, A. J., Nogee, P., and DeMario, A. Two kinds of conformity: a study of the Riesman typology applied to standards of parental discipline. *J. Psychol.*, 1956, **41**, 23-45. (35)
78. Brownell, W., and Hendrickson, G. How children learn information, concepts, and generalizations. In *Learning and Instruction,* 49th Yearbook of N.S.S.E. Part I. Chicago: Univ. of Chicago Press, 1950. (209)
79. Bruce, William F., and Freeman, F. S. *Development and learning.* Boston: Houghton, 1942. (58)
80. Bruner, Jerome S. On coping and defending. Presidential address for Div. 8, Am. Psychol. Assn., Sept. 1959. (Unpubl.) (39, 209, 306)
81. Buehler, Charlotte. *The first year of life.* New York: Day, 1930. (107, 108, 151)

    Buker, M. E. See **211.**

    Burri, C. See **344.**
82. Burt, Cyril. The trend of Scottish intelligence—critical notice. *Brit. J. educ. Psychol.*, 1950, **20**, 55-61. (309)

83. Cabot, P. S. de Q. The relationship between characteristics of personality and physique in adolescents. *Genet. Psychol. Monogr.*, 1938, **20**, 3-120. (255)
84. Caille, Ruth K. Resistant behavior of preschool children. *Child Develpm. Monogr.*, 1933, no. 11. (28)
85. Caldwell, Otis W., and Wellman, B. Characteristics of school leaders. *J. educ. Res.*, 1926, **14**, 1-13. (255)
86. Cameron, Norman. Psychological trends and emotional theory. In Midwest conference on character development, *The child's emotions.* Chicago: Univ. of Chicago Press, 1930. (94)
87. Campbell, Elise H. The social-sex development of children. *Genet. Psychol. Monogr.*, 1939, **21**, 461-552. (412)

    Cantril, H. See **389.**
88. Carlson, Earl R. *Born that way.* New York: Day, 1941. (263)
89. Carmichael, Leonard. The onset and early development of behavior. In **90.** (107, 108)
90. Carmichael, Leonard (ed.) *Manual of child psychology.* (2d ed.) New York: Wiley, 1954.
91. Carter, V. E., and Chess, S. Factors influencing the adaptations of organically handicapped children. *Am. J. Orthopsychiat.*, 1951, **21**, 827-839. (261, 262)
92. Cassirer, Ernst. *An essay on man.* Garden City, N. Y.: Doubleday Anchor, 1953. (134)

    Castner, B. M. See **167.**
93. Cattell, Raymond B. Sentiment or attitude? the core of a terminological problem in personality research. *Character and Pers.*, 1940, **9**, 6-17. (386)
94. Cattell, Raymond B. *General psychology.* Cambridge, Mass.: Sci-Art, 1947. (386)
95. Cattell, Raymond B. *Personality, a systematic and factual study.* New York: McGraw, 1950. (377)
96. Challman, R. C. Factors influencing friendships among preschool children. *Child Develpm.*, 1932, **3**, 146-158. (410, 419)

97. Champney, Horace. Parent behavior as related to child development. Unpub. paper read before Am. Assn. for Adv. of Sci., December, 1939. (49, 51, 307)

98. Champney, Horace. The variables of parent behavior. *J. abn. soc. Psychol.*, 1941, **36,** 525-542. (51)

Chant, S. N. F. See **61.**

99. Chapman, Dwight W., and Volkmann, J. A social determinant of the level of aspiration. *J. abn. soc. Psychol.*, 1939, **34,** 225-238. (219)

100. *Character education inquiry.* 3 vols. New York: Macmillan. Vol. I. Hartshorne, H., and May, M. A. *Studies in deceit,* 1928. Vol. II, Hartshorne, H., and May, M. A. *Studies in service and self-control,* 1929. Vol. III, Hartshorne, H., May, M. A., and Shuttleworth, F. K. *Studies in the organization of character,* 1930. (192, 226, 227)

101. Charters, W. W. *Motion pictures and youth: a summary.* New York: Macmillan, 1933. (128)

Chess, S. See **91.**

102. Child, I. L., and Bacon, M. K. Cultural pressures and achievement motivation. Ch. 10 in **205.** (405)

103. Child, I. L., Potter, E. H., and Levine, E. M. Children's textbooks and personality development—an exploration in the social psychology of education. *Psychol. Monogr.*, 1946, **60,** no. 3. (59)

104. Child, I. L., and Whiting, J. W. M. Determinants of level of aspiration: evidence from everyday life. *J. abn. soc. Psychol.*, 1949, **44,** 303-315. (218)

105. Chittenden, Gertrude E. An experimental study in measuring and modifying assertive behavior in young children. *Monogr. Soc. Res. Child Develpm.*, 1942, **7.** (361, 362)

106. Clark, B. Binocular anomalies and reading ability. *Amer. J. Ophthal.*, 1940, **23,** 885-892. (273)

107. Clarke, A. D. B. and Clarke, Ann M. Some recent advances in the study of early deprivation. *J. Child Psychol. and Psychiat.*, 1960 **1,** 26-36. (298, 299)

108. Cohen, John and Hansel, C. E. M. The idea of independence. *Brit. J. Psychol.*, 1955, **46,** 178-190. (327)

Cook, Walter W. See **130.**

109. Coons, M. O. Rosenzweig differences in reaction to frustration in children of high, low, and middle sociometric status. *Group Psychother.*, 1957, **10,** 60-63. (193)

110. Corbin, Charles E. The attitude of high school pupils toward various methods of discipline. *Purdue Univ. Stud. higher Educ.*, 1936, **37,** 214-224. (15)

111. Courtney, Paul D. Identification and learning: a theoretical analysis. Unpubl. dissertation, Harvard Univ., 1949. (27)

112. Cruickshank, W. M. The relation of physical disability to fear and guilt feelings. *Child Develpm.*, 1951, **22,** 291-298. (261)

113. Davis, Allison. *Social class influences upon learning.* Cambridge, Mass.: Harvard Univ. Press, 1948. (232)

114. Davis, Allison, and Havighurst, Robert. *Father of the man: how your child gets his personality.* Boston: Houghton, 1947. (157)

Davis, D. Russell. See **247.**

115. Davis, Harvey H. Corporal punishment and suspension. *Sch. and Soc.,* 1928, **28,** 632. (16)
116. Dawe, Helen C., Ekern, D., and Berger, H. Differences in adult contacts with children. *J. Home Econ.,* 1949, **41,** 85-87. (361)
117. Dearborn, W. F., and Rothney, J. Predicting the child's development. Cambridge, Mass.: Sci-Art, 1941. (294)
DeMario, A. See **77.**
118. Dembo, T. Der Aerger als dynamisches Problem. *Psychol. Forsch.,* 1931, **15,** 1-144. (188)
Dembo, T. See **35** and **277.**
119. Dermigny, Louis. *U.S.A.-essai de mythologie americaine.* Paris: Presses Universitaires de France, 1956. (42)
120. Deutsche, Jean M. *The development of children's concepts of causal relations.* Minneapolis: Univ. of Minn. Press, 1937. (327)
121. Dewey, John. Education and social direction. *The Dial,* 1918, **64,** 333-335. (62)
122. Ding, G. F., and Jersild, A. T. A study of laughing and smiling of school children. *J. genet. Psychol.,* 1932, **40,** 452-472. (113)
123. Dockeray, F. C. *Studies in infant behavior.* Columbus: Ohio State Univ. Press, 1934, 88-92. (107, 109)
124. Dolger, L., and Ginandes, J. Children's attitudes toward discipline as related to socio-economic status. *J. exp. Educ.,* 1946, **15,** 161-165. (15)
125. Dollard, J., Doob, L. W., Miller, N. E., Mowrer, O. H., and Sears, R. R. *Frustration and aggression.* New Haven, Conn.: Yale Univ. Press, 1939. (186)
Dugger, Harriet. See **69.**
126. Dunbar, F. Effect of the mother's attitude on the infant. *Psychosom. Med.,* 1944, **6,** 150-159. (124)
127. Dymond, R., Hughes, A., and Roabe, V. Measurable changes in empathy with age. *J. consult. Psychol.,* 1952, **16,** 202-206. (147)

Eagleson, B. M. See **244.**
128. Eckert, Eileen J. The elimination of the pre-school child's fear. Unpubl. thesis, Ohio State Univ., 1945. (136)
129. Edelston, H. Separation anxiety in young children: a study of hospital cases. *Genet. Psychol. Monogr.,* 1943, **28,** 3-95. (131)
130. Edson, W. H., Bond, G. L., Cook, Walter W. Relationship between visual characteristics and specific silent reading abilities. *J. educ. Res.,* 1953, **46,** 451-457. (273)
Ekern, Dorothy. See **116.**
131. England, A. O. Non-structural approach to a study of children's fears. *J. clin. Psychol.,* 1946, **2,** 364-368. (131)
English, Ava C. See **139.**
132. English, Horace B. Three cases of the "conditioned fear response." *J. abn. soc. Psychol.,* 1929, **24,** 221-225. (116, 124)
133. English, Horace B. The ghostly tradition and the categories of psychology. *Psychol. Rev.,* 1933, **40,** 498-513. (260)
134. English, Horace B. Symbolic vs. functional equivalents in the neurosis of deprivation. *J. abn. soc. Psychol.,* 1937, **32,** 392-394. (196)
135. English, Horace B. Authority not authoritativeness. *Prog. Educ.,* Oct. 1946, pp. 22-23, 41-42. (22)

136. English, Horace B. Review of J. Nesbitt, *The road to Avalon,* and of Betsy Barton, *And now to live again. J. appl. Psychol.,* 1946, **30,** 571. (281)
137. English, Horace B. What is emotion? *Ohio J. Sci.,* 1946, **47,** 62-66. (94)
138. English, Horace B. Learning as psychotechnology. Columbus: mimeographed, 1949. (217)
139. English, Horace B., and English, Ava C. *A comprehensive dictionary of psychological and psychoanalytical terms.* New York: Longmans, 1958. (22)
English, Horace B. See **361.**
140. English, O. S., and Finch, S. *Emotional problems of growing up.* Chicago: Science Research Associates, 1951, p. 6. (161)
141. Escalona, S. K. Feeding disturbances in very young children. *Am. J. Orthopsychiat.,* 1945, **15,** 76-80. (124)
142. Estes, William K. An experimental study of punishment. *Psychol. Monogr.,* 1944, **57,** no. 263. (71, 219)
Estess, F. See **363.**

143. Fairchild, Hoxie N. The scholar-teacher. *Am. Scholar,* 1946, **15,** 209. (42)
144. Fajans, S. Erfolg, Ausdauer und Activität beim Säugling und Kleinkind. *Psychol. Forsch.,* 1933, **17,** 268-305. (188)
Farrell, M. J. See **52.**
145. Fenichel, O. *The psychoanalytic theory of neuroses.* New York: Norton, 1945. (125)
146. Ferguson, Mrs. Walter. Our over-privileged children. Columbus (O.) *Citizen,* Dec. 30, 1950. (14)
Festinger, L. See **200** and **277.**
147. Fields, Sidney L. Discrimination of facial expression and its relation to personal adjustment. *Am. Psychologist,* 1950, **5,** 309. (151)
Finch, S. See **140.**
Fite, M. D. See **228.**
148. Flesher, William R. The beginning teacher. *Educ. Res. Bull.,* 1945, **24,** 14 ff. (15)
149. Frank, L. K. *Feelings and emotions.* New York: Random House, 1954. (164)
150. Frankiel, Rita V. *A review of research on parent influences on child personality.* New York: Family Serv. Assn. of Am., 1959. (49)
151. Fredericson, E. Competition: the effects of infantile experience upon adult behavior. *J. abn. soc. Psychol.,* 1951, **46,** 406-409. (222)
Freeman, F. S. See **79.**
152. French, V. V. A restatement of the theory of sentiments. *J. Personality,* 1946, **15,** 247-282. (386)
Frenkel-Brunswik, Else. See 4.
153. Freud, S. *The problem of anxiety* (trans. H. A. Bunder). New York: Norton, 1936. (102, 125)
154. Freud, S. *General introduction to psychoanalysis* (trans. J. Riviere). Garden City, N. Y.: Garden City Publ., 1943, pp. 323-324. (125)
155. Freud, S. *Collected papers, 1906-1924.* London: Hogarth Press and Institute of Psychoanalysis, 1949. (125)
156. Fries, Margaret E., and Woolf, Paul J. Some hypotheses on the role of the congenital activity type in personality development. *Psychoanal. Study Child,* 1953, **8,** 48-62. (110)
157. Fry, P. C. A comparative study of "obese" children selected on the basis of fat pads. *J. clin. Nutrition,* 1953, **1,** 453-468. (255)

158. Fulcher, J. S. Voluntary facial expression in blind and seeing children. *Arch. Psychol.* (N. Y.), 1942, no. 272. (147)
159. Furfey, Paul H. Some factors influencing the selection of boys' chums. *J. appl. Psychol.,* 1927, **11,** 47-51. (254, 418)
160. Furfcy, Paul H., Bonham, M. A., and Sargent, M. K. The mental organization of the newborn. *Child Develpm.,* 1930, **1,** 48-51. (103)

161. Gallagher, James J. *The gifted child in the elementary school.* Washington, D. C.: Dept. of Classroom Teachers, Am. Educ. Res. Assn. of N.E.A., 1959. (344)
162. Gardner, L. Pearl. A survey of the attitudes and activities of fathers. *J. genet. Psychol.,* 1943, **63,** 15-54. (58)
163. Garrett, J. F. (ed.) *Psychological aspects of physical disability.* Fed. Security Agency Rehab. Service Series, no. 120. Washington, D. C.: Government Printing Office, 1952. (262)
164. Gates, Georgina S. An experimental study of the growth of social perception. *J. educ. Psychol.,* 1923, **14,** 449-461. (151)
165. Gayle, Margaret. Dramatic lessons for youngsters. *Parents' Magazines,* Jan. 1948 (condensed in *Reader's Digest,* 1948, **52,** 49-51). (139)
Geisel, J. B. See **51.**
166. Gesell, Arnold, and Ilg, Frances L. *Infant and child in the culture of today.* New York: Harper, 1942. (215)
167. Gesell, Arnold, Castner, B. M., and Thompson, Helen. *Biographies of Child Development.* New York: Hoeber, 1939. (106, 107, 108)
168. Gesell, Arnold, and Thompson, Helen. *The psychology of early growth.* New York: Macmillan, 1938. (117)
Ginandes, J. See **124.**
Girdany, B. R. See **18.**
Gjerde, Clayton M. See **376.**
Goldman, B. See **229.**
169. Goldsmith, L. C. The children's war. *Nation,* Aug. 6, 1949, **169,** 130. (192)
170. Goldstein, Kurt. *The organism.* New York: American Book, 1935. (199)
Gonick, M. See **38.**
171. Goodenough, Florence L. Anger in young children. *Univ. of Minn. Inst. Child Welf. Monogr.,* 1931, no. 9. (113, 115, 117, 120, 146, 148, 157, 158)
172. Goodenough, Florence L. The expression of the emotions in infancy. *Child Develpm.,* 1931, **2,** 96-101. (106, 107, 148)
173. Goodenough, Florence L. The expression of the emotions in a blind-deaf child. *J. abn. soc. Psychol.,* 1932, **27,** 328-333. (111, 112, 147)
174. Gorer, G. *The American people.* New York: Norton, 1948. (58)
175. Graham, B. F. Neuroendocrine components in the physiologic response to stress. *Ann. N. Y. Acad. Sci.,* 1953, **56,** 184-199. (110)
176. Green, E. H. Friendships and quarrels among preschool children. *Child Develpm.,* 1933, **4,** 237-252. (418)
177. Green, E. H. Group play and quarreling among preschool children. *Child Develpm.,* 1933, **4,** 302-307. (418)
178. Greenacre, P. Quoted by F. A. Montague, Constitutional and prenatal factors in infant and child health. In **385.** (110)
179. Greenberg, P. J. Competition in children. *Am. J. Psychol.,* 1932, **44,** 221-248. (219)

180. Greisbach and Kunz. Quoted by Wilson, J. F. Adjustments to blindness. *Brit. J. Psychol.,* 1948, **38,** 219. (244)
181. Grosslight, J. H. Goal setting and probability expectations as a function of the order and relative amounts of success and failure. Unpubl. disser., Yale Univ., 1947. Cited in **104.** (219)
182. Gruen, E. W. Level of aspiration in relation to personality factors in adolescence. *Child Develpm.,* 1945, **16,** 181-188. (219)
183. Guilford, Joy P. An experiment in learning to read facial expression. *J. abn. Psychol.,* 1929, **24,** 191-202. (152)
Gump, Paul V. See **254.**

184. Haggerty, M. E. The incidence of undesirable behavior in public school children. *J. educ. Res.,* 1925, **12,** 102-122. (19, 311)
185. Hagman, E. P. The companionships of preschool children. *Univ. of Ia. Stud. Child Welf.,* 1933, **7,** no. 4. (416)
186. Hagman, R. R. A study of the fears of children of preschool age. *J. exp. Educ.,* 1932, **1,** 110-130. (128, 131)
187. Halliday, N. Quoted by F. A. Montague, Constitutional and prenatal factors in infant and child health. In **385.** (110)
188. Hanley, C. Physique and reputation of junior high school boys. *Child Develpm.,* 1951, **22,** 247-260. (256)
Hansel, C. E. M. See **108.**
189. Hardy, Martha C. Social recognition at the elementary school age. *J. soc. Psychol.,* 1937, **8,** 365-384. (415)
190. Hardy, Martha C. Some evidence of an inverse relation between health history and behavior adjustments during childhood. *J. abn. soc. Psychol.,* 1937, **31,** 406-417. (268)
191. Harlow, Harry. The nature of love. *Am. Psychologist,* 1958, **13,** 673-685. (25, 172, 410, 411)
192. Harris, Dale B. The climate of achievement. *Child Study,* 1958, **35,** 8-14. (62)
193. Harris, Dale B. (ed.) *The concept of development—an issue in the study of human behavior.* Minneapolis: U. of Minn. Press, 1957.
194. Harris, J. A., Jackson, C. M., Paterson, D. G., and Scammon, R. D. *The measurement of man.* Minneapolis: Univ. of Minn. Press, 1930. (250)
Hartshorne, H. See **100.**
Havighurst, Robert. See **114.**
195. Heathers, Glen. Emotional dependence and independence in a physical threat situation. *Child Develpm.,* 1953, **24,** 169-179. (136)
196. Heathers, Glen. Acquiring dependence and independence: a theoretical orientation. *J. genet. Psychol.,* 1955, **87,** 37-57. (23)
197. Hebb, D. O. Emotion in man and animal. *Psychol. Rev.,* 1946, **53,** 88-106. (104)
198. Hebb, D. O. *The organization of behavior.* New York: Wiley, 1949. (298)
199. Hendrick, I. Instinct and the ego during infancy. *Psychoanal. Quart.,* 1942, **11,** 33-58. (103)
Hendrickson, G. See **78.**
200. Hertzman, M., and Festinger, L. Shifts in explicit goals in a level of aspiration experiment. *J. exp. Psychol.,* 1940, **27,** 439-452. (219)
201. Highfield, M. E., and Pinsent, M. B. E. *A survey of rewards and punishments in schools.* London: Newnes Educ. Publ. Co., 1952. (19)

202. Hilgard, Ernest R., and Russell, D. H. Motivation in school learning. In *Learning and instruction,* 49th Yearbook of N.S.S.E., Part I. Chicago: Univ. of Chicago Press, 1950. (204)
203. Hilgard, Ernest R., Sait, E. N., and Magaret, G. A. Level of aspiration as affected by relative standing in an experimental social group. *J. exp. Psychol.,* 1940, **27,** 411-421. (219)
204. Hoashi, Kiyoko. Need as a function of frustration. *Psychologia* (Tokyo), 1959, **2,** 183-185. (188)
205. Hoch, P. H., and Zubin, J. (eds.) *Psychopathology of childhood.* New York: Gruen and Stratton, 1955.
206. Hofstaetter, P. R. The changing composition of "intelligence"—a study in T-technique. *J. genet. Psychol.,* 1954, **85,** 159-164. (286)
207. Holmes, F. B. An experimental investigation of a method of overcoming children's fears. *Child Develpm.,* 1936, **7,** 6-30. (137)
Holmes, F. B. See **230.**
208. Honzik, M. P., Macfarlane, J. W., and Allen, L. The stability of mental test performance. *J. exp. Educ.,* 1949, **17,** 309-324. (293, 294)
Honzik, M. P. See **292.**
209. Horney, Karen. *New ways in psychoanalysis.* New York: Norton, 1939. (125)
210. Horowitz, Eugene L. Spatial localization of the self. *J. soc. Psychol.,* 1935, **6,** 379-387. (401)
Horowitz, Ruth. See **33.**
211. Horrocks, J. E., and Buker, M. E. A study of friendship fluctuations of preadolescents. *J. genet. Psychol.,* 1951, **78,** 131-144. (416, 417)
212. Horrocks, J. E. *The psychology of adolescence.* Boston: Houghton, 1951. (218)
213. Hubbard, F. W. Teacher opinion on pupil behavior, 1955-56. *N.E.A. Res. Bull.,* 1956, **34,** 52-107. (16)
Hughes, A. See **127.**
Hughes, B. D. See **339.**
Hunt, William. See **25.**
214. Hunter, E. C., Changes in teachers' attitudes toward children's behavior over the last thirty years. *Mental Hygiene,* 1957, **41,** 3-11. (19)
215. Hutt, Max L., and Miller, D. R. Social values and personality development. *J. soc. Issues,* 1949, **5,** no. 4. (27)

216. Ilg, F. L., Learned, J., Lockwood, A., and Ames, L. B. The three-and-a-half-year-old. *J. genet. Psychol.,* 1949, **75,** 21-31. (131)
Ilg, F. L. See **166.**
217. Irwin, O. C. Infant response to vertical movements. *Child Develpm.* 1932, **3,** 167-169. (103, 104)
218. Isaacs, S. *The nursery years.* New York: Vanguard, 1936. (103, 105)

219. Jack, Lois M. Experimental study of ascendant behavior in pre-school children. *Univ. of Ia. Stud. Child. Welf.,* 1934, **9,** no. 3, 7-65. (361, 365)
Jackson, C. M. See **194.**
220. Jackson, K., and others. Emotional trauma in hospital treatment of children. *J. Am. med. Assn.,* 1952, **149,** 1536-1538. (124)
221. James, H. W. Causes of teacher-failure in Alabama. *Peabody J. Educ.,* 1930, **7,** 269-271. (15)

222. James, William. Principles of psychology. 2 vols. New York: Holt, Rinehart and Winston, 1890. (102, 359, 398)
Jaynes, J. See **48.**
223. Jenkins, R. L. The constructive use of punishment. *Ment. Hyg.,* 1945, **29,** 561-574. (81)
224. Jennings, Helen. Structure of leadership—development and sphere of influence. *Sociometry,* 1937, **1,** 99-143. (364)
225. Jenss, Rachel M., and Souther, S. P. *Methods of assessing the physical fitness of children.* Washington, D. C.: Government Printing Office, 1940. (251)
226. Jersild, A. T. *Child psychology.* 3d ed. Englewood Cliffs, N. J.: Prentice-Hall, 1947. (221)
227. Jersild, A .T. Self-understanding in childhood and adolescence. Presidential address, Div. on Childhood and Adolescence, Am. Psychol. Assn., Sept. 1950. (339, 351)
228. Jersild, A. T., and Fite, M. D. The influence of nursery school experience on children's social adjustment. *Child Develpm. Monogr.,* 1939, no. 25. (362)
229. Jersild, A. T., Goldman, B., and Loftus, J. J. A comparative study of the worries of children in two school situations. *J. exper. Educ.,* 1941, **9,** 323-326. (133)
230. Jersild, A. T., and Holmes, F. B. Children's fears. *Child Develpm. Monogr.,* 1935, no. 20. (131, 132)
231. Jersild, A. T., and Markey, F. V. Conflicts between pre-school children. *Child Develpm. Monogr.,* 1935, no. 21. (113, 120, 146)
232. Jersild, A. T., Markey, F. V., and Jersild, C. L. Children's fears, dreams, wishes, daydreams, likes, dislikes, pleasant and unpleasant memories. *Child Develpm. Monogr.,* 1933, no. 12. (113)
Jersild, A. T. See **122.**
Jersild, C. L. See **232.**
233. Johnson, Marguerite W. The influence of verbal directions upon behavior. *Child Develpm.,* 1935, **6,** 196-204. (214)
234. Johnson, Robert. How parents' attitudes affect children's illness. *Bull. Inst. Child Stud.,* Toronto, 1955, **17** (3), 5-8. (267)
235. Jones, Harold E. Environmental influences on mental development. In **90.** (296)
236. Jones, Harold E., and Jones, M. C. Fear. *Childh. Educ.,* 1928, **5,** 136-143. (116)
237. Jones, M. C., and Bayley, Nancy. Physical maturing among boys as related to behavior. *J. educ. Psychol.,* 1950, **41,** 129-148. (254, 255, 261)
238. Jones, Mary C. A laboratory study of fear: the case of Peter. *Ped. Sem.,* 1924, **31,** 308-316. (122)
Jost, H. See **392.**
239. Jucknat, M. Leistung, Anspruchsniveau und Selbstbewusstsein. *Psychol. Forsch.,* 1937, **22,** 89-179. (218)

Kalhorn, J. See **29.**
240. Kanner, Leo. *Child psychiatry.* New York: Wiley, 1954, p. 599. (100)
241. Kantor, J. R. *A survey of the science of psychology.* Bloomington, Ind.: Principia, 1933. (95)

242. Keister, Mary E. The behavior of young children in failure. In **36.** (218)
Keister, Mary E. See **452.**
243. Kelley, Ida B., and Perkins, K. J. An investigation of teachers' knowledge of and attitudes toward child and adolescent behavior in everyday school situations. Purdue Univ., *Stud. higher Educ.*, 1941, no. 42. (19, 311)
244. Kellogg, Winthrop N., and Eagleson, B. M. The growth of social perception in different racial groups. *J. educ. Psychol.,* 1931, **22,** 367-375. (151)
245. Kemper, H. D. Cheating among high school pupils. Unpublished thesis, Univ. of Ia. Quoted by Tuttle, H. D. *Dynamic psychology and conflict.* New York: Harper, 1949. (226)
246. Kenderdine, M. Laughter in the preschool child. *Child Develpm.,* 1931, **2,** 228-230. (113)
247. Kent, Norma, and Davis, D. Russell. Discipline in the home and intellectual development. *Brit. J. med. Psychol.,* 1957, **30,** 27-33. (49)
248. Keys, Noel. *The underage student in high school and college.* Berkeley: Univ. of Calif. Press, 1938. (341, 342)
249. Kierkegaard, Sören. *Sickness unto death.* Garden City, N. Y.: Doubleday Anchor, 1954. (53)
Kirschbaum, R. M. See **358.**
250. Klausmeier, H. J., Beeman, Alan, and Lehman, I. J. Comparison of organismic age and regression equations in predicting achievements in elementary school. *J. educ. Psychol.,* 1958, **49,** 182-186. (251)
Klebanoff, S. G. See **368.**
251. Klein, R. Die Autorität als eine Form der socialen Beeinflusung. *Zeitsch. der Kinderforsch.,* 1932, **39,** 348-399. (215)
252. Klineberg, Otto. *Social psychology.* New York: Holt, Rinehart and Winston, 1940. (212)
Knief, L. See **63.**
253. Komazaki, Tsutomu. Reward-punishment and learning in extroversion and introversion. *Jap. J. educ. Psychol.,* 1956, **4,** 41-45. (223)
254. Kounin, Jacob S., and Gump, Paul V. The influence of punitive teachers upon children's attitudes toward misbehavior. *Am. Psychologist,* 1959, **14,** 378. (53)
Kounin, Jacob S. See **36.**
255. Krogman, Wilton M. The concept of maturity from a morphological viewpoint. *Child Develpm.,* 1950, **21,** 25-32. (156)
Kunz. See **180.**
256. Kwint, L. Ontogeny of the motility of the face. *Child Develpm.,* 1934, **4,** 1-12. (148)
Kymer, K. See **51.**

257. Landis, Carney. The interpretation of facial expressions of emotions. *J. gen. Psychol.,* 1929, **2,** 59-72. (148, 151)
258. Landis, Carney, and Hunt, William. *The startle pattern.* New York: Holt, Rinehart and Winston, 1939. (106, 107)
259. Langdon, G., and Stout, I. W. *The discipline of well adjusted children.* New York: Day, 1952. (19)
260. Lasko, Joan Kalhorn. Parent behavior toward first and second children. *Genet. Psychol. Monogr.,* 1954, **49,** 97-137. (421)
261. Lawton, G. Fears: their cause and prevention. *Child Develpm.,* 1938, **9,** 151-159. (131)

262. Lazarsfeld, M., and Zeisl, N. Die Arbeitslosen von Marienthal. *Psychol. Monographen,* 1933, **5.** (394)
Learned, J. See **216.**

263. Lehman, Harvey C., and Witty, P. A. *The psychology of play activities.* New York: Barnes, 1927. (379)
Lehman, I. J. See **250.**

264. Leuba, C. J. Tickling and laughter: two genetic studies. *J. genet. Psychol.,* 1941, **58,** 201-209. (113)

265. Leuba, C. J. An experimental study of rivalry in young children. *J. comp. Psychol.,* 1933, **16,** 367-378. (220)
Levin, Harry. See **381.**
Levine, E. M. See **103.**
Levinson, D. J. See **4.**

266. Levitt, Eugene E. Effect of a "causal" teacher-training program on authoritarianism and responsibility in grade-school children. *Psychol. Reports,* Dec. 1955. (56)
Levitt, Eugene E. See **289.**

267. Levy, David M. Hostility patterns in sibling rivalry experiments. *Am. J. Orthopsychiat.,* 1936, **6,** 183-257. (113, 421)

268. Levy, David M. Primary affect hunger. *Am. J. Psychiat.,* 1937, **94,** 643-652. (201)

269. Levy, David M. On instinct-satiation: an experiment on the pecking behavior of chickens. *J. gen. Psychol.,* 1938, **18,** 327-328. (201)

270. Levy, David M. *Maternal overprotection.* New York: Columbia Univ. Press, 1943. (201)

271. Levy, David M. Oppositional syndromes and oppositional behavior. In **205.** (28, 30)

272. Levy, John and Munroe, Ruth. *The happy family.* New York: Knopf, 1941. (27)

273. Lewin, Kurt. *A dynamic theory of personality* (trans. D. K. Adams and K. E. Zener). New York: McGraw, 1935. (76)

274. Lewin, Kurt. Field theory of learning. In *The psychology of learning,* 41st Yearbook of N.S.S.E. Chicago: Univ. of Chicago Press, 1942. (221)

275. Lewin, Kurt. Cultural reconstruction. *J. abn. soc. Psychol.,* 1943, **38,** 166-173. (59)

276. Lewin, Kurt. Constructs in psychology and psychological ecology. *Univ. of Ia. Stud. Child Welf.,* 1944, **20,** 1-29. (187)
Lewin, Kurt. See **35** and **42.**

277. Lewin, Kurt, Dembo, T., Festinger, L., and Sears, P. S. Level of aspiration. In Hunt, J. McV. (ed.), *Personality and the behavior disorders.* New York: Ronald, 1944, pp. 333-378. (219)

278. Lewin, Kurt, Lippitt, R., and White, R. K. Patterns of aggressive behavior in experimentally created "social climates." *J. soc. Psychol.,* 1939, **10,** 271-299. (46, 47, 67)

279. Lewis, Drayton. Teachers' judgments as to intelligence. *J. genet. Psychol.,* 1947, **70,** 29-51. (6)
Lewis, Paul. See **69.**

280. Lewis, W. D. Influence of parental attitude on children's personal inventory scores. *J. genet. Psychol.,* 1945, **67,** 195-201. (49)

281. Liberman, S. *A child's guide to a parent's mind.* New York: Abelard, 1951. (170)

282. Lieb, A. Vorstellungen und Urteile von Schűlern űber Fűhrer in der Schulklasse. *Zsch. f. angew. Psychol.,* 1928, **20,** 341-346. (255)

283. Lindbergh, Anne Morrow. Airliner to Europe. *Harper's Magazine,* 1948, **197,** 44. (246)

284. Lippitt, Ronald. An experimental study of authoritarian and democratic group atmospheres. *Studies of topological and vector psychology, No. 1. Univ. of Ia. Stud. Child Welf.,* 1940, **16,** no. 3. (56)

285. Lippitt, Ronald. From domination to leadership. *J. natl. Assn. Deans Women,* 1943, **6,** 147-152. (60)

Lippitt, Ronald. See **278.**

286. Lippitt, Rosemary. Popularity among preschool children. *Child Develpm.,* 1941, **12,** 305-332. (415)

287. Littledale, Clara S. A long time growing up. *Parents' Magazine,* Feb. 1943, p. 15. (239)

288. Lockhart, E. G. The attitudes of children toward law. *Univ. of Ia. Stud. Charact.,* 1930, **3,** no. 1. (226)

Lockwood, A., See **216.**

Loftus, J. J. See **229.**

Long, L. See **469.**

Lonihan, E. A. See **358.**

Lukes, A. J. See **51.**

289. Lyle, W. H., and Levitt, Eugene E. Punitiveness, authoritarianism, and parental discipline of grade school children. *J. abn. soc. Psychol.,* 1955, **51,** 42-46. (50)

290. Lynd, R. S., and Lynd, H. M. *Middletown: A study in contemporary American culture.* New York: Harcourt, 1929. (218)

291. Maccoby, Eleanor E. Why do children watch television? *Publ. Opin. Quart.,* 1954, **18,** 239-344. (187)

Maccoby, Eleanor E. See **381.**

292. Macfarlane, J. W., Allen, L., and Honzik, M. P. *A developmental study of the behavior problems of normal children between 21 months and 14 years.* Berkeley: Univ. of Calif. Press, 1954. (100)

Macfarlane, J. W. See **208.**

293. Macmurray, John. *Reason and emotion.* London: Faber, 1935. (102, 166)

294. Macmurray, John. Developing emotions. *Sat. Rev.,* 1958, **41,** 22. (102, 166)

Magaret, G. A. See **203.**

295. Maller, J. B. *Cooperation and competition: an experimental study of motivation.* New York: Teach. Coll., Columbia Univ., 1929. (220)

Markey, F. V. See **231** and **232.**

296. Maslow, A. H. Deprivation, threat, and frustration. *Psychol. Rev.,* 1941, **48,** 364. (196)

297. Maslow, A. H. Some theoretical consequences of basic need-gratification. *J. Personality,* 1948, **16,** 402-416. (201, 393)

298. Maslow, A. H. Our maligned animal nature. *J. Psychol.,* 1949, **28,** 273-278. (199)

May, M. A. See **100.**

McCandless, Boyd. See **341.**

299. McCarthy, Dorothea. Infant speech as a possible predictor of later intelligence. *J. Psychol.,* 1954, **38,** 203-209. (287)

300. McCarthy, Dorothea. Language development in children. Ch. 9 in **90.** (318)

301. McClelland, D. C. *The achievement motive.* New York: Appleton-Century-Crofts, 1953. (220, 405)

302. McClure, S. C. The effect of varying verbal construction on motor responses of pre-school children. *Child Developm.,* 1936, **7,** 276-290. (215)

303. McDougall, William. *An introduction to social psychology.* 20th ed. London: Methuen, 1926. (228)

304. McGregor, Douglas. Conditions of effective leadership in the industrial organization. *J. consult. Psychol.,*1944, **8,** 55-63. (60)

McIntosh, R. See **18.**

305. McKinney, Fred. Personality adjustment of college students as related to factors in personal history. *J. appl. Psychol.,* 1939, **23,** 660-668. (49)

306. McNeil, E. B. Psychology and aggression. *J. Conflict Resolution,* 1959, **3,** 195-293. (363)

Martin, Barclay. See **62.**

307. Maudry, M., and Nekula, M. Social relations between children of the same age during the first two years of life. *J. genet. Psychol.,* 1939, **54,** 193-213. (220)

308. Mead, Margaret, *Sex and temperament in three primitive societies.* New York: Morrow, 1935. (121, 133)

309. Menninger, K. Psychiatric aspects of physical disability. In **163.** (261)

310. Meyer, C. T. The assertive behavior of children as related to parent behavior. *J. Home Econ.,* 1947, **39,** 77-80. (361)

311. Meyer, H. D. A perceptual-motivational theory of the occurrence and intensity of emotion. *J. genet. Psychol.,* 1950, **43,** 105-124. (101)

312. Meyers, C. E. The effect of conflicting authority on the child. *Univ. of Ia. Stud. Child Welf.,* 1944, **20,** 31-98. (215)

313. Miles, Catherine C. Gifted children. In **90.** (340)

314. Miles, Catherine C. Sex in social psychology. In Murchison, C. (ed.), *Handbook of social psychology.* Worcester, Mass.: Clark Univ. Press, 1935. (414)

Miller, D. R. See **215.**

Miller, N. E. See **125.**

Millichamp, D. A. See **60.**

315. Mirsky, J. The Dakota. In Mead, Margaret (ed.), *Cooperation and competition among primitive peoples.* New York: McGraw, 1937. (177)

316. Misbach, Lorenz. Psychoanalysis and theories of learning. *Psychol. Rev.,* 1948, **55,** 143-156. (125)

317. Mohr, G. J. Psychosomatic problems in childhood. *Child Develpm.,* 1930, **24,** 597-611. (261)

318. Moncur, J. P. Symptoms of maladjustment differentiating young stutterers from non-stutterers. *Child Develpm.,* 1955, **26,** 91-96. (100)

319. Montagu, F. A. Constitutional and prenatal factors in infant and child health. In **385,** quoting **178** and **187.**

Morgan, Christina D. See **332.**

320. Morgan, J. J. B. *Child psychology.* 3d ed. New York: Holt, Rinehart and Winston, 1942. (211, 324, 325, 349)

321. Morgan, J. J. B., and Banker, M. H. The relation of mental stamina to parental protection. *J. genet. Psychol.,* 1938, **52,** 347-460. (49)

322. Morrison, Robert H. Factors causing failure in teaching. *J. educ. Res.,* 1927, **16,** 98-105. (15)

323. Morton, G. F. *Childhood's fears.* New York: Macmillan, 1925. (28)

Mowrer, O. H. See **125.**

324. Munroe, Ruth. Unpublished material quoted by Gardner Murphy in **325,** p. 225. (126)
Munroe, Ruth. See **272.**
325. Murphy, Gardner. *Personality, a biosocial approach to origins and structure.* New York: Harper, 1947. (27, 175, 185, 229, 380, 398)
326. Murphy, Gardner. *The minds of men.* New York: Basic Books, 1953. (138)
327. Murphy Gardner, Murphy, L. B., and Newcomb, T. *Experimental social psychology.* 2d ed. New York: Harper, 1937. (225, 226, 351, 369, 420)
328. Murphy, Lois B. Emotional development and guidance in nursery school and home. *Childh. Educ.,* 1936, **12,** 306-311. (161)
329. Murphy, Lois B. *Social behavior and child personality.* New York: Columbia Univ. Press, 1937. (113, 361, 368, 369 ff.)
330. Murphy, Lois B. In **326.**
331. Murphy, Lois B., and Horowitz, Ruth. Projective methods in the psychological study of children. *J. exp. Educ.,* 1938-1939, **7,** 133-140. (150)
332. Murray, Henry A., and Morgan, Christina D. A clinical study of sentiments. *Genet. Psychol. Monogr.,* 1945, **32,** 1-311. (386)

333. National Opinion Research Center. *The public looks at education.* Annual report. Denver: 1944. (15)
Nekula, M. See **307.**
Nelson, A. K. See **356.**
Nelson, V. L. See **408.**
Newcomb, Theodore. See **327.**
334. Newsweek, July 22, 1940. (241)
Nogee, P. See **77.**
335. Northway, M. L. Outsiders. *Sociometry,* 1944, **7,** 10-25. (415)

336. Obrien, F. P. The conditional value of a longer school year in one-teacher schools. *Nature and nurture:* Part II, *Their influence upon achievement.* 27th Yearbook of the N.S.S.E. Bloomington, Ill.: Public School Pub. Co., 1928. (269)
Odbert, H. S. See **5.**
Oden, M. H. See **439.**
Offerman, E. M. See **405.**
337. Olson, Willard, C. The organism as a whole: interrelationships in physical, mental, and emotional development. Ch. 10 in *Pupil development and curriculum* by staff members of School of Educ., Univ. of Mich. Ann Arbor: Bur. of Education, Reference and Research, 1937. (250)
338. Olson, Willard C., The parents request an extra promotion. *Childh. Educ.,* 1941, **18,** 24-28. (338)
339. Olson, Willard C., and Hughes, B. D. Growth of the child as a whole. In **36.** (250)
Orbison, W. D. See **67.**
340. Orlansky, H. Infant care and personality. *Psychol. Bull.,* 1949, **46,** 1-48. (105, 124)
341. Otis, Nancy Barker, and McCandless, Boyd. Responses to repeated frustration of young children differentiated according to need area. *J. abn. soc. Psychol.,* 1955, **50,** 349-353. (187)
342. Overstreet, H. *The mature mind.* New York: Norton, 1949. (26)

343. Page, Marjorie L. The modification of ascendant behavior in pre-school children. *Univ. of Ia. Stud. Child Welf.*, 1936, **12**, no. 3. (361)
344. Park, G. E., and Burri, C. The effect of eye abnormalities on reading difficulty. *J. educ. Psychol.*, 1943, **34**, 420-430. (273)
345. Parten, M. L. Social participation among pre-school children. *J. abn. soc. Psychol.*, 1932, **27**, 243-269. (352 ff., 356)
346. Pastore, N. A neglected factor in the frustration-aggression hypothesis. *J. Psychol.*, 1950, **29**, 271-280. (187)
Paterson, D. G. See **194.**
347. Pearson, G. Some early factors in the formation of personality. *Am. J. Orthopsychiat.*, 1931, **1**, 284-291. (124)
348. Pelone, Anthony J. *Helping the visually handicapped child in a regular class.* New York: Teach Coll., Columbia Univ., 1957. (279)
Perkins, K. J. See **243.**
349. Phillips, Margaret. *The education of the emotions through sentiment development.* London: Allen and Unwin, 1937. (377)
350. Piaget, Jean. *The language and thought of the child.* New York: Harcourt, 1926. (324)
Pinneau, S. P. See **47.**
Pinsent, M. B. E. See **201.**
351. Podolsky, Edward. Physical ailments and the frightened child. *Ment. Hyg.* (N. Y.), 1955, **39**, 489-497. (267)
352. Porter, Robert M. Student attitudes toward child behavior problems. *J. ed. Res.*, 1959, **52**, 349-352. (19)
353. Potashin, R. A sociometric study of children's friendships. *Sociometry*, 1946, **9**, 48-70. (418)
Potter, E. H. See **103.**
Powell, Johnny. See **66.**
Poyntz, L. See **395.**
354. Pratt, K. C. A study of the "fears" of rural children. *J. genet. Psychol.*, 1945, **67**, 179-194. (128, 131)
355. Pratt, K. C. The neonate. Ch. 4 in **90.** (104, 105)
356. Pratt, K. C., Nelson, A. K., and Sun, K. H. *The behavior of the newborn infant.* Columbus: Ohio State Univ., 1930. (104, 107, 109)
357. Pressey, Sidney L. *Educational acceleration—appraisals and basic problems.* Columbus: Ohio State Univ., 1949. (340, 342 ff.)
358. Prugh, D. G., Staub, E. M., Sands, H. H., Kirschbaum, R. M., and Lonihan, E. A. A study of the emotional reactions of children and families to hospitalization and illness. *Am. J. Orthopsychiat.*, 1953, **23**, 70-106. (131)

359. Radke, M. *The relations of parental authority to children's behavior and attitudes.* Minneapolis: Univ. of Minn. Press, 1946. (17, 19)
360. Rank, O. *Modern education: a critique of its fundamental ideas.* New York: Knopf, 1932. (102)
Rayner, R. See **466.**
361. Reader, Natalie, and English, H. B. Personality factors in adolescent female friendships. *J. consult. Psychol.*, 1947, **11**, 212-220. (419, 420)
362. Redl, Fritz. Group psychological elements in discipline problems. *Am. J. Orthopsychiat.*, 1943, **12**, 77-81. (65)
Redl, Fritz. See **393.**

363. Renaud, H., and Estess, F. Childhood traumata in normals. *Am. Psychologist,* 1955, **10,** 371. (126)
364. Reynolds, M. M. Negativism of preschool children. *Teach. Coll. Contr. Educ.,* 1928, no. 288. (28)
365. Richardson, H. M. Studies of mental resemblance between husbands, wives, and friends. *Psychol. Bull.,* 1939, **36,** 104-120. (419)
366. Ritholz, Sophie. *Children's behavior.* New York: Bookman Associates, 1959. (19)
Roabe, V. See **127.**
367. Robinson, F. P. *Effective study.* New York: Harper, 1946. (10)
368. Rodnick, E. H., and Klebanoff, S. G. Projective reactions to induced frustration as a measure of social adjustment. *Psychol. Bull.,* 1942, **39,** 489. (188)
Rosen, Victor. See **370.**
369. Ross, B. M. Some traits associated with sibling jealousy in problem children. *Smith Coll. Stud. soc. Work,* 1930, **1,** 364-376. (421)
Rothney, J. See **117.**
Russell, David H. See **202.**
370. Russell, Harold, and Rosen, Victor. *Victory in my hands.* New York: Creative Age, 1949. (280)
371. Rust, M. M. The effect of resistance on intelligence test scores of young children. *Child Develpm. Monogr.,* 1931, no. 6. (28)

Sait, E. M. See **203.**
Sands, H. H. See **358.**
372. Sanford, R. N., and others. Physique, personality and scholarship. *Monogr. Soc. Res. Child Develpm.,* 1943, no. 1, (254)
Sanford, R. N. See **4.**
Sargent, M. K. See **160.**
373. Sargent, S. S. Reaction to frustration: a critique and hypothesis. *Psychol. Rev.,* 1948, **55,** 108-114. (187)
Sargent, S. S. See **431.**
Scammon, R. D. See **194.**
374. Schaeffer, Robert. Come to have our fears loved away. *Fellowship,* 1952, **18,** 8. (133)
375. Schaffner, Bertram. *Father land—a study of authoritarianism in the German family.* New York: Columbia Univ. Press, 1948. (57)
Schoggen, M. See **33.**
Schonfeld, M. See **405.**
376. Schrupp, Manfred H., and Gjerde, Clayton M. Teacher growth in attitudes toward behavior problems of children. *J. educ. Psychol.,* 1953, **44,** 203-214. (19)
377. Schutz, William C. *Firo: a three-dimensional theory of interpersonal behavior.* New York: Holt, Rinehart and Winston, 1958. (349)
378. Scott, John P. *Aggression.* Chicago: Univ. of Chicago Press, 1958. (186, 225)
379. Seagoe, M. V. Factors influencing the selection of associates. *J. educ. Res.,* 1933, **27,** 32-40. (416)
380. Sears, Pauline S. Levels of aspiration in academically successful and unsuccessful children. *J. abn. soc. Psychol.,* 1940, **35,** 498-536. (218, 219)
Sears, Pauline S. See **277.**
381. Sears, R. R., Maccoby, E. E., and Levin, Harry. *Patterns of child rearing.* Evanston, Ill.: Row, 1957. (75)

382. Sears, R. R. Non-aggressive reactions to frustration. *Psychol. Rev.,* 1941, **48,** 343-346. (188)

383. Sears, R. R. Success and failure: a study in motility. In McNemar, Q., and Merrill, M. A. (eds.), *Studies in personality.* New York: McGraw, 1942, pp. 235-258. (188)

384. Sears, R. R. *Survey of objective studies of psychoanalytic concepts.* New York: Social Science Research Council, 1943.
Sears, R. R. See **125.**

385. Senn, M. J. E. *Symposium on the healthy personality.* New York: Josiah Macy, Jr., Foundation, 1950. (110)

386. Sewall, Mabel. Some causes of jealousy in young children. *Smith Coll. Stud. Soc. Work,* 1930, **1,** no. 1. (113, 421)

387. Shand, Alexander F. *The foundations of character.* London: Macmillan, 1941. (383)

388. Sheldon, William H., Stevens, S. S., and Tucker, W. B. *Varieties of human physique: an introduction to constitutional psychology.* New York: Harper, 1940. (254)

389. Sherif, M., and Cantril, H. *The psychology of ego-involvements, social attitudes, and identifications.* New York: Wiley, 1947. (Quoting Baldwin, **30.**) (27)

390. Sherman, Mandel, and Sherman, I. C. *The process of human behavior.* New York: Norton, 1929. (104)

391. Sherman, Mandel. The differentiation of emotional responses in infants: I. Judgments of emotional responses from motion picture views and from actual observation. II. The ability of observers to judge the emotional characteristics of the crying of infants, and of the voice of an adult. *J. comp. Psychol.,* 1927, **7,** 265-284, 335-351. (104, 116, 148)

392. Sherman, Mandel, and Jost, H. Frustration reactions of normal and neurotic persons. *J. Psychol.,* 1942, **13,** 3-19. (188)

393. Sheviakov, G. V., and Redl, F., Rev. by S. K. Richardson. *Discipline for today's children and youth.* Wash., D. C.: Assn. for Supervision and Curriculum Development, 1956. (66)

394. Shirley, Mary M. *The first two years, a study of twenty-five babies.* Minneapolis: Univ. of Minn. Press. Vol. I, 1931; Vol. II, 1933; Vol. III, 1933. (107, 109, 116, 117)

395. Shirley, Mary M., and Poyntz, L. Children's emotional responses to health examinations. *Child Develpm.,* 1945, **16,** 89-95. (116)

396. Shoben, E. J., Jr. The assessment of parental attitudes in relation to child adjustment. *Genet. Psychol. Monogr.,* 1949, **39,** 101-148. (124)

397. Shock, Nathan W. Physiological factors in mental development. *Rev. educ. Res.,* 1947, **17,** 362-370. (266)

398. Shuttleworth, F. K. The adolescent period. *Monogr. Soc. Res. Child Develpm.,* 1938, no. 3. (413)
Shuttleworth, F. K. See **100.**

399. Siegel, Saul M. The relationship of hostility to authoritarianism. *J. abn. soc. Psychol.,* 1956, **52,** 368-372. (49)
Skeels, H. M. See **400.**

400. Skodak, Marie, and Skeels, H. M. A final follow-up study of one hundred adopted children. *J. genet. Psychol.,* 1949, **75,** 85-125. (308)
Slater, M. D. See **61.**
Smith, J. W. See **414.**

401. Smith, Mary K. Measurement of the size of general English vocabulary through the elementary grades and high school. *Genet. Psychol. Monogr.,* 1941, **24,** 311-345. (317)
Smith, M. W. See **431.**
402. Smith, Theodate L. Obstinacy and obedience. *Ped. Sem.,* 1905, **12,** 27-54. (65)
403. Smoke, K. L. An objective study of concept formation. *Psychol. Monogr.,* 1932, **42,** no. 4. (325)
404. Snyder, Lawrence H. The Rh factor in feeble-mindedness and other diseases. *Minn. Med.,* 1946, **29,** 121-129. (263)
405. Snyder, Lawrence H., Schonfeld, M., and Offerman, E. M. Rh factor and feeble-mindedness. *J. Hered.,* 1945, **36,** 9. (263)
Snyder, M. M. See **43.**
406. Sollenberger, R. T. Quoted in **398.**
407. Sontag, L. W. Differences in modifiability of fetal behavior and physiology. *Psychosom. Med.,* 1944, **6,** 151-154. (110, 117)
408. Sontag, L. W., Baker, C. T., and Nelson, V. L. Mental growth and personality: a longitudinal study. *Monogr. Soc. Res. Child Develpm.,* 1958, **23,** no. 2. (294)
Souther, Susan P. See **225.**
409. Spitz, René A. Hospitalism: an inquiry into the genesis of psychiatric conditions in early childhood. *Psychoanal. Study Child,* 1945, **1,** 53-74. (27)
410. Spitz, René A. Anaclitic depression. *Psychoanal. Study Child,* 1946, **2,** 313-342. (27)
411. Spitz, René A. The role of ecological factors in emotional development in infancy. *Child Develpm.,* 1949, **20,** 145-155. (27)
412. Spitz, René A. Psychoanalytische Begriffsbildung u. physiologisches Denkmodell. *Schweiz. Zeitsch. psychol. Anwendung,* 1953, **12,** 24-39. (27)
413. Spitz, René A., and Wolf, K. M. The smiling response: a contribution to the ontogenesis of social relations. *Genet. Psychol. Monogr.,* 1946, **34,** 57-125. (110, 118, 410)
414. Staples, R., and Smith, J. W. Attitudes of grandmothers and mothers toward child rearing practices. *Child Develpm.,* 1954, **25,** 91-97. (19)
Staub, E. M. See **358.**
415. Staver, Nancy. The child's learning difficulty as related to the emotional problem of the mother. *Am. J. Orthopsychiat.,* 1953, **23,** 131-141. (307)
416. Stendler, Celia B. How well do elementary school teachers understand child behavior? *J. educ. Psychol.,* 1949, **40,** 489-498. (17)
417. Stendler, Celia B. Sixty years of child training practices. *J. Pediat.,* 1950, **36,** 122-134. (17)
418. Stendler, Celia B. Possible causes of overdependency in young children. *Child Develpm.,* 1954, **25,** 127-146. (23, 41)
419. Stern, William Louis. *Psychology of early childhood.* New York: Holt, Rinehart and Winston, 1930. (106)
Stevens, S. S. See **388.**
420. Stogdill, Ralph M. Experiments in the measurement of attitude toward children: 1899-1935. *Child Develpm.,* 1936, **7,** 31-36. (311)
421. Stogdill, Ralph M. The measurement of attitudes toward parental control and the social adjustment of children. *J. appl. Psychol.,* 1936, **20,** 259-267. (19)

422. Stogdill, Ralph M. Personal factors associated with leadership: a survey of the literature. *J. Psychol.*, 1948, **25**, 35-71. (255)

423. Stoke, Stuart M. An inquiry into the concept of identification. *J. genet. Psychol.*, 1950, **76**, 163-190. (27, 402)

424. Stott, D. H. Infantile illness and subsequent mental and emotional development. *J. genet. Psychol.*, 1959, **94**, 233-251. (268)

425. Stott, L. H. Research in family life in Nebraska. *J. Home Econ.*, 1945, **37**, 80-83. (15)

426. Stouffer, G. A. W. Behavior problems of children as viewed by teachers and mental hygienists. *Ment. Hyg.*, 1952, **36**, 271-283. (19)

Stout, I. W. See **259.**

427. Stratton, George M. Emotion and the incidence of disease: the influence of the number of diseases and of the age at which they occur. *Psychol. Rev.*, 1929, **36**, 242-253. (268)

428. Strecker, Edward S. *Their mothers' sons.* Philadelphia: Lippincott, 1946. (41)

429. Stroud, J. B. *Psychology in education.* New York: Longmans, 1946. (217)

Stroud, J. B. See **63** and **64.**

430. Sullivan, Harry S. The human organism and its necessary environment. *Psychiatry,* 1940, **3**, 20. (418)

431. Sullivan, Harry S., Sargent, S. S., and Smith, M. W. (eds.) *Culture and personality.* New York: Viking, 1949. (197)

Sun, K. H. See **356.**

432. Suttie, I. D. *The origins of love and hate.* London: Kegan Paul, 1935. (424)

433. Symonds, P. M. *The psychology of parent-child relationships.* New York: Appleton-Century-Crofts, 1939. (27)

434. Taft, Jessie. *The dynamics of therapy in a controlled relationship.* New York: Macmillan, 1933. (27)

435. Taylor, C., and Thompson, G. G. Age trends in preferences for certain facial proportions. *Child Develpm.*, 1955, **26**, 97-102. (151)

Taylor, H. C. See **18.**

436. Taylor, J. H. Innate emotional responses in infants. *Ohio State Univ. Contr. in Psychol.*, 1934, no. 12, 69-81. (103, 104)

437. Terman, Lewis M. A preliminary study of the psychology and pedagogy of leadership. *Ped. Sem.*, 1904, **11**, 413-451. (255)

438. Terman, Lewis M., and Almack, J. C. *The hygiene of the school child.* Boston: Houghton, 1929. (260)

439. Terman, Lewis M., and Oden, Melita H. *The gifted child grows up* and *The gifted group at mid-life: thirty-five years' follow-up of the superior child* (Vols. IV and V of *The genetic study of genius*). Stanford, Calif.: Stanford Univ. Press, 1946, 1959. (339, 343)

440. Thompson, G. G. Social and emotional development of preschool children under two types of educational programs. *Psychol. Monogr.*, 1944, **56**, 29. (361)

Thompson, G. G. See **21** and **435.**

441. Thompson, Helen. Physical Growth. Ch. 5 in **90.** (247)

Thompson, Helen. See **167** and **168.**

442. Thompson, Jane. The development of expressions of emotion in blind and seeing children. *Arch. Psychol.* (N. Y.), 1941, no. 264, 1-47. (147)

443. Thompson, W. R. Ch. 8 in **205.** (117)

444. Thomson, Godfrey H., and others. *The trend of Scottish intelligence.* London: Univ. of London Press, 1949. (309)
445. Thorndike, E. L. *Human learning.* New York: Appleton-Century-Crofts, 1931. (123)
446. Thorndike, E. L. The organization of a person. *J. abn. soc. Psychol.,* 1950, **45,** 137-145. (378)
Tucker, W. B. See **388.**
447. Tuckman, Jacob. The influence of varying amounts of punishment on mental connections. *Teach. Coll. Contr. Educ.,* 1933, no. 590. (71)
448. Tuddenham, R. D. Studies in reputation. *Psychol. Monogr.,* 1952, **64,** no. 333. (410)
Turner, Masal. See **69.**
449. Turner, William D. Altruism and its measurement in children. *J. abn. soc. Psychol.,* 1948, **43,** 502-516. (373)
450. Tyler, Fred T. Organismic growth: P-technique in the analysis of longitudinal growth data. *Child Develpm.,* 1954, **25,** 83-90. (251)
451. Tyler, Leona E. *The psychology of human differences.* 2d ed. New York: Appleton-Century-Crofts, 1956. (283, 296)

452. Updegraff, Ruth, and Keister, Marjorie. A study of children's reactions to failure and an experimental attempt to modify them. *Univ. of Ia. Stud. Child Welf.,* 1937, no. 13. (188, 201)

453. Valentine, C. W. The innate basis of fear. *J. genet. Psychol.,* 1930, **39,** 394-420. (116)
454. Valentine, C. W. *The difficult child and the problem of discipline.* 4th ed. London: Methuen, 1947, ch. 5. (15, 19)
455. Van Alstyne, D. The environment of three-year-old children. *Teach. Coll. Contr. Educ.,* 1929, no. 366. (305)
456. Vance, Eleanor Merrick. Parental attitudes toward school and home discipline. Unpubl. thesis, Ohio State Univ., 1948. (58)
Vincent, E. L. See **73.**
Volkmann, J. See **99.**
457. Vollmer, H. Jealousy in children. *Am. J. Orthopsychiat.,* 1946, **15,** 660-671. (421)

458. Wallis, R. S. Overt fears of Dakota Indian children. *Child Develpm.,* 1954, **25,** 185-192. (118)
459. Walsh, Ann Marie. *Self concept of bright boys with learning difficulties.* New York: Teach. Coll., Columbia Univ., 1956. (307)
Walters, R. H. See **31.**
460. Walton, W. E. Empathic responses in children. *Psychol. Monogr.,* 1936, **48,** no. 1, 40-67. (151)
461. Washburn, Ruth W. A study of the smiling and laughing of infants in the first year of life. *Genet. Psychol. Monogr.,* 1929, **6,** 398-537. (113, 118)
462. Watson, Goodwin. Comparison of the effects of lax versus strict home training. *J. soc. Psychol.,* 1934, **5,** 102-105. (49)
463. Watson, Goodwin. Some personality differences in children related to strict or permissive parental discipline. *J. Psychol.,* 1957, **44,** 227-249. (47)
464. Watson, Goodwin. The "spoiled" child. *McCall's,* 1958, **85,** 33, 170-172. (47)

465. Watson, John B. *The psychological care of infant and child.* New York: Norton, 1928. (122)
466. Watson, John B., and Rayner, R. Conditioned emotional reactions. *J. exp. Psychol.,* 1920, **3,** 1-14. (121)
467. Welch, Livingston. The span of generalization below the two-year age level. *J. genet. Psychol.,* 1939, **55,** 269-297. (322)
468. Welch, Livingston. The genetic development of the associational structures of abstract thinking. *J. genet. Psychol.,* 1940, **56,** 175-206. (322)
469. Welch, Livingston, and Long, L. The higher structural phases of concept formation of children. *J. Psychol.,* 1940, **9,** 59-95. (322)
470. Welch, Livingston, and Long, L. A further investigation of the higher structural phases of concept formation. *J. Psychol.,* 1940, **10,** 211-220. (322)
471. Wellman, Beth. The school child's choice of companions. *J. educ. Res.,* 1926, **14,** 126-132. (254)
Wellman, Beth. See **85.**
472. Wenar, Charles. The effects of a motor handicap on personality. I. The effects on level of aspiration. *Child Develpm.,* 1953, **24,** 123-130. II. The effects on integrative ability. *Child Develpm.,* 1954, **25,** 287-294. III. The effects on certain fantasies and adjustive techniques. *Child Develpm.,* 1956, **27,** 9-15. (280)
473. West, Rebecca. Another man's poison. *Harper's Magazine,* 1945, **191,** 57. (34)
474. White House Conference. *Social hygiene in the schools.* New York: Appleton-Century-Crofts, 1932. (410, 413)
White, Ralph K. See **278.**
Whiting, J. W. M. See **104.**
475. Wickman, E. K. *Children's behavior and teachers' attitudes.* New York: Commonwealth Fund, 1928. (19)
476. Wightman, C. S. The teacher's diary as an instrument of follow-up work. *J. educ. Res.,* 1936, **30,** 237-240. (15)
477. Willoughby, Raymond Royce. A study of some poorly adjusted families. *Am. sociol. Rev.,* 1942, **7,** 47-58. (49)
478. Winker, J. B. Age trends and sex differences in the wishes, identifications, activities, and fears of children. *Child Develpm.,* 1949, **20,** 191-200. (131)
Witty, Paul A. See **263.**
Wolf, K. M. See **413.**
479. Wolf, Katherine. Observation of individual tendencies in the first year of life. In *Problems of infancy and childhood* (ed. Milton Senn). New York: Josiah Macy, Jr. Foundation, 1953, pp. 97-137. (110)
480. Wolf, Thelma H. The effect of praise and competition on the persisting behavior of kindergarten children. *Univ. of Minn. Inst. Child Welf. Monogr.,* 1938, no. 15. (220)
481. Wolfle, Dael L., and Wolfle, H. M. The development of co-operative behavior in monkeys and young children. *J. genet. Psychol.,* 1939, **55,** 137-175. (368)
482. Woodruff, Asahel D. Motivation theory and educational practice. *J. educ. Psychol.,* 1949, **40,** 33-40. (405)
Woolf, Paul J. See **156.**
483. Wright, Beatrice A. *Physical disability—a psychological approach.* New York: Harper, 1960. (262)
Wright, Beatrice A. See **37.**

484. Wright, H. F. Psychological development in Midwest. *Child Develpm.,* 1956, **27,** 265-286. (65)
485. Wright, H. F. The effect of barriers upon strength of motivation. Ch. 22 in **21.** (212)
Wright, H. F. See **36** and **39.**
486. Wright, M. Eric. The influence of frustration upon the social relations of young children. *Character and Pers.,* 1944, **12,** 111-122. (185)

487. Xydias, N. Attitude du corps enseignment de Vienne (Isere) vis-a-vis de divers traits de comportment des écoliers. *Travail humaine,* 1955, **18,** 249-256. (19)

488. Yarrow, Leon J. The effect of antecedent frustration on projective play. *Psychol. Monogr.,* 1948, **62,** no. 293, 1-40. (188)
489. Yarrow, Marion Radke. Authority roles are differently reported by mother, father, and 10-year-olds. Paper read at the Bethesda, 1959, meeting of Soc. Res. Child Develpm. (51)
490. Young, M. C. The partially seeing. In **163,** pp. 162-178. (270)

491. Zander, Alvin F. A study of experimental frustration. *Psychol. Monogr.,* 1944, **56,** no. 256. (187)
492. Zazzo, René. Images du corps et conscience de soi. *Enfance,* 1948, **1,** 29-43. (402)
Zeisl, H. See **262.**
493. Zilborg, Gregory. In Introduction, pp. 14f., to S. Freud, *Beyond the pleasure principle.* New York: Bantam Books, 1959. (404)
Zubin, J. See **205.**

Index of Subjects